Personality:
Current Theory and Research

Personality:
Current Theory and Research

Janet Beavin Bavelas
University of Victoria

Brooks/Cole Publishing Company
Monterey, California
A Division of Wadsworth Publishing Company, Inc.

Core Books in Psychology Series
Consulting Editor: Edward L. Walker, University of Michigan

Printed in the United States of America

10 9 8 7 6 5 4 3 2

Library of Congress Cataloging in Publication Data

Bavelas, Janet Beavin, 1940-
    Personality.

    Bibliography: p. 275
    1. Personality. I. Title.
BF698.B3189   155.2'34   77-13213
ISBN 0-8185-0253-3

Acquisition Editor: *Charles T. Hendrix*
Project Development Editor: *Claire Verduin*
Manuscript Editor: *Margaret C. Tropp*
Production Editor: *Marilu Uland*
Interior and Part-Opening Designs: *Sharon Marie Bird*
Cover Design: *Katherine Minerva*
Typesetting: *Column Type Co., Inc., Salt Lake City, Utah*

Progress, far from consisting in change, depends on retentiveness. When change is absolute there remains no being to improve and no direction is set for possible improvement: and when experience is not retained . . . infancy is perpetual. Those who cannot remember the past are condemned to repeat it. . . .Old age is as forgetful as youth, and more incorrigible; it displays the same inattentiveness to conditions; its memory becomes self-repeating and degenerates into an instinctive reaction, like a bird's chirp.

The Life of Reason
Santayana

Preface

The purpose of this book is to present current personality theory and research as a field alive with controversy, to show how the lines are drawn and how the issues might be resolved by present and future theory and research. The aim is to bring personality as taught at the undergraduate level not merely into the second half but into the last quarter of the 20th century.

The organization of the book reflects its major themes: (1) the emergence of two competing metatheoretical paradigms, the individual and social views of personality, and (2) the importance of theory and research to each other. The first theme has determined the sequence of topics, which is historical, from where we began to where we are now. Part 1 introduces and examines the traditional, individual personality theories. Part 2 considers the social approach—principally the social-learning theories, plus Lewin. Those who favor the traditional, individual theories will undoubtedly wince at the level of criticism handed out in Part 1. Be assured that the same standard is applied to social approaches, including the social-learning theories and behavioral assessment. Part 3 compares these two paradigms and looks for compromises and even alternatives to both (including interactionism in its many forms). The last two chapters consider broader lessons derived from the book as a whole: how better to build and test a personality theory and what the implications of theory and research are for applied psychology, especially clinical practice. Students who want this incentive might read the last chapter first. Overall, the text is addressed to the following questions: Where did we start and how did it go? Where are we now? Where might we go from here?

The second theme—the relation between theory and research—is integrated into the book as a whole. The current empirical status of each theory is evaluated as soon as that theory has been introduced. There is an introductory chapter on the goals and methods of psychology, but these are better understood as they arise naturally in the course of critically examining the research on each theory. Theory and research are treated throughout as two sides of the same problem; each has little meaning without the other. This balance is especially important in the field of personality. The empirical status of most personality theories has typically not been given the weight it deserves for a balanced approach. It is appropriate to evaluate any personality theory, at least in part, according to whether it has any basis in observed human behavior.

Each theory has been presented with some brevity, so that only its central and identifying aspects are included. There are three reasons for this departure from the usual, more encyclopedic approach. First, there are already available excellent sources of detailed treatment, especially the original sources. The second reason for distilling the theories is to make room for other material, especially critical and empirical analyses of each theory, as well as new approaches. Finally, I am inclined to share Sechrest's (1976) dismay at the teaching of historical theories as contemporary psychology. I have tried to find a balance between living in the past and rejecting it altogether.

I would like to acknowledge and thank Walter Mischel of Stanford University, a teacher whose influence is obvious; Douglas Lawrence of Stanford University, a teacher whose influence is more subtle; Alex Bavelas of the University of Victoria and Donald Fiske of the University of Chicago, who made detailed comments on sections concerning their own and related work; Richard May of the University of Victoria, who sharpened my vocabulary on the issues in Chapter 1; Edward L. Walker and Warren T. Norman of the University of Michigan, Lawrence Wrightsman of the University of Kansas, Jack L. Bodden of Texas Tech University, Joseph C. Speisman of Boston University, Mark Sherman of Syracuse University, and Ian Begg of McMaster University, who read and commented on the manuscript at various stages; Julius Ozioko of the University of Nigeria, for his able bibliographic assistance; and the Brooks/Cole staff for their help from beginning to end.

As a student, it seemed to me either incomprehensible or condescending for an author to thank his or her students and to acknowledge the contribution they made "merely" by being students. It has since been my good fortune to discover the validity of such an acknowledgment. The undergraduates at the University of Victoria inspired and shaped this book in the classroom, the hallways, and my office. It is to them, as a well-known and respected audience, that I have been writing. For those who choose to teach, I can only wish similar experiences with open, demanding, good-humored, and eminently teachable individuals.

Janet Beavin Bavelas

Contents

Personality:
Current Theory and Research

1

Ground Rules

The study of personality is one of psychology's broadest and most freely defined areas of inquiry. It includes research and speculation on needs and motives, thinking, interests and values, perceptions of self and of others, psychopathology, emotions, and a virtually unlimited array of other such diverse topics. Personality is often loosely defined as the study of the individual or as "personology"—the study of the whole person. Such a definition would seem to make almost any human behavior or psychological process a suitable topic for the field of personality.

Far from making the entire field a wastebasket of general psychology, this omnibus definition of the subject matter actually distinguishes personality from other areas within psychology. Most other areas deal with particular processes (for example, with learning or perception) or with a particular level of analysis (for example, the physiological or social aspects of behavior). Personality aims to deal with no less than the whole person; with most of his or her psychological processes; and at any level of analysis necessary.

In other words, personality theories, however they may differ—and they do differ strikingly from one another—have at least one thing in common. They aim to encompass the widest conceivable variety of internal processes, observable behaviors, and human situations. In the most superficial sense, this means that many unrelated topics are found in the field. Virtually all theories of personality, however, share a more significant aspect in that they seek to integrate many aspects of human behavior into a single theoretical framework. Not satisfied with an inventory of psychological facts, personality theorists derive and explain these facts from a central theme. Freud's concept of the unconscious and the social-learning theorists' sweeping use of learning principles are good examples of such integrative theories. Any personality theory able to catch the imagination, and then to remain interesting and influential enough to become a major theory, has sought to encompass and to unify the many facets of the individual human being. These are "theories of the normal,

1

unique totality which is variously described as person, personality, self, or organism" (Woodworth & Sheehan, 1964, p. 336). Each of the theories described and evaluated in this book has made a unique, and in some sense appealing, attempt to encompass this totality.

This is obviously a very ambitious endeavor, and however laudable it may be, some caution and reservations are in order. First of all, human beings are indeed very complex, and it is easier to praise the idea of a comprehensive theory than it is to build one. The personality theorist must walk a narrow road with pitfalls on either side: either extend, elaborate, or qualify the theory until it is so complicated and unwieldy as to lose its integrative appeal; or effectively reduce the required coverage by simplifying the subject matter. The latter alternative is usually accomplished by assumption. Examples of simplifying assumptions are: human behavior is always sexual or aggressive in origin; all human processes are stimulus-response links; or all human behavior results from a finite set of needs. Such assumptions or definitions reduce the phenomenon to a manageable size, but again at a cost. The result is a complete theory, but of a far simpler human being than many of us would recognize. The specialist outside the field of personality who studies only color vision or the conditioned reflex rarely claims that this is the essence of all human behavior, but rather only an aspect of a vast unmapped whole. Paradoxical as it may appear at first, the narrow, modest theory may be a greater respecter of the ultimate breadth and complexity of human nature than is the general theory, if the latter can succeed only by oversimplification.

The second reservation regarding personality theories is one that applies in any area of psychology but seems to arise most often in the field of personality. No matter how satisfactorily integrative, no matter how intuitively obvious or appealing it may be, a scientific theory is not complete until it can make objectively verifiable predictions derived from its assumptions. In less stuffy terms, a theory without facts is only an opinion. Until adequate empirical support has been gathered, such a theory—any theory—has only a tentative status. Many (and especially the older) personality theories have never had their basic assumptions seriously tested. This is not to say that we should ignore ideas until supporting evidence has been secured, but rather that an untested theory has a provisional status and little authority, no matter how authoritative its proponent may be. There is always the possibility that the theory is merely a fanciful construction contradicted by human behavior.

The importance of making such tests goes beyond scientific orthodoxy and involves a serious practical issue. Given the great diversity of personality theories, *not all of them can be right.* Personality theories seem to proliferate, and few of them are subsequently eliminated on empirical grounds. Yet Freud and Rogers cannot both be entirely right. Skinner's and Kelly's theories can coexist only as two unsupported opinions, for the evidence that would verify one would decrease the credibility of the other. Science is a marriage of theory and data, and many personality theories still await consummation.

These issues—how to formulate an encompassing theory of personality, what to include and exclude in such a theory, and the means of testing the theory—are the important continuing issues in the field. Their particular current manifestations will be the subject of the remaining chapters.

THE GOALS AND METHODS OF PSYCHOLOGY

All of the foregoing implies certain standards, or a set of rules, by which we judge work in personality or in any other area of psychology. For example, I have mentioned a preference for theory over unrelated collections of data, but also a preference for theories supported by data. More precisely, the ideal is a balanced marriage of theory and data, as equal partners complementing one another. The beauty, intricacies, and difficulties in this metaphorical marriage will be seen throughout this book. Here some general points and definitions will be given, primarily to give us a common language for talking about theory and research in the pages ahead. With apologies to the philosophers of science, this will be in the simplest working language that will still serve the purpose. The reader who is interested in further reading may wish to look at any of the following sources, which are listed in order from introductory to advanced treatments: Matheson, Bruce, and Beauchamp (1974); Kerlinger (1964); Coombs, Raiffa, and Thrall (1954); Rudner (1966); and Hempel (1952).

A note of encouragement for the beginning student: don't be intimidated by the very idea of theory and methodology. Both are, in the end, refined common sense. If you can keep yourself from being afraid, they will appear as straightforward as they really are. Furthermore, don't worry if everything isn't completely clear by the end of this chapter. I find that I learn better from actual examples than general, abstract statements. The rest of this book illustrates the material in this chapter. So relax and get the general idea; it's the job of the rest of the book to make these ideas clearer and to demonstrate their usefulness.

What Are Concepts, Data, and Theories?

A theory identifies several concepts, their properties, and their relations to one another. Take, for example, the theory that "mother knows best." The concept, or category, *mother* is equated with the concept of *knowing best*. Each of these is a *concept* because each refers to a class of people or events, not merely to a particular instance (for example, my mother knows more about golf courses than anyone else in the world does). Besides being a general notion, a concept may not even be observable. While all the living mothers in the world could, in principle, be observed, this is not true for *knowing best*. All the actions and judgments made by mothers might also, in principle, be observed—but whether these constitute or reflect *knowing best* would still have to be inferred from these observations. In fact, most of the concepts of psychology are of this kind: intangible inferences from behavior. Not that psychology is alone in using concepts that are not even potentially observable. One cannot see *evolution, energy,* or *atomic weight,* yet these are useful scientific concepts. They correspond to observable data (although the data are not the concept), and they summarize all instances of such data into a single concept. As we shall see, concepts and data have an interesting reciprocal relation to each other.

One last point for now about concepts in psychology. These are frequently all-or-none, like motherhood (you have it or you don't). But consider *motherliness*, which is more a matter of degree. Many psychological concepts, especially in personality, represent a hypothetical continuum that includes all points along a dimension. Just as there might be more or less energy or atomic weight, there might be more or less motherliness, ability, friendliness, desire, reward, or punishment. These concepts encompass all possible degrees and therefore refer to the characteristic in general, not to any particular amount. For example, the concept of intelligence includes not merely the higher levels that we would colloquially call intelligent, but all conceivable levels of intellectual ability.

To return to the relation of concepts to data, it is vital that they be defined together: *data* are the observable aspects of a concept. Strictly speaking, *data* is the plural form, and *datum* is the singular. But, perhaps because datum sounds so tiny and precise, most psychologists use the word *data* whether referring to a single observation or several. In any case, data are *empirical*—that is, based on our direct experience. These can be seen, heard, felt, or somehow observed. One of the simplest forms of data is a single example. If I do not understand exactly what someone means by the term *weird*, an example from among our common acquaintances will probably make it clearer than any dictionary definition would. A more elaborate form of data would be a variety of scores for several individuals on an intelligence test, as data representing the concept of intelligence.

Thus, data and concepts define each other. Concepts can be clarified by pointing to their observable aspects—the data that represent them empirically. For this reason, the procedures for gathering data for a particular concept are often called the *operational definition* of that concept. These procedures are a set of operations, or instructions, that one carries out in order to obtain data consistent with the conceptual definition. On the other hand, data are dictated by the concept they represent. If the concept of aggression is defined as an attempt to do intentional harm to someone, then certain data are appropriate representations of that concept. If aggression is, on the other hand, defined as actual harm to anyone or anything, regardless of intention, then other data would be appropriate, and these data would include some instances that are not consistent with the first definition. It follows that a vague concept is going to be very difficult to find data for, since it would not be clear which data are appropriate. Problems can occur in the other direction as well. The wrong data will misrepresent the concept intended. It is obvious that hair length is a silly operational definition of academic ability. But is overall grade-point average necessarily the best kind of data for this concept?

I have two strong mental images of the relation between concepts and data. The first is a classical one: concepts exist in the intangible world of ideas, suspended over the world of realities. As scientists, we try to make connections—strong ropes or ladders—between the two worlds. The other image, which is much more vivid when I am doing research rather than talking about it, is that of translating from one language to another. The challenge is to find the right empirical expression for the concept to be studied. It must represent the concept as faithfully as possible, or else there is no purpose in the translation. If the concept is unclear in its own language, then it must first be clarified by examining the context (the theory) in which it exists. Then the suitable phrase in the other language (data) must be carefully selected. To choose an operational definition of, for example, self-esteem merely by finding a test with that name on it is as careless and useless (or comical) as translating a passage from French into English, one word at a time, using the first English definition of each French word listed in the dictionary.

Recall that a *theory* is several concepts with specified properties and relations to one another. The minimum would be a single, simple statement— for example, "Absence makes the heart grow fonder"—in which a cause/effect relation is proposed between two concepts. Or "Once a thief, always a thief"; the property of being a thief is, according to this theory, unchanging or unchangeable. A full-blown theory is usually much more elaborate, with many concepts, properties, and relations. This book is devoted to many such complex theories of personality. Some comments can be made now about what the above, simple "theories" have in common with more serious, formal ones.

First, theories aim for some generality, not just one particular absence or one individual thief. A fact alone has little interest. Who cares if Sam agreed with Martha on Tuesday morning of last week? That is close to a purely descriptive event. We might be more interested in whether Sam usually agrees with Martha, or in whether other people like Sam usually agree with anyone, or if other people in the same situation usually agree. These are general statements going beyond a specific instance; in short, they are theories.

Some psychologists are coy about theorizing and propose to stick to facts instead. But on close examination there is usually a theory wrapped around these supposedly bare facts. For example, B. F. Skinner, who describes himself as an analyst of behavior rather than a theorist, recalls when he first saw the cumulative graph of responses of a rat who had stopped receiving reinforcement:

> I can easily recall the excitement of that first complete extinction curve. . . . It was an orderly change due to nothing more than a special contingency of reinforcement. It was pure behavior! [1959, p. 367.]

Those of you who have not yet studied the concepts of learning in psychology probably find that statement incomprehensible. You can therefore appreciate first-hand that *extinction curve, contingency,* and *reinforcement,* not to mention *orderly* and *change,* are abstract concepts that require definition. Any of us can recognize that the phrase "due to nothing more than" is a strong cause/effect hypothesis. A great deal more than "pure behavior" is being described here, and well it should be. Generalizations from behavior can lead to organizing theories, whereas facts can only be recorded, accumulated, and memorized. Pure empiricism is sterile.

It is not necessary for a theory to cover all possible cases—that is, all human beings in all situations—but it is a good idea to specify which are covered by the theory. Often unthinkingly, psychologists base their theories on normal adults in their own subculture (North American, English-speaking, educated, middle-class) but do not make it clear whether or not they mean to include other groups in their theory. Similarly, the theory may not hold for all situations (for example, absences caused by desertion may not increase fondness), and this too should be clear. In summary, a useful theory should have some generality, but it need not be universal.

How Can We Judge a Theory?

These considerations lead to a second point, which concerns the criteria by which theories can be evaluated. Positive criteria for what properties a theory should have—how broad, how simple, how formal, how much inference, and so on—are hard to find agreement on. This is partly a matter of taste. Perhaps some such criteria will grow out of experience with how well theories of certain kinds work out over the long haul. (As we shall see, the breadth of most personality theories seems to be both their glory and their weakness.)

Negative criteria are easier to give. The concepts should be clearly defined. It is surprising how often this is not done, to everyone's loss and confusion. It is never impolite to ask of a theory or theorist: exactly what is meant by your concept of reinforcement, authoritarianism, self, or whatever? The theory as well as its concepts should be clear, stating what relations exist between concepts; for example, when does frustration lead to aggression and when does it not? Finally, there are useful logical standards that can be applied to theories. All theories should be cleared of illogical propositions, such as circularities and tautologies. These two terms will be defined as they arise in particular theories, where they are unfortunately common. Finally, a theory should not pretend to be anything it is not. If the theory is really a collection of hunches, better to say so than to disguise it as a complex and rigorous framework.

The third general characteristic of a theory is that it can be wrong. It is an idea that someone has proposed, but it is not right or wrong because of that. The theory, or at least important parts of it, should be empirically testable, leading to modification of the theory if necessary. The statement "That's all right in theory, but... " should never be left at that. If theory and practice or data disagree, then either the theory is wrong or there is a bad empirical translation of the theory. Either suggests that some kind of change is necessary. Notice that one of the goals of psychology is to test theories with empirical data. This implies that there are bound to be differences of opinion about theories, and these have to be sorted out. Science is, among other things, *a way of settling disagreements*.

There are other ways of settling such disagreements—that is, of deciding to believe a certain theory or not. Some of them are worth considering as alternatives to the empirical method. We could adopt the theory of the most powerful protagonist. Let everyone fight it out and the one left alive or in power decides which theory is to be accepted: might makes right. While there are many historical precedents for the use of raw power to coerce beliefs, it is not an appealing alternative. One reason is that it does not seem convincing. People may be coerced by physical, legal, or economic power, to say that they accept a theory, but it is doubtful whether they really do.

A more subtle form of power often used to uphold theories is authority. The parent, the teacher, and the boss all may use their positions of authority to assert a wide variety of theories, which the child, student, or employee must accept. More often, the person chooses to accept a theory on the basis of authority because of the prestige he or she attributes to the authoritative figure. Being a scientist, a psychologist, a successful person, even a celebrity is sometimes sufficient to lend authority to one's pronouncements. Besides the authority of personal prestige, there is the diffuse authority of social consensus, sometimes called common sense. We accept many informal theories of human nature, such as the "naturalness" of greed or aggression, solely because we have always heard them and most people act as though they believe them. An even more subtle form of authority is our own personal authority—that is, personal opinion or intuition. We believe something because it is consistent with what we already believe, because we can find an example in our own life, or because it simply "feels right."

None of these kinds of authority has the coercive influence of sheer power, so that when people believe something because of prestige, common sense, or intuition, they are likely truly to believe it. The disadvantage is that this belief is still arbitrary, and when people disagree because they believe different authorities, there is no way to resolve the argument ("My expert is more expert than your expert"). So, for the special purpose we call scientific, there is a better alternative: the empirical method. A theory is accepted or rejected because of its congruence with data observable by anyone.

By resorting to empirical observation, the debate is removed from irrelevant personal criteria, such as who is more persuasive, who has a Nobel prize, or whose intuitions are more special or revered. The only arbiter is the set of data relevant to the issue. It is an essentially democratic process, and many historians of science have pointed out that science only grew as the feudal system broke up and individuals were able to act independently of a fixed social structure. In principle, anyone can challenge any scientific theory successfully by producing the appropriate data.

There are two qualifications on this, however. For most areas of science today, including psychology, some technical training is necessary to be able to do the work. This is not because outsiders must be initiated into a closed society; it is because knowledge about how best to proceed has accumulated, and one would otherwise have to relearn it the hard way. The training is not for the purpose of maintaining the status quo. It is for the essentially radical purpose of putting the means of proof into the hands of anyone motivated to use them, whether to extend or to attack the current beliefs. This first qualification, that of suitable training (*not* brainwashing), seems a reasonable one, particularly since scientific training is so broadly available in universities. When such training is not practical—for example, in areas of specialization too far from our own interests—we expect the specialists to "police" one another.

There is a second qualification to any sweeping characterization of science as an open, democratic community. This qualification is unfortunate, because it reveals a tendency antithetical to this very goal. Science in the 20th century has become the new authority. It is often as autocratic as the medieval church ever dreamed of being, holding special powers to itself or being given them by a willing public. Even among scientists within the field, personal prestige and status carry weight—we're only human—and these may override the need for data. A statement by a psychologist, a physicist, a professor, may be accepted merely because of who proposed it, and we are back to the authority of prestige. It is an uphill battle to keep ourselves honest, in the sense of remaining true to empirical evidence above all other kinds. Data are often disappointing, ego-bruising, and downright risky because the outcome is not certain. But research is also exciting and satisfying in a very special way. The world where theory and data meet is, in its best form, a world apart from petty personal issues yet full of passionate curiosity and belief and the means of satisfying that curiosity or testing that belief.

By no means can every belief or theory be subjected to empirical test. Only a fairly small set of all the beliefs we hold can be made into formal theories for which data are even available. Furthermore, highly personal beliefs, such as religious, moral, social, or political convictions, seem more suitable to other kinds of support, including especially faith and personal conviction. But for other topics where data are at least potentially available, it is well worth the effort to try this method.

FROM THEORY TO RESEARCH

Suppose we now have a theory and are eager to set about testing it. There is no cookbook of recipes for producing the appropriate data for any theory. There are, however, significant common aspects in any psychological research. These will be described and illustrated here so that the same language can be used to describe the research process as it appears throughout the book.

Theories are often too broad to be tested in a single study. Virtually all research focuses not on the entire theory but on a selected part of it, called the *conceptual hypothesis.* This is the minimum meaningful form to which some part of the theory can be reduced for the purpose of testing. Suppose a theory proposed that personality is entirely inherited. This very broad notion could be restricted, for the purpose of beginning empirical work on the theory, to a single conceptual hypothesis: the more similar the genetic heritage, the more similar the personalities. Another conceptual hypothesis from the same theory would be that personality would change only as a function of maturation, not of experience. You might try to think of other, different conceptual hypotheses which can be derived from this illustrative theory. Several conceptual hypotheses follow from most theories. Even poor theories can usually generate a conceptual hypothesis. That is, a theory that is only a loose collection of assumptions or no more than a "point of view" can usually be forced to yield at least one conceptual hypothesis.

The next step is into the empirical world. The conceptual hypothesis is translated into a *research hypothesis*, which states the conceptual hypothesis in the language of data. For example, the conceptual hypothesis above about similar genetic heritages might lead to the following research hypothesis: identical twins will be more alike in their social behavior, as measured by an introversion/extraversion questionnaire, than fraternal twins will be. Note that everything is suddenly more specific. Similarity of genetic heritage has been expressed as identical versus fraternal (nonidentical) twins. Personality has been narrowed to social behavior, then even further to a particular question-naire aimed at introversion/extraversion. There are virtually always several, alternative research hypotheses. Try to think of other, different research hypotheses that would serve the same conceptual hypothesis, which was that the more similar the genetic heritage, the more similar the personalities. Everything at this point depends on the research hypothesis being a good expression of the conceptual hypothesis. Each concept must have a suitable operational definition, and the relation between operational definitions must be equally clear.

Another way of defining *research hypothesis* is as the predicted relations among operational definitions of the concepts. Since the research hypothesis is an empirical reflection of the conceptual hypothesis, the prediction is always of the same general form as the conceptual hypothesis. If the conceptual hypothesis says that a concept will have certain properties, then the research hypothesis proposes that the operational definition of this concept will demonstrate these properties empirically. If the conceptual hypothesis proposes X causes Y, then the research hypothesis should attempt to demonstrate such causality. The conceptual hypothesis should be mirrored in its research hypothesis.

Nothing has been said so far about statistics. To the above phases of research we can now add a last, the *statistical hypothesis*, which is a further refinement of the research hypothesis. For the inheritance example, the statistical hypothesis might be that the average correlation between scores for identical twins will be significantly higher than the average correlation for fraternal twins. Alternatively, it might be that the average difference between scores for identical twins (that is, twin A minus twin B) would be significantly smaller than the average difference for fraternal twins. In either case, statistical *significance* refers only to the plausibility of concluding that the numbers involved are not due to chance. It does not refer to the theoretical, practical, or social significance of the findings. The statistical hypothesis must adequately express the conceptual and research hypotheses. A statistical test for differences between the mean scores of identical versus fraternal twins would have no bearing on the illustrative conceptual and research hypotheses. It might tell us whether identical twins are more extraverted, on the whole, than are fraternal twins. But that would be an answer to a different question than the one at hand.

Statistics are thus the servant of research, not its master. It is convenient to use available statistics that have good properties. For example, the first statistical hypothesis suggested above is better than the second because comparing difference scores is rather tricky statistically. Testing whether two correlations are further apart than chance fluctuations would suggest is a little unusual, but it involves a straightforward statistic. Neither human nature nor theories about it come packaged neatly for the available statistics. The researcher must walk a line between letting the available statistics dominate his or her conceptual and research hypotheses and, on the other hand, ignoring statistical issues only to find out later that these hypotheses cannot be subjected to statistical test.

In practice, the research need not actually begin with a theory. The impetus to research might be at any of the other levels—for example, thinking of a research hypothesis first and going on to wonder why, conceptually, it might be true. Regardless of how it begins, the final research should be describable at all four levels—theory, conceptual hypothesis, research hypothesis, statistical hypothesis—and some critical questions should be aimed at each level.

CRITERIA FOR EVALUATING RESEARCH

At the level of the theory, some negative criteria have been mentioned in an earlier section. The next question concerns the connection between the theory and the conceptual hypothesis. Is it accurately derived from the theory? Is it important to the theory? It is a good idea to select among the available conceptual hypotheses one which will get to the heart of the theory. Confirming results will then make us more inclined to accept the theory, and negative results will make us more likely to reject it. Many studies merely nibble around the edges of a theory, never brave enough to face being blatantly wrong, but at the price of never being convincingly right. The conceptual hypothesis itself should be clear and logically satisfactory. "Either this or that or something else is so" is not a good conceptual hypothesis.

A conceptual hypothesis must, finally, be more than a description of the data; that is, it should be more abstract than the research hypothesis. The statement "Men will score higher than women on the Wechsler Adult Intelligence Scale" is a research hypothesis. The conceptual hypothesis might be "There are sex differences in intelligence, favoring men." Note that forcing oneself past a description of the data to a conceptual hypothesis raises issues that should be raised about the theory or assumptions behind the hypothesis: Are these proposed differences hereditary, environmental, or both? What is meant by intelligence? Does the particular intelligence test matter? The answer to these questions might properly lead to a different, more precise research hypothesis than the first one that came to mind.

The research hypothesis must be an accurate translation of the conceptual hypothesis. When it is, there is an almost tangible feeling of fit, of locking together two vital pieces in a chain. When it is not, the result is a sorry mess. When I was a graduate student (and of course knew everything), we used to play a game called "Read only the research procedures and guess the conceptual hypothesis." The prize went to the one who could think of more, or more bizarre, conceptual hypotheses for the same research hypothesis. The point was to show how often published articles do not convincingly connect the two. While this game was rigged because irrelevant aspects of the procedures were not distinguished from vital ones, it still makes that point. Good insurance for authors against arrogant graduate students can be obtained easily: state explicitly the correspondence between the conceptual and research hypotheses. Connect the Introduction and the Method sections.

There is a second important criterion for the research hypothesis. It should be free of *artifacts* and *alternative explanations*. These terms can best be defined by example. Suppose in the identical versus fraternal twin study, all the identical twins had been reared together, while all the fraternal twins had been separated at birth and reared apart. If the expected similarity between identical twins were found, it might well be due to a common environment, rather than to the common heredity that the conceptual hypothesis proposes. The difference in experience between the two groups is an artifactual difference, an unwanted by-product of a particular research hypothesis. Furthermore, it constitutes a plausible alternative explanation for any positive results, since an environmental explanation would be just as plausible as the hereditary one for those data. The empirical world is full of potential artifacts that do not exist in the purely conceptual world. One of the challenges of doing research is to spot and avoid these traps. Many of the more common ones have been identified for us, complete with research designs for overcoming them. The standard treatment of this topic is Campbell and Stanley's (1966) book.

Using standard designs, however, is only a partial solution, just as using standard grammatical forms is only a part of becoming a good writer. Each research hypothesis presents its own unique problems. Before proceeding, one must look carefully for artifacts; enlist the aid of friendly but candid colleagues; and, finally, be prepared to be gracious if critics find artifacts when the research is completed and it's too late to do anything about it! We shall see that some artifacts and alternative explanations are only discovered as our methodology develops over time, so that no one sees the problem until much later. There is no shame, especially in the latter. Those who come later learn by our errors. We can only do the best we can with the methods available at the time, but we must not use them once they have been outmoded by new insights.

Finally, there are some rules for examining the statistical hypothesis. Again, accurate translation is vital, this time from the research to the statistical hypothesis. This requires that some thought be given to the statistical analysis *before* the data are gathered, so that the data are amenable to some appropriate statistical test. Added to this consideration are those imposed by the statistics themselves. Most psychological statistics can be used only on condition that certain assumptions are met by the data. Fortunately, as luck would have it, most research in personality requires only very simple statistics with few assumptions, so we will seldom be bothered by statistical issues in this book. If the reader is familiar with the correlation coefficient, its statistical significance, and the interpretation of r^2, that will be sufficient. These concepts can be found in many introductory psychology textbooks or, for example, in Hays's (1967) brief explanation.

To summarize the key issues, the four levels of research should be aligned so that each expresses the aim of the research in its own terms. The statistical hypothesis should agree with the research hypothesis, which should agree with the conceptual hypothesis, which should accurately express some part of the overall theory.

This chapter has aimed to introduce the way psychologists go about their business and to develop a vocabulary and a set of standards by which the theories and research in this book will be examined. Personality theories and research can be judged just as any other psychological work—that is, by using the standards set out above. After seeing repeatedly how these are applied to particular cases, the main points of this chapter will probably become much clearer than they are now, in the abstract.

Part 1

Individual
Personality Theories

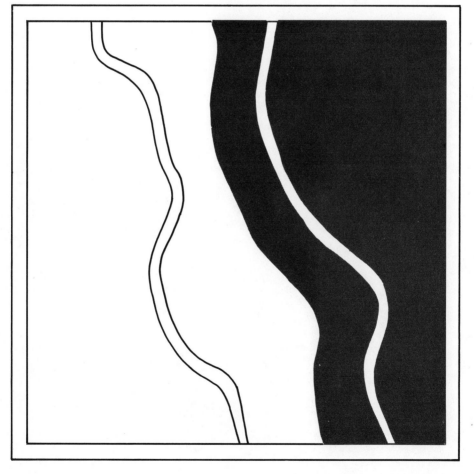

2

Introduction to the Individual Theories

During the first half of the 20th century, theories of personality were concerned almost exclusively with the individual. Since the early sixties, however, theories of personality that emphasize external, and especially social, influences on the person have challenged these earlier theories. This has led to a lively and continuing controversy, and this controversy is a major theme of this book.

To understand this debate, it is necessary to grasp the essential, common characteristics of many theories as a group. Each of the traditional theorists—Freud, Allport, Cattell, Sheldon, Murray, Rogers, Kelly, and many others—emphasizes the uniqueness of his own theory. Each stresses the different perspective with which he approaches the individual. This emphasis on differences is quite appropriate; the variety among theories focused on the individual is impressive and should not be overlooked. Yet these same theories share many common assumptions, which have only recently become clear. These common assumptions are fundamental ones, and the theories built on them form a distinct class despite their differences in other respects. I will call these theories as a group the *individual personality theories*. The similarities among them all stem from their common assumption that personality is basically a characteristic of the *individual* human being, whereas the *social personality theories* (which will be described in Part 2) propose that the study of personality must also include the social influences and processes that surround the individual.

The common view held by the family of individual personality theorists is stated clearly by Sanford (1968):

> Personality, in its most widely accepted technical sense, refers to dispositions *in the person that help to determine his behavior and that differ from one person to another* [p. 587; italics original].

There are two important parts to this definition. First, it focuses on *dispositions*—for example, temperament, instincts, motivation, or character—that are *inside* the individual. Second, it proposes *individual differences*—in other words, that people differ from one another in significant and consistent ways. These two ideas are found in all individual personality theories. They will be explained here and then illustrated repeatedly in the particular theories. After each theory has been introduced, the features that make it an individual personality theory will be pointed out.

Every theory of personality tries to describe people with its own particular set of terms, terms that convey a particular perspective on human behavior. Each emphasizes aspects that others ignore; many give different interpretations for the same behavior. This may sound like the aftermath of the Tower of Babel, but there is a common tongue. Virtually all the descriptive and explanatory terms that individual personality theories use refer to the individual alone and rarely to social or environmental events around the individual. An individual personality theory emphasizes internal dispositions, whether as needs, traits, or complexes. Few of these theories even have words to describe external events, such as reinforcement, communication, or discriminative stimuli, which are part of the language of social personality theories. And the formal vocabulary of a theory reveals its view of human nature. The person whom individual personality theories describe is an internally complex but isolated individual. Each person is seen as if in close-up, with his or her own features clear and detailed, against a blurred and indistinct background.

Given this focus, it is natural that individual personality theories would use internal terms and concepts when discussing the causes of an individual's behavior. The "dispositions in the person that help to determine his behavior" include, for example, traits, needs, cognitions, fixations, motives, and self-images; they do *not* include immediate or current environmental influences. Virtually all propose that personality (in the form of traits, needs, or whatever) is shaped at a relatively early age and that the adult's behavior is guided mainly by this enduring personality. The current environment is not very influential. Note that this corresponds to a common idea, both older and broader than the psychology of personality, that childhood is the critical period in the development of adult character.

It follows from this that enduring personal characteristics will be of great interest to individual personality theorists. But none proposes that everyone is stamped in the same mold. People differ from one another in which dispositions they have. That is, all individual personality theorists believe that there are individual differences in personalities. Further, these are not just transient differences but enduring ones. They are consistent over time and across situations. A man who reveres and obeys his father might continue to do so, in any situation, and he would show the same attitude toward other fatherlike persons. That is, he would be characterized by submission to authority figures. *Individual differences* is the term that psychologists use to refer to three related assumptions about people: (1) that individuals do differ from one another in significant ways; (2) that any particular individual's difference from others is true in many situations; and (3) that each individual maintains this characteristic difference over a considerable period of time. Whereas other psychologists are interested in how people in general behave (according to the situation), individual personality theorists are interested in how people in particular behave (regardless of the situation).

These assumptions lie behind all personality tests,[1] whether in the psychological clinic, in personnel departments, or in popular magazines. The aim of personality assessment is to identify the significant, relatively permanent characteristics of individuals. The test may be objective, subjective, projective, or observational. The trait may be dependency, aggressiveness, empathy, anxiety, extraversion, leadership, spontaneity, femininity, or motivation to achieve. There may be a limited number of categories into which everyone must be sorted, or each person may be uniquely described. But the purpose is the same: to find and measure individual differences.

One of the first questions a traditional personality theorist must answer is, which individual differences are the broad and enduring ones? Each theory either sets forth particular, important traits from the premises of the theory or indicates a general method for finding the important traits. In either case, one of the major goals of an individual personality theory is taxonomic—that is, the classification of people or their behavior, and especially the discovery of the dimensions on which individuals should be classified. Each theory presents its own taxonomy, a set of individual differences that aim to cover the significant consistencies in human behavior.

One final point before describing specific individual personality theories. The assumptions on which these traditional individual theories are based are remarkably similar to intuitive or common-sense ideas about personality. We think of personality as something everyone "has," something that is "typical" of him or her; we think that there are "different kinds of people." This is probably part of our sense of the inherent uniqueness of everyone—especially ourselves. But common sense is often inconsistent ("Absence makes the heart grow fonder," yet "Out of sight, out of mind"). Even more important, common sense is often wrong. For example, the sun does not "rise" and "set" over a geocentric world as common sense tells us. In the case of personality, common sense is hopelessly vague. For example, proposing that everyone has a unique personality says almost nothing. Each personality theory to be discussed has abandoned this comfortable vagueness and sought to say specifically what personality is and how people vary. This is what distinguishes a theory from intuition or common sense.

---

[1]which should really be called personality *assessments*. The word *test* implies success or failure. How could one fail to have a personality?

3

Freud: The Theory

Most students have the impression that there is one Freudian theory, a single and systematic set of ideas with straightforward definitions and hypotheses, but this is not true. Sigmund Freud's psychoanalytic theory is a complex and subtle one, which he continually revised between 1895 and 1939, and which finally filled 24 volumes in the *Standard Edition*. Many of Freud's revisions are inconsistent with his earlier ideas, and he did not resolve these differences or produce a final version of his theory. Some later psychoanalysts (including Fenichel, 1945, and Rapaport, 1959) have attempted to consolidate and refine Freudian theory, but no subsequent version is recognized as the definitive theory. More often, his followers have extended and modified his theory substantially, creating many new versions or "schools" of psychoanalytic thought. The result is a wide variety of Freudian, or psychoanalytic, theories.

Still, most of Freud's own important ideas—those that distinguish his from other theories and that have had the greatest influence on subsequent work—can be grasped fairly readily by understanding his central concept, the unconscious. To understand what Freud means by the unconscious mind and its processes is to understand how he defines and explains the human personality.

We will see that Freud makes four basic assumptions about personality: (1) the unconscious portion of the mind is the largest and most important part; (2) the unconscious consists of sexual and destructive instincts which are the individual's basic motives; (3) these impulses are forbidden by society and are therefore censored and actively kept out of the conscious mind; (4) in spite of this "censorship," the instinctual impulses break through the barriers to consciousness and determine all conscious thoughts, feelings, and behavior, although in disguised form. The brief introduction to Freud's theory to be given below will consist of explaining these assumptions and the consequences that Freud derived from them.

It may help if you recognize the ways in which Freudian theory does and does not resemble popular views of human nature. In many ways, Freud's theory is quite old. It has often been said, and still is, that humans are basically animals; that their powers of reason are ephemeral and often clouded by passion; that humans deceive themselves easily, in various ways; that people seek pleasure or self-interest above all; that society is hypocritical or even harmful in its regulation of human nature. But, as noted at the end of the last chapter, a true theory does not merely reaffirm vague generalities. It chooses certain generalities and stakes its value on them, on their capacity to account for all human behavior. Thus, Freud was proposing a model of human nature, constructing a hypothetical personality with particular, specified characteristics. He, as any other theorist, is permitted and encouraged to sketch such a model in any way he chooses, limiting his version of human nature to "nothing but. . . . " Then we can evaluate whether this model is logically coherent and whether it can be matched to observable human behaviors.

PSYCHODYNAMICS

The Unconscious

Let's begin with the outline of Freud's psychodynamic theory: his assumptions about the workings of the unconscious mind. First, according to Freud, there exists a part of the mind that is *unconscious*—that is, completely outside our subjective awareness—and the unconscious is the largest and most important part of the mind. This core of personality ultimately determines an individual's behavior and all conscious thoughts and feelings. The relation between unconscious mental processes and either behavior or conscious thought may be indirect and often hard to trace, but it is certain. There can be no other cause than an unconscious one. The mind, in Freud's theory, is often described as analogous to an iceberg. Only the smaller part is visible (conscious), while the greater part is not visible at all (unconscious). Furthermore, the conscious "tip of the iceberg" is only a minor portion of the whole; it suggests vaguely, or even deceptively, what might lie below. "Below," in this analogy, is the unconscious mind—immense, unknown, and potentially dangerous.

The Freudian unconscious is different from other ideas of the unconscious that refer simply to temporary lack of awareness. Freud proposes that what is unconscious ordinarily remains unconscious and cannot come into awareness. A person may be merely unaware of background music or traffic noises; or of the details in a painting when looking at the composition as a whole; or of the individual letters in the words while reading; or of the exact nature of something that was seen only very briefly. But as soon as attention is drawn to these events, the person notices them; they become conscious easily. These are all neutral events, with no emotional importance, and they are temporarily out of awareness only because a person cannot attend to everything at once. Freud calls such thoughts or perceptions *preconscious*. He reserves the term *unconscious* for those events that are truly unavailable to the conscious mind. Thus, our subjective experience of the world consists of what Freud calls *conscious* and *preconscious*. He assumes that we are totally unaware, and mostly incapable of becoming aware, of the most important aspect of personality—the unconscious part of the mind.

Instincts

Freud's second major assumption about the unconscious suggests both why it is so important and why it is kept from consciousness: it is the reservoir of the instincts that motivate the individual. Satisfaction of these instincts is the sole concern of the unconscious mind. In most of his writings, Freud spoke only of the instinct for sexual gratification, so that this part of his theory is best developed and best known. Later in his life, he added a second basic instinct, for death or aggression, but this destructive instinct is not well integrated into the rest of the theory.

Note that Freud does not include other "instincts," such as hunger, avoidance of pain, survival or self-preservation. These, he felt, are actually more complex processes than unconscious instincts are: they require coming to grips with reality. This the unconscious instincts are unable to do:

> The one and only urge of these instincts is towards satisfaction. . . . But immediate and unheeding satisfaction of the instincts . . . would often lead to perilous conflicts with the external world and to extinction. . . . The processes which are possible in [the unconscious] differ widely from those which are familiar to us through conscious perception in our intellectual and emotional life; nor are they subject to the critical restrictions of logic, which repudiates some of these processes as invalid and seeks to undo them [Freud, 1938/1964, p. 198].

So much for what the unconscious instincts are not: they are not conscious, not realistic, not logical. What they are is raw energy, urges toward satisfaction. When this urge was toward sexual satisfaction, Freud called it the *libido*, or sexual energy. The two instincts, sexual and destructive, are the *only* sources of psychological energy, or motivation. All behavior is ultimately caused by instinctual impulses. Without these unconscious impulses, the person would be psychologically inert.

Suppression and Repression

Third, Freud assumed that society forbids the free and direct expression of these instincts, especially sexual impulses. This assumption may seem less credible now than when Freud began to develop his theory, in Victorian times. But Freud assumed that the critical sexual instincts began to seek expression very early, in infancy. We can probably agree with him that overt sexuality in young children is largely disapproved—even disbelieved—by contemporary society.

With just these assumptions, the stage is set for active conflict. The child has powerful and necessary sexual motives that are denied expression or even acknowledgement by society and its agents (especially parents). The first consequence of this suppression by society is that the individual learns to repress his or her sexual impulses into the unconscious. What is unconscious is so because it is actively censored. In contrast to the preconscious, the unconscious is filled with emotionally charged motives and thoughts. These are unconscious not because of inattention, but precisely because they deal with powerful and threatening motives and must be denied conscious acknowledgement, not to mention direct expression.

Freud's fourth assumption about the nature and role of the unconscious—that unconscious impulses break through and determine all conscious thoughts, feelings, and behavior, although in disguised form—follows necessarily from what has already been assumed. The individual's most powerful, indeed only, motives are repressed. So they must be "harnessed," or expressed indirectly in acceptable forms. Coming at it from the other direction, a Freudian assumes that all behavior is the expression of unconscious, probably sexual, impulses. The task of the psychoanalyst, then, is to discover the exact nature of the impulse and the nature of the disguise.

Id, Ego, Superego

Freud often expressed the above assumptions using his own terminology for each of the mental processes involved: id, ego, and superego. It is important to note here that, although he used the nouns *id, ego,* and *superego,* Freud did not mean to imply mental structures or "little people" inside the head. These terms, like the conscious and unconscious, refer not to entities but to different mental processes or functions that are inferred from behavior. The unconscious instinctual drives are called the *id.* The id operates according to the *pleasure principle*—that is, solely for the satisfaction of its impulses. The id is incapable of dealing with reality. If, for instance, an infant is deprived of oral satisfaction because the nipple comes out of its mouth, then the id is frustrated but incapable of remedying the situation. The id would wish the nipple to return and might even fantasize that it has returned, but the id could not act on reality in order to accomplish this.

The child soon develops the capacity to act according to the *reality principle:* the *ego* develops out of the id in order to serve the id by dealing with reality (for example, finding the nipple and getting it back in the mouth). Thus Freud meant to distinguish between two mental processes, one guided by pleasure, one by reality. The ego is the servant of the id, the middleman with reality. One of the realities the ego must cope with is that the id's impulses are forbidden by others. These are therefore repressed by the ego. The child eventually internalizes (that is, brings inside its own mind) society's prohibition against the expression and satisfaction of sexual instincts. This part of the mind, which reflects the moral code presented to a child, is called the *superego.* The superego represents the child's identification with the parents' and society's values, including their censure of its own impulses. Feelings of guilt and conscience are superego functions. Since the superego is internalized in childhood, it may be more rigid and unrealistic than adult values are. The superego reflects the stereotyped, "right or wrong" morality that parents often present to the child.

Anxiety and Defense

The ego must mediate between id and superego as well as between id and reality. This sets the stage for Freud's theory of *psychodynamics*, which is the resolution of unconscious forces. The impulses of the id must be expressed, both because they are powerful and because they are the only motivation the individual has. Since these impulses conflict with reality or the superego or both, they are repressed—that is, not permitted to become conscious or to be directly expressed. However, repression does not end the dynamic process; it only hides the exact nature of the impulse. What the individual feels instead is anxiety, a vague but intense uneasiness. Consciously, the person does not feel the real (usually sexual) motive, which is repressed. He or she feels only the *free-floating anxiety* left by the conflict of impulse and repression—that is, anxiety without any apparent, or at least conscious, cause.

The ego defends against the direct expression of the impulse and acts to reduce the anxiety as well. The means by which the ego does this is called a *defense mechanism*. As we have just seen, *repression* is the first defense mechanism; but it is not satisfactory for long. Freud's view of motivation is an hydraulic one, analogous to the force of rushing water. This force can be temporarily stopped, but the pressure will build up until it must be released somewhere. Thus, repression will stop the expression or acknowledgement of the original impulse, but this impulse remains unsatisfied and must therefore take some other outlet.

Freud suggested several other defense mechanisms that would express the impulse in disguised form. *Sublimation* channels the impulse into a socially acceptable form. For example, Freud (1910/1957) suggested that Leonardo da Vinci had a passion for his mother that was sublimated into painting beautiful madonnas (mother figures). *Intellectualization* expresses the impulse but without any personal emotional involvement. An anthropologist might study kinship systems and incest taboos as an intellectualized form of his or her own incestuous desires.

Sublimation and intellectualization both retain some aspect of the original impulse. Most other defense mechanisms reveal nothing of the true impulse. Repression and *denial* ("I don't feel that way at all!") are this sort of defense mechanism; they forswear the impulse entirely. *Reaction formation* is a defense mechanism that expresses the exact opposite of the true impulse, wherein love is expressed as hate, or hate as love. An unconsciously jealous older child who fusses adoringly over a new sibling might be displaying the defense mechanism of reaction formation. *Projection* turns the impulse into someone else's. Freud (1911/1958) proposed that a man with repressed homosexual desires might see himself as a heterosexual who is pursued, annoyed, or even persecuted by *other* men's homosexual intentions. Freud proposed that, distorted though they may be, these mechanisms of defense serve their function, which is a compromise between expression by the id and censorship by the ego.

It is important to remember that although Freud proposes a sequence of

$$\text{impulse} \longrightarrow \text{conflict} \longrightarrow \text{anxiety} \longrightarrow \text{defense}$$

this sequence is not observable in human behavior. If the defense mechanism is successful, then nothing will remain, either in consciousness or in behavior, of the original impulse or even the anxiety it engendered. Observation or inquiry would show only a person who specializes in painting madonnas; or who feels he is frequently approached by homosexuals; or who is devoted to her younger brother. Freud's hypothesis is that these are only appearances and that they disguise other, truer feelings. Obviously, this sort of inference will require considerable evidence that it is the true one. The problem of evidence for Freud's theory will be reviewed in Chapter 4.

PSYCHOSEXUAL DEVELOPMENT

So far, we have focused on the dynamics of Freud's theory: the unconscious influences on conscious thought and behavior. This process was of great interest to Freud, one that he studied especially through the analysis of dreams (1900/1953), through slips of speech and other mistakes (1901/1960), and in neurotic behavior. The other major part of his theory defines more clearly what is being repressed and defended against—that is, exactly what is in the unconscious. It is true that the unconscious consists of instincts, especially sexual drives, but Freud is much more specific than that. One of his original and lasting contributions is his theory of sexuality or, to use Freud's term, *psychosexuality*, which includes both the physical and psychological aspects as inseparable.

The common-sense notion of sexuality includes only adult heterosexual intercourse and some other acts, such as homosexuality and masturbation (which are considered by some to be perversions of or substitutes for the real thing). This viewpoint emphasizes sexual acts, not attitudes or feelings, and only a limited variety of acts at most. What Freud means by libido, or the sexual drive that dominates the unconscious, is much broader. For Freud, sexuality means anything pleasurable. Genital sex and orgasm are only part of the spectrum and not necessarily the most important part. Furthermore, Freud was less interested in the physical mode of sexual expression than in the psychological themes that accompany it. These psychological concomitants determine the adult personality.

The Oral Stage

Freud proposed a sequence of universal, normal psychosexual stages through which every child must pass and thereby acquire its adult personality characteristics. In each stage, the id seeks pleasure in a different way. Although

Freud did not study children directly, he inferred from the reports of his adult patients that three crucial stages occurred in the first five years of life. From birth until about the age of 2, the infant takes pleasure by the mouth. Since nursing and eating are the major satisfactions, Freud called this the *oral stage*. The mouth and lips are the *erogenous zone* of the oral stage—that is, the physical locus of pleasure. Remember that Freud equates sexuality with pleasure, and it is in this sense that he speaks of nursing as the oral gratification of sexual instincts during this stage.

There are distinct psychological aspects of oral pleasure in this stage. In the earliest phase, the child is completely passive and dependent. Psychologically as well as physically, the oral child is receptive. Later, teething and weaning lead to more active oral gratification, which may become voracious, biting, or even aggressive. In both parts of the oral period, the child is psychologically as well as physically dependent for this pleasure. It can suck a thumb or otherwise manipulate the mouth but cannot provide much real oral gratification for itself; this is in another's power. The child may be mild or hostile, according to whether it is in the early or late oral period, but its psychosexual state is essentially dependent.

Freud proposed that these psychosexual characteristics might be seen in the adult if something went wrong during the childhood stage—that is, if the child was overindulged or especially if the child was severely frustrated, for instance, by early weaning. Then the adult would retain some degree of *oral character*, a personality pattern of dependence that might include passivity, trust, talkativeness, insecurity, envy, or passive aggression such as nagging or sarcasm ("biting" speech). Such an adult might also continue to seek oral forms of gratification by smoking, drinking, or even fussing absent-mindedly with the lips.

The Anal Stage

Whether or not the child has successfully completed the oral stage will be revealed in adulthood. Meanwhile, inevitable maturational changes in physical capacities and activities carry the child into the second psychosexual period, the *anal stage*. Freud proposes that around ages 2 and 3 the erogenous zone shifts from the mouth to the anus, so that the child receives intense pleasure from its bowel movements. Like the oral stage, the anal stage has two phases. At first, gratification comes from expelling feces, later from retaining them. In contrast to the oral period, the child now controls its own gratification, so the child has become more independent. The psychological characteristics of the early, expulsive anal phase are messy disorderliness, wanton destructiveness, and temper tantrums. Anal expletives ("crap," "shit") typically have this destructive, degrading meaning.

The psychology of the later, or retentive, anal period is more complex. The child has more physical control over its anal muscles and can withhold as well as expel feces. At this point, the parents are trying to toilet-train the child, who is able to comply with or to defy them, as it chooses. In this period, the classic *anal character* of Freudian theory develops, with the "anal triad" of characteristics—namely, orderliness, obstinacy, and stinginess. All are related to the retention of feces. Retention, in contrast to expulsion, emphasizes cleanliness, tidiness, and, in general, orderliness—the first characteristic of the anal triad. Since the parents are trying to control when and where the child will defecate, retention also implies stubbornness, resistance, and therefore obstinacy—the second anal characteristic. Freud also proposes that the combination of the child's pleasure in its bowel movements and the parents' efforts to obtain them results in a childish belief that the feces are valuable in themselves. Therefore the child "hoards" them and dispenses them grudgingly, adopting a miserly, possessive attitude—in short, stinginess, the final anal characteristic.

These psychological aspects of anal gratification may appear as adult anal character if the child is overly gratified or frustrated in this period—for example, by early or severe toilet-training. A preference for anal intercourse or an undue concern with constipation would be unusually direct consequences of the anal period. More commonly, the individual would be overly tidy, close with money, and stubborn with other people.

The Phallic Stage and the Oedipus Complex

Between about 3 and 5, the child enters the most intricate and probably the most influential period, the *phallic stage*. The erogenous zone is the phallus, or penis, although this is still not the truly genital stage of adult sexuality, which occurs after puberty. The phallic stage begins with the child's pleasure and pride in his penis. Obviously, if true, this can be valid only for a boy, so at this point Freud's theory of psychosexual development diverges for males and females. The basic theory follows male development and only parenthetically or incompletely describes a parallel sequence for the female.

Throughout this period, the erogenous zone is the penis, but there are at least four distinct phases. As he enters the phallic stage, the young boy becomes sexually aware of his penis, which replaces the mouth and anus as a locus of pleasure. The attitude which accompanies the early phallic period is one of pride, even vanity, self-assurance, and courage or recklessness. An adult *phallic character* would have the same qualities—a narcissistic kind of masculinity, with great pride in his physique and daredevil courage. (The parallel for the girl is supposed to be *penis envy* and a resulting jealous desire to castrate or excel men.)

The second phase of the phallic period is the beginning of the *Oedipus complex*. The mother becomes the first love-object. To Freud, the oral and anal impulses as well as the early phallic phase are essentially autoerotic—that is, directed to the child's own body. In the Oedipal phase, the sexual instinct seeks an external object, the opposite-sexed parent. The little boy loves his mother both mentally and sensually. If he does not outgrow this passion, it will be the prototype of all his future heterosexual relationships.

The third phase of the phallic period follows as a consequence of loving and desiring the mother. The mother belongs to the father, so the father becomes a hated and feared rival. The boy longs to do what the Greek king Oedipus did inadvertently—kill his father and possess his mother—but he fears the father's greater power. Imagining that his father knows his thoughts, he fears that his father will harm him in the most fearful manner he (the child) can think of, by castrating him. The third phase is therefore one of *castration anxiety*, in which the boy dreads losing his most precious organ.

The fourth phase is the solution to this dilemma. The way out, according to Freud, is for the boy to identify with his father—that is, to try to become as much like him as possible. During this last, *identification* phase, the boy imitates his father and seeks to be a "little man." Presumably, this serves the function of allaying his fear both by ingratiating the father and by acquiring the qualities of the feared "aggressor." Identification with the same-sexed parent, which Freud also proposed for girls, is the beginning of the general process of socialization, in which the child adopts society's rules and values as its own. The superego is fully incorporated during this period, so that the child becomes its own critic and conscience.

Note that since the castration anxiety and its solution, identification, follow directly from phallic sexuality (specifically the Oedipus complex), Freud is proposing that even this accommodation to society is ultimately motivated by libidinal impulses. In the case of successful ("normal") resolution of the Oedipus complex, the libidinal energies are turned around and channeled into forms that actually oppose their further expression (for example, the superego).

Later Stages

At this point—around the age of 5 or 6—Freud feels that the basic personality has been formed. What's done is done and will be revealed when the individual becomes an adult. Meanwhile, the child enters a tranquil period, called *latency*, in which the strong urges of the early years are repressed or inactive, while the child engages in the task of entering the larger culture by, for instance, beginning school. With the physical onset of adolescence, all the old themes are revived and briefly recapitulated, then the adult either shows the characteristics of an unresolved earlier period (oral, anal, or especially Oedipal) or successfully enters the *genital stage*. In this final, mature period, the adult becomes free of the parents, finds an appropriate love-object, integrates residuals of the earlier periods into normal functioning, and channels sexual instincts into acceptable behavior. Narcissism gives way to altruism; the normal adult is able "to work and to love."

All of this, and what went before, has been on the unconscious level. What the child and the adult feel consciously are only disguised or distorted forms of the real impulses and the true course of personality development. No one, in fact, has observed this saga first-hand. Freud and other psychoanalysts have inferred the sequence from their interpretations of dreams and free-associations and of the current lives of their adult patients. The validity of such interpretation and reconstruction, as well as other means of corroborating the theory, will be discussed in the next chapter.

FREUD'S THEORY AS AN
INDIVIDUAL PERSONALITY THEORY

Freud's theory is a completely traditional, individual personality theory, with its emphasis on the internal life and characteristics of an individual. It is interesting that we are able to identify the point at which Freud's thinking took this turn rather than looking for more social influences.

In 1897, Freud had been treating cases of female hysteria (a form of neurosis sometimes resulting in psychosomatic paralysis) with the novel "talking technique" that Joseph Breuer and he had developed a few years earlier. Previously such patients had been treated medically or written off as malingerers. Freud was intent on understanding the cause of this as a psychological illness and, based on his patients' reports, he had tentatively formulated a "seduction hypothesis." A child with weakened psychological defenses was the victim of seduction (or attempted seduction) by a parent. Although a child with stronger defenses could presumably handle such an experience without permanent psychological damage, the child whose defenses were already weak became the adult hysteric.

But by the summer of 1897, Freud had begun to see flaws in this theory, and he expressed these doubts in a letter to his friend and confidant, Wilhelm Fliess:

> [It was an] astonishing thing that in every case... blame was laid on perverse acts by the father, ... though it was hardly credible that perverted acts against children were so general. (Perversion would have to be immeasurably more frequent than hysteria, as the illness can only arise where the events have accumulated and one of the factors which weaken defence is present.) [1957, pp. 218-219.]

Thus, Freud reasoned that, if his seduction theory were true, the incidence of incest would have to be much higher than the incidence of hysteria. In Freud's opinion, this was implausible. But he was still left with the stories his patients had told him. He consequently came to

> the definite realization that there is no "indication of reality" in the unconscious, so that it is impossible to distinguish between truth and emotionally-charged fiction. (This leaves open the possible explanation that sexual phantasy regularly makes use of the theme of the parents.) [1957, p. 219.]

From this last, parenthetical remark, Freud eventually made the leap to the Oedipus complex, which he considered one of his greatest discoveries and central to psychoanalytic theory. While the particular form that an Oedipus complex may take is mediated by environmental events, its origin and its universality are intrapsychic. Having rejected the possibility of real seduction, or a real disturbance in parent/child relations, Freud shifted the sexual drama into the child's fantasy: every child may not have been seduced, but every child has wanted to be.

It is this shift of emphasis from environmental trauma to internal fantasy that marks Freud's as an individual personality theory. Social and especially familial events are not totally ignored, but none of the major terms of the theory refers to such external factors. This is a theory of mental, not social, life. Every technical term in the preceding introduction to Freud's theory refers to a disposition, process, or structure *inside* the individual. This is true of the unconscious; the pleasure and reality principles; id, ego, and superego; all of the defense mechanisms; the psychosexual zones, stages, and adult characteristics. Recall that this is the first characteristic of an individual personality theory.

The second characteristic of an individual personality theory, the emphasis on individual differences, is also clear. An individual may be an oral-aggressive or anal-retentive character, with an unresolved Oedipus complex, or some combination of these characteristics. He may have a weak or strong ego or superego; or she may characteristically use denial, projection, reaction formation, or some other defense mechanism. Freud proposes these and many other individual differences.

As noted above, Freud does not picture a person as an instinctual robot, driven only by innate behavior patterns. Environmental influences help to shape individual differences, but only to a degree. Instinct is primary, and the period of external influence is relatively brief: for Freud, the personality is formed before the latency period. Since adolescent and adult life are considered essentially as reruns of earlier periods, psychoanalytic assessment of personality seeks to describe the result, and psychoanalytic therapy seeks to reconstruct those crucial years.

AFTER FREUD

Quite a few of Freud's colleagues and followers disagreed with him enough to form distinct, new psychodynamic theories. The disagreement was usually about sex. His first collaboration, with Joseph Breuer, ended because Breuer believed that Freud's emphasis on sexual factors was exaggerated. Later, Carl Jung, Otto Rank, and Alfred Adler also disagreed enough on this point for each, in his turn, to break with Freud and to author a new theory that bears his own name. (The recently published letters between Freud and Jung [1974] over the period of their collaboration and through their parting are fascinating reading and suggest, to me at least, that Freud resisted strongly any modification of his theory by others.)

Even later, the "ego psychologists" (especially Heinz Hartmann and Ernst Kris) continued this revision by upgrading the ego, consequently de-emphasizing the id and its sexual energy. Finally, psychoanalysts such as Karen Horney, Erich Fromm, Harry Stack Sullivan, and Erik Erikson, who were personally less influenced by Freud and his European tradition, but greatly impressed by the vigor of North American social science, authored the "social psychological" theories of psychoanalysis. Each of these newer theories is still considered psychodynamic, not only because of its historical origin, but because each retains the basic skeleton of Freud's theory, although the details differ. This skeleton, made up of Freud's "metapsychological assumptions," has at least two parts. First, there is an emphasis on unconscious processes, anxiety, and defense: some fundamental psychological energy (need, drive, or motivation) is seen to be present but repressed and transformed. Second, there is a fixed developmental sequence with critical periods for environmental influence and/or the resolution of conflicts. Perhaps these theories are what Freud's would have become had he moved to the New World and continued to work into the middle of the 20th century.

Erik Erikson's neo-Freudian theory (1963, 1968) is a good example of both the continuity and the change that characterizes these theories. Erikson remains most strongly Freudian in his emphasis on developmental stages in life, which he calls the *epigenetic principle*:

> that anything that grows has a ground plan, and that out of this ground plan the parts arise, each part having its time of special ascendancy, until all parts have arisen to form a functioning whole [1968, p. 92].

Erikson proposes a life cycle comprised of eight distinct, sequential stages extending from birth to mature adult life: trust versus mistrust; autonomy versus shame and doubt; initiative versus guilt; industry versus inferiority; identity versus identity confusion (this stage is typical of adolescence); intimacy versus isolation; generativity versus stagnation; and integrity versus despair.

Erikson's proposed stages differ from Freud's in two ways. First, obviously, they go much further than Freud's, which essentially climax at the resolution of the Oedipus complex around age 5. Erikson extends the sequence into adolescence, young adulthood, parenthood, and beyond. The other difference is that Erikson's stages are much more psychological than sexual. Recall that for Freud, the oral stage was equally as important for a psychological attitude as for the erogenous zone from which pleasure was derived. With Erikson, the issues of pleasure and sexuality are so muted as to be invisible. His stages describe important personal or interpersonal issues that must be resolved in order to reach healthy adulthood. Indeed, one could suggest that Erikson has replaced Freud's biological focus with his own social and cross-cultural emphasis.

All psychodynamic theories—with the possible exception of Fromm's and Sullivan's, which will be discussed briefly below—remain strictly within the family of individual personality theories. Their disagreements are over such issues as which internal processes are basic, whether these are innate or culturally determined, and the nature and origin of individual differences. For example, Erikson frequently refers to the importance of the family's or the society's actions or reactions at certain stages. But this influence is diffuse, theoretically, and seems to fade in later life. Indeed, even differences across societies and cultures are limited:

It is important to realize that in the sequence of his most personal experiences the healthy child, given a reasonable amount of guidance, can be trusted to obey *inner laws of development*, laws which create a succession of potentialities for significant interaction with those who tend him. While such interaction varies from culture to culture, *it must remain within the proper rate and the proper sequence* which govern the growth of a personality as well as that of an organism. . . . Personality can be said to develop *according to steps predetermined in the human organism's readiness* to be driven toward, to be aware of, and to interact with, a widening social radius [Erikson, 1961, p. 187; some italics changed].

To give another example, Horney (1939) points out that if women show penis envy, it may not be literal or even anatomical but may reflect, symbolically, the favored position of men in most societies. Presumably, in a sexually egalitarian society, this phenomenon would disappear; therefore, she too disagrees with Freud about biological determinism. Adler, Erikson, and Horney propose that early social experiences are important. But all are extremely vague about what these influences are or the processes behind them. None of the technical vocabulary of these theories describes a social process.

Erich Fromm (1955) did propose differences in social environments that would affect personality development. For example, he felt that a capitalistic society produces different personality types than would a "humanistic, communitarian socialism." These observations on large-scale political and economic organization take the social aspects of Fromm's theory outside the domain of psychology into sociology or political science. The rest of his theory is psychodynamic, focusing principally on universal major needs and the consequences of their frustration.

Harry Stack Sullivan tried earnestly to get rid of the notion of personality as an individual phenomenon, defining it instead as "the relatively enduring pattern of interpersonal *situations* which characterize a human life" (1953, pp. 110-111, italics added). He constantly stresses the malleability and openness of the individual to interpersonal influence and situational change. Some of his students (such as Jackson, see pages 485-493) did in fact become more social theorists who studied interpersonal influences on the individual. But Sullivan's own theory is ambivalent. His theory consists of intrapsychic terms such as *energy transformation, dynamism* (a sort of personal trait), *personifications* (stereotypes), and other terms for cognitive processes or ways of thinking. Only his concept of *consensual validation,* which is the establishment of shared meanings in social intercourse, clearly refers to a process outside the individual psyche.

Each of these "social psychological" theorists proposes that human conflicts and motivations are more social than instinctual. But the result is more a change of labels than of the unit of study. Early interpersonal experiences replace early sexual experiences as a major cause of subsequent behavior. But personality is still seen as a relatively fixed entity, influenced more by the enduring traces of previous experiences than by current interactions. The individual's internal struggle with social motives, rather than the condition of the social environment, dominates these theories.

4

Freud: Empirical Status

A few ideas and terms from Chapter 1 should be reviewed or defined briefly here. A theory, such as Freud's, is a set of ideas, of defined terms and relations between those terms. (For example, the anal stage follows the oral stage; libidinal impulses and ideas will always be repressed.) A scientific theory should be clear and logical; in addition, some of its major parts or consequences should correspond to actual observations. *Empirical* means, simply, observed: for a psychological theory to have empirical support means that the theory should correspond to observed human behavior. (Nonempirical support for a theory would be, for example, endorsement by a respected or authoritative person.)

Empirical, or observed, events are even better if they are also *objective*— that is, observable and interpretable in the same way by more than one person. If I claim to have seen the Loch Ness Monster, you may well say this is not an objective observation (although it is an empirical observation), for no one else saw what I saw, or others may have seen something but interpreted what they saw as merely a log floating on the water. But if we arrange for several observers to be present, and if we agree in advance on some criteria for deciding between a log and a serpent (for example, a large undulating motion counter to the wind or waves), then we can observe objectively. If we all understand the observation rules and techniques, then no one's opinion is any more important than anyone else's. Science is, among other things, an effort to replace authority with evidence open to everyone. So scientific theories strive for data that are there for all to see. Obviously everyone cannot be present at every scientific study. Therefore, this goal is served by making the reasoning and procedures so explicit that anyone who has mastered them—that is, anyone who becomes a specialist in the field—could actually repeat the study. This replication would show that the observed facts that support the theory exist independently of the person who first reported them. The case of empirical support for psychoanalytic theory illustrates almost every problem that can arise when these standards are used.

CLINICAL EVIDENCE

The psychodynamic theories, particularly Freud's psychoanalytic theory, have had a great impact on modern intellectual life. Psychoanalytic analogies and applications abound not only in psychiatry and psychology but in anthropology, literature, political science, interpretive history, and the arts. But broad acceptance and use do not qualify as empirical support; they simply mean that the ideas are appealing to many people. It is sobering, then, to discover that, although psychoanalytic theory has been amply illustrated, it has not yet been confirmed by empirical evidence. Nor has it been disconfirmed; rather, it is virtually untested. To understand this odd situation, we must take into consideration both the state of psychoanalytic theory and the change in standards for testing any theory since Freud's time.

Freud regarded his theory as indisputably true. For example, in 1934, an American psychologist, Saul Rosenzweig, sent Freud reports on his experimental efforts to study repression. Freud wrote back, briefly, as follows:

> I have reviewed with interest your experimental investigations for verifying psychoanalytic propositions. I cannot value these confirmations very highly since the abundance of reliable observations upon which these propositions rest makes them independent of experimental verification. Nevertheless, it [experimental verification] can do no harm.[1]

Freud had been trained in the late 19th century when an "abundance of reliable observations" meant his clinical observations, which were then sufficient evidence in many sciences (as were Darwin's observations). But standards of evidence change with the growth of a science, as flaws in the old methods are uncovered, and new, less fallible methods are found.

The problem with clinical evidence is that, while it is empirical, it is not objective. One person, the therapist, obtains the data, records and reports them, and interprets them. Moreover, this person is at the same time interacting and intervening with the patient in order to change him or her. There are three defects in this procedure. First, it is not repeatable. Each patient is a unique case, whose story will not happen again. No one now can reproduce Freud's famous cases, such as Dora (1905/1953), the "Rat Man" (1909/1955b), or the "Wolf Man" (1918/1955). The best that can be done is to attempt an objective analysis of such data—that is, independent interpretations by other people. This is possible only if all the facts are available.

The second problem with clinical case histories, however, is that there is no guarantee that all the salient facts have been reported. Even if it is not true that Freud, as Glover (1952) and Wolpe and Rachman (1960) suggest, applied "a touch of revision" to his cases, Freud would have been more than human if he had been able to identify and record all relevant facts. If unique events are to

---

[1]Reprinted by permission of S. Rosenzweig and of Sigmund Freud Copyrights Ltd., London. The original German text and this translation by Professor Rosenzweig are from his book, *Freud, Jung and the Kingmaker: The Visit to America 1909* (St. Louis: Rana House, 1977), which also contains a more detailed discussion of the meaning of the letter and its context.

be recorded for later analysis (a common situation, for example, in astronomy, where many unique events such as a new meteor occur), then a recording system as complete and faithful as possible must be devised. Clinical case methodology has no such system.

The third and as yet unsolved problem with clinical case evidence is that it is not the facts but the *interpretation* of these facts that is offered as evidence: for example, Leonardo da Vinci painted madonnas (fact) because of his unresolved Oedipus complex (interpretation). There is no objective guide to how these interpretations are to be made or to which interpretation is correct if several are possible (perhaps da Vinci painted madonnas because the church was the primary patron of the arts).

Just such disputes have arisen with Freud's cases. Take two cases in which Freud was working from independent data, data that he had not gathered himself; this separates issues pertaining to the interpretation of data from those concerning the gathering and reporting of data. Freud's most important evidence for the Oedipus complex is the case of "Little Hans," a young boy in whom Freud found the conflict expressed as a phobia (Freud, 1909/1955a). His analysis of Little Hans was based solely on reports from Hans's father, a physician and follower of Freud, whose account Freud gives along with his own interpretation. Freud interprets Hans's fear of horses as a disguised fear of castration by his father. Wolpe and Rachman (1960), even accepting the facts of the case as described by Freud, disagree completely with his interpretation and offer their own. They point out that Hans had literally been frightened by a horse and had developed a simple, specific phobia, for which he received a good deal of warm and concerned attention. By what rules shall we decide that Freud's interpretation is more true than Wolpe and Rachman's?

In the case of Schreber (Freud, 1911/1958), Freud made his classic analysis of paranoia from Daniel Schreber's published, autobiographical account of his madness (Schreber, 1903/1955). Recently, Schatzman (1971) has given a startling, new interpretation. Schatzman notes that, as Freud knew, Schreber's father was a child-rearing expert of the period. The books by Dr. Schreber (the father) describe some grim practices (such as cold baths for infants after three months of age) and some mechanical aids to accomplish specific goals (including a device, to be worn by the child, that pulled his hair if he did not hold his head perfectly straight). The senior Schreber proposed to achieve "complete mastery of the child," and his means could easily be called sadistic. After matching Schreber's paranoid fantasies with excerpts from his father's books, Schatzman concludes that "Schreber did not imagine he was persecuted; he was persecuted" (1971, p. 177).

The point is not to decide whose interpretation is right for any particular case but to seek a means of deciding on an objectively defensible interpretation from among several. Our inability to resolve or to justify interpretations based on clinical observation is the main reason that today, in contrast to Freud's day, clinical evidence is accepted as valuable for illustration and exemplification but not as evidence for a theory. One of the most respected Freudian scholars, David Rapaport, summarizes the modern situation in these words:

Much of the evidence for the theory remains phenomenological and anecdotal, even if its obviousness and bulk tend to lend it a semblance of objective validity. . . . The extensive clinical evidence . . . fails to be conclusive in terms of the usual criteria of science, because there is no established *canon for the interpretation of clinical observations* [1959, pp. 141-143; italics original].

LOGICAL PROBLEMS

Once the necessity for objective as well as empirical evidence has been accepted, it is still not easy to test Freudian theory, because of problems within the theory itself. As noted at the beginning of Chapter 3, there is no single Freudian theory, only an extensive but incomplete and sometimes contradictory body of writings. Therefore, supposing that one sets out to collect evidence for psychoanalytic theory—what is to be tested? Schultz (1969) gives this answer:

It seems that, except in the broadest sense of the word, there is no such thing as a psychoanalytic theory! There are a large number of generalizations and hypotheses but there seems to be no orderly framework of theorems, postulates, or precise relationships so necessary to a scientific theory [p. 286].

Lacking an organized body of ideas that would put important premises first and integrate more particular phenomena logically into these assumptions, the researcher can only pick away randomly at whatever strikes the fancy: dreams, perceptual defense, psychosexual stages, and so on. We may find something interesting, but we have at best verified a particular phenomenon, not the entire theory. Studies that claim to disconfirm Freud's theory must have a similarly limited impact. Evidence that the latency period is not found in all cultures (Malinowski, 1927, 1932) or that infants are not very oral (B. L. White, 1967) are isolated facts that cannot destroy psychoanalytic theory as a whole, because no one knows the relative importance of these issues within the theory.

Anyone who wants to test Freudian theory undoubtedly has to make many decisions about exactly what the theory means. These decisions might then be criticized as not being true or orthodox interpretations of the theory. But such criticism is fatuous. Freud's theory is incomplete, and anyone may finish it as he or she chooses. That person will be responsible for what is chosen and may be right or wrong empirically. But this can never be considered heretical:

Neither psychoanalysis nor psychology . . . is the possession of any group, the property of the members of any organized association. They belong to man. . . . As the discipline most directly involved, it is up to a mature psychology to understand, develop, incorporate and change this heritage as imagination, coupled with careful observation and experiment, indicate [Shakow, 1969, p. 115].

Another serious problem that can only be solved by a more rigorous statement of psychoanalytic theory is the presence of tautologies in the theory. A *tautology* is an assertion that is true in every conceivable case. Since it cannot be wrong, it is both logically and empirically meaningless. Tautologies are the specialty of that annoying species, the amateur Freudian: "Why are you so defensive?", "I'm not defensive," "Aha! Your denial proves you are defensive!" Unfortunately, many tautologies are built into the theory itself by the doctrine of defense mechanisms, by which almost any behavior can be interpreted as a disguised form of any motive. The philosopher of science, Abraham Kaplan, discusses one case:

> The psychoanalytic doctrine of reaction formation seems to some to secure the theory against falsification by making it tautologous. Boys are sexually attracted to their mothers; if they express such an attraction, good [for the theory]; if on the contrary they behave as though their mothers were detestable, this conduct only indicates a reaction against their own forbidden desires, and again the claim holds good; so it is true no matter what [1964, p. 100].

Kaplan goes on to propose that what is needed is a clear specification of what constitutes love, hate, and *all alternative attitudes that would not support the theory*. That is, a testable psychoanalytic theory must describe the data that would make it untenable as well as those that would support it. The absence of an impulse cannot automatically be interpreted as repression and therefore as evidence for the presence of the impulse at an unconscious level. (Which reminds me of the comedian who proves he has an invisible uncle: "You don't see him, do you?")

What is needed is a systematic statement of psychoanalytic theory, or at least of some parts of the theory, that makes clear predictions that could be right or wrong. To make such predictions is always risky: the experimenter could be proven wrong by the data to be gathered. But it is this risk that makes the evidence meaningful. Not incidentally, it also makes research interesting, exciting, and suspenseful.

AN OBJECTIVE STUDY

Kline (1972) has filled an urgent need in the area of psychoanalytic research by bringing together all the studies that attempt to satisfy the criteria set out above—namely, those featuring logically testable hypotheses, objective evidence, and defensible interpretations. Each of these several dozen studies deals with a specific aspect of psychoanalytic theory, not with the theory as a whole (which, as previously mentioned, is not possible). Some studies show positive results for the theory, some negative; some are well designed, many have weaknesses that require further research. None is a "crucial experiment" that conclusively confirms or disconfirms any aspect of Freudian theory. But this is usually the case in any area of psychology. Only a series of studies, including replication of important results by others, is conclusive. In short, the studies reviewed by Kline provide a starting place for further, more definitive research.

The reader is referred to Kline (1972) and especially to his "summary of verified concepts" (pp. 345-359) for a review that will not be repeated here. One of the most promising studies will be described briefly as an example. Hall and Van de Castle (1965) analyzed the dreams of men and women for evidence of the Oedipus and castration complexes. They accepted the early Freudian assumption that dreams reveal unconscious phenomena in thinly disguised form (Freud, 1900/1953). Hall and Van de Castle derived from the Freudian theory of psychosexual development the conceptual hypothesis that males would be anxious about castration while females would have more castration wishes or penis envy. Therefore, the research hypothesis was that these themes (dependent variable) should be evident in dreams according to the sex of the dreamer (independent variable).

Judges scored the written reports of dreams by 120 college students for the three themes, as follows:

Criteria for [Inferring] Castration Anxiety

1. Actual or threatened loss, removal, injury to, or pain in a specific part of the dreamer's body; actual or threatened cutting, clawing, biting, or stabbing of the dreamer's body as a whole or to any part of the dreamer's body; defect of a specified part of the dreamer's body; some part of the dreamer's body is infantile, juvenile, or undersized.

2. Actual or threatened injury or damage to, loss of, or defect in an object or animal belonging to the dreamer or one that is in his possession in the dream.

3. Inability or difficulty of the dreamer in using his penis or an object that has phallic characteristics; inability or difficulty of the dreamer in placing an object in a receptacle.

4. A male dreams that he is a woman or changes into a woman, or has or acquires female secondary sex characteristics, or is wearing women's clothes or accessories.

Criteria for [Inferring] Castration Wish

The criteria for castration wish are the same as those for castration anxiety except that they do not occur to the dreamer but to another person in his dream.

Criteria for [Inferring] Penis Envy

1. Acquisition *within* the dream by the dreamer of an object that has phallic characteristics; acquisition of a better penis or an impressive phallic object.

2. The dreamer envies or admires a man's physical characteristics or performance or possession that has phallic characteristics.

3. A female dreams that she is a man or changes into a man, or has acquired male secondary sex characteristics, or is wearing men's clothing or accessories which are not customarily worn by women [pp. 22-23].[2]

The tendency for men to have more themes of the first category (castration anxiety) than of the second and third (castration wish and penis envy) and for women to show the opposite pattern was statistically significant. So Hall and Van de Castle's hypothesis was confirmed. But is it really that simple?

While this is a fairly good example of logically straightforward as well as objective research, there are some defects in both the logic and the objectivity of the scoring system that are basic to the research hypothesis. Some of the criteria that resulted in scores for one category or the other are tautological in that they can only result in scores favorable to the conceptual hypothesis.

Recall the fourth criterion for castration anxiety ("A male dreams that he is a woman . . . ") and the third for penis envy ("A female dreams that she is a man . . . "). The sex of the dreamer (the independent variable) enters into the scoring decision (the dependent variable), so that only males can have this particular type of castration-anxiety dream and only females can have this particular type of penis-envy dream. Suppose that males and females dream of becoming the opposite sex exactly the same number of times. This identical dream theme would be scored as castration anxiety for men but penis envy for women, thereby confirming the Freudian hypothesis, even though transsexual or transvestite content was equally present in both. Therefore, these criteria should not be used, because they "stack the cards" in favor of the researchers' hypothesis.

Furthermore, the use of these criteria means that the judges who scored the dreams knew the dreamer's sex. Thus, although the judges demonstrated good interscorer reliability (they could agree without consulting one another on how to score the dream), the judges as a group could still have been biased by knowing the sex of the dreamer. An ambiguous dream, for example, in which the dreamer compares his or her physique unfavorably to a man's, could be scored either as castration anxiety (criterion one: dreamer's body is defective or undersized) or as penis envy (criterion two: envies a man's physical characteristics). The decision could easily be made on the basis of the dreamer's sex, in accordance with the theory being tested. A replication needs to be done that not only removes the tautological criteria but that would also keep the judges "blind" to the sex of the dreamer.

A final criticism of this study was made by the authors themselves, who pointed out that

the greater incidence of injuries and accidents [castration anxiety, criteria one and two] in male dreams may merely reflect the nature of the activities in which they engage in waking life as compared with the activities of women. It is believed that men engage in more dangerous activities and

[2]From "An Empirical Investigation of the Castration Complex in Dreams," by C.S. Hall and R. L. Van de Castle, *Journal of Personality*, 1965, 33, 20-29. Copyright 1965 by Duke University Press. Reprinted by permission.

take more risks than women do. If this is the case it might be expected that their dreams would be in accord with their waking life experiences [p. 28].

While the authors do not agree with this alternative, non-Freudian explanation of their findings, they do not offer evidence for their opinion.

Two steps could be taken to answer this criticism. First, it should be established whether the themes of injuries and accidents are solely responsible for the difference in male and female scores of castration anxiety. Only if these themes are the major contributors to castration anxiety scores (as the authors imply) do they pose a serious alternative explanation. If this is true, if there is a difference in castration anxiety scores between men and women only if accident and injury themes are included, then a serious effort should be made to explore the "waking life" hypothesis. For example, it might be possible to ascertain objectively whether or not the dreamers' waking lives really differ in this regard. If so, groups could be selected and matched on this basis, so that both men and women in the study would have the same degree of danger in their waking lives. If the themes were still found, then the difference in waking lives could no longer be invoked.

This study is described and criticized in some detail in order to illustrate research on Freudian theory. It also illustrates the general principles of empirical research discussed at the outset. Imagine a clinical study that concluded, on the basis of a few cases seen in therapy by the author, that Freud's theory of psychosexual development was true because the men's dreams showed (in some unspecified way) more castration anxiety than castration wishes or penis envy, while the reverse was true for women. The author might give several examples and detailed interpretation, but no explicit research procedures.

Hall and Van de Castle's study has many advantages over such a clinical study. As readers, we know how they got their data, how they made inferences from it, and exactly what they found (50% of women had no castration-anxiety themes at all, and so forth). Thus, we are able to find flaws in their scoring system—*flaws that would not be detectable in clinical evidence,* because no objective system of inference would be used or reported. Furthermore, we could reanalyze their data ourselves. Even better, we could repeat the entire study exactly as they did it, or with whatever modifications or improvements seem desirable on the basis of our criticisms. This is only possible because the authors practiced the principle of open, objective research.

It should not ever be surprising that criticisms can be made—of anyone's research. Researchers try to find as many errors as they can themselves, either before the study so they can avoid them, or afterwards so they can caution the reader. But any outsider can usually find problems that have been overlooked. One of the advantages of conducting and reporting research objectively is that others can praise or criticize specific points. But criticism cannot be mere opinion any more than evidence can be mere opinion. Criticism must be logical or empirical, not just "I don't believe it." Good criticism suggests a new study, one that would answer a question left by the previous study. Research should proceed as a vigorous dialogue until the answer has been hammered out. This process can only begin when objective evidence is gathered and fully described. This process still lies ahead for psychoanalytic theory.

5

Allport

By 1930, psychoanalysis and behaviorism (see pages 185-187) were the major influences in personality theory, if not in all of psychology. But in the thirties and forties, several psychologists proposed new theories of personality that owed little to either Freud or experimental psychology. Within a ten-year period, at least five of the classic theories were first published: Allport (1937), Murray (1938), Sheldon (1940), Rogers (1942), and Cattell (1946). Different as they are from one another, these theories taken together form the solid center of individual personality theories.

THE THEORY

Gordon Allport is known as a trait psychologist. Although this label neglects other, more dynamic parts of his broad, eclectic theory, it does emphasize one of his major contributions to personality theory. *Trait* is a term often used in everyday descriptions of people. We say a child inherited her father's good traits; or we don't like one of John's traits. Allport took this casual use of the term and made it formal and explicit, the basis of his personality theory.

Allport conceptualizes individual differences as traits. Earlier psychologists used a notion like trait only implicitly or in a purely practical sense. Freud, for instance, implies traits of anality and orality, as well as pathological traits such as hysteria or paranoia. The success of early practical work on ability traits such as intelligence, reaction time, and other capabilities by Francis Galton, Alfred Binet, and James McKeen Cattell undoubtedly impressed personality psychologists, who began to apply the same framework to problems in personality. But it was Allport who finally made the trait assumptions clear and explicit. He gave traits theoretical status and definition by making them the basic structural units of his theory and by elaborating the various forms that a trait might take.

The Concept of Trait

Allport's definition of a *trait* is a bit hard to comprehend in its condensed form:

> a neuropsychic structure having the capacity to render many stimuli functionally equivalent, and to initiate and guide equivalent (meaningfully consistent) forms of adaptive and expressive behavior [1961, p. 347].

Essentially, this definition formalizes our everyday observation of *consistency* in human behavior and the inference we make from this apparent consistency—namely, that a person has certain personal qualities, or traits. For example, saying that Mary is aggressive implies that she is not simply aggressive to her younger sister, but that she seems to find many other persons and situations to be suitable occasions for aggression (the trait "renders many stimuli functionally equivalent"). Moreover, Mary's aggressiveness is not limited to pushing and shoving. She might also be sarcastic, insulting, or bossy (the trait of aggression "guides equivalent forms of behavior"). That is, among any choice of behaviors presented by a situation, Mary will choose the aggressive one. The point is that Mary's behavior is not a series of unrelated incidents, such as hitting her sister, crowding to the front of a line, ridiculing another child, and arguing for her own way. Rather, these behaviors all belong in one category, aggressiveness, and the consistent recurrence of behaviors from this category is evidence for a personality trait. Allport proposes that there is something in Mary that transcends many situations and responses, so that a more general pattern of behavior is seen. A person with the trait of sociability would, similarly, find many occasions for gregariousness and would have a number of ways of expressing this outgoing nature.

In short, consistent behavior is the evidence for a trait. Not a single incident, but a repetition of behaviors of the same sort forms the basis for inferring a trait. Having observed such consistency, one can then predict future behavior. Most individual personality theorists expect individual differences to be expressed as traits in Allport's sense of lasting, transsituational consistencies of behavior. In fact, individual personality theories, as a class, are often called trait theories.

Classification of Traits

Allport classifies traits in three different ways: by breadth, by content, and by individuality. The first important characteristic of a trait is how broad or pervasive the consistency is. Allport proposes that, in rare cases, a trait might encompass almost the entire personality. For example, Hitler seemed preoccupied with power; every stimulus was seen only as it reflected, challenged, or confirmed his power, and every response expressed personal power. A strongly religious person might see everything in terms of religious principles and, on the response side, would bend all efforts to the assistance, enlightenment, and salvation of souls. Allport calls such thoroughgoing consistency a *cardinal* trait and emphasizes that few people are so simple as to have a cardinal trait. Most traits are less general, but still quite broad; these are the *central* traits. Perhaps six to ten of these would virtually capture a single personality. For example, his analysis of Jenny (Allport, 1965) led him to describe her with eight central traits: quarrelsome, self-centered, independent, dramatic, aesthetic, aggressive, cynical or morbid, and sentimental. Allport proposed that each of us could quite adequately describe ourselves or those we know well in about this many terms. Finally, each of us has more limited regularities of behavior, little habits that persist but are specific to certain situations (such as smiling when talking, or chewing on pencils in exams). These are *secondary* traits—numerous but not very important to Allport.

A second way in which Allport classifies traits is according to whether they are adaptive or expressive in nature. Here Allport wants us to notice not only what people do but how they do it. Two individuals might both perform the same task (*adaptive* or necessary behavior), but they can still differ noticeably in their manner of doing it—that is, in their *expressive* or stylistic behavior. These expressive behaviors can be regular enough to constitute traits in themselves (for example, carefulness, boldness, humility, expansiveness, acquiescence). In fact, Allport is inclined to think that adaptive behaviors are often pressed by environmental demands into so much of the same mold that individual differences are obscured. This leaves expressive behaviors, which are not so circumscribed, to reveal the variety of individual personalities.

For instance, walking is an ubiquitous adaptive behavior, and there is little to be learned by noting that an individual walks. But how an individual walks may be described as sauntering, plodding, tripping, waddling, shuffling, swaying, slinking, marching, or any of a great many more styles that would constitute an informative array of potential expressive traits. Recent research interest in "response style" on personality inventories (such as Couch and Keniston, 1960; see also page 102 below) may reflect the rediscovery of the distinction Allport is making.

Finally, Allport points out that there are both common and individual traits. The *common* traits are dimensions on which everyone can be placed (for example, height), whereas *individual* traits, or personal dispositions, are those that characterize single lives and do not imply comparison with others. Common traits are studied in *nomothetic* research, which involves a relatively small amount of standard information from many people. For example, Allport has done a great deal of work on how prejudiced individuals are: each person is assessed and assigned a score that represents his or her degree of prejudice; this score can be compared to anyone else's score.

In contrast, individual traits are studied in *idiographic* research, which gathers a relatively large amount of information from perhaps only one person. Jenny, who was characterized above, was studied only as Jenny, with no comparison to anyone else. Allport was interested in whether Jenny was independent, but not in whether other people were independent, nor in whether she was more or less independent than anyone else. Individual traits,

Allport argues, are unique trends to be followed in the intensive, preferably longitudinal, study of an individual. The details of this individualized research strategy are well discussed by Hall and Lindzey (1970, pp. 278-290) and will reappear here in Chapters 10 (Kelly) and 15 (new developments).

In everyday descriptions, we are often vague about whether a trait is intended to be individual or common. When we describe someone as generous, it may mean generous in an absolute sense, or more generous than most people. Most personality research, including Allport's, focuses on common traits, each of which is conceived as a continuum on which any person can be placed relative to others. The numerous "single-trait" theories (Chapter 13) usually study what Allport would call common, central, adaptive traits. Hereafter, the term *trait* will be used to refer to the common dimension (such as orderliness), which includes all possible degrees of that trait (ranging from disorderly to very orderly).

Thus, Allport's theory aims at a more precise and refined conception of traits. A trait should be defined explicitly in terms of how pervasive or specific it is (cardinal, central, or secondary); by what kind of behavior it refers to (adaptive or expressive); and by whether it is intended to encompass all personalities or only one (common or individual). These are choices that one must make in order to use trait psychology with maximum precision.

A final choice, one that Allport implies by taking a strong position on one side, is between traits as real or as hypothetical entities. Recall that, in Allport's definition, a trait is a "neuropsychic structure"—that is, a part of the brain—even though he leaves the physical location and characteristics unspecified. In this regard, Allport is probably in the minority of trait theorists. Most are content to say that a trait is a hypothetical entity, merely a concept that summarizes in a convenient way the consistency one observes (see MacCorquodale & Meehl, 1948). This sort of intangible concept is quite familiar in other sciences. Gravity, for instance, refers to a variety of regular phenomena but has no tangible reality. Although we see its effects all around us, we do not expect ever to see gravity itself. Similarly, we can observe regularities of personality such as Allport proposes and call these a trait, without having to expect ever to see it physically.

The difference between the two positions is one of expectation. Allport expects that traits are ultimately tangible, although they are not now. Others do not expect to identify traits physically and consider the term only a convenient abstraction. For example, Freud referred to "our psychoanalytic mythology," meaning the analogies he used, such as id, ego, and superego. He did not intend that future neuroanatomists would discover these structures. Rather, he wanted to summarize three different kinds of consistency that he saw in human behavior: the push of instinct (id), adaptation to reality (ego), and moral concerns (superego). While it is very important in some respects, this distinction does not affect present research. Traits must be inferred from behavior. Behavior that is consistent over time and across situations is the basic phenomenon, and all trait theorists expect to find this. Indeed, they must find it to demonstrate that traits (conceptual or physical) exist at all.

Allport's Theory as an Individual Personality Theory

Emphasizing Allport's theory of traits means bluntly ignoring other, equally influential and distinctive aspects of his theory: his emphasis on the whole person, on the functional autonomy of motives, and on the proprium (self) and its functions. Allport's is unashamedly an eclectic theory, and no single concept can accurately portray it. However, the trait concept is so central to all individual personality theories that, in this context, it deserves the major emphasis. Other aspects of Allport's theory do not modify his individual viewpoint; they are internal concepts or hypotheses about the nature of the individual personality, without reference to social circumstances:

> [Allport] has taken a biophysical rather than a biosocial position on the issue of personality. According to his view, personality exists "within the skin" of each individual, notwithstanding the important influence of its transactions with the social and physical environments. ...he has given thoughtful consideration to the impact of culture and cultural roles and situations, but has maintained his original stand on the subject [Woodworth & Sheehan, 1964, p. 378].

Allport's advocacy of the individual position extended over 40 years. In an "anniversary" paper late in his life, Allport (1966) reviewed his position. He admitted there was evidence for considerable social or situational influence on personality. For example, both prejudice and lack of prejudice may be found in the same person, depending on the circumstances. Still, Allport does not relinquish the concept of trait, for two reasons. First, he believes that these apparent inconsistencies can ultimately be resolved and shown to be in fact consistent: the unsuspected complexity of human behavior does not mean that it is not determined by traits. (The dangers of tautology should be obvious here. If inconsistency is redefined as consistency, then the trait hypothesis can never be disproven. Just as with psychoanalytic theory, the banner of "complexity" cannot be used as a cover for unsightly evidence. Rather, the nature of the complexity must be made explicit, and the conditions under which consistency will be confirmed or disconfirmed must be specified.)

Allport's second reason for preferring traits to situations is his fear that the social theories propose an "empty organism," a stimulus-response robot, a role-playing nonentity—in short, a nonperson. Allport argues that action by an individual must originate within the individual, and that the locus of these tendencies to act must be the individual, whose existence is therefore being challenged by those who put the cause of action outside the person. Even if social influence is admitted, Allport insists, "My capacities and my tendencies lie within" (1966, p. 2). To deny traits, then, is to deny the validity of the individual human being. Many other theorists, especially Carl Rogers, have argued in the same way for the individual position and against the social theories. When both sides have been presented, we will return to evaluate this argument (Chapter 23).

EMPIRICAL STATUS

The most natural empirical test of Allport's theory is a search for such consistency of behavior as would justify inferring traits. Allport and Vernon's *Studies in Expressive Movement* (1933) is the most straightforward test of the trait hypothesis to be found in Allport's research. In one of the earliest objective studies of nonverbal behavior, the authors chose to study expressive traits, particularly in physical actions such as walking, drawing, pressure of grip, muscular tonus, and speed. Other activities such as reading, counting, and estimating sizes or distances were also included. Although they did both nomothetic and idiographic analyses of their subjects, we will look only at their nomothetic search for common, central traits of expressive movement.

Allport and Vernon proposed to find dimensions of expressive behavior that would fit the requirements of individual differences as common, central traits. These dimensions would differentiate individuals from one another, be consistent over time, and show some considerable generality across situations. This was their conceptual hypothesis. This led to several research hypotheses. For example, they felt they might find a speed trait. People high on this dimension would read, walk, count, draw, and even tap their fingers at a faster pace than others at the low end of the dimension, who would conduct all their activities at a more leisurely pace. Similarly, there might be traits of forcefulness (grip pressure, writing pressure, muscular tonus) or of expansiveness (size of writing, overestimation of sizes, and the like).

Twenty-five men each came to three research sessions over an 11-week period. A total of 300 different objective measures of performance were made. Most of the tests did differentiate clearly among the subjects; that is, there was a variety of scores on any particular measure. Naturally, the subjects did not vary much in what they said when counting, for instance, and any small difference was probably due to error. But each counted with a different speed, loudness, clarity, and so forth. Similarly, they drew the required figures (for example, a circle on the blackboard) in different sizes, with different amounts of pressure, and at different speeds. As expected, expressive behaviors were a fruitful source of individual differences.

The next question was whether these initial differences were consistent over time. The loud, fast talker should not be soft and slow on the same material when tested later. Therefore, Allport and Vernon calculated correlation coefficients between the two sets of scores for each of their measures, in order to assess test/retest reliability. They reasoned that

> wherever satisfactory reliability is found among our measures, we have prima facie evidence of consistency among the expressive acts of our subjects [p. 176].

The results revealed that when the act was repeated in the same experimental session (no more than an hour after the first performance), the average correlation was .75. When the act was repeated in different experimental sessions (between 4 and 11 weeks apart), the average correlation dropped to .64. These correlations are too large to be chance occurrences, so there was definitely a relation between the first and second instance of the same behavior. But in absolute terms, the relationship is not impressive. If only traits were determining the behavior, then there would be no reason for any variation at all. Allport and Vernon themselves concluded that temporary, nontrait factors played an appreciable role, even in what should be identical behaviors. These other factors might be mood, fatigue, or any of dozens of other aspects of the immediate situation. Note that the behaviors being evaluated were very specific, yet even these were not particularly stable.

Finally, they looked for consistency across behaviors of similar kinds— that is, for central traits. Here the results were even poorer. There were no central traits. For example, 14 different measures of speed in different activities did not correlate significantly with one another. That is, a subject's speed score on one task had nothing to do with his speed score on another task: they were independent acts. Three specific speed traits were found. Behaviors reflecting rhythmic speed, such as tapping a finger or a pencil, correlated .76 with each other. Two other kinds of speed, drawing speed and verbal speed, had intercorrelations of .58 and .46 respectively. But these three kinds of speed did not relate to one another: a fast talker might draw painstakingly slowly. Thus, these were secondary rather than central traits.

Having found none of their predicted traits (speed, forcefulness, and so on), the authors proceeded from the other direction and looked at their data again, this time for *any* meaningful general traits that might be there, regardless of whether they had been predicted in advance. The factors that emerged (for example, "emphasis," which included voice intensity, tapping pressure, and overestimation) exhibited the best intercorrelations to be found across diverse situations of testing. Even these provided no support for central traits, however, having average intercorrelations from .25 to .33, none of which is statistically significant.

This study of expressive movement, then, did not find consistency of the kind Allport needs in order to infer the presence of traits as major determinants of behavior. But the evidence does not necessarily disconfirm his theory. Allport later described this particular research as "wholly characteristic" of his theory (1968). However, he does not say it is vital to his theory, and he seems satisfied with the degree of consistency found there. Thus, the problem is similar to that of testing Freudian theory. Allport's theory is not stated in a systematic form that permits specific prediction and confirmation or disconfirmation. How much consistency is necessary to infer a trait? How stable should simple behaviors be over time? In other words, what statistical hypotheses correspond to his conceptual and research hypotheses?

Like many personality theorists, Allport uses research to illustrate, rather than to test, his theory. The failure to find consistent central expressive traits could mean, at most, that expressive traits of the kind studied are not general or even stable. But nowhere does Allport say whether or to what degree this would make his theory untenable. Is the consistency of expressive traits a crucial research hypothesis, or only an expendable one of several alternatives? This failure to connect theory and research firmly, which is not at all unique to Allport, weakens the force of any evidence gathered because no important issue is put at risk.

6

Cattell

THE THEORY

Raymond B. Cattell is a thoroughgoing trait psychologist. For Allport, traits are an important part of his theory. For Cattell, traits are the basis of his entire theory: personality, which includes all of human behavior, is a complex structure composed of traits. The traits are the building blocks, the basic units to which personality can always be reduced. The main problem, as Cattell sees it, is to find out which traits are the fundamental ones. These would be analogous to the chemical elements that are the basis for all compounds.

Although this analogy expresses his goal, it should not imply that Cattell is necessarily looking for tangible traits of any kind, chemical or otherwise. Cattell usually defines a trait as a hypothetical entity, or a shorthand for the consistencies observed in an individual. Even though he does suggest that some traits have a "psycho-physical" basis, he is not concerned with locating the trait in the brain but rather with demonstrating the usefulness of such a concept for predicting behavior. "Personality is that which permits a prediction of what a person will do in a given situation" (1950, p. 2). The structural units of personality are traits, and they too are no more or less than information about the person that may help us predict what he or she will do in the future.

Classification of Traits

Before going into how Cattell proposes to identify and verify the basic traits, it is useful to look at the various ways in which he proposes to classify traits. Like Allport, Cattell says that traits may be general or specific, and they may be unique or common (although he is inclined to believe that even unique traits can be fitted onto a continuum common to everyone).

In addition to these two classifications, Cattell proposes that traits fall in one of three modalities: dynamic traits, which reflect interests and motivation (drives, attitudes, and sentiments); ability traits, which reflect capacities to perform (intelligence, coordination, skill, and so on); and temperament traits, which are defined mainly by exclusion — that is, they are personal characteristics that are not abilities or motivations. These include, for example, emotional reactivity, energy, and the qualities and tempos of our actions.

A fourth independent characteristic of traits is their presumed origin, which can be constitutional (that is, physiological, though not necessarily inherited), or what he called "environmental mold" (acquired through early experiences with the environment). Like all individual personality theorists, Cattell thinks that the acquired traits reflect mostly social influences, but that these influences are "imprinted" early in life. Social factors do not continue to operate so pervasively throughout life.

Finally, Cattell's most important distinction is between *surface traits* (clusters of behavior that typically go together) and *source traits,* which are the roots of such behavior patterns. Source traits are the basic elements of personality that Cattell is seeking to identify. They are the building blocks that create the observed pattern of surface traits. The surface traits of vocabulary, arithmetic ability, and reasoning might spring from the source trait of general mental ability. Similarly, a source trait of emotional stability may account for the surface traits of poise, calm, composure, and lack of hypochondria. Once a source trait has been identified, it becomes a common dimension on which personalities can be located. A particular individual could be described by a series of scores on each source trait (for example, high on mental ability, average on emotional stability, and so on), with the precise combination of all source traits being a description of this unique personality. In seeking source traits, Cattell is trying to discover the basic dimensions that underlie all personalities.

The key to this ambitious theory, then, is in naming and measuring the source traits. Most individual personality theorists face the same question: which are the vital, common dimensions of personality? Most answer it from intuition based on observation of the human scene. For example, Freud decided that oral, anal, and phallic characteristics were universally important. Allport also made educated guesses, for example, about expressive movements. Cattell, however, rejects the possibility of guessing what the source traits are and chooses instead to locate them by an objective analysis of human behavior.

Identification of Traits

Just as a centrifuge separates physical materials into their constituent parts, so Cattell proposes to separate psychological data into their underlying dimensions. For his psychological centrifuge, he chose the statistical technique of *factor analysis* (Cattell, 1952). He obtains many measures on each of many individuals and then analyzes all these scores statistically in order to find those that tend to go together. Groups of variables that all correlate highly with one another are surface traits. These surface traits (groups of correlated variables) are assumed to spring from some underlying statistical *factor,* which Cattell equates with his concept of source trait. The way to identify source traits, then, is to factor-analyze a large number of variables from a large number of people. The essence of Cattell's theory is that he outlines the general structure of personality and then gives a method for finding the specifics.

Cattell's Theory as an Individual Personality Theory

In choosing the trait as the core of his theory, Cattell is automatically an individual personality theorist. He proposes that people have inherent, typical ways of acting and feeling—in other words, they have traits. If you can assess an individual's traits accurately, you will know that person and be able to predict his or her behavior—almost. For surprisingly, Cattell adds that behavior is a function of the individual *and the situation.* Specifically, he says that it matters whether or not a trait is relevant in a particular situation. An ability trait such as perfect musical pitch is unlikely to be useful for a mathematical problem. But arithmetic ability and concentration are very important to such a problem, while impulsiveness is relevant in a negative sense. Thus, Cattell would weight arithmetic ability and concentration positively, impulsiveness negatively, and perfect musical pitch zero or neutral in predicting a person's performance on mathematical problems.

Cattell has not developed this "specification equation," as he calls it, in any detail. He has not classified situations in the same way he has classified traits, and therefore he has not developed any weights for the relevance of particular traits in particular situations, except in hypothetical examples. The ardent social theorist would add that Cattell's equation does not really say that the situation has a direct influence on behavior. Rather, it only permits the situation to qualify (weight) the primary influence of the trait. If, in the example of the mathematics problem, the answer were written on the blackboard for all to see, this would be a powerful situational variable that would eliminate all individual differences in performance. All traits would be irrelevant (weighted zero), and the situation itself would be the only predictor of behavior. This degree of situational influence cannot be easily expressed in Cattell's specification equation, which remains more of a gesture toward immediate environmental influence than a revision of individual personality theory on that issue. In any case, all of Cattell's research, to which we ought to turn next, has been on the identification of source traits.

EMPIRICAL STATUS

The logic of Cattell's theory is easy to follow. There are common, general source traits; these are dimensions that underlie everyone's behavior. Since the source traits are supposed to emerge from factor analysis, Cattell makes two related predictions. First, successive factor analyses of different kinds of data on the *same* people should always yield the same factors (source traits). That is, having discovered the source traits in his first factor analysis of one kind of data, Cattell can test his hypothesis that these are the ubiquitous source traits underlying all behavior by factor analyzing different kinds of behavior from the same subjects. The same factors should emerge.

Second, and for the same reasons, the same source traits should be found in *all* subjects. Factor analysis of data from different groups of people should produce the same factors. Both predictions emphasize the replicability of the results of the first factor analysis. We cannot believe that factor analysis is locating source traits unless, at the very least, it locates the same set of source traits each time. Cattell has followed exactly this strategy through an impressive program of research, particularly on temperament traits (1946, 1950, 1957), and he remains optimistic about the ultimate verification of his theory. However, attempts to date have not been successful in corroborating any of his basic premises.

Limitations of Factor Analysis

The first and probably most fundamental problem is that factor analysis has not turned out to be the infallible objective device for which Cattell had hoped. It does not automatically locate the basic dimensions underlying the data on which it operates (Humphreys, 1968). It appears that there are usually several different factor structures in any set of data, and a subjective decision by the investigator is required in order to settle on one particular solution. Even the question of how many factors to extract from a set of data is a matter of choice by the analyst.

In any case, factor analysis actually produces only a weighted listing of surface traits that go together; inferring and naming the dimensions (the source traits) that might underlie them is left to the investigator. Thus, different researchers can and do get different results from the same data. Even when the true factor structure is known (for instance, when simulated data have been generated directly from a known factor structure), the factor analysis does not find exactly that structure (Kerlinger, 1964, pp. 654-655).

Finally, there is no hard and fast method for assessing whether the factors that emerge from one set of data are in fact a good replication of previously obtained factors. It would be easy if the question were simply whether individuals have more or less the same scores in two different sets of data. This could be computed by a correlation coefficient, as Allport and Vernon did, for example. But Cattell is not initially interested in individual cases. He wants to show that the same groupings or dimensions emerge from the population as a whole. So he must somehow match these factors (which come from an entire sample, not from individuals) with another set of factors, again based on an entire sample. The question is, does "extraversion" emerge as a common dimension—not whether any particular individual is consistently high, medium, or low on extraversion.

About the method for answering this question, Peterson (1965) says

> The most common procedure involves a combination of inspection, intuition, and preconception. The investigator gazes thoughtfully at the salient variables, and decides whether one factor "appears" to be the same as another.... The criteria are seldom explicit [p. 51].

In short, although factor analysis may be an improvement on guesswork for identifying the important traits, it is not as pure and objective as its intimidating statistical complexity implies to the novice. More important, it is not at all what Cattell had hoped for and counted on for the purpose of testing his theory.

Cattell's Evidence

With these limitations in mind, we can look at Cattell's efforts to test his two major conceptual hypotheses. The first—that the same source traits underlie all behavior—requires evidence that the factor analyses of different kinds of behavior from the same people yield the same factors. For example, people should not have different source traits for a questionnaire and a performance test. To test this, Cattell has divided data from individuals into three kinds. The "life record" includes all behaviors of the person in the course of everyday life. Specifically, Cattell uses ratings by other persons who have known the subject for some time and who have observed this person in a variety of situations. Cattell hopes to replicate the source traits from these ratings in the two other kinds of data: questionnaires filled out by the subject describing him- or herself; and what he calls objective tests, such as physiological measures or other responses to standardized situations. In practice, Cattell's main research hypothesis has been that the same factors emerge from the ratings and the questionnaires—that is, from descriptions of the subject by others and by self.

Recall that whether or not factors match is largely a matter of the researcher's criterion for matching. It is obviously impossible here to go into the technical controversies that have arisen because of this ambiguity. In the end, Cattell believes he has shown several matches between rating and questionnaire factors (see, for example, Cattell, 1957). But the overwhelming judgment of his peers is that his criteria are too liberal and that he has not demonstrated any matches from one kind of data to another (Becker, 1960; Peterson, 1965; Tyler, 1965; Vernon, 1964). Researchers using the same methods themselves have also failed to find any common factors (see Becker, Peterson, Hellmer, Shoemaker, & Quay, 1959). The source traits being identified by factor analysis are not general across situations. Different dimensions of behavior emerge depending on the context in which the data are gathered.

The next question is whether these source traits are at least found universally in a given kind of data. Cattell has attempted to show that the same factors appear repeatedly in any sample of people on whom ratings by others (such as roommates, classmates, or friends) are gathered. Early studies by Cattell seemed to yield "twelve very stable and two or three less definite primary personality factors" (Cattell, 1957, p. 73). Other investigators, using the same methods, and sometimes even reanalyzing Cattell's own data, found only five significant recurring factors (see Norman, 1963). Still, these five source traits were being replicated in every sample of subjects, and this in itself was an impressive intermediate success for factor theory.

Problems with Rating Data

One investigator (Norman, 1963), however, began to wonder if the results weren't a little too good. Specifically, he noted that "even groups with rather limited histories of interpersonal association . . .produce a highly similar factor structure" (p. 581). That is, whether the rater knew the subject for three days or three years seemed to make no difference; the same five factors emerged from the data. This might mean that the average person can quickly and accurately assess the basic characteristics of anyone just met. If so, it also means that further contact, even intimate friendship, does not uncover any new or different dimensions.

To explore this curious situation, Passini and Norman (1966) went one step further: they used the same rating method for complete strangers. These were students who had simply been in the same room with one another for 15 minutes of the first class meeting of a psychology course. Although they had never even talked to one another, they were asked to rate their fellow students "as you would imagine them to be." Although it was deliberately made impossible for these ratings to be accurate, the data from this control group produced the same five factors as in earlier studies! This is a case of a theory being wounded by success. Passini and Norman concluded that these factors could not reflect anything about the personalities of their subjects—not in their study, and probably not in any of the earlier studies. Since the ratings could not have reflected characteristics of the subjects, they must have sprung from the heads of the raters. That is, they must reflect stereotypes that we all have about others (and possibly about ourselves).

These stereotypes seem to operate to make people consistent. An example from the ratings and factors of these studies will make this clear. In all the studies, the raters were asked to judge each person on many dimensions including these:

talkative—silent

frank and open—secretive

adventurous—cautious

sociable—reclusive

Having decided, on any basis, that a person is more on the silent than the talkative side, it seems reasonable to call this same person more secretive than frank. Surely, silent people are not frank and open. Similarly, a silent, secretive person is not adventurous or sociable, so cautious and reclusive are also chosen. A person initially identified as talkative would receive the opposite rating on all four characteristics. The result would be a high correlation among the four ratings, hence a factor.

Thus, the rater probably does not think about each characteristic separately. Instead, he or she tends to put together terms that seem nearly synonymous. If most people use these terms in the same way, it is this common semantic structure that the factor analysis will discover. In fact, when the ratings are factor-analyzed, the four dimensions in this example do emerge as one factor. This means that most raters put them together; they treat each rated characteristic as a repetition of the same underlying dimension. This would explain why the same dimensions emerge whether or not the rater has any knowledge of the personality of the subject. It is quite possible that, in all these studies, the factors that emerge reflect the *raters'* ways of describing people and not the personality structure of the subjects.

Norman and Goldberg (1966) have developed this argument more rigorously. They reaffirm, first, that

> it [is] possible to obtain factor structures that are similar to those derived by previous investigators in situations where the results could not possibly be attributable to the personality characteristics of the ratees [pp. 681-682].

But they also point out that it is not possible, in some cases, to prove that the factors that emerged were *not* attributable to the ratees' personalities. The factors may, in some cases, be a bit of both—raters' preconceptions about traits and ratees' actual traits. They discuss some methods for sorting these out in rating data. Shweder (1975) offers more evidence on this issue.

Such possible solutions were not used, however, in Cattell's or any of the earlier data. So Cattell has failed thus far to demonstrate the replicability of source traits across different groups of people. The early, apparent replication may well be, in whole or part, due to an artifact—namely, the raters' common stereotypes. This artifact might be corrected by, for instance, using a specific rather than a global rating system. Raters would count particular behaviors (such as amount of time spent talking) rather than supplying global impressions (such as "talkative"). This would relieve the rater of making inferences that have been shown to be frequently interdependent.[1] Alternatively, the research hypothesis could be shifted to a different kind of data altogether, such as standardized tests.

Cattell is one of the personality theorists who has worked hardest toward the ideal of verifying his theory. Since he has stated his hypotheses and methods quite clearly, it is possible to find out directly whether he is right or wrong. Although some feel that Cattell himself is inclined to see positive results when others cannot (Hall & Lindzey, 1970, p. 409), there is not room for much disagreement about the current status of his theory. The results are not convincing so far, but it would be hasty to say that it has all been for nothing, as the process of testing a theory is usually productive in itself.

If Cattell's theory had seemed farfetched at the outset, it would not have been worth much to show that its status is moot. But Cattell's is a reasonable and almost inevitable individual theory of personality. Therefore it is useful to

---

[1]For other purposes, one might not wish to get rid of the artifact at all. This interdependence of inferences is a significant aspect of "person perception," or how we make judgments about other people. In studies of person perception, however, the subject is always the perceiver (rater), not the person whose personality is being judged.

know about its empirical trials and tribulations. Furthermore, when a particular research hypothesis fails, the reasons for the failure are usually clear. In Cattell's case, we now know that factor analysis is not as definitive as it might be; that the situation in which personality data is gathered makes a difference; and that raters' stereotypes can contaminate personality data. Each of these is a useful bit of knowledge, and, more important, each suggests a modification of Cattell's original theory that might be more successful. Only a theory that has been tested has the possibility of growing into a more accurate theory on the basis of the data it encounters.

7

Sheldon

THE THEORY

William H. Sheldon's theory of personality is a simple and straightforward one—namely, that inherited physique helps determine an individual's character. Like most personality theories, this one has a folk basis: it formalizes commonly held beliefs. For example, the Fowlers's *Phrenology: A Practical Guide to Your Head* (1969) is an amusing but historically accurate collection of psychological interpretations of face, body, and so on.

Sheldon has proposed, in scientific terms, the old and widespread notion that we can accurately judge personality by looks. There are many different folk theories of this type. Some emphasize the set of the eyes or the shape of the face; others propose that beauty or strength reflect moral virtue. Sheldon has focused on physique, or the shape of the body and its various parts. By physique, he means especially the relative dominance of fat, muscle, or skeleton.

Physique and Temperament

Sheldon took a taxonomic approach. His first goal was to discover the dimensions on which physique could be classified. After intensive study of thousands of photographs, Sheldon and his colleagues (1940) concluded that there were three primary components of physique: *endomorphy* (fat), *mesomorphy* (muscular), and *ectomorphy* (skeletal, frail), as well as a number of secondary components. In assessing these dimensions of physique, Sheldon tries to look past the effects of the environment (such as diet and exercise) in order to measure the genotype—that is, the inherited structure of the body. His estimate of this true structure is called the *somatotype*.

Contrary to a common misunderstanding about Sheldon's system, he does not simply classify people into three types corresponding to the three primary components. Rather, he assumes that each of us has some degree of each component and therefore can be rated on each dimension. Only in rare cases, with the highest possible rating on one dimension and the lowest possible ratings on the other two, would we find a physical "type."

Sheldon proposes that the amount of each component will correspond to differences in temperament. To describe differences in temperament, he developed a parallel system of dimensions on which temperament might vary. Using an informal kind of factor analysis, he proposed three universal components of temperament: *viscerotonia*, with predominant love of food and comfort, in which "the soul has its seat in the splendid gut" (Sheldon, 1942, p. 248); *somatotonia*, with a craving for vigorous action; and *cerebrotonia*, characterized by restraint, inhibition, and apprehensiveness. These are Sheldon's basic personality trait dimensions.

The exact manner in which body type shapes personality is not of great concern to Sheldon. He can accept that temperament might be inherited, in a genetic pattern shared with physique. However, he seems to favor environmental mediation—that is, the different experiences that different body types are likely to engender (Hall & Lindzey, 1970, pp. 363-365). For instance, fat people are expected to be affable, gregarious food-lovers. Athletically built individuals are more likely to be recruited onto the playing field and out of the classroom. A frail child is not expected to be athletic and seldom succeeds even on trying. Thus, the body type controls social expectations, makes some experiences more likely than others, and determines success and failure in various activities. All these experiences, according to Sheldon, can ultimately be traced to the body type. That is, the body type is a stimulus for certain responses from other people, responses which in turn affect the personality in the body.

Sheldon's Theory as an Individual Personality Theory

Sheldon's theory is an anomaly among personality theories, for two reasons. First, Sheldon emphasizes genetic causes of behavior. Most psychologists have remained on the environmental side of heredity/environment debates. Individual personality theorists usually argue that the influence of the current environment on an adult's behavior is small relative to the enduring influence of his or her traits. But they do propose that those traits originated in early interaction with the environment. Only Cattell thinks enough of inherited personality traits to make an explicit, though small, place for them in his theory. Sheldon, on the other hand, traces most of personality to genetic endowment, with environment serving only to implement genetic effects. Sheldon does credit the social influences to which the person has been exposed with shaping less significant aspects of temperament.

The viscerotonic may of course express his temperamental predominance in a wide variety of ways. He may be culturally polished and urbane, or crude and uneducated. He may be bishop or bumpkin, scholar or butcher, aggressive or meek, energetic or lazy—in short he may live out *any* role in life which permits the expression of a predominant viscerotonia [Sheldon, 1942, p. 249].

Sheldon's second eccentricity is his choice of physical, rather than psychological, causes of behavior. His genetic theory might be palatable to more psychologists if he proposed the direct inheritance of psychological characteristics, such as innate differences in intelligence, activity, or aggressiveness. Instead, he proposes that physique is a primary cause of human behavior, so that a person must first be classified physically in order to be understood psychologically. Modern psychologists regard constitutional theories (such as Hippocrates's humors, Lombroso's criminal faces, and the art of phrenology) as quaint, naive, historical oddities. This prejudice tends to be extended to any constitutional theory, including Sheldon's, even though it is not at all quaint or naive.

Yet for all his isolation on these issues, Sheldon is definitely a traditional, individual personality theorist. It would be hard to find concepts more individual, with less reference to the environment, than physique and temperament, as Sheldon uses them. Recall that Sheldon believes that the important physical characteristics are not influenced by environmental vicissitudes but can be assessed just as they come from the genes, so to speak. Temperament, too, may be inherited or may be the result of some interaction with the social environment, as described above. But even in the latter case, Sheldon does not expect variations in social environment to determine temperament. Rather, the innate variation in physique automatically creates an environment that will shape temperament according to body type. Thus, the social environment is at best only a "go-between" that implements the influence of body type on temperament but does not have any influence in itself. Thus the primary—indeed, the only—cause of behavior that Sheldon discusses lies within the individual.

Sheldon's pursuit of individual differences is also typical of the individual personality theorist. His primary goal is to identify the dimensions of physique and temperament on which individuals can be compared—that is, their physical and psychological traits. He assumes explicitly that the somatotype rating would not change throughout a lifetime and that temperament is similarly enduring. He also expects temperament to pervade the broad range of an individual's activities. For example, the cerebrotonic is described as tense, self-conscious, easily fatigued, insomniac, susceptible to alcoholism or schizoid escape from reality, introverted, more inclined to thought than to action, and rarely able to sing! (Sheldon, 1942, pp. 271-279.) Sheldon's individual-difference dimensions obviously assume the stability over time and generality across situations that is typical of individual personality theories. In fact, although there has been considerable debate over the permanence and causal importance of Sheldon's physique dimensions, there has been little debate about the temperament dimensions, which are indistinguishable in form from most other proposed personality traits.

EMPIRICAL STATUS

Considering how far Sheldon's theory is from the mainstream of psychology, it may be surprising to find that the empirical basis of the theory is more substantial than that of most personality theories. Not that his theory has been wholly confirmed. But it has been subjected to the kind of research that goes to the heart of the issue. Sheldon has made a serious effort not just to illustrate but actually to prove his theory. Perhaps it was the very lack of intuitive acceptance for a constitutional theory that made this necessary. As scientists, we are supposed to require evidence for any theory, but, as humans, we often demand more evidence from theories that jar our preconceptions than from those that fit them easily.

Sheldon's Evidence

Sheldon's research is aimed directly at his basic premise—that inherited physique largely determines temperament. To test this conceptual hypothesis, he needs three kinds of data: a comprehensive and objective measure of genetic physique; a comprehensive and objective measure of temperament; and correlations between the two. Sheldon directed most of his research efforts to exactly these goals (1940, 1942, 1954).

The first two steps have already been described briefly. First, he derived the dimensions of physique (endomorphy, mesomorphy, and ectomorphy) from the study of nude photographs of literally thousands of men.[1] He quantified this classification into his somatotype rating system, which is quite objective in use (Sheldon, Lewis, & Tenny, 1969; Rees, 1961). Next, he observed and interviewed a small group of men intensively for a year, until he derived his temperament dimensions (viscerotonia, somatotonia, and cerebrotonia).

Finally, he applied both sets of measures to a new sample of 200 men and obtained the following high correlations between somatotype and temperament: endomorphy and viscerotonia, .79; mesomorphy and somatotonia, .82; ectomorphy and cerebrotonia, .83 (Sheldon, 1942). This confirmed his research hypothesis, that particular physical characteristics are significantly related to particular temperaments. Sheldon had followed the logic of his theory to this final result, which appeared to be a success unparalleled in personality research.

Problems with Sheldon's Data

Unfortunately, it is not that clear. Both proponents and opponents of constitutional psychology have criticized Sheldon's work extensively. Four of the less technical but more important objections will be given here.

[1]Sheldon planned but did not complete a similar study of women, principally because of conventional sanctions against the necessary photographing of nude females. It is unclear whether he considered his findings to be general across sexes.

First, Sheldon asserts that the somatotype that he measures is a direct estimate of the genotype. If this measure of body type is genetically determined, then identical twins should have perfectly correlated somatotype scores. In fact, these correlations are more on the order of .36 for males and .61 for females (Lindzey, 1967)—too low to claim exclusively genetic influence. Further, some investigators have found that the somatotype changes significantly under environmental pressures, such as partial starvation (Lasker, 1947), and perhaps even with age alone (Newman, 1952).

If the somatotype is not constant, then either it is not measuring the genetic body type, or the body type itself changes. Either alternative is bad for Sheldon's theory. Acknowledging the first possibility, Sheldon has proposed a new method of measurement which should not be susceptible to change (Sheldon, Lewis, & Tenny, 1969). Only further research will tell whether this is true. When the new measure has been shown to be higher for twins and stable over time, then the correlations with temperament will have to be obtained anew, because the original correlations, however impressive, were based on the questionable somatotype measure.

The second and most common objection to the remarkable correlations that Sheldon found between physique and temperament is that Sheldon made both sets of ratings himself. Since the ratings, especially the temperament ratings, involve considerable subjective inference, he may have inadvertently biased the results in favor of his hypothesis. That is, he may have seen what he expected to see. The appropriate check on this possibility is to separate the two measurement procedures. Child (1950) gave questionnaires to his subjects instead of rating their temperaments himself. Walker (1962) had two different groups of judges do the physical and psychological ratings; some of these judges did not even know the hypothesis being tested. Both these studies confirmed Sheldon's original findings, *but to a lesser degree*. Child's highest correlation was .39, compared to Sheldon's high of .83. Similar positive but weak relationships were found between unbiased measures obtained by Hanley (1951) and by Davidson, McInnes, and Parnell (1957). These studies show that Sheldon probably did inadvertently bias his results but that there is still a small, significant relationship between body type and temperament. These correlations are just as high as Allport and Vernon's best correlations on a much smaller sample (recall pages 44-45). It is evidence of a double standard that Sheldon's correlations are commonly discounted, whereas Allport and Vernon's are cited as evidence for expressive traits.

The third problem with Sheldon's evidence is not so easily resolved. Correlations do not necessarily tell us anything about causality. While there are correlational research designs that may sort out causality, Sheldon's was not one of them. Even if replicated with a more stable somatotype measure, the positive correlations between somatotype and temperament ratings could mean that body type causes temperament, as Sheldon proposes. They could also mean that temperament causes body type; or that a single factor is being measured by both. This last possibility is especially plausible when one looks at the items on the temperament scales—which are surprisingly "physical" for temperament scales. Viscerotonia, for example, includes love of eating, slow reactions, and relaxation of posture and movement. Somatotonia includes love of exercise, overmaturity of appearance, and being energetic. Thus, Sheldon's ideas of temperament and physique seem to blend together into a single, hybrid concept, which both scales may be measuring. A test that needs to be made is whether larger correlations with physique are found for these physical aspects of temperament than for the more psychological items on the scale—for example, the viscerotonic's amiability.

This question is related to the fourth problem in Sheldon's data: how homogeneous are the behaviors within each temperament category? When he uses the term *temperament*, Sheldon seems to mean two different things. Each of the three basic components of temperament refers to the dominance of a single *motive*; for example, viscerotonia is "a manifest desire to embrace the environment and to make its substance one with [oneself]" (Sheldon, 1942, p. 248). But each component is also characterized by a remarkably heterogeneous set of specific *behaviors* that may or may not be related to the central motive (recall the cerebrotonic's varied characteristics, page 56). Sheldon cannot simply assume that these specific behaviors go together and that they reflect the motive. He must, at a minimum, demonstrate that each correlates highly with the others. Although his initial cluster analysis was aimed at guaranteeing this, later research by Sheldon and others has used an assortment of indicators of each temperament dimension without showing that they in fact correlate highly. (This problem of consistency among specific manifestations of a hypothetical general trait is the same one that Allport and Vernon faced. It will be discussed in further detail in Chapter 12.)

With all of these qualifications, which indicate the need for further research, one should not lose sight of Sheldon's unusual commitment to the empirical verification of his theory. Like Cattell, he did not nibble around the edges with anecdotes or illustrative experiments. He stated his entire theory in a testable form and set out to test it. Theories that are put to the test have the healthy effect of presenting something tangible to debate. It should not be surprising that further work is required to confirm or disconfirm Sheldon's theory. But his theory is further ahead than those that have not been tossed into the fray.

8

Murray

THE THEORY

Henry A. Murray's enduring interest has been in long-term, intensive understanding of the individual case. Thus, he shares with Allport and Freud a preference for idiographic study. As much as any personality theorist, Murray has taken the risk of an overwhelmingly elaborate theory, in his effort to carve out a satisfactory statement of individual human nature. He incorporates and modifies many of Freud's concepts. For example, he fits "claustral," or pre-natal, and "urethral" complexes into the oral/anal/phallic sequence. But Murray's theory is too much his own to be considered psychodynamic or simply a derivative of psychoanalysis. His writings are immediate evidence of his originality. Murray's neologisms spring at the reader, one after the other, each forcing us to stop and pay close attention to yet another aspect of personality that might otherwise be ignored. *Regnancy, proceeding, thema, subsidiation*, and *actone* join dozens of other newly coined or newly defined terms, all of which aim at a true personology: an encompassing theory of the individual in all his or her aspects, from birth to death.

The Concept of Need

Not even Murray would try to summarize his theory in a few pages. But not all of his theory is equally important for our purposes. Central to Murray's theory, and his major contribution to individual personality theory, is his emphasis on motivation, particularly his concept of *need*. Murray formalizes a tendency we all share, the inclination to ascribe motivation to behavior (Heider, 1958). The child who doesn't perform well lacks the "desire to excel"; tidy persons have a "need for order"; and even frolicking animals have a "need (or instinct) to play." Murray does for needs what Allport did for traits: he focuses on a widely used term and makes its meaning and uses clearer.

Just as Allport infers traits from behavioral consistencies, Murray infers needs from organized behavioral sequences. For example,

restlessness $\longrightarrow$ searching $\longrightarrow$ eating $\longrightarrow$ satiation

is a sequence from which we can infer a need for food. Similarly, a sequence that includes

a difficult problem $\longrightarrow$ tension $\longrightarrow$ mastery $\longrightarrow$ pride

may reveal a need for achievement.

Murray is careful to require that a consistent sequence be observed before a need is inferred. In this way, he avoids the circular and sterile use that often befalls motivational terms. For example, the observer sees one person strike another, infers a need for aggression in the attacker, then explains the attack by this need for aggression. Why did he hit him? Because he has a need for aggression. How do you know he has this need? Because he hit him. In this "circle of interpretation" (Kaplan, 1964, p. 362), the need is inferred from a single piece of behavior and then used to explain that same behavior. Murray escapes this circularity by requiring several independent events, in a particular sequence, as the basis of his inference—namely, a particular emotion (such as anger); selective attention to certain objects (such as male peers); a particular mode of behavior (such as sarcasm or hitting); a particular goal or effect (such as pain to the other); and satisfaction or disappointment, depending on whether or not the effect is achieved (Murray, 1938). Furthermore, he aims to predict *new* behaviors and not simply to account for what has already been observed.

From long-term observation and the reports of his subjects, Murray attempted a complete taxonomy of needs. Through several revisions, he has produced the standard list of eight physical and 20 psychological needs seen in many psychology texts (Murray, 1938). Using his own notational system, from *n Abasement* (the need to abase or submit oneself) to *n Understanding* (the need to understand ideas and events), Murray commits himself to a list of needs, one or more of which should apply to any human activity. Sexual activity, for example, may be motivated both by the physical need for sex and by a psychological need for affiliation, dominance, play, or even exhibition.

Having proposed this universal list of human needs, Murray uses a number of additional ideas to account for individual differences in behavior. Needs may take on different objects. For example, the child reared in a single-child nuclear family would express n Affiliation differently than would the communally reared child. Similarly, characteristic modes of behavior are used to satisfy the same need in different persons: some achieve in the hockey rink and others in the library. Finally, certain needs can, for one reason or another, become dominant and be observed much more frequently in some persons than in others.

Murray uses *need* as more than a static, descriptive term, useful for classifying behaviors into meaningful groups. He also implies a dynamic process—an active, goal-directed sequence that begins with arousal and ends with some form of satisfaction. Although he is careful to define needs in terms of observable behavior, there is no doubt that Murray believes that people experience their needs subjectively, whether consciously or unconsciously. This additional degree of inference, beyond merely descriptive usage, is the primary difference between the concepts of need and trait. Both can account for the same observed consistencies in behavior, but traits are not so "anthropomorphic."

Murray's Theory as an Individual Personality Theory

Despite these differences in degree of inference, Murray is completely the individual personality theorist in his treatment of needs. He predicts a substantial consistency in human behavior; he locates the cause of this consistency in the individual's personality (in the form of needs); and he expects systematic differences among individuals either in kind or amount of behavior. In all other aspects of his theory not discussed here, Murray is equally a traditional, individual personality theorist.

In all aspects, that is, but one. The exception in his concept of *press*, or situational influence. Both need and press refer to forces on the individual that lead to behavior. But press is external, rather than internal, in origin. Objects or situations that can initiate and direct behavior are press.[1] For example, an insult or frustration from another person may elicit aggression. Murray calls this situation *p Aggression*—that is, an environmental pressure to aggress as opposed to a self-generated inner need. Again, Murray cautions against too quickly inferring press from behavior; and again he proposes a taxonomy, in his several lists of press, including p Danger, p Lack or Loss, and p Dominance. But both his methods and his taxonomies are more cursory on the topic of press than of need.

Murray says, in effect, that there are external influences as well as internal ones, but he does not become much more specific than this. He does break with individual personality theories to the extent that he includes this term for ongoing or immediate environmental influences in the language of his theory. But he devotes so little to developing the concept that one must conclude either that he thought press were relatively unimportant (compared to needs), or that he was not particularly interested in these external conditions.

EMPIRICAL STATUS

Murray made some distinctive additions to the available techniques for measuring personality, but he did not test his own theory. His best-known contribution to personality research is the *Thematic Apperception Test*, or *TAT* (Murray, 1938). Subjects are asked to tell stories about each of a standard set of pictures. These stories are analyzed with the assumption that, in creating the stories about the pictures, an individual "is apt to expose his own personality as much as the phenomenon to which he is attending" (p. 531). The subject is

---

[1]Murray uses the same term, *press*, for both singular and plural.

assumed to project personal needs and experiences into the stories he or she makes up. Thus, if a male subject says that the man in the picture is unhappy because he wants to travel and see the world, the tester assumes that the subject himself has this problem. The subject's freedom to respond with any story he can think of, plus the assumption that the story is about himself and not the picture, make this a *projective* test, like the Rorschach (inkblot) test.

Murray and his colleagues used this technique extensively in their clinical analysis of individuals (Murray, 1943), but they did not develop formal rules for its use. Later McClelland, Atkinson, and their coauthors (McClelland, Atkinson, Clark, & Lowell, 1953) selected the need for achievement from Murray's list and formalized its measurement by the TAT in quantitative terms. That is, they worked out a scoring system whereby the amount of need for achievement a subject has can be measured from his or her TAT stories. This line of research has evolved into something quite different from Murray's original theory, and it will be discussed in Chapter 13.

In his research, Murray provides another example of an already familiar problem in the field of personality. He has illustrated his theory extensively with cases and examples, but he has not tested any of his ideas. That is, he has never said: if what I propose is true, then such-and-such must be found, or else I am wrong. Although he has defined needs, for example, carefully and in empirical terms, he has not suggested how his comprehensive list of all human needs is to be verified, nor how individual differences in the strength, mode, or object of a need are to be confirmed. As Hall and Lindzey conclude after an overview of Murray's research:

> In Murray's system there is definitely a set of concepts, and a related set of empirical definitions, but . . .there is *no* set of explicitly stated psychological assumptions linked to these concepts in such a manner as to produce testable consequences . . . .[T]he research which Murray and his students have done is not to be considered in any direct way the consequence of his theory. His investigations have not been focused on testing predictions which derive explicitly from his theoretical position [1970, p. 204].[2]

To understand this conspicuous deficiency, it is necessary to understand that, at the time Murray (and Freud, Allport, and others) wrote, it was not considered much of a deficiency. Personality theorists concerned themselves with theories of human nature in the broadest terms, and not with the additional, formidable task of testing those theories. The field of personality has traditionally been a sanctuary for free speculation within the science of psychology, and one cannot blame Murray retroactively because this tradition is changing.

In addition, Murray's personal view about research is skeptical, at best. He equates validation and precision with narrowness and trivial specialization (1940, p. 154). Since his first priority is a completely encompassing theory,

---

[2]From *Theories of Personality* (2nd Ed.), by C.S. Hall and G. Lindzey. Copyright © 1970 by John Wiley & Sons, Inc. Reprinted by permission.

testing any particular part of the theory seems to Murray to emphasize that part out of proportion to the whole. That is, to test is necessarily to specialize, and in Murray's opinion this would shred the elaborate fabric that he is trying to weave together. Logically, then, one cannot begin anywhere.

There are two counterarguments against this position. First, while everyone would agree that trivial research is worthless (by definition), it is not necessary to equate explicit and limited aims with triviality. The difference lies in the time perspective that a researcher has. Murray's arguments against starting anywhere imply that the researcher would inevitably go no further. If, on the other hand, he or she starts somewhere with the explicit intention to explore the entire theory, then the immediate necessity to focus is far less threatening. Further, if the theory is arranged in logical order as are Cattell's and Sheldon's, then the starting place and the series of tests required are clear. In other words, to the extent that the theory does not give a clue where to begin, it is deficient as a theory—both because it is insufficiently organized as a body of thought, and because it is not amenable to sensible empirical testing.

The second defense of empirical tests of any theory is that it matters, in the end, whether the theory is accurate in what it says about human nature. No matter what objections one may have about the way research is often done (and it is often done poorly), one cannot dismiss the *principle* of empirical support for a theory without both leaving the realm of science entirely and shedding one's scientific credentials. A philosophy or opinion about human nature is, in a scientific sense, an unfinished work.

9

Rogers

The two individual personality theories to be described last are often called *phenomenological* theories. *Phenomenology* has taken on a meaning in psychology different from its original meaning in philosophy. Here it means "the systematic investigation of conscious experience" (Drever, 1952, p. 210), especially in preference to the study of behavior or of the subconscious. Both Carl Rogers and George Kelly reject the perspective of the other theories described so far, which view the person from outside, as an object under the observer's knowing eye. Instead, they propose to study me in my own terms, entering as much as possible into my consciousness, to learn how I see both world and myself. These are theories in the first person rather than the third person.

This position is not new, nor is its subjectivity necessarily antiscientific, as it may sound at first. The famous historian of experimental psychology, E.G. Boring, showed that "experimental psychology began as phenomenology, as the taxonomy of consciousness" (1957, p. 21). For example, early work in perception was marked by the discovery of the difference between the objective characteristics of the stimulus (say, wave length of light) and its subjective impact (color). So Rogers and Kelly adopt an old perspective and use it to build their personality theories. Beyond this common point, however, they go in different directions.

THE THEORY

Like Freud, Rogers's first interest is clinical psychology. However, in treating his clients (a term he preferred to "patients"), Rogers began, quite naturally, to make inferences about the nature of their troubles. This led to an informal theory of personality—what people must be like, given their behavior

(1947, 1951). Subsequently, Rogers (1959) has systematized some of his ideas, but this has never been his primary goal, and the job is largely unfinished.

The Phenomenological Perspective

In his most formal paper (1959, pp. 221-234), Rogers presents his theory developmentally, beginning with the infant and continuing through the normal and abnormal development of personality. He begins with the basic phenomenological position: the infant's reality is what it experiences. Thus, as one would expect of a phenomenological theory, Rogers is interested in an individual's conscious mind. He defines personality largely in terms of conscious events—in contrast to Freud, who focused on the unconscious, and to trait theorists, who were not particularly concerned with dividing the mind into levels at all.

Rogers believes that most experience is conscious. He proposes that for each individual this takes the form of an *experiential* (or *phenomenal*) *field*. This is the world as I see it. It is the private and unique view that each person has at any particular moment. We can only imagine someone else's experiential field by empathy, by pretending we are in that person's skin, seeing the world through his or her eyes. The phenomenal field is neither an accurate nor a complete picture of the person's objective world; but it is not wrong in any sense, because it is completely subjective and idiographic. Returning to the infant, its reality is what it experiences. Even the infant has better knowledge of its own internal frame of reference than does anyone else, and this is the reality that will regulate its behavior.

Self-Actualization and Self-Concept

Rogers ascribes a second important characteristic to the infant: an inherent tendency for the organism to *actualize* itself. *Self-actualization* is the drive to enhance, to develop, to become one's best self. Jung, Goldstein, Maslow, Angyal, and others, as well as Rogers, have proposed this basic motive to grow and to change (see, for example, Maddi, 1976, Chapters 3 and 7; or Hall & Lindzey, 1970, Chapters 8 and 13-14). It is often contrasted to the more usual motives or needs (such as hunger or loneliness) that aim only to make up deficits and to reduce all needs to zero. Self-actualization is positive and additive. Rogers goes on to propose that the infant values and seeks experiences that are perceived as either maintaining or actualizing and avoids those that negate maintenance or enhancement. This is the first motive.

The actualizing tendency leads to differentiation and refinement of experience. A most important part of this process is the development of a concept of *self*. There are many events and objects in the experiential field. Most change, but some are permanent. One that emerges early and persists for life is the self. Each person sees him- or herself as an important object in the phenomenal world: *I* perceive *me*. Self-experience (awareness of one's own being) becomes differentiated from the rest of the individual's experiences. Everyone has a phenomenal field, and within it there is always a self. This concept is so important to Rogers's theory that his is often called "self theory."

Positive Regard and Self-Regard

As the awareness of self emerges, how the self is valued by others becomes important. A pervasive, persistent, and universal need emerges: the need for *positive regard*—that is, the need to know that others think well of oneself. Rogers proposes that this second motive is a very potent one and can even override the actualizing motive. The individual may seek to gain the positive regard of others rather than to develop and self-actualize.

Part of the importance of positive regard from others is that it becomes independent of those who give it and is incorporated into the self. This is experienced as *self-regard*, an evaluation of the self by oneself, independently of others. That is, the person perceives others as evaluating the self and subsequently does so as well. The experience "Mother thinks I am good" becomes "I am good." Like positive regard (by others), self-regard is a broad disposition. The person does not merely feel "I am a good (or poor) tennis player," but "I am a worthwhile (or worthless) person."

Conditions of Worth

Furthermore, the individual tends to seek out those experiences that yield positive regard (and, therefore, self-regard). These become *conditions of worth*, or contingencies, usually imposed by the parents, that must be satisfied in order for the person to receive positive regard and avoid negative evaluation of the self. In Rogers's view this is a bad, although inevitable, step in development. If an individual received unconditional positive regard, then self-regard would be similarly unconditional, and neither would interfere with self-actualization.

Rogers illustrates the usual course of development as follows:

> The infant learns to need love [positive regard]. Love is very satisfying, but to know whether he is receiving it or not he must observe his mother's face, gestures, and other ambiguous signs. He develops a total gestalt as to the way he is regarded by his mother and each new experience of love or rejection tends to alter the whole gestalt. Consequently each behavior on his mother's part such as a specific disapproval of a specific behavior tends to be experienced as disapproval in general. So important is this to the infant that he comes to be guided in his behavior not by the degree to which an experience maintains or enhances the organism, but by the likelihood of receiving maternal love.
>
> Soon he learns to view himself in much the same way, liking or disliking himself as a total configuration. He tends, quite independently of his mother or others, to view himself and his behavior in the same way they have. This means that some behaviors are regarded positively which are not actually experienced organismically as satisfying. Other behaviors are re-

garded negatively which are not actually experienced as unsatisfying. It is when he behaves in accordance with these introjected values that he may be said to have acquired conditions of worth. He cannot regard himself positively, as having worth, unless he lives in terms of these conditions [1959, p. 225].[1]

Thus, the developing individual can be alienated from his or her own feelings. For a child, sitting still and keeping quiet are probably very unsatisfying and contribute nothing to self-actualization. But—from the child's-eye view—I come to value this behavior and engage in it because it is praised, and I feel I am a good person when I do it. This, according to Rogers, is the beginning of psychological maladjustment.

The effects of conditions of worth are insidious. Not only do I choose to satisfy them rather than to actualize myself, but I will even distort or deny reality in order to do so. Impulses or experiences that are incongruent with the conditions of worth are distorted and made congruent, or denied altogether. The individual begins to perceive selectively and drives a wedge of *incongruence between self and experience*. I relabel or am no longer even aware of feelings or behaviors that threaten my self-regard. A "wrong" thought or action, one that violates a previous condition of worth, is threatening and leads to anxiety. This is handled by defenses such as rationalization, projection, fantasy, and so forth. Even the normal person maintains self-regard by denying a mistake, by blaming others, or by imagining a better outcome. Abnormal development, even psychotic states, are only different in the degree of incongruence or in the necessity to deal with it in socially unacceptable ways.

This is the core of Rogers's theory: the adult is the product of these hypothesized early experiences. Rogers has gone on to describe abnormal development, psychotherapy, and interpersonal relations in similar terms. For example, the critical element of therapy is unconditional positive regard, in order to remove the conditions of worth that cause distortion. This and other proposals are all applications derived from the basic assumptions about people, their motives, and their experiences, that have been summarized here.

Rogers's Theory as an Individual Personality Theory

Is Rogers an individual personality theorist? Phenomenological theories are concerned with the person's view of the world. Since they include both the person and this world, they have the potential to be either individual or social theories, or even to combine these two perspectives. It all depends on which aspect the theorist chooses to emphasize. An individual personality theorist considers personality to be a relatively fixed property of the individual, not varying or changing with the current environment; consequently, the terms in an individual theory refer to characteristics of the individual, not the environ-

---

[1]From "A Theory of Therapy, Personality, and Interpersonal Relationships, as Developed in the Client-Centered Framework," by C.R. Rogers. In S. Koch (Ed.), *Psychology: A Study of a Science* (Vol.3). Copyright 1959 by McGraw-Hill, Inc. This and all other quotations from this source are used with permission of McGraw-Hill Book Company.

ment. Individual personality theorists also propose differences among individuals in the degree to which they have particular characteristics.

Of all the events and objects in the experiential field, Rogers is almost exclusively interested in the self, its characteristics and processes. As mentioned above, Rogers's theory is a "self theory." Because he emphasizes characteristics of the individual (self-concept, self-regard, congruence of self and experience), Rogers is an individual personality theorist. External influences, such as the imposition of conditions of worth, are hypothetical, *past* events that are significant only for their residual in terms of conditional self-regard. Individual differences are one result of this past experience, and Rogers proposes individual differences in degree of incongruency, of self-actualization, of denial or distortion of experience, of adjustment, and so forth.

EMPIRICAL STATUS

Theoretical Problems

Even in the most thoroughgoing statement of his theory, Rogers was quite explicit that his theory was not as complete or as rigorously stated as it might be:

> This is a developing system, in which some of the older portions are being formulated with considerable logical rigor, while newer portions are more informal, and contain some logical and systematic gaps and flaws, and still others (not presented) exist as highly personal and subjective hunches [1959, p. 244].

And, despite his often critical attitude about empirical testing, Rogers added:

> Still another urgent need . . .is the translation of the present theory into terms which meet the rigorous requirements of the logic of science. Although progress in this direction has been made there is still a woefully long distance to go. Such a development, carried through by competent persons, would greatly sharpen the deductive hypotheses which might be drawn from the system, and hence provide more crucial tests of it [1959, p. 251].

Rogers did suggest several predictions based on his theory, some of which will be discussed below. But the ambiguities left in his theory may make empirical testing impossible (Wylie, 1968, 1974[2]). There are substantial difficulties in Rogers's theory, as presently stated, in at least three areas: (1) his phenomenology, (2) his definition of self, and (3) the relationship between motives. These will be explained in turn.

The phenomenological position that Rogers takes emphasizes the in-

---

[2]Wylie, 1974, is a particularly good summary of research on the self-concept. The 1961 and 1974 editions differ considerably, and both are useful.

fluence of conscious experience on behavior. "Reality is what is experienced." Yet Rogers stresses the possibility, even the likelihood, of incongruence between self and organismic experience. Thus, "some behaviors are regarded positively [for the self] which are not actually experienced organismically as satisfying" (1959, p. 225). Which, then, is phenomenological reality?

In handling this problem, Rogers introduces ideas that amount to a kind of unconscious. When self and experience conflict, Rogers proposes a process he calls "subception" (in contrast to perception), in which information that is seen as threatening to the self-concept is kept out of awareness. While this is not unconscious in the full-blown Freudian sense, it does propose a part of the mind that is being actively kept from consciousness. Indeed, Rogers sounds very much like Freud when he describes a sequence of threat (to self-regard), anxiety, and defense. The threat is not necessarily an instinctual impulse, and the self rather than the superego resists it. But the result is still a substantial role for unconscious events in determining anxiety and defensive behavior. This is an awkward position for a phenomenologist of conscious experience.

A similar difficulty is Rogers's considerable emphasis on the enduring influence of past events. The conscious mind exists *now*. Although Rogers claims to be appropriately ahistorical, he in fact presents his theory developmentally, indicating the critical and lasting influence of past events on adult life. Neither the unconscious nor the influence of past events is inherently deplorable in a theory of personality. But these ideas, which he uses heavily, are inconsistent with Rogers's avowed emphasis on conscious influence (Wylie, 1974, Chapter 2).

A second major problem is in Rogers's definitions of *self* (Smith, 1950). Originally, he clearly defines the self as an object in the experiential field. It is like the image one sees in a mirror—a perceived entity like any other object of perception, except for the importance of its being perceived as good or valuable. But other self-like concepts are also implied in the theory. The organism has experiences and seeks actualization. The self-as-object cannot experience or seek anything; it is not the agent but the object of experience. Therefore, the organism must be a second, separate concept.

Then there is the self who feels threatened by organismic or external experiences incongruent with the self-concept. This self resorts to subception and defense to maintain self-regard. Who is this third self? It cannot be the self-as-object, which is an object of perception, incapable of feeling or acting. Nor can it be the organism, which has the experiences that are so threatening to this other self. This third use of the term *self* is quite similar to Freud's concept of the ego with its defense mechanisms. In any case, it will not be possible to study the self (or selves) without clearer definitions and distinctions.

Finally, Rogers is inconsistent regarding the relative importance of the motives he proposes. He has said that self-actualization is "the only motive which is postulated in this theoretical system" (1959, p. 196). But, as indicated earlier, he also suggests that self-actualization can easily give way to the need for positive regard or self-regard when conditions of worth are imposed. (Rogers also implies, less explicitly, a need for congruence within the self-concept, between self and ideal self, and between self and experience.)

Probably Rogers means that self-actualization *should*, in an ideal world, be the primary motive, but that society and child-rearing practices too often stifle this motive. If so, then it is human nature to serve self-regard before self-actualization, and society should be remedied to make this unnecessary. But Rogers confuses what would be the only motive (in a Utopia) with what actually is the primary need. Any research involving the motivational aspect of Rogers's theory must choose between what he says (self-actualization is primary) and what he implies (self-regard will dominate). A study to be described below—one that Rogers particularly praises—assumes the latter: that individuals will shut out information that is threatening to the self-image. Yet shutting out information is the antithesis of self-actualization.

The point of these three criticisms is not to be pedantic or overly fussy about details. It is that Rogers bases his theory on a relatively few, simple concepts: phenomenological experience, the self, and some basic motives. If these are not clearly defined, then it will be difficult if not impossible to derive straightforward deductions and tests from Rogers's theory.

Most research on Rogers's theory has been done in the course of psychotherapy. Effective therapy is seen as confirmation of the theory. Unfortunately, this logic is not strong. Too often, the results of therapy are evaluated without the necessary untreated control group (Bergin, 1971), so that even if improvement occurs, we do not know whether similar people would have improved during the same time period even without therapy. Attention of any kind, or even the fact of seeking therapy, may be sufficient to produce some improvement. But suppose that Rogers's brand of therapy, which emphasizes nondirective, unconditional positive regard and encourages self-actualization, were found to be effective. This might at most prove that disturbed persons can be made to function better under these conditions. It does not prove that the course of normal development is as Rogers proposes; nor that the self-as-object exists; nor even that experience is phenomenological. These hypotheses, which are basic to Rogers's theory, are too indirectly connected to the therapeutic situation to gather any support from the therapeutic success. They will have to tested separately.

An Empirical Study

Anticipating this objection, Rogers (1959, pp. 231-233) deduced several hypotheses from his theory and focused on one particular study that tested some of them directly. Although he cites other studies, Rogers repeatedly refers to the research by Chodorkoff (1954) as the strongest and most direct evidence for his theory. Therefore, this study will be described and evaluated in some detail.

Chodorkoff (1954) summarizes parts of Rogers's theory as follows:

> Defensiveness is described as primarily a perceptual phenomenon which follows as a consequence of threat to the individual's self. Defense, in essence, is the prevention of accurate perceptions of what is threatening from reaching awareness. As a result, aspects of the environment and of the

person himself may be denied to awareness or may be misperceived. It is in this way that the individual insures the stability of his self. Furthermore, the adequacy of the individual's personal adjustment is considered to be inversely related to the degree to which experiences are denied awareness [p. 508].

This leads to three conceptual hypotheses:

1. The greater the agreement between the individual's self-description and an "objective"[3] description of him, the less perceptual defense he will show.
2. The greater the agreement between the individual's self-description and an "objective" description of him, the more adequate will be his personal adjustment.
3. The more adequate the personal adjustment of the individual, the less perceptual defense he will show [1954, p. 508; quotation marks added].

In other words, if a person has a self-concept that agrees with other people's view of him or her, then there is congruency between self and experience and consequently no need to distort perceptions or experiences. But if the self-concept is quite different from other people's view of the self, then a state of incongruency exists, and the individual will handle this by defending the self from threatening perceptions, principally by denying them awareness (hypothesis one). Such incongruency will lead to abnormal development and poor personal adjustment, whereas congruence will lead to normal development and good adjustment (hypothesis two). Since they are both related to congruency, perceptual defensiveness and personal adjustment should also be (negatively) related to each other (hypothesis three).

Therefore, Chodorkoff needs to measure three characteristics of individuals: (1) the degree to which self-description is congruent with an "objective" description, which Chodorkoff calls *accuracy of self-description*; (2) the degree to which threatening experiences are denied awareness, called *perceptual defense*; and (3) the degree to which the individual is personally well adjusted (*adjustment*).

Chodorkoff's research hypotheses are that measures of these three variables on a number of people will correlate. Accuracy of self-description and perceptual defense will be negatively related (hypothesis one). Accuracy of self-description and adjustment will be positively related (hypothesis two). Adjustment and perceptual defense will be negatively related (hypothesis three). If the positive and negative relationships are confusing, recall that a positive correlation means that high scores go with high scores, and low scores go with low (for example, high adjustment with high accuracy of self-

---

[3]By *objective*, Chodorkoff means a description by others, rather than by oneself; he implies that this is a truer description than a self-description. Whether or not this is a reasonable assumption, or even an assumption consistent with a phenomenological theory, it should not be confused with the scientific sense of the term *objective* (p. 31). The latter refers to any explicit, repeatable procedure and inference system (including self-description). Chodorkoff's special use of the term *objective* will be identified by quotation marks.

description). A negative correlation means that high scores on one variable (such as adjustment) go with low scores on the other variable (such as perceptual defense).

Since one cannot simply walk up to a person and either ask or guess the degree to which he or she accurately describes the self, is perceptually defensive, or is adjusted, these qualities have to be inferred from indirect measures. Therefore, Chodorkoff gave each of 30 subjects (male undergraduates) a series of personality tests, from which he would derive the three basic scores for each person. The relation between the personality tests and each measure, to be described below, is summarized in Figure 9-1.

Each subject attended three testing sessions, within two weeks. In the first session, he filled out a biographical inventory, which asked for personal background information with multiple-choice questions. He then took the standard Rorschach test, in which he was asked to tell what he saw in each inkblot picture.

In the second session, soon after the first, he took a word-association test. He was to give his first association to each of 100 words, half of which were considered neutral words and half of which carried emotional connotations. The experimenter measured the subject's reaction time (how fast he gave his association) to each word. Then he took the Thematic Apperception Test, in which he made up stories about a standard set of pictures.

In the third session, one week later, each subject took a perceptual-defense test. Ten words were selected from his previous word-association test because they were the emotional words to which this particular subject had the longest reaction time. Since he had previously taken a relatively long time to react to them, these were assumed to be personally threatening words. Another ten words were also used, those from the neutral list for which he had the lowest reaction time. Therefore, each subject was given his own list of the 20 words that should be personally most and least threatening. Each word was presented (in random order) by a tachistoscope, which is essentially a *very* fast slide projector. Each word was shown for only .01 second the first time; then the subject was asked to tell what the word was. If he did not recognize it, the exposure time was gradually increased, by .01 second each time, until he did recognize the word. Chodorkoff assumed, as have many others, that a subject who is perceptually defensive would "shut out" threatening words and so would not recognize them at very fast speeds. That is, he would require longer exposure times to recognize threatening than neutral words. Exactly how much longer he took was his perceptual-defense score.

After this procedure, the subject was given his last test, called the Q-sort. He was asked to describe himself with a standard set of 125 short statements by telling to what degree (on a 13-point scale) each statement (such as "I am impulsive") was true of him personally.

Then the investigator began to put all the results for each subject together in order to derive the scores for adjustment and accuracy of self-description. (See Figure 9-1.) For adjustment, he gave the results of the four tests from the first two sessions to another clinical psychologist, who discussed all this material with the investigator until they agreed on a score on an adjustment rating scale. They also agreed on a Q-sort description of the subject, using the same statements that the subject had used. That is, they decided to what degree they believed each statement was true of the subject. This Q-sort was called the "objective" description of the subject, and the discrepancy between it and the subject's self-description was the accuracy of self-description score.

The three scores were then intercorrelated, and the results confirmed the predictions: (1) accuracy of self-description correlated negatively with perceptual defense; (2) accuracy of self-description correlated positively with adjustment; and (3) adjustment correlated negatively with perceptual defense. Most of the correlations were statistically significant—that is, too large to be considered chance deviations from zero.

Nonindependence of Chodorkoff's data. There may, however, have been artifacts that are alternative explanations for the correlations that Chodorkoff found. This is a successful confirmation of Rogers's theory only if the three variables were measured independently, and unfortunately this is not true. Chodorkoff (1954, p. 510) points out what is obvious by inspection of Figure 9-1: that the same tests and the same judges determined both the adjustment and the accuracy of self-description scores. This is analogous to Sheldon's doing both temperament and physique ratings (see page 58), and again the possibility of bias is present. Not only were the judges the same, but the same data (the results of the first four tests) went into the two scores.

Furthermore, as Wylie (1961, pp. 300-301) notes, the word-association results affected all three scores! They were part of the information from which the adjustment and accuracy of self-description ratings were made. And the perceptual-defense procedure was very similar to the word-association procedure, using 20 words selected from the 100 and measuring required exposure time instead of reaction time. It is quite possible that the judges noticed the very long reaction times to certain words on the word-association test and that they inferred that these words were threatening to the subject. This inference would probably influence their adjustment and accuracy ratings. Thus, the judges virtually knew the perceptual-defense score when they made their ratings.

Noting especially these sources of contamination, Wylie concludes:

> Although all of [Chodorkoff's] hypotheses were supported, a number of uncontrolled features of the design make it seem likely that the results are artifactual and do not warrant the psychological interpretation given them [1961, p. 300].

These problems could be corrected by better research procedures, especially by obtaining independent measures of the three important variables. For example, one set of tests could be given to one pair of judges to rate adjustments. Another, completely different source of information could be given to a different pair of judges for the "objective" Q-sort, which determines the accuracy of self-description score. Better yet, the "objective" description could be obtained from people who knew the subject well in everyday life, rather than from judges who never met him or her. In any case, the manner in which

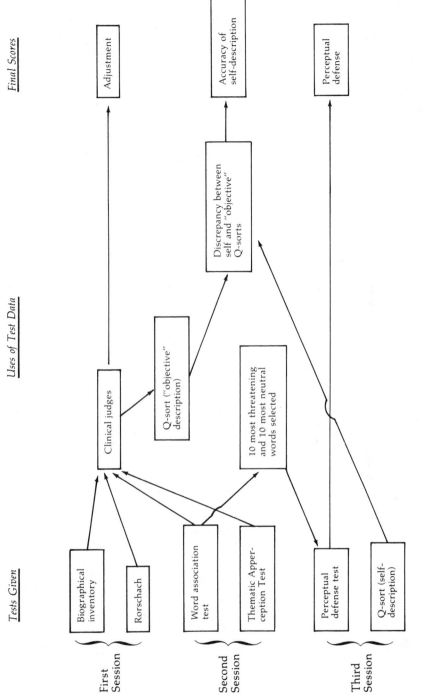

Tests Given

Uses of Test Data

Final Scores

Adjustment

Accuracy of
self-description

Perceptual
defense

Discrepancy between
self and "objective"
Q-sorts

Clinical judges

Q-sort ("objective"
description)

10 most threatening
and 10 most neutral
words selected

Biographical
inventory

Rorschach

Word association
test

Thematic Apper-
ception Test

Perceptual
defense test

Q-sort (self-
description)

First
Session

Second
Session

Third
Session

Figure 9-1. Research definitions of the concepts in Chodorkoff's study

the ratings are arrived at should be objective, in the sense of a clearly defined system of inference, rather than a pooling of clinical judgments in an unspecified way. Finally, the word-association results should not be given to any judges, since they influence and are very similar to the perceptual-defense procedure.

In short, the story of Rogers's theory ends as so many before—incomplete. Rogers and others (for example, Pervin, 1970, pp. 294-296) emphasize that Chodorkoff's study, in particular, supports and confirms Rogers's theory. Having examined Chodorkoff's study, however, we find that it is inadequate to do so. The necessary research for this popular theory, research that would be both interesting and worthwhile, has barely begun.

10

Kelly

THE THEORY

In 1955, George Kelly published his two-volume *Psychology of Personal Constructs*, which introduced both his theory of personality and the methods suitable for research on this theory. Like Rogers, Kelly advocates a personality theory that emphasizes the person's own view of the world: it is a first-person theory. But Kelly's person has a great deal more than self-concept in view.

Kelly objects strongly to most psychologists' view of the human as a rather simple-minded creature. Freud sees the individual as an instinctual animal, with a weak and illusory conscious mind. Trait theorists look at bundles of traits and ignore the mind. Even Rogers describes a simple person, preoccupied with self-esteem and inclined to distort reality. Yet, Kelly points out, none of these theorists would describe himself that way! Each uses his own mind in subtle and complex ways to interpret the world around him. In other words, their cognitive (thinking) processes dominate their lives. All persons, according to Kelly, are primarily cognitive: they think, they learn, they interpret and organize the world around them in their minds. Therefore, cognitive processes, especially those that describe an individual's subjective view of the world, must be the basis of personality.

Like some other personality theories, Kelly's theory has come to mean many things to many people. Especially in the apparently mechanical, deterministic, statistical world of contemporary psychology, both Kelly's philosophy and his witty needling of his contemporaries have been a welcome change to many converts. We, however, will not approach Kelly at such a broad and diffuse level. In addition to (or in spite of) his rebellious spirit, Kelly has a formal theory of personality. This theory and the data that bear on it will be considered here.

What Are Personal Constructs?

Any theorist who insists on looking at a person's subjective view of the world must propose exactly *how* people in general view the world—that is, what structures and processes for knowing the world are common to all people. Then the theorist can propose individual variations and differences within this general format. But without such a general theory, we could do no more than report the stream-of-consciousness of various individuals, each uniquely different from the others.

For Rogers, the basic phenomenological experience is the experiential field and especially the self-concept. For Kelly, *personal constructs,* or categories for the interpretation of events, are the basis of subjective experience. Kelly presents his theory of personal constructs formally, if somewhat cryptically, in one "fundamental postulate":

> A person's processes are psychologically channelized by the ways in which he anticipates events [1955, p. 46].[1]

He adds to this eleven corollaries, all annotated at some length (1955, pp. 46-104). These will be summarized below, first by defining personal constructs further, then by discussing how personal constructs might influence behavior.

Kelly proposes that cognitive processes consist primarily of the ways in which individuals anticipate—that is, interpret and classify—things, especially other people. Although Kelly speaks very generally of the classification of "elements" and "events," he strongly implies that the most important elements are people and the most important events are their behaviors. Thus, an individual may think, this person is "nice," that one is "pushy" but "successful," while I myself am "emotional" and "sensitive." All these terms refer not to specific behaviors or actions but to interpretations of whatever occurred; many different, specific actions could lead to the interpretation "nice."

Kelly's fundamental postulate is that as an individual I am completely influenced by the labels I put on people or events. Furthermore, my ways of construing events are personal, by which Kelly means idiographic. Each individual will develop and use his or her own category system so that, for example, a person may see most interactions with others in terms of "winning versus losing" or "friendly versus unfriendly." In short, Kelly is saying that people have their own categories by which they find similarities in diverse events. These categories are their personal constructs. Personal constructs guide an individual's perceptions, actions, expectations, and responses—all the psychological processes that we call personality.

A *construct* is an interpretive category that describes more than one unique element. Some constructs that might apply to people are "honest with me," "religious," and "a little lazy." Kelly thinks all people form and use

---

[1]From *The Psychology of Personal Constructs,* Volume One, by George A. Kelly. Copyright 1955 by George A. Kelly. This and all other quotations from this source are reprinted by permission of W.W. Norton & Company, Inc.

constructs, but the exact content of these constructs is personal. When asked to describe a common friend, three different people might say "honest with me," "religious," and "a little lazy," respectively. Kelly is not at all interested in which label is true of that friend; in fact, he would deny that any one is truer than any other. Instead, he is interested in the person who uses the construct and how this person uses it.

In order to understand the construct, one must understand both what it means and what it does not mean to the person who uses it. Each construct is actually a *dichotomy*, indicating what things are not, as well as what they are. For example, saying that someone is "good" may mean that the person described is "not bad": the construct is not simply "good" but "good versus bad." An interesting part of Kelly's theory is his assertion that "bad" is not necessarily the psychological opposite of "good" in a personal construct. The opposite of "good" for some people might be "fun." The opposite pole is just as individual and personal as the main pole of the construct. Several people may all use the label "intellectual," but for one person the opposite is "stupid," for another the opposite is "practical," while for a third person the opposite is "warm and emotional." Kelly says that these are three different, dichotomous constructs: intellectual versus stupid, intellectual versus practical, and intellectual versus warm and emotional. To understand a construct, then, it is necessary to understand both sides of the construct, or the psychological opposites that it expresses.

It is also necessary to understand to what elements the construct can be applied. Each construct can be used to categorize only a finite *range* of events, and this range is also personal. "Intellectual/stupid" applies at most to people, not to roses. It may not even apply to all people but only to adults, or only to peers. At a minimum, each construct must apply to three elements (usually people): two who are alike in some respect and therefore constitute a category rather than a unique event, and one who is different and therefore illustrates the opposite pole.

A child, for example, cannot have the construct "parent" until it understands that both mother and father are parents (not simply unique people) and that there is at least one other person (say, a sibling) who is not a parent. At first, the range of this construct is likely to be limited to just these three people, or to parents versus everyone-else-in-the-world. But when the child comes to understand that a friend also has parents, the range of this category is extended. Note that even this common construct may take on personal meanings by its ranges of application. "Parent" may be applied only in a genetic sense; or to those who rear a child (including adoptive and foster parents); or even more broadly to anyone who is helpful and nurturant (a "parent-figure"). To understand a particular construct of a particular individual, one must know the range of elements included, as well as the similar and opposite poles.

Personal constructs and choice. But personal constructs are not simply static pigeonholes for sorting the world. Recall Kelly's fundamental postulate: that personal constructs direct all of a person's psychological processes. Constructs determine how an individual will interpret events, and how I interpret events will obviously affect my expectations and actions. If I construe a situation as "impossible" or "dangerous," I will behave differently than if I construe it as "challenging."

Kelly goes beyond this obvious effect of perception on behavior and proposes that an individual actually chooses courses of action that will improve the construct system. This amounts to proposing a basic motivation—namely, to extend or define the construct system and thereby to improve one's ability to predict and control events. But Kelly's statements on motivation are ambiguous. He rejects all theories of motivation which, he says, propose that the person is basically inert and must either be pushed (by instinct) or pulled (by self-actualization) into action. Instead, Kelly says that the problem can be solved by assuming that each individual "is delivered fresh into the psychological world alive and struggling" (1955, p. 37). Subsequent actions will be channeled into directions determined by personal constructs. But, as noted above, Kelly says that an individual actively chooses "in favor of the alternative which seems to provide the best basis for anticipating the ensuing events" (p. 64). Specifically, I will either refine my constructs so that they are sharper and more discriminating, or I will extend them to include new elements. Either way, my constructs are further elaborated and

> there is a continuing movement toward the anticipation of events, rather than a series of barters for temporal satisfactions, and this movement is the essence of human life itself [p. 68].

Kelly's Theory as an Individual Personality Theory

To this point, Kelly is an individual personality theorist. The theory focuses on the individual construing the world and on the nature of these psychological constructs. Kelly's terms and definitions refer to structures or processes occurring inside the individual. He discusses constructs rather than the external elements that elicit those constructs. In emphasizing *personal* constructs, Kelly is incorporating the second characteristic of an individual personality theory—the study of individual differences. He is as idiographic as Allport would like to be, being more interested in individual differences in the construction of events than in common constructs. Kelly is fascinated by the possibility that "individuals can be found living out their existence next door to each other but in altogether different subjective worlds" (1955, p. 56). Kelly devised his research instrument, the Role Construct Repertory Test (described below), to elicit personal, not common, constructs.

In one of his corollaries, however, Kelly mentions the influence of *experience* on personal constructs, noting that experience will modify personal constructs by validating or invalidating them. If developed further, this idea could make Kelly's theory social as well as individual by including systematic and important effects of the environment. But Kelly defines experience as

> the successive construing of events. . . . It is not what happens around him that makes a man experienced; it is the successive construing and reconstruing of what happens, as it happens, that enriches the experience of life [p. 73].

At best, this definition of experience is incomplete. Nothing in the environment is functionally distinguished from anything else in the environment; that is, everything acts as experience, in the same way. Kelly does not tell us what kinds of experience invalidate constructs or cause them to be reconstrued, yet this is the only way in which the external world can influence the internal world. It may even be that Kelly's definition of experience has nothing at all to do with the external world ("It is not what happens around him") but only with changes inside the person's head that cause things to be seen the same or differently. Thus Kelly's is still an individual theory, in which the person somehow develops a unique set of constructs which thereafter determine behavior.

EMPIRICAL STATUS

The Role Construct Repertory Test

Any research on Kelly's theory depends on identifying personal constructs as Kelly has defined them. Fortunately, Kelly suggests an empirical and objective means of doing this, the *Role Construct Repertory Test*, which he abbreviates to Repertory Test, or *Rep Test* (1955, Chapters 5 and 6). With this test, Kelly aims to elicit constructs about people, especially about people who fill certain important roles in the individual's life (such as mother, spouse, best friend). Since Kelly is particularly interested in how people construe other people rather than, for example, how they construe rocks or buildings, it is entirely appropriate that he limit the test to constructs whose range of elements is persons whom the individual knows.

The basic idea of the Rep Test is simple and follows almost directly from the definitions in Kelly's theory. Imagine that you are the subject (the person taking the test). You are given a "role title list," which is a list of several kinds of people you are likely to know: self, father (or person who has had the role of a father to you), most successful person known to you personally, and so on. For each of these roles, you are to think of an actual person in your life; Kelly calls these people *figures*. As the subject, you are then asked to think of three specified figures—say, the most successful, the happiest, and the most ethical persons you know. Keeping in mind the actual people who fill these roles in your life, you are to answer, "In what *important way* are two of them alike but different from the third?" (1955, p. 222).

For example, a particular subject might say that the most successful and happiest acquaintances are alike in being "understanding," while the most ethical acquaintance is different by being "cold." "Understanding versus cold" would be one of this subject's personal constructs: it is a dichotomous category in which at least two elements occur and which has an identifiable opposite pole. Kelly assumes that this subject has and uses a personal construct that is verbalized as "understanding versus cold." The subject is repeatedly given three new figures to consider and gives a new construct each time.

In the commonly used *Grid Form* of the Rep Test (see Figure 10-1), the subject is also asked to apply each construct to *all* of the figures. Thus, in

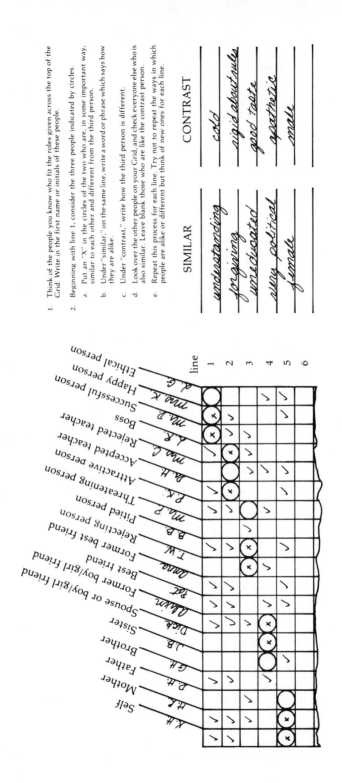

1. Think of the people you know who fit the roles given across the top of the Grid. Write in the first name or initials of these people.

2. Beginning with line 1, consider the three people indicated by circles.
   a. Put an "X" in the circles of the two who are, in some important way, similar to each other and different from the third person.
   b. Under "similar," on the same line, write a word or phrase which says how they are alike.
   c. Under "contrast," write how the third person is different.
   d. Look over the other people on your Grid, and check everyone else who is also similar. Leave blank those who are like the contrast person.
   e. Repeat this process for each line. Try not to repeat the ways in which people are alike or different but think of new ones for each line.

line	SIMILAR	CONTRAST
1	understanding	cold
2	forgiving	rigid about rules
3	uneducated	good taste
4	very political	apathetic
5	female	male
6		

Figure 10-1. Sample Grid Form of Kelly's Rep Test (Adapted from *The Psychology of Personal Constructs*, Volume One, by George A. Kelly. Copyright 1955 by George A. Kelly. Reprinted by permission of W. W. Norton & Company, Inc.)

addition to indicating which two of the three are alike, you also check any of the other figures who are like these two in the same way. In the case of "understanding versus cold," everyone who is "understanding" is checked and everyone who is "cold" is not checked. For each row, a different group of three figures (indicated by the circles) is used to elicit the construct, which is then applied to all the remaining figures.

The completed Grid should contain the important personal constructs and the way in which each construct is applied to all the persons listed. From these raw data, research can go in many different directions, which are reviewed by Bonarius (1965) and Bannister and Mair (1968).

Basically, the Rep Grid can be analyzed either idiographically or nomothetically. Idiographic uses of the Grid emphasize which constructs are used and how they are used by each individual subject. Since the constructs elicited are entirely up to the subject—indeed, since the whole point is to elicit *personal* constructs—these constructs cannot be compared with those of any other subject. Some nomothetic analysis of the Grid was suggested by Kelly (1955, pp. 267-318) and further developed by his colleagues and students. The Grid with its pattern of checks and blanks (ignoring the verbalized constructs) is examined for structural qualities, such as complexity, which will be described below. This kind of analysis results in a single score for each subject, and this score can be compared on a common dimension with the scores of other subjects.

The Rep Test and Personal-Construct Theory

With this brief introduction to how Kelly proposed to identify and analyze personal constructs, we can consider how well Kelly's test suits his theory and assumptions. First, the relatively open format of the Rep Test fits Kelly's phenomenological theory. It is much more appropriate than a forced-choice questionnaire using terms and phrases chosen by the tester or than a projective test in which the subject's responses are completely reinterpreted by the tester. The Rep Test, at least in its idiographic uses, is in the subject's own words and, therefore, presumably elicits a personal view of the world.

Second, the Rep Test does elicit dichotomous labels with at least two similar elements and one opposite element. In noting that this fits Kelly's assumption about the nature of personal constructs, however, it is important to point out that this procedure does not provide any independent evidence that personal constructs have these properties, or that personal constructs exist at all. The dichotomous nature of the subject's response is built into the test, not put there spontaneously by the subject. Kelly explicitly proposes (1955, pp. 59-64, 299-301) that people construe dichotomously (black versus white) and not in separate "class concepts" (just "black") or on continuous dimensions (black to white with shades of gray between). But the fact that subjects give dichotomous adjectives or phrases on the Rep Test does not confirm that they ordinarily think this way. It only demonstrates that they are able and willing to respond this way when asked. A subject who responds with only a class concept and no opposite is required by the tester to think of an opposite before proceeding further. If the subject feels that the similar and opposite labels are points on a continuum, not dichotomous poles, there is no way of indicating this on the test. The format is appropriate to Kelly's theory, but it does not, in itself, confirm the theory.

Kelly's third assumption, that the constructs elicited are the important ones for each subject, has no guarantee of being met. Recall that the constructs are limited to those covering figures that Kelly initially assumes are important in anyone's life. Specific constructs are elicited by triads of these persons, and not all possible combinations of three figures are used. The triads chosen are guided by Kelly's preconception as to which figures will provide important similar-and-opposite comparisons (for example, the "authority triad" compares a well-liked teacher, a disliked teacher, and a boss; 1955, p. 275).

If Kelly's preconception about how figures are grouped is wrong, then these triads will not necessarily elicit important or even frequently used constructs. Each triad will at most elicit a construct on which two are similar and one is different. An important construct on which all three are similar, or one that is not relevant to these three figures, cannot be given. So the final list of constructs is arbitrarily determined first by the role-titles used and then by the triads given to elicit the constructs. One could, of course, leave the persons to be described entirely up to the subject and also let each person pick the groupings ("In what important way are *some persons* on your list alike but different from at least one person there?"). However, this would make the test even more different for each subject than it is now. The phenomenological theorist walks a fine line between honoring the assumption about the validity of each individual's experience and achieving some standardization in assessment techniques.

Finally, Kelly acknowledges (1955, pp. 271-272) that the Grid form of the Rep Test violates one of his theoretical assumptions: the unique range of each construct. In requiring the subject to indicate which pole of the construct applies to every figure on the list, the test forces the subject to include all these figures as elements in this construct. For example, the construct "understanding versus cold" may not apply to "the most interesting person known to me personally." The subject must either make it apply or respond arbitrarily (recall that a blank is interpreted as the opposite pole). Fjeld and Landfield (1961) have proposed a modification that would permit the subject to indicate when neither pole of the construct applies to the figure being considered, but their version is seldom used, probably because the "not applicable" option is hard to analyze.

The Reliability of the Rep Test

With all these qualifications in mind, it is still possible to ask whether the Rep Test reveals anything significant about the way in which the subject sees the world. If the responses are indeed personal constructs, then certain research hypotheses should be true. One simple yet important prediction is that the constructs elicited are relatively stable; that is, they are ways in which the subject typically structures the world and are not merely transient descriptions. While Kelly expects personal constructs to change with experience, he implies that such change would be slow unless dramatic events intervened. It is therefore appropriate to ask whether the Rep Test yields the same results over short time intervals. Recall that this is the same question asked for Allport and Vernon's "expressive traits." Simple reliability over time is the first criterion for any proposed individual difference. If each testing produces substantially different personal constructs, then either personal constructs are not being measured by the test, or they are not consistent characteristics of the individual.

The test/retest reliability, or stability, of personal constructs is not easy to evaluate. What constitutes stability? How much stability is required? For any test that yields a quantitative score, these questions are easily answered by the correlation coefficient, which indicates the degree to which the second test score is numerically close to the first. But when the responses are qualitative, as the verbal labels elicited by the idiographic version of the Rep Test are, this is not possible. A subject who gives exactly the same construct labels on the second test is perfectly consistent. But if there are some differences, then it is not obvious how to judge the amount of consistency. I might use new words that mean the same thing to me—or nearly so—as my original words.

To evaluate consistency, the researcher must make three empirical decisions: whether or not any given pair of responses on the two tests are the same; how to count up the amount of similarity found in the two tests as a whole; and how much similarity is required. Several studies have tackled these problems, each in a different way.

D. E. Hunt (1951) asked 30 subjects to fill out two Rep Tests, one week apart, with 20 different figures each time. He then asked each subject to judge whether a construct used on the second test was the same as one used on the first. By this method, an average of about 70% of the constructs used the first time were repeated on the second test. Hunt's means of deciding which constructs were the same is consistent with the subjective basis of personal construct theory, which implies that no one knows about personal constructs better than the subject. It is an objective procedure as well, since the method of asking subjects whether or not a construct is the same is clearly described by Hunt and could be repeated by anyone.

But the resulting 70% agreement is difficult to deal with. Is it a large or small amount of agreement? Could it be due to chance alone? Hunt seems pleased with the number, but a skeptic could point out that the remaining 30% of these supposedly important and lasting constructs were completely different one week later. How do we decide who is right? The percentage is a purely descriptive statistic and does not permit us to infer anything beyond this description. Kelly, who was Hunt's teacher at the time, describes this study in his book (1955, pp. 231-232) with the implication that it is a positive result for his theory. But neither Kelly nor Hunt says anything about how much consistency the theory requires; that is, they do not specify a statistical hypothesis that would express the research hypothesis. Since we do not know how much consistency would support the hypothesis that personal constructs are stable, we cannot say whether Hunt's study was successful or not.

A later study tried to set statistical standards for the amount of agreement required. Mitsos (1958) gave ten subjects the same Rep Test three months after the first test. He counted only verbatim repetitions of a construct; that is, agreement was scored each time the subject used exactly the same word for a construct as was used the first time. (Actually, agreement was scored if either pole of a construct was repeated verbatim; for example, "intellectual versus warm" would count as a repetition of "intellectual versus stupid.")

Mitsos's main purpose was to compare the amount of agreement that did occur with the amount that might be due to chance. He implies that the amount of consistency that would support Kelly's theory is any amount too large to have arisen by chance. This line of reasoning requires that he specify how much repetition might have occurred merely by chance. Therefore, he proposed that there is a 50-50 chance that any construct will be repeated. Since he elicited 22 constructs from each subject, he assumed that 11 would be repeated by chance alone and would not be meaningful examples of consistency. Of course, 12 or 13 repetitions might be chance as well, since these are only slightly above the 50-50 point. But he calculated[2] that 16 or more repetitions were not likely to have arisen by chance. Therefore, when nine of his ten subjects repeated 16 or more constructs, he concluded that significant consistency had been shown.

While it is to Mitsos's credit that he tried to establish a baseline for consistency, his method of doing so is completely arbitrary and probably invalid. He assumes that the odds that a construct would be repeated on the second test were 50-50. That is, half of the constructs given on the first test would automatically appear on the second test, not because the constructs were stable but merely by chance. Mitsos gives no reason for assuming that the odds are 50-50 (rather than 60-40, 75-25, or 90-10), and it is difficult to find one. If a fair coin is tossed, the odds that the result will be repeated on the second toss are 50-50. But when a pair of dice are thrown, the odds that the sum will be repeated on the second throw are very different from 50-50; they are even different depending on which numbers were rolled the first time. *To know what might occur by chance in any situation, it is necessary to know all the things that might happen and how frequently they happen.* Mitsos did not know which constructs occur how frequently, so he chose 50-50 arbitrarily. Suppose that 90% of all persons taking Rep Tests used the construct "good versus bad"; then the probability that this construct would appear by chance on another Rep Test would be 90-10 rather than 50-50. One would have to get this kind of information—that is, how frequently each construct is given by people taking Rep Tests—in order to set any odds on how likely a construct is to appear by chance.

Two other studies attempted to assess the reliability of personal constructs by substantially revising the Repertory Grid method. Fjeld and Landfield (1961) put each construct that a subject had used at each testing into one of 16 categories that these researchers had developed. Their test/retest data, therefore, reflected the consistency with which subjects (unknowingly) used those categories—not the consistency of the subject's own constructs. Since the

---

[2]Using the binomial expansion to establish 5% significance levels (Mitsos, 1958, p. 312)

subject did not know the 16 categories, the relation of the constructs to the categories was a decision made by the investigators. This is an extreme departure from Kelly's notion that the personal constructs represent the individual's *own* categorization of events, not someone else's.

Finally, Gathercole, Bromley, and Ashcroft (1970) used a rank-order form of the Rep Grid (described in Bannister and Mair, 1968, pp. 61-63) as a solution to the reliability problem. In this form, the subject first supplies a construct in the usual manner. But when the subject subsequently applies the construct to the other figures, he or she does not check those to whom the similar pole applies and leave blank those to whom the opposite pole applies, in the usual way. Instead of this dichotomy, the subject ranks the figures on a dimension, from the one who shows the similar pole most to the one who shows it least (that is, who shows the opposite pole most). Thus, the subject uses each construct as a continuum rather than a dichotomy, ranking figures from, for example, warm to cold rather than classifying them as either warm or cold. Whereas Fjeld and Landfield found rather good reliability coefficients, Gathercole et al. obtained very poor ones. But both the procedures are so different from Kelly's original intention that these studies, too, leave unanswered the question of reliability of personal constructs as defined by Kelly.

Let us turn now to the reliability of nomothetic scores. As noted earlier, the Rep Grid can be scored nomothetically, producing scores that are quantitative and comparable across subjects. For example, Kelly (1955, pp. 267-318) and especially Bieri (1955, 1966) suggest that individuals show a characteristic amount of *cognitive complexity* in their Rep Grid responses.

The complexity/simplicity dimension refers to the number of functionally distinct constructs used. If each individual is asked to give 19 constructs, most will comply, but this does not necessarily mean that each has 19 different constructs. For example, in the Rep Grid illustrated in Figure 10-1 (page 83), lines 1 and 2 have different verbal labels ("understanding versus cold" and "forgiving versus rigid about rules"), but these are applied in exactly the same way to the same people. Anyone described as understanding is also forgiving; the pattern of check marks is identical for the two rows. Therefore, Kelly and Bieri propose, these constructs are not functionally distinct, and this subject is a little less complex cognitively than a subject whose rows never match. A subject who checks all the rows in the same pattern would score at the bottom of the scale as very simple cognitively.

There are many ways of assessing the degree to which the row patterns match, including by factor analysis. Bavelas, Chan, and Guthrie (1976) used all known scoring systems to assess the reliability of complexity/simplicity as a personality trait. Seventy-six subjects took the grid form of the Rep Test a first time, then each repeated it 1, 2, or 3 weeks later. Three different retest periods were used in order to detect any trends over time, and each subject was assigned to a 1-, 2-, or 3-week interval randomly. The results revealed *no* reliability for complexity/simplicity (or for any of the other nomothetic measures). The average correlation was .45, with a range of -.15 to .70. Most of the correlations were statistically significant. But more than a departure from chance is required of a reliability coefficient (see Chapter 12); the absolute size should be much larger, above .90. The reliability was as poor after 1 week as after 3, so it could not be attributed to meaningful changes over time. The results indicated that cognitive complexity (and indeed any of the nomothetic traits purportedly measured by the Rep Grid) is not a stable individual difference. In fact, Grids filled randomly were indistinguishable in many ways from those completed by real subjects!

It is unfortunate that so much research using the Rep Test, both idiographically and nomothetically, has been conducted before this basic problem has been solved. Further work on Kelly's theory awaits a more satisfactory measure of personal constructs. We (Bavelas et al., 1976, pp. 35-36) made some positive suggestions but also cautioned that these should be empirically verified before being counted on.

11

Summing Up:
The Individual Paradigm

In addition to providing an introduction to some important theories of personality, the purpose of Chapters 2 through 10 has been to show how this group of theories shares a common set of assumptions about the nature of personality. These assumptions were described in Chapter 2 and then illustrated explicitly for each theory. Now we can return to them somewhat more abstractly.

A common pattern that can be found in several different theories is called a *paradigm* (see Kuhn, 1962). This word originally meant "to show, side by side." Imagine lining up all these theories, side by side. At first, their differences are striking. But looking closer, and especially seeing them one after the other, all together, their similarities begin to show. They are like houses of the same basic design, but with different exteriors. The basic design, the framework from which each begins, is the paradigm.

The paradigm of individual personality theories is that personality is (1) a property of the individual that (2) includes aspects that vary from individual to individual. These two assumptions of the individual paradigm correspond to a focus on intrapsychic events and on individual differences. These assumptions might also be called a *metatheory*, or the theory behind the other theories.

The first assumption is reflected in the important terms of each theory—for example, unconscious, trait, somatotype, need, self, personal construct. Each of these is the characteristic of an individual that the theorist wants to describe because he believes it is an important cause of behavior. As we have seen, every individual personality theorist looks "inside" the individual for the intrapsychic structures and processes that might explain human behavior.

If you look back at all the major terms, which appear in italics for each theory, you will see that virtually all of them refer to such intrapsychic processes or characteristics. Put another way, with few exceptions, none of these terms requires that the individual's environment be included or described.

Certainly none contributes substantially to our understanding of the individual's environment. Nor did any intend to, for the focus was within.

The role of the environment in an individual personality theory is seldom explicitly described and therefore must be inferred. It would be against common sense to state flatly that people are impervious to influence from outside themselves. All individual personality theories do acknowledge environmental influence, although the exact nature of this influence is not included as part of the theory. In fact, since few individual personality theorists propose that psychosexual character, traits, self-regard, or whatever are inherited, it must be that the environment shapes personality—if only by default. Thus, the individual position on the environment seems to be that it does operate, in some vaguely specified way, early in life. But by adulthood, the effects of the environment are fixed, the personality has formed, and these personal characteristics now *inside* each individual determine behavior. The individual personality theories center around this later stage in life and therefore on causes fixed inside the individual.

The second assumption in the individual personality paradigm is that some of these fixed characteristics of individuals vary from person to person. Each of the seven individual personality theories described so far is quite broad in scope. These general theories take as their subject matter "human nature," or at least the nature of humans as individual persons—for example, as primarily conscious or unconscious, biological or cognitive, and so on. Within each theory, an intricate set of relationships is proposed to account for the development and functioning of the individual. Some properties ascribed to individuals are intended to be universal (for example, the unconscious, source traits, or self-actualization). Others are aspects in which individuals systematically *differ* (such as resolution of the Oedipal conflict, degree of mesomorphy, or personal constructs).

Each theory proposes that there are significant individual differences that are consistent over time and across situations. These individual differences appear in different forms. Some theories propose that each person is in some ways unique (Allport, Kelly). Others imply that there are discrete personality types (for example, Freud's oral, anal, or phallic characters). But these and other theories most often use the notion of a personality trait—that is, a common dimension—by which to measure individual differences. Implicitly or explicitly, these theories usually describe individual differences in the form of traits as dimensions on which individuals can be placed indicating the *degree* to which a quality is present. Allport, Sheldon, and Cattell explicitly propose common traits as a basic unit of study. But, as we have seen, studies investigating Freud's theory have measured the degree of castration anxiety or penis envy (number of times the theme appeared in dreams). Rogerian studies typically measure the degree to which the self is accurately perceived, or how highly the self is regarded. Even Kelly's idiographic technique has been used to measure traits such as cognitive complexity. In short, the major individual personality theories propose both a broad, intrapsychic view of human nature and a number of dimensions on which important individual differences might occur.

In addition to the broad theories presented so far, there is a second group of individual personality theories, which will be called here the *single-trait theories*. These theories, of which there are easily dozens and possibly hundreds, are narrower in scope than the general theories in that they focus on one particular personality trait. Such theories never propose that their single trait is the only trait that individuals have. But they have limited themselves to defining this one trait, measuring it, and studying its antecedents and consequences. In Chapter 13, the following well-known examples will illustrate more concretely what a single-trait theory is: authoritarianism, need for achievement, extraversion/introversion, anxiety, and internal/external locus of control.

One difference between the general theories of personality covered so far and these single-trait theories is that the former are associated with a person, the author of the theory, while the latter are associated with a trait and a test. Single-trait theories are also less grand in conception, less interested in the complete nature of individuals, although they do connect their trait to a surprising diversity of human behaviors. Finally, the single-trait theories typically lead to much more (although not necessarily better) empirical research than do the general theories. Clearly, single-trait theories are the ultimate individual personality theories. Everything is devoted to a characteristic inside the individual, to individual differences that are supposed to be the primary cause of all the behavior studied under the theory.

There are other elements of the individual personality paradigm that follow from the two basic assumptions emphasized here. These will be discussed in Part 3, because they are clearer when they can be contrasted with the paradigm behind the social personality theories, to which Part 2 is devoted. This delay will also reflect the historical development of awareness of the two paradigms. As Kuhn (1962, especially Chapters 2 and 5) points out, we tend to become aware of a paradigm—of the theory behind the theories—only when a new paradigm is proposed or discovered. Until then, the paradigm or metatheory is often unquestioned and implicit or unverbalized. It becomes clearer when an alternative, such as the social paradigm, becomes available for contrast.

Meanwhile, however, the reader should be able to recognize a theory that belongs in the individual paradigm, even one not described here. The key is in examining the fundamentals of the theory, its basic terms and concepts. Do these refer primarily to the individual? Do some also describe important individual differences? If so, then it is an individual personality theory.

12

Validation of Personality Trait Measures

This chapter will deal with the problem of establishing the validity of a personality measure. In 1959, Donald T. Campbell and Donald W. Fiske proposed a validation method that is still, in my opinion, the best available for this purpose. This chapter will describe and elaborate on their method. The next chapter will illustrate its use by examining the current empirical status of several important trait measures.

Many students see words such as "method" and "validation" as signals for the onset of obscure, technical jargon or—worst of all—statistics. But the essence of Campbell and Fiske's method of validation is straightforward and nontechnical, based on common-sense reasoning. Moreover, it is a natural extension of one of the major themes of this book so far: what are the major characteristics of a trait according to individual personality theory and how do we get evidence to verify such traits? The only statistic referred to is the correlation coefficient.

From now on, I will try to avoid the term *personality test*, using instead such terms as *measure, assessment,* or *assessment procedure*. Although the term *test* is quite commonly used (and is also shorter), it has the misleading connotation of success or failure—a carryover from classroom or ability testing. Personality trait measures aim to assess only what kind of personality an individual has. The term *personality test* implies that, in addition, the individual might be graded on this test. A personality measure itself, and even the theory on which it is based, might be said to be tested empirically and might even be judged to pass or fail. But an individual's personality cannot be said to pass or fail and is therefore not being tested.

The validation of personality trait measures is a vital issue in the theory and study of personality because, as will be recalled from the previous chapter, virtually all individual personality theories formulate individual differences as traits. Although they may disagree about which traits to study, both general and single-trait theorists stake a great deal on the existence of common dimensions on which individuals vary systematically. In order to proceed from theory to data, we must be able to measure these traits. Real people must be assessed by some method that translates their behavior into a score on a trait dimension. For example, check marks on a Rep Grid are translated into cognitive complexity scores; stories told about TAT pictures are scored for achievement themes or personal adjustment; the events in dreams become castration wishes; the amount of agreement with questions on the California F Scale is said to measure authoritarianism. But are these valid translations of behavior into trait scores?

Validation is, simply, any objective way to answer this question: does the procedure measure what it says it measures? If the evidence shows that a personality assessment does measure the trait it aims to measure, then and only then can the trait be said to exist. Otherwise, its status is moot. Thus, there is an intimate, reciprocal relationship between the conceptual definition of a trait and its empirical form, the measurement data. The conceptual definition of a trait determines what properties the measure must have (such as consistency over time and across situations). The empirical data indicate whether or not the trait exists as defined—that is, whether the assumptions made about the trait are true when it is actually measured. The assumptions made about a trait are therefore conceptual hypotheses, and good empirical validation identifies and tests the appropriate research hypotheses.

Campbell and Fiske (1959) proposed a method of validation that checks on three assumptions, or conceptual hypotheses, implicitly made about any trait and its measurement. Both logic and previous experience with personality assessment suggest that these assumptions should have high priority. In a nutshell, they are: (1) The trait is consistent despite minor variations within a single method of measurement; that is, the measure is relatively free of error. This is traditionally called *reliability*. (2) The trait is not tied to one particular method of measurement; that is, it will show itself when measured by several appropriate methods. Campbell and Fiske call this *convergent validity*: different measures should converge on the same point on the trait dimension for the same person. (3) The trait as measured is independent of other traits from which it can be conceptually distinguished. This amounts to checking that a trait as measured does not turn out, after all, to be some other trait. Campbell and Fiske call this *discriminant validity*: an assessment procedure should discriminate well between different traits.

If a personality trait measure can empirically satisfy these three criteria—reliability, convergent validity, and discriminant validity—then it is probably measuring what we think it is measuring. If not, there is reason to doubt its validity. Let us look more closely at each of these criteria in turn.

RELIABILITY

Reliability has already appeared as a fundamental test of trait assumptions. Reliability concerns precision of measurement—that is, the elimination of variation caused by certain specific factors in the assessment procedure used. Such variation is usually called measurement error, because it is not what we want to measure. It is certainly reasonable to assume that trait measures should not contain much error—which is to say that they should be reliable.

As there are several different kinds of errors that can influence personality scores, it is useful to talk about a different kind of reliability for each kind of error. Fortunately—and rather surprisingly—there are only three major classes of error in personality assessments. (None will be brand new here, as each has been at least mentioned in earlier chapters.)

Interjudge Reliability

If a measure requires a *judgment*, or inference, to be made about the score, then that human judgment could be faulty. For example, an observer might be asked to judge how "outgoing" a child is during a class discussion. If the observer does not pay attention, then we could have little confidence in the score given to the child. There is another, more common, and more important kind of error associated with judgment. This type of error arises when the basis for judgment is not clear to the observer. If "outgoing" has not been clearly defined, then the observer, no matter how attentive, can only guess at what the trait consists of and, therefore, what score should be given a particular child. Even if some rules for inferring the trait have been given, if they are not clear enough, then errors of judgment will occur. This is particularly problematic with projective methods, where judgment inevitably plays an important role.

We can check for errors of judgment simply by having two observers, each working independently on the same judgments from the same data. The scores that the two judges give to each individual should agree—that is, they should correlate highly. Good reliability requires a very high correlation coefficient—definitely over .80 and preferably over .90. If good interjudge reliability is found, then the kind of errors just described have been eliminated. While it may sometimes be just a mundane check for sloppiness, interjudge reliability usually has an important relation to objectivity. Recall (page 31) that objective data are data that can be observed and interpreted in the same way by virtually anyone. This requires that the rules of inference be explicit and clear. Interjudge reliability is the appropriate way to find out if this is true.

Internal Consistency

A second source of error or unreliability is the *content*, or particular items, of a measure. Most personality questionnaires, for example, consist of many questions, all assumed to be getting at the same thing in slightly different ways. But some of the questions might be "bad" ones in the sense that they are imprecise in some way. A question may be too vague, with different meanings to different people; or it may be too specific to measure a general trait. For example, "Do you like your neighbors?" may be a poor item for measuring sociability because it depends on which neighbors, on how new the individual is to the neighborhood, on how much time is spent at home, and so on. Answers to this item might not agree with other items measuring sociability.

The question of the homogeneity of Sheldon's temperament traits (see page 59) is also a matter of the reliability of content.

There are several obscure-sounding ways to evaluate the reliability of the content of a measure (item-total or interitem correlations, split-half correlations, and the construction of parallel forms), but they are all analogous to interjudge reliability: see if the items agree. For the purpose of demonstration only, you can get an idea of the internal consistency of a "personality test" in, say, a popular magazine by answering all the questions carefully as directed, but scoring it as follows: instead of adding up your total score, get two separate totals based on the same number of items (the first half and the second half of the test, or odd-numbered and even-numbered items). Do these two scores agree? If they do not, you have an example of imprecise measurement, or unreliability caused simply by which items happened to be included in each half. In general, if different items yield similar scores for the same person, then no error is being introduced by the content of the measure; the measure is said to be internally consistent.

Temporal Stability

Although it is necessary that interjudge reliability and internal consistency be demonstrated, these are essentially technical requirements—more a matter of avoiding rather obvious errors than of testing important assumptions. The third kind of reliability involves the effects of time: the *temporal stability* of the trait is measured. This is a more substantive issue, because it is a direct test of the assumption that a trait is a relatively enduring characteristic of the individual. Someone may behave in a particular way only because of a passing mood; such behavior should not be used as evidence of a lasting trait. A good personality measure would include only behaviors that do not change from day to day, because this is the conceptual hypothesis behind such measures.

The procedure called test/retest reliability, as we have already seen, usually consists of giving the measure twice, with a moderate interval between, and then correlating the two scores. Recall that, for Allport and Kelly, the assumption of temporal stability was not supported empirically, even over periods of a few weeks (see pages 44-45 and 87-88).

What these different kinds of reliability have in common is that they evaluate how well certain minimum standards have been met for any given assessment procedure, in order to eliminate errors of measurement. If judgment is involved, then independent judgments should agree. If the measure has varied content (more than one item), then subsets of the items should all yield similar scores. Note that some kinds of personality assessment may not require one or both of these kinds of reliability. But all must show temporal stability, or the same score at different times of testing, since it is a fundamental assumption of individual personality theories that the trait is consistent over time.

High reliability correlations mean that little error is being made in assigning a score. If reliability is not evaluated by the above procedures, we are vulnerable to what will be called here "the fallacy of the first score." That is, if we accept the score of a personality measure based on only one judge, or one set of items, given only once, then we will never know whether that score might have been quite different if measured by a second judge, a second set of items, or at a second time. Reliability testing will not only spare us this fallacy of assuming without evidence that the score obtained is the one true score, it can also identify the source of the error. If, for example, a measure shows good interjudge reliability and good internal consistency, but poor test/retest reliability, then it is obviously measuring behaviors that can be carefully and objectively scored and that are similar in content, but that are not inclined to remain the same over the time interval used.

Reliability Coefficients

Before leaving this section, I would like to mention in passing a more technical but interesting aspect of reliability. The correlation coefficient obtained for reliability can tell us even more than the above, provided certain statistical assumptions are met. For the reader who wishes to follow this up, Nunnally (1970, Chapter 5) is a good introductory source, and McNemar (1969, pp. 163-165) is a thorough one.

In brief, the value

$$1 - reliability\ coefficient$$
(for example, $1.00 - .90 = .10$)

can be interpreted as the proportion of error in the measurement. For example, if the .90 were a measure of interjudge reliability, then the proportion .10 represents 10% error owing to judgment, as only judges were varied, not items or time.

Suppose now that we have three independent tests of reliability, corresponding to the three major sources of error (judgment, content, and temporal stability). In this case, each proportion of error is independent, so they are additive. For example, these three reliability coefficients for the same trait measure might each be a respectable-looking .80. But if each is based on a different, independent, source of error, then the total error is 3 times .20, or .60. The measure contains 60% error! This is why reliability standards are so high. Even three independent reliabilities of .95 add up to 15% error, or a true reliability of .85. (See Anastasi, 1976, pp. 119-122, for further information about this interpretation. The formidable book by Cronbach, Gleser, Handa, and Rajaratnam, 1972, is an even more general treatment of this basic idea.)

CONVERGENT VALIDITY

Convergent validity is the next requirement, after reliability has been established. (Without reliability, it would be foolish to proceed further, since the test would be full of error.) Convergent validity is a test of the conceptual hypothesis that a trait is a broad and general disposition that will be evident in a wide variety of situations. For any particular measure, it tests the research hypothesis that scores are not primarily associated with one method—that they are not method-specific.

According to trait theory, a "cautious" person should be cautious at home and at work, with people as well as with money, and in most other situations. Personality measures can be thought of as merely different situations or modes by which the individual can be observed. Thus, for example, one rationale for giving a personality measure to a job applicant is that responses on the test (one situation) will be an indicator of behavior on the job (another situation).

Convergent validity goes to the heart of the individual personality theorists' assumption of the breadth of personality traits by checking whether a trait shows up in different situations—that is, whether two methods of measuring the same trait correlate highly. There are many ways proposed to measure, say, chronic anxiety—a questionnaire, an interview, ratings by an observer, even physiological measures such as heart rate or sweating. While some, such as the questionnaire, may be more convenient than others, all should give the same person the same relative score on the trait of anxiety. If they do, it is strong evidence that these measures are convergently valid—that is, that they are measuring a trait that is as broad and general as it is assumed to be. If they do not correlate highly, then it is likely that the trait being measured by at least one of the methods is limited to just that measurement situation and is therefore too narrow to be considered a personality trait of any consequence.

Convergent Validity Coefficients

The rules for how high a convergent validity correlation should be are not as clear-cut as for reliability, but the correlation should be quite high. This is because the usefulness of a correlation coefficient drops very rapidly with its size. One way of expressing this is the fact that r^2 (not r) tells how much the two measures have in common. So if $r = .70$, then $r^2 = .49$, which can be interpreted as the proportion or percentage (49%) of shared variance.

The scores in any sample show a certain amount of variability. We hope that this variability reflects true individual differences—in other words, that it is due to the trait being measured. If we treat this variability in scores as variance in the statistical sense (s^2), then we begin to "account for it," or say what it probably is due to (see, for example, Hays, 1967, p. 103; or McNemar, 1969, pp. 142-145). The convergent validity correlation, squared, tells us the proportion of variance accounted for by whatever both measures have in common—namely, the trait. The rest of the variance ($1 - r^2$) is the variance *not* accounted for by the shared trait. For example, $1 - .70^2 = 51\%$ variance unaccounted for! This variability may be due to measurement error, the method used for each measure, or another trait being picked up by one of the measures. If the two convergent measures are both measuring only the trait, then r, and r^2, would have to be very high.

Another way to look at the value of the convergent validity correlation is by means of a "relative validity" criterion, in which convergent validity is compared with discriminant validity. This will become clearer after discriminant validity has been explained.

Choosing a Convergent Method

There are often several choices available for convergent methods. Suppose that a true/false questionnaire to measure leadership is given to a large number of people. As a second measure, the same people might take a multiple-choice questionnaire, entirely different in format and questions, that is also a measure of leadership. Alternatively, the behavior of each individual in a group situation might be (reliably) rated by observers for leadership. If only one additional measure could be obtained, which would be the better evidence for convergent validity—that is, which second measure should be used?

To answer this, recall that convergent validity is a test of the generality of a trait across different situations. Highly similar situations do not test this generality very much. Therefore, the situations should be as different as possible. The ratings of group behavior would be a better convergent measure than a second questionnaire because they measure the individuals' behavior in an entirely different situation. A second questionnaire is, after all, another paper and pencil test, given in a highly structured situation with only written material for stimuli and check marks for responses. A high correlation would mean at best that people are consistent in the way they describe themselves. The group situation, however, presents entirely different stimuli and demands different kinds of responses than does the questionnaire. A high correlation with the questionnaire would indicate true generality across situations. *The more different the testing situations are from each other, the stronger the evidence for convergent validity.* In this sense, a projective test would be a good choice of convergent measure for dream interpretation; a questionnaire could be compared with a physiological measure; an interview with peer ratings; and so forth. (Fiske, 1971, Chapter 5, gives a useful classification of the major modes, or families, of personality assessment methods.)

There is only one qualification on the desirability of obtaining maximally different convergent measures. Each measure should be appropriate to the trait being measured. For example, cognitive complexity probably cannot be measured physiologically. Oedipal conflicts cannot be measured by a direct questionnaire ("Do you love your mother?"), since it is basic to Freudian theory that the subject is unaware of such conflicts: projective or other indirect methods must be used. A phenomenological theorist would probably not be interested in peer ratings of self-esteem, since they do not reflect the person's own view but a view from outside. Traits are defined in the context of a particular theory, and this context cannot be ignored without changing the meaning of the trait. The research hypothesis must suit the conceptual hypothesis and the theory behind it. Convergent validity involves demonstrating the generality of a trait by obtaining evidence that it can be measured by a variety of suitable methods. It does not require that every trait be measured by every conceivable method.

DISCRIMINANT VALIDITY

Reliability and convergent validity involve a series of check points that a personality trait measure must pass in order to assure its validity. These procedures check on accuracy and objectivity of scoring; homogeneity of content; stability over time; and consistency across situations or methods. Together they would make quite a strong case for the validity of a particular assessment procedure as a measure of a broad, enduring trait. Indeed, what more could reasonably be required? As mentioned at the outset, the criteria set out here have grown partly out of experience with the kinds of problems that typically invalidate personality measures. While positive evidence of reliability and convergent validity is convincing, there is a third and final difficulty that can only be assessed by discriminant validity—that is, by showing that the measure is uncontaminated by other traits that it is *not* supposed to be measuring.

Discriminating a Single Trait

Take the example of need for achievement. As described in Chapter 8 (and ahead, in Chapter 13), Murray's concept of achievement motivation was measured by McClelland, Atkinson, and others as a trait, using the TAT. The *motivation*, or need, to achieve should be distinguished from the *ability* to achieve. It is one thing to want something and quite another to be able to do it. These researchers are interested only in the motivational component of performance. While both ability and motivation undoubtedly go into every kind of performance, they are two different concepts and should be empirically separable. The TAT test of nAch aims to measure only the motivational component—the drive, the desire to overcome obstacles and accomplish difficult things. Individuals might have a great deal of this need, only a moderate amount, or none at all.

It is easy to imagine that this trait need not be correlated with ability. There are highly capable people who do not care about achievement; depending on one's perspective, they might be called lazy, underachievers, or free spirits. There are also people who want very much to succeed but who are not able to because they lack the capacity to match their motivation. Any level of achievement motivation might therefore be found with any level of ability. This suggests that empirical measures of achievement motivation and of ability should not be correlated. If these two measures were shown to correlate zero (or nonsignificantly), then the TAT measure of achievement motivation would be demonstrably capable of measuring purely the motivational trait as intended. It would discriminate in practice as well as in theory between ability and need. But the evidence says no: the TAT measure of achievement motivation often correlates significantly with measures of intelligence (see, for example, Morgan, 1953). So this measure has not succeeded in "distilling" ability out of motivation. It is not discriminantly valid because it cannot make a discrimination that it aims to make.

Discriminant validity, then, tests the assumption that a trait as measured is in fact independent of those traits from which it should be independent. We do not want wide-ranging measures of personality traits that pick up a little bit of everything. Anyone who has used a metal detector to try to locate a lost object knows how annoyingly responsive the device is to every kind of metal—not just to the lost gold ring. Analogously, the ideal personality measure should identify one and only one trait—the one it aims to measure.

Note that this is one instance in which the researcher wants a nonsignificant correlation—that is, one that is either zero or only a chance deviation from zero. Such a correlation means that scores on one measure have no relation to scores on the other: they are empirically independent. A negative correlation would be as undesirable as a positive one, since it also reflects a systematic relationship between the two variables. Good reliability and convergent validity correlations are high; good discriminant validity correlations are low, preferably zero. *Relative validity* would be shown when the reliability and convergent-validity correlations are at least higher than those of discriminant validity—that is, when a trait measure correlates better with another measure of itself than it does with a measure of something else.

Relative validity is a very useful standard. For example, it may have occurred to you that the criticism of the correlation between achievement motivation and intelligence was unfair. Perhaps achievement motivation—as a truly measured, "pure" trait—is indeed correlated with intelligence. For example, the bright child may be more encouraged to be an achiever, to need to excel, than a child who is less bright. Tempting as this after-the-fact explanation is, it runs afoul of the convergent validity results for this measure. The TAT measure of achievement motivation correlates virtually zero with every other way to measure this trait (see page 118). If it were measuring achievement motivation, it would surely correlate better with measures of itself than with a measure of another trait (intelligence). This discriminant validity correlation tells us something about a contaminant of the TAT measure, in particular, and not about achievement motivation in general. In other words, the TAT measure of achievement motivation is not *relatively* valid, and so more abstract explanations of its correlations with intelligence are implausible.

Discriminant validity does not require that a trait measure correlate zero with every other trait. Indeed, what would be the use of a trait that was not associated with anything else? It requires independence of only certain other traits. These other traits for which discriminant validity must be shown are of three kinds. First, as illustrated above, a trait should be shown to be independent of traits of which the author says it is independent. If one intends to measure motivation and not ability, then it is necessary to check whether this has been accomplished. Similarly, if "dogmatism" (Rokeach, 1960) is defined as a trait independent of political orientation (that is, there can be dogmatic left- and right-wingers), then any scale to measure dogmatism so defined should be shown not to correlate with political attitudes on a "left/right" dimension. (Rokeach's measure of dogmatism may not have the independence he assumed; see Thompson & Michel, 1972.) Good definitions of any trait should say what the trait is *not* as well as what it is, and discriminant validity is a test of this part of the definition.

Separating Traits Measured Simultaneously

A second kind of discriminant validity is usually required when a particular method is used to measure two or more different traits. For example, the Eysenck Personality Inventory includes two interspersed sets of questions measuring extraversion/introversion (see Chapter 13) and neuroticism, respectively. These two traits were especially developed (by factor analysis) to be independent of each other. They are measured at the same time only for convenience and comprehensiveness. Therefore, the Inventory as a whole should be shown to be discriminating between the two; ideally, the two traits as measured in this way should not correlate.

Similarly, if raters are asked to observe and score several purportedly different personality characteristics, such as honesty, courtesy, and charm, then a low correlation should be found among the three ratings. This would demonstrate that each rating is in fact unique and independent of the others. A high correlation among such ratings is often called the "halo effect," because raters seem to give some subjects all the positive ratings (and others all the negative attributes). A person described as honest would also be rated high on courtesy and charm, not because that person has all these fine attributes but because the rater does not discriminate among them.

This second kind of discriminant validity, then, requires that any method that claims to be able to measure two or more independent traits should show zero correlations between them, or at least demonstrate relative validity. If it can, then we know that two different traits are indeed being measured; if not, the method may only be measuring one trait—but we don't know which or what.

Avoiding Some Common Contaminants

The first two kinds of discriminant validity are theoretical and methodological, respectively. The first requires that conceptual distinctions be shown to hold up empirically. The second requires that a method that aims to measure different traits demonstrate its capacity to do this. In each case, the discriminant validity variable (the trait that must correlate zero) is determined by the particular theory or method.

The third and final class of discriminant validity variables is more general; it might be called "old favorites," although perhaps "old enemies" would be more accurate. These are traits that, while not explicitly disowned by a particular theory or method, have all too frequently been found to contaminate personality tests aimed at measuring other traits.

One such trait is intelligence. In an example already given, achievement motivation was defined as a personality trait independent of ability or intelligence. In general, although intelligence is an interesting trait in itself, it is not a personality (temperament) trait. Intelligence refers to maximum performance, whereas personality refers to typical performance (Cronbach, 1970, pp. 35-41). For example, the upper limit of an individual's vocabulary is an intelligence trait; his usual amount of talkativeness is a personality trait. Personality traits include motives, personal styles, preferences, and emotional states. Intelligence includes abilities such as verbal capacity, reasoning, and quantitative skills. Thus, by definition, a personality trait should be independent of intelligence.

There are already many good measures of intelligence: personality measures should aim to be precise and to measure only the new personality trait, not ability as well. (The only exception to the requirement of zero correlation with intelligence would be any personality trait that the author asserts *should* be related to intelligence, for a sound theoretical reason.) A personality measure that correlates highly with intelligence is incapable of discriminating between the personality and ability traits. Besides its technical impurity, such a test is vulnerable on practical grounds. For example, Cohn (1952) has shown that a measure that correlates highly with IQ can be easily "faked" by intelligent subjects (see also page 112).

Many personality measures, particularly questionnaires, need to show discriminant validity from *response sets* (or *styles*), such as social desirability (the tendency to present oneself in a good light). A response set is a highly specific trait: the tendency to give a certain kind of response to all questions on personality measurements, regardless of content. Social desirability is the systematic tendency to choose answers that are socially acceptable or desirable and to avoid alternatives that are socially disapproved. This is especially a problem in questionnaires or interviews involving psychopathology because abnormal behavior is, by definition, socially undesirable. Thus, an individual might say no to a question about bed-wetting, extreme fears, or depression because it is truly not a problem *or* because of not wanting to admit that this is a problem.

There are two distinct social-desirability measures (Crowne & Marlowe, 1960; Edwards, 1957). Both are questionnaires full of items for which one alternative is clearly socially desirable and the other clearly socially undesirable. As the items have nothing else in common, a high score would reflect a tendency to choose the socially desirable alternative. The appropriate one of these measures should be used as a discriminant validity variable whenever the possibility of socially desirable responding exists.

These and other common contaminants of personality measures are described by Campbell (1960). The main point here is that we should gain from the experience of others and test for discriminant validity with respect to variables known to contaminate personality assessments.

INTEGRATING THE THREE CRITERIA

The previous sections have defined and illustrated the three stages of Campbell and Fiske's validation strategy: reliability, convergent validity, and discriminant validity. I hope that a case has been made for each as a reasonable and useful kind of information to require of a personality trait measure. However, no connections have been made among the three. Each has been presented as if unrelated to the others, whereas in fact they are only different aspects of a common principle. In this section, the unity behind these three procedures will be explained. No new procedures or concepts are involved, only restatements of the above material in a more systematic way.

Trait, Method, and Error

Any personality assessment score is an irreducible compound of (1) the personality trait, (2) the method used to measure it, and (3) errors of measurement. Although we want to measure only the "pure" personality trait, there is no way of doing this without some actual testing situation (the method), and this method may or may not contain error. Hypothetically each of these three factors could be influencing the score to any degree. To give a very literal and simplified example, suppose that an individual has a true score of 10 on, say, open-mindedness. There is no way of knowing that this is the true score without measuring it by some method. But suppose that the method used also influenced the score. A questionnaire, for example, would give only the person's self-description of her open-mindedness. Suppose that this underestimated the true score by 2. Suppose further that errors of measurement (the particular items, or certain events on the day of taking the questionnaire) further reduced the score by 3. The resulting score, which is the only one we will ever know, is 10 minus 2 minus 3, or 5. On the other hand, the method and error may be having no influence at all, and the real score could in fact be 5. How do we tell which is the case?

We cannot simply eliminate the method and its attendant error because some method must be used. The "true score" is not directly accessible. Every personality assessment score is an indivisible trait/method/error unit (see Figure 12-1a). The problem is somehow to look "inside" that unit and find out the relative contributions of each part to the final score. Each might, logically, be there, but dissection is impossible.

The answer is an old and indispensable strategy in experimental psychology: instead of trying to break the unit apart, compare it to a unit similar in all but one respect. This "method of similarities and differences" will reveal the importance of the part that has been varied. For example, in testing for reliability, the trait and the method remain the same, but the source of error is changed (Figure 12-1b). If the trait is dependency and the method is observation, then the error due to one particular rater can be compared with the error due to another rater. If neither made any mistakes, the scores would be identical; if either or both made mistakes, the two scores would be different. The correlation of such pairs over a number of subjects tells us the reliability of this method of measuring this trait. By deliberately obtaining two different sources of error, and by assuring that these errors are independent of each other, the errors can be, in effect, canceled out. A high correlation would show that the errors do not interfere with the score: the scores remained the same with an independent source of potential error. A low correlation would mean that part of the score is error, because the score changed when only the source

a. Score = | Trait (T) | Method (M) | Error (e) |

b.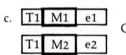
Reliability (varying the source of error)

c.
Convergent Validity (varying the method of measurement)

d.
Discriminant Validity (varying trait)

e.
Discriminant Validity (varying trait and method)

Figure 12-1. Hypothetical components of a score

of error changed. The source of error could be the rater or judge, the items or content, or the time of testing, depending on which was varied. The reasoning and interpretation of results are the same.

Convergent validity also involves varying an aspect whose importance one wants to evaluate. In this case, the focus moves to the method used. To test the assumption that the particular method used is essentially unimportant—that is, that any appropriate method would converge on a similar trait score—the method is varied (Figure 12-1c). If the individual's trait position remains the same, then the method cannot be influencing it, because two different methods yield the same result. Therefore, it must be the trait that determines the score, and the score obtained is probably the true score. (Notice in Figure 12-1c that changing the method inevitably introduces different sources of error, so in fact both method and error are being varied. This illustrates why it is sensible to evaluate reliability first and to proceed only when satisfactory reliability has been found. Otherwise, the difference could be interpreted as due to method, error, or both.)

Thus, in both reliability and convergent validity testing, the strategy is to vary something that should not matter and to hope that the scores remain the same (that the correlation will be high). Finally, for discriminant validity, we vary something that *should* matter, namely the very trait being measured, and hope that the scores *do* change—that the correlation will drop to zero (Figures 12-1d and 12-1e). If traits 1 and 2 really are different from and independent of each other, individuals should get different and unrelated scores on measures of the two. If they are not in fact different, the scores would correlate and the measure would lack discriminant validity.

Notice that when the traits are varied for discriminant validation, the same or different methods could be used. The case in Figure 12-1d (different traits, same method) would tell whether the particular *method* is capable of discriminating the two traits. The case in Figure 12-1e (different traits and different methods) would indicate whether the traits are independent regardless of method (for example, a projective measure of achievement motivation and a questionnaire measure of intelligence).

The Multitrait/Multimethod Matrix

All of the above can (but need not) be summarized in a table or matrix that bears the formal name of Campbell and Fiske's validation procedure: the *multitrait/multimethod matrix*. This describes a procedure in which more than one trait and more than one method have been compared in all possible combinations in order to obtain the desired information. Some students will enjoy the tidiness and unity with which this entire validation scheme can be neatly wrapped up in the matrix. Others will blanch at the name and the format. To the latter, it should be emphasized that this matrix is no more or less than a condensed and systematic summary of all that has been described verbally before. There are no new concepts, only a different way of presenting the same ones.

Figure 12-2 summarizes the smallest possible multitrait/multimethod matrix, with two traits and two methods for measuring each trait. More convergent and discriminant measures could be added. In reading the matrix, notice first that the labels (variables) are the same on both sides (T1, M1; T1, M2; T2, M1; and T2, M2). The cell where a row and column intersect represents the correlation between the two variables. Thus, the entire matrix must contain all possible correlations among the four variables.

	Trait 1, Method 1	Trait 1, Method 2	Trait 2, Method 1	Trait 2, Method 2
Trait 1, Method 1	RELIABILITY of T1, M1 (should be very high positive correlation)			
Trait 1, Method 2	CONVERGENT VALIDITY of Trait 1 (should be high correlation)	RELIABILITY of T1, M2 (should be very high positive correlation)		
Trait 2, Method 1	DISCRIMINANT VALIDITY of Method 1 (should be zero correlation)	DISCRIMINANT VALIDITY of Traits 1 & 2 (should be zero correlation)	RELIABILITY of T2, M1 (should be very high positive correlation)	
Trait 2, Method 2	DISCRIMINANT VALIDITY of Traits 1 & 2 (should be zero correlation)	DISCRIMINANT VALIDITY of Method 2 (should be zero correlation)	CONVERGENT VALIDITY of Trait 2 (should be high correlation)	RELIABILITY of T2, M2 (should be very high positive correlation)

Reliability—Does the same measure of the same thing usually produce the same score for the same person?

Convergent validity—Do two different measures of the same thing produce similar scores for the same person?

Discriminant validity—Do two traits that should not be related show different scores for the same person?

Figure 12-2. Campbell and Fiske's multitrait/multimethod matrix

The first cell of the first row, at the upper left, represents the correlation between Trait 1 measured by Method 1 and Trait 1 measured by Method

1—that is, the same trait and method correlated with itself. Since it would be silly to correlate the same set of scores with itself, it is implicit and not written in the matrix that the source of error would be different—for example, test and retest. This cell therefore represents reliability. In fact, all four cells on this diagonal represent reliability information, for each of the four variables.

The next step is to notice that the blank cells above the diagonal are a mirror image of those below: for example, the lowest left and highest right cells represent the same correlation (T1, M1 with T2, M2). Thus, only one triangular half needs to be considered; by custom, the lower triangle is used.

The first cell of the second row is Trait 1, Method 1 correlated, or compared, with Trait 1, Method 2. Since this is the same trait measured two different ways, it is the convergent validity of Trait 1. The convergent validity of Trait 2 can be found on the bottom row.

This leaves a square of four cells in the lower left of the matrix that must, by process of elimination, represent discriminant validity. This is confirmed by noting that the trait label is 1 on both columns, but 2 on both rows—two different traits, which can only be discriminant validity. But why four cells? Because the matrix presents all the possible combinations of two different traits using two different methods.

On inspection, three of the four possibilities have differences of some interest. The first (labeled "Discriminant Validity of Method 1") represents the correlation of Traits 1 and 2 when both are measured by the same method (recall Figure 12-1d). This answers directly the question whether a particular method (Method 1) can discriminate between two traits that it claims to be able to measure as separate entities. The cell diagonally below represents the analogous discriminant validity for Method 2.

The last two cells (first cell of the last row and second cell of the row above) are similar to each other, in the sense that both trait and method differ (recall Figure 12-1e). A nonzero correlation here would most likely mean that the two traits are not independent no matter what method is used.

A Sample Matrix

Rather than going further into the abstract meanings of various patterns of correlations in the matrix, let us consider one last figure, filled with real data. Figure 12-3 contains data from a study by Bavelas, Chan, and Guthrie (1976), which used the multitrait/multimethod matrix design to assess the reliability and validity of traits measured by Kelly's Rep Grid (see Chapter 10). The Grid can be used to measure several traits, including cognitive complexity (the number of different constructs the subject uses) and identification (the degree to which the subject sees himself or herself as similar to or different from the other figures on the Grid). Recall that the self is the first column on the Grid; this column can be compared to all other columns for similarity. A rating scale developed by Bieri (1966) to measure cognitive complexity was used as a convergent measure for each trait.

	Cognitive Complexity, Rep Grid (T1, M1)	Cognitive Complexity, Rating Scale (T1, M2)	Identification, Rep Grid (T2, M1)	Identification, Rating Scale (T2, M2)
Cognitive Complexity, Rep Grid (T1, M1)	r = .54			
Cognitive Complexity, Rating Scale (T1, M2)	r = .24	r = .67		
Identification, Rep Grid (T2, M1)	r = .65	r = .17	r = .64	
Identification, Rating Scale (T2, M2)	r = .27	r = .53	r = .13	r = .69

N = 76 subjects

Trait 1 = Cognitive complexity

Trait 2 = Identification

Method 1 = Rep Grid

Method 2 = Rating Scale

Figure 12-3. Actual data from a study using the multitrait/multimethod matrix design. All reliabilities are test/retest, over a period of one to three weeks.

There are four test/retest reliabilities,[1] one for each combination of trait and method, on the main diagonal. These range from .54 to .69, which is below the usual standard. Thus, the same measure of the same trait, given only a little while later, reveals a considerable difference in scores for individuals.

The convergent validities are even worse, .24 for cognitive complexity and .13 for identification; the latter is not even statistically significant. Thus,

[1]Interjudge reliability and internal consistency are not necessary for this kind of test.

there is a very low correlation between scores for cognitive complexity on the two different methods and only a chance association between scores for identification on the two methods. Clearly, these are not very broad or pervasive traits.

Of the four discriminant validity correlations, the two highest (.65 and .53) are those that share the same method. That is, when the Rep Grid is used to measure both cognitive complexity and identification, individuals get very similar scores for the two different traits. The Rep Grid does not discriminate well between the two; nor does the rating scale. The two traits are not the same thing, however, because the correlations drop to .27 and .17 when two different methods are used.

In summary, the matrix tells us that these traits measured by these methods do not have even relative validity, as the discriminant validity correlations (ranging from .17 to .65) are the same size or even higher than the reliability and convergent validity correlations (.13 to .69). These poor results mean that the Rep Grid does not measure these traits, because scores obtained by the Rep method have none of the empirical characteristics the traits should have. They are not consistent, broad, or distinct from each other. This pattern is an extreme but not an unusual one, as will be seen in the next chapter.

(The reader should be aware that the form of the matrix presented and illustrated in Figures 12-2 and 12-3 is slightly different from the way Campbell and Fiske displayed it. First, Campbell and Fiske (see, for example, 1959, p. 82) would list the variables, reading across the top or down the side, in the following order: Trait A, Method 1; Trait B, Method 1; Trait A, Method 2; Trait B, Method 2. As a result, the convergent and discriminant validity values appear in different cells in the matrix. Second, as noted at the outset, most matrices are bigger, containing several traits and several methods. The form I have used is easier to understand initially, and once you have the basic idea you can easily read another format by checking the system of labeling and reasoning out what the intersection of two variables must represent. For example, the value that appears in the cell in which Trait A, Method 1 and Trait A, Method 2 meet *must* be a convergent validity correlation, no matter where it is found in the matrix.)

A NOTE ON CONSTRUCT VALIDITY

Some readers will recognize that the validity described in this chapter is of the class known as *construct validity*, which is the validity of a method of measuring a particular abstract construct or concept, in this case a personality trait. However, construct validation usually refers to a procedure quite different from Campbell and Fiske's multitrait/multimethod matrix. To explain this apparent confusion, it is necessary to give a brief history of construct validity.

In a classic paper, Cronbach and Meehl (1955) described construct validity and set out a general guideline for establishing it empirically: study the "predicted relations among observables" (1955, p.300). "Observables" are any kind of empirical data—here, personality measures. For example, if a theory proposes that a personality trait (the construct) arises out of certain childhood experiences (another construct), then there should be a correlation between measures of the trait and of the experiences (the observables). Similarly, if a theory proposes that a personality trait is stable over time, then the theory is predicting that successive empirical measures of the trait will have a certain relationship—namely, agreement or high correlation. In other words, if a method really measures a trait, then the data should mirror any conceptual hypotheses about the trait.

Cronbach and Meehl pointed out that construct validation is therefore identical with hypothesis testing, which is basic to psychology in general, not just personality measurement. This suggests that the measure and the theory are validated simultaneously—a sort of "two birds with one stone" approach, in which positive results both validate the measure and affirm the theory behind it. All the research examples in Chapters 4-10 are in fact construct validation by this hypothesis-testing strategy. Evidence that castration anxiety is more common in men's than women's dreams should both support Freud's theory *and* establish dream analysis as a valid measure of this personality trait.

Following Cronbach and Meehl, most psychologists have assumed that testing their theories would also validate their personality trait measures. Thus, they have concentrated on hypothesis testing, particularly on the antecedents and consequences of personality traits. This kind of research is not only interesting and creative but, by the above reasoning, it should be more efficient and comprehensive than any other procedure for construct validation.

What Campbell and Fiske pointed out in 1959, but is still not universally understood or accepted, is that equating construct validation with *general* hypothesis testing is not satisfactory. There are three serious defects in the general hypothesis-testing strategy: the first two were anticipated by Cronbach and Meehl, and the third was added by Campbell and Fiske.

Theoretical Vagueness

First, the procedure is too vague. The "predicted relations among observables" are not at all obvious for a particular personality measure and a particular theory. For each proposed trait measure, the investigator must build or derive enough of a theory to know what predictions to make. Different investigators working with even slightly different theories can and often do make different predictions for the same trait! The procedure is often vague because of the vagueness of many present psychological theories:

> *Since the meaning of theoretical constructs is set forth by stating the laws in which they occur, our incomplete knowledge of the laws of nature produces a vagueness in our constructs.* . . . . . [For example,] we will be able to say "what anxiety is" when we know all of the laws involving it; meanwhile, since we are in the process of discovering these laws, we do not yet know precisely what anxiety is [Cronbach & Meehl, 1955, p. 294; italics original].

Thus, the development of a simple personality assessment for, say, anxiety is impeded by the lack of detailed and sophisticated knowledge of the theory in which it might fit.

Ambiguity of Negative Results

The second defect in the hypothesis-testing strategy is that negative results are hard to interpret. Cronbach and Meehl pointed out that when "predictions and data are discordant" there are three interpretations:

1. The test does not measure the construct variable.
2. The theoretical network which generated the hypothesis is incorrect.
3. The experimental design failed to test the hypothesis properly [1955, p. 295].

Suppose that, in order to validate a measure of construct A, it is correlated with a measure of construct B, which is hypothesized to be a consequence of A. If the two do not in fact correlate, where is the problem? It may be that the measure is not a valid measure of construct A (interpretation 1, above). But it may also be that the measure is valid but the theory is wrong: A and B are not really related (interpretation 2). A simple example of the third interpretation would be as follows: the measure of A is valid, the theory is right, but B has not been validly measured.

These three very different situations or combinations of them would all, indistinguishably, produce the same negative result: no correlation between measures of A and B. The most useful experimental design (for validation or any other purpose) is one that yields a clear result. If the results are negative, it is very desirable to know exactly why, so that the investigator can either correct the problem or abandon the personality measure as invalid. The general hypothesis-testing approach leaves the investigator (and the topic) in a quandary when results are negative.

Artifacts

The third defect in this strategy arises, ironically, when results are positive. It may be erroneous to conclude from positive results that the personality measure and the theory are home free. The positive results may be artifactual—that is, caused *not* by the factors that the investigators intended but instead by some unintended error in the design or execution of the study. Two examples of precisely this problem were encountered in tests of Freudian and Rogerian theory (see pages 37-38 and 75-76).

A more general possibility is pointed out by Campbell and Fiske:

> For example, a conceptual framework might postulate a large correlation between Traits A and B and no correlation between Traits A and C. If the experimenter then measures A and B by one method (e.g., questionnaire) and C by another method (such as the measurement of overt behavior in a

situation test), his findings may be consistent with his hypotheses solely as a function of method variance common to his measures of A and B but not to C [1959, p. 100].

Method variance is that part of the score attributable to the method alone (recall Figure 12-1a). It may cause an artifactual correlation.

Precisely this problem of method variance was encountered by Burwen and Campbell (1957) in a study of attitudes toward authority figures. These investigators explored their theory that men's attitudes toward authority figures are an extension of their attitudes toward their own fathers. They measured each subject's attitude toward his own father and toward his present boss by an interview and then correlated the two scores. Their strong positive finding (r = .64, highly significant for the sample of 57) seemed to confirm the hypothesis. However, Burwen and Campbell also had some other pieces of information. In the same interview, the subjects were asked about their attitudes toward their peers. Although peers are by definition not authority figures, this variable correlated .65 and .76 with attitudes toward father and boss, respectively. In other words, the interview did not discriminate among attitudes. When all attitudes were measured by a paper and pencil test, none correlated well with the interview method. The original correlation, which is the only one required by a general hypothesis-testing strategy, was purely the result of the interview's lack of discriminant validity.

Another example of misleading positive results is our old friend, the TAT measure of achievement motivation. An obvious hypothesis would be that students with high need for achievement would obtain better grades than those with low need for achievement. Results showing this correlation have been found. However, when we recall that the TAT measure of achievement motivation is often highly correlated with intelligence, these results are less impressive: bright students are likely to get better grades, and no further explanation is needed or justified. One reviewer concluded:

> Of the literally hundreds of articles in the achievement motivation literature, only a handful try to link the motive to academic performance. The evidence . . .suggests that verbal productivity and/or IQ may be sufficient to account for the few positive relationships that do exist. [TAT] measures of achievement motivation appear to have little or no independent predictive validity for school performance [Entwisle, 1972, p. 389].

Similarly, after reviewing the research on dozens of correlates of the F-scale measure of authoritarianism, from prejudice to leadership, Titus and Hollander pointed out:

> It is well to recall that intelligence and educational level have both been found to relate negatively to the [F] scale. It is not astonishing, then, that a general intelligence factor may operate here to provide the basis for a good many of the r's which have been so zealously garnered [1957, p. 62].

It is sobering to consider how many other positive results filling the research journals may be equally misleading.

First Things First

In summary, the approach to construct validation that leads to just any plausible hypothesis being tested is potentially vague and misleading. What Campbell and Fiske have proposed is that *certain specific hypotheses should be tested first*. Since it is clear that reliability, convergent validity, and discriminant validity are implicit conceptual hypotheses for any individual personality theory, validation should begin with these. There is then no vagueness about where to begin. The ambiguity of negative results is also reduced, since each hypothesis is highly specific and failure at any point can be easily interpreted. Finally, the possibility of artifactual positive results is virtually eliminated, since discriminant validity in particular aims precisely at known artifacts.

The two approaches are not mutually exclusive; rather, the multitrait/ multimethod matrix should simply come first. If a personality measure successfully "passes" these tests, it could then be used with confidence in a program of general hypothesis testing. Let Campbell and Fiske, whose insights have dominated this chapter, have the last word:

> We believe that before one can test the relationships between a specific trait and other traits, one must have some confidence in one's measures of that trait. Such confidence can be supported by evidence of convergent and discriminant validation. Stated in different words, any conceptual formulation of [a] trait will usually include implicitly the proposition that this trait is a response tendency which can be observed under more than one experimental condition and that this trait can be meaningfully differentiated from other traits. The testing of these two propositions must be prior to the testing of other propositions to prevent the acceptance of erroneous conclusions [1959, p. 100].

13

Single-Trait Theories

Although the general, "name" theories of personality have dominated individual personality theory, empirical activity has been focused principally on what I have called the single-trait theories. As introduced in Chapter 11, these are theories clearly in the individual paradigm, although they are less comprehensive than those described so far. In this chapter, five prominent examples will be given. Of the dozens or even hundreds to choose from, these are both typical and highly influential. They are: (1) authoritarianism, (2) need for achievement, (3) extraversion/introversion, (4) anxiety, and (5) internal/external locus of control.

Different as they are from one another, these examples of single-trait theories have several common, identifying features. First, they select *one* trait (although admitting that many others exist as well) that is proposed to be of central importance in every individual's personality. Second, this trait is defined in the context of a theory of personality—not so broad a theory as Freud's, Allport's, and others we have seen, but a substantial theory nonetheless. The function of the theory is to connect the trait to other aspects of the individual's life, indicating how the trait has developed and what other traits or behavior it leads to.

Third, these theories always devise an empirical and objective measure, which is often synonymous with the trait itself—for example, the F scale and authoritarianism. Because of the emphasis on standardized measurement of a trait or dimension common to everyone, single-trait theories are often associated with the psychometric and assessment tradition in psychology. But they are not simply isolated "personality tests," because these measures are the means by which an entire theory of the trait is studied empirically. The measure of a single trait may be used for assessment in an applied setting, but it was originally developed to test a theory of personality built around the trait.

This is the fourth characteristic of single-trait theories: they lead to very active research in which the trait measure is correlated with whatever might be relevant, especially with hypothesized antecedents and consequences of the trait. This research has typically been of the general hypothesis-testing kind proposed by Cronbach and Meehl (1955; see also pages 109-113 of the preceding chapter).

The logic and procedures that Campbell and Fiske have developed for investigating the construct validity of personality trait measures are especially valuable for evaluating the empirical status of single-trait theories. Each of these theories is based on one particular trait measure. Its empirical status, therefore, depends on the validity of that measure. In this chapter, the five single-trait measures will be reviewed for validity. We will be asking whether the empirical definition of each trait meets the conceptual assumptions that underlie any individual personality measure. This chapter should therefore be read in close conjunction with the previous chapter.

Unfortunately, a single study obtaining all the necessary information has not been done for any of these traits. However, it is possible to put together a picture from several studies, one establishing reliability, another examining convergent validity, and so on. As these studies necessarily involve different samples and different procedures, it might be best to view them as a prelude to a comprehensive study for each trait. That is, the combined results raise questions that should be answered by a major, overall validation study of each trait in which the entire multitrait/multimethod matrix design is used.

AUTHORITARIANISM

Authoritarianism was first described by Adorno, Frenkel-Brunswik, Levinson, and Sanford (1950) as a personality trait characteristic of potentially fascistic individuals. This trait is a complex one, including, among other things, prejudice, political conservatism, puritanical sexual attitudes, admiration for strong authority figures, and uncritical obedience.

Adorno and colleagues used psychoanalytic ideas in their theory of the authoritarian personality. For example, they assumed that a punitive attitude toward sex was a projective defense mechanism, based on a fear of one's own uncontrolled sexual impulses. But they were not primarily concerned with Freudian theory. Instead, they aimed to define the characteristics and dynamics of an important personal quality, authoritarianism, so that they could study how it developed in the family and what consequences it had for the individual's behavior.

After definition, the next step for a single-trait theory is measurement of the trait. These authors developed the *California F* (for fascism) *Scale,* a 29-item questionnaire including such items as:

People can be divided into two distinct classes: the weak and the strong.

Homosexuals are nothing but degenerates and ought to be severely punished.

What the youth needs most is strict discipline, rugged determination, and the will to work and fight for family and country [Adorno et al., 1950, pp. 248-250].

Subjects are asked to indicate their degree of agreement with each of these items by use of a scale from −3 (strong opposition) to +3 (strong support). A subject's F score is the sum of his or her agreement levels on these items, all of which are intended to reflect authoritarian attitudes. The higher the score on the F scale, the more authoritarian the subject is assumed to be.

With this instrument, a very large amount of research has been done relating F-scale scores to such antecedent and consequent variables as the disciplinary techniques used by the subject's parents, the political and social beliefs of the subject, and personal adjustment. Good sources of further details are the original volume by Adorno et al. (1950); a review of subsequent research by Titus and Hollander (1957); and a chapter devoted to authoritarianism in Byrne's text (1966, 1974; note that these two editions differ somewhat in their coverage). My review of the empirical status of authoritarianism will examine only the reliability, convergent validity, and discriminant validity of the F scale.

Empirical Status

Reliability.   The F scale does not require interjudge reliability because it is an objective questionnaire: no judgment is needed to decide which point a subject marked on a scale from −3 (strong disagreement) to +3 (strong agreement), nor to convert these numbers to a scale of 1 to 7 and add them up to score the questionnaire. The authors of the scale (Adorno et al., 1950) report very high internal consistency ($r = .91$). But they do not mention test/retest reliability nor, strangely enough, has this kind of reliability been described in any major review. We do not actually know, therefore, whether, as a student of mine once said, it lasts past teatime.

Convergent validity.   The convergent validity of the F scale presents some problems, since what is needed is another way of measuring the *same* trait. The trait of authoritarianism is defined as very diverse, aiming to include nine different aspects of personality: conventionalism; authoritarian aggression; authoritarian submission; anti-intraception (intraception means introspection and attention to one's own feelings); superstition and stereotypy; power and toughness; destructiveness and cynicism; projectivity; and concern about sex. A convergent measure should contain all these aspects. Questionnaires on different particular aspects (such as traditional family ideology, misanthropy, rigidity, dogmatism, and religious orthodoxy) have correlated .50 or better with the F scale (see, for example, Byrne, 1974; Webster, Sanford, and Freedman, 1955).

Only two measures have attempted to encompass the entire authoritarian spectrum. Webster, Sanford, and Freedman (1955) devised a new questionnaire with 123 items covering most aspects of authoritarianism, which correlated .78 ($N = 441$) and .74 ($N = 402$) with the original F scale. Encouraging as these correlations are, they involve highly similar measures—namely, questionnaires. The only evidence that authoritarianism can be found in other behavior is McGee's (1954) study in which F-scale scores correlated .58 with ratings of authoritarian classroom behaviors.

Discriminant validity. As for discriminant validity, a negative correlation between the F scale and intelligence is well established. The original authors found correlations of −.13 to −.48 between the F scale and five different measures of intelligence. Over twenty years later, Thompson and Michel (1972) replicated the same relationship. Byrne (1966, pp. 267-268) summarizes nine more studies that found significant negative correlations, from −.18 to −.53, with intelligence measures, as well as −.40 to −.60 with grade-point average.

In summary, the F scale has good internal consistency but unknown temporal stability; convergent validity is moderately good but mostly limited to the same general method; and the discriminant validity for intelligence is definitely poor.

Recall (page 112) that this correlation with intelligence is especially a problem for general hypothesis testing. If, for example, high F-scale scores are negatively correlated with creative problem solving, then the authoritarian's supposed conventionalism may not be the only explanation. Given that high F-scale scores are associated with low intelligence, it is equally plausible to propose that this relative lack of intellectual ability is responsible for the lack of creative problem solving. Although it is tempting to conclude that authoritarianism (the concept) is characterized by low intelligence, the correlation may in fact arise from the lack of subtlety in the items on the empirical measure: Cohn (1952) found that his more intelligent subjects were better able to fake low F-scale scores when asked to do so.

NEED FOR ACHIEVEMENT

The need for achievement, or achievement motivation, is one of several basic needs originally proposed by Murray, who developed the Thematic Apperception Test (see pages 62-63) for measuring this and other motives. Later, McClelland, Atkinson, and others (McClelland, Clark, Roby, & Atkinson, 1949; McClelland, Atkinson, Clark, & Lowell, 1953) selected this need as a particularly important one and fashioned a single-trait theory around it.

Achievement motivation is the need to compete, to overcome obstacles, and to strive for success. Persons high in achievement motivation possess these qualities to a high degree, whereas those lower in achievement motivation are not particularly concerned with success, competition, or accomplishment. McClelland et al. formalized Murray's projective TAT method so that each of four stories told by the subject about four different pictures could be objectively scored for the presence of achievement themes. An example of an achievement theme is when the person in the picture is described as trying to accomplish a difficult professional goal, such as studying in order to be first in the class.

These and other investigators went on to study child-rearing practices, academic performance, time perception, and many, many other proposed antecedents and consequences of this trait. (See Byrne, 1966, 1974, for a review.)

Empirical Status

Reliability. The TAT measure of achievement motivation requires all three kinds of reliability. A thorough scoring manual is available, which reports interjudge reliability over .90 (McClelland et al., 1953), so that objective scoring is possible. The internal consistency (agreement among scores for each picture-story) is very poor, however, rarely exceeding .30 or .40 (Entwisle, 1972). McClelland et al. (1953) reported one-week test/retest reliability of only .22. Subsequent studies of temporal stability have not improved the results, yielding reliabilities of .03 to .64 (Byrne, 1966), with the lower figures being more common.

Convergent validity.   A variety of convergent measures such as direct questioning, observer ratings, and questionnaires do not correlate at all with the TAT measure (Byrne, 1974; Entwisle, 1972). For example, French (1958) created a variation in which a situation is described verbally rather than being presented in a TAT picture. All other procedures are the same: the subject tells a story about the situation, and the same scoring system is used as for TAT-stimulated stories. Yet the correlation between this way of measuring achievement motivation and the original method is zero (Weinstein, 1969, pp. 161-162). Since both methods are projective and have many other similarities, it is hard to account for their failure to agree. One self-rating questionnaire (Mehrabian, 1968) showed some positive relationship to the TAT measure, but the highest correlation was .28, and nonsignificant r's were also obtained in the same study.

Discriminant validity.   The lack of discriminant validity for intelligence (and attendant problems of interpretation) has already been mentioned in Chapter 12. It is generally agreed that there is a moderate and troublesome positive relationship between achievement motivation and intelligence: Morgan (1953) found correlations ranging from .03 to .73. Finally, the TAT does not discriminate finely between the need to achieve and other needs. Achievement motivation correlates .20 to .28 with need for affiliation; for men, the need to aggress is negatively correlated to about the same degree (Groesbeck, 1958; Skolnick, 1966).

These correlations among needs have been interpreted by some as valid "configurations of motives": interesting patterns rather than lack of discriminant validity. There are two problems with this interpretation. Fiske (1973) has shown that the relationships among needs vary with the measurement used. Second, when the reliability and convergent validity correlations are the same size or even lower than the discriminant validity correlations, then this (or any) interpretation is hard to support. That is, correlations with measures of the *same* need measured by different pictures, times, or methods are typically lower than correlations with *different* needs using the same method.

EXTRAVERSION/INTROVERSION

A popularly known single-trait theory is extraversion/introversion. Extraversion (outgoing sociability) and introversion (inward-turning shyness) were originally proposed as two personality types by Jung (1921/1971), but later they emerged as a single dimension in Eysenck's (1947) factor analyses. Eysenck considers extraversion/introversion a fundamental, constitutional personality trait responsible for many diverse attitudes, behaviors, and even physiological responses.

This trait can be measured by the *Eysenck Personality Inventory* (Eysenck & Eysenck, 1965), which is a short, direct questionnaire. A subject with a high extraversion score would agree with items describing himself or herself as sociable, impulsive, carefree, active, and changeable. A subject scoring low (introverted) on this trait would be self-described as quiet, retiring, introspective, serious, and controlled. Naturally, an individual can score anywhere in between the two extremes.

Eysenck has proposed several, similar measures of extraversion/ introversion, the latest of which is the Eysenck Personality Questionnaire (1975), which is too recent to have accumulated detailed evidence for validity. Therefore, we will focus on the earlier Eysenck Personality Inventory (EPI). This questionnaire measures both the extraversion/introversion dimension and an independent trait, neuroticism (instability). The E score from this test is extraversion/introversion, with high scores indicating relative extraversion and low scores, introversion.

Empirical Status

Reliability. The reliability of the E score is good, with internal consistency of .76 to .86 for 2000 normal subjects, and test/retest reliability of .80 to .97 for periods of nine months to one year (Eysenck & Eysenck, 1965).

Convergent validity. Two investigations have correlated E scores—that is, extraversion as measured by the Eysenck Personality Inventory—with other measures of extraversion. Vingoe (1968) asked students to rate themselves and their dormitory peers on extraversion. Self-ratings correlated .60 to .65, and peer ratings correlated .52, with the E score from the EPI. The peer ratings are the preferred convergent method, because they are more different and independent of the EPI than are self-ratings. White, Stephenson, Child, and Gibbs (1968) obtained peer ratings from small groups of psychology students who had worked together for one and a half years. For only two of the five groups were these convergent correlations significant; the average of the five correlations was .32. In a second investigation, White et al. interviewed 15 university students about their social activities such as dances, parties, and meetings, in order to assess whether real-life behavior correlates with the E score. Extraverts and introverts (according to the EPI) differed significantly on only 3 of 16 different social activities. Thus the evidence that E scores reflect a broad behavior pattern ranges from moderate to minimal.

Discriminant validity.   The E scale has been examined for three kinds of discriminant validity. First, Eysenck wanted this scale to be independent of neuroticism; in fact, this was the essential reason for developing the EPI to replace the older Maudsley Personality Inventory, on which the two scales were not independent. For the EPI, Eysenck and Eysenck (1965) reported correlations ranging from $-.06$ to $-.12$ between the E and N scales for 2000 normals. Thus there was a small but often statistically significant tendency for introverts to get high neuroticism scores. Among neurotic and psychotic populations, the correlations were slightly higher ($-.04$ to $-.22$, with one correlation of $+.05$; Eysenck & Eysenck, 1965). Subsequent studies have had mixed results. Farley (1967) found no significant correlations between the scales for a total of 1478 males. However, Richardson (1968), also using all-male samples (totaling 3427), found some larger correlations than even Eysenck and Eysenck's, ranging from $-.06$ to $-.33$, with five of six correlations significant. It is important to note that all three studies used samples much larger than is usual for validation purposes, and therefore should have shown highly stable and consistent results. Yet the matter remains unresolved.

The second kind of discriminant validity for which the E scale has been tested is social desirability. Farley (1966) found that the E scale correlated significantly ($r = -.22$) with a general social-desirability measure, but nonsignificantly with a social-desirability measure focusing on psychopathology. The third discriminant validity variable is, of course, intelligence. Farley (1968) found no relationship between the E scale and intelligence.

In summary, the EPI measure of extraversion has acceptable reliability, only fair convergent validity, and some problems with discriminant validity. However, since the discriminant validity correlations are virtually always lower than the convergent validity correlations, the E scale has relative validity, in Campbell and Fiske's sense. The major improvement would be broader convergent validity.

ANXIETY

Anxiety has long been important to personality theorists, especially those interested in psychopathology. Anxiety can be a temporary state into which an individual occasionally falls; or it can be a chronic trait, with individuals differing in how anxious they usually are. The best known trait measure of anxiety is Taylor's (1953) *Manifest Anxiety Scale.*

Taylor constructed the MAS by selecting items from the Minnesota Multiphasic Personality Inventory. (The MMPI is the 500-item grandparent of many personality questionnaires.) She chose a set of questions that reflect the clinical manifestations of chronic anxiety such as worry, lack of confidence, insomnia, and other physical symptoms. This test has had many uses, but two have been typical: relating anxiety to psychopathology, and studying anxiety as an aroused "drive" that might act analogously to hunger and thirst in learning situations. (See Byrne, 1966 & 1974, for further details.)

Empirical Status

Reliability. This questionnaire has good reliability. In its original form (65 items in length), the internal consistency was .92 (Hilgard, Jones, & Kaplan, 1951). The more common 50-item form was made up of the most consistent items, so that this correlation, although not reported by Taylor, is probably quite high as well. Test/retest reliability was .89 after 3 weeks, .92 after 5 months, and .81 for 9 to 17 months (Taylor, 1953).

Convergent validity. A good summary of correlations between the MAS and other measures of anxiety (convergent validity) can be found in Byrne (1966, pp. 357-361). Several other questionnaires have correlated .30 to .68 with the MAS. Correlations of about the same size have been found with substantially different methods, including the Rorschach ($r = .38$) and judges' ratings (.44 to .61). It is not yet clear whether physiological measures of anxiety, such as sweating, skin conductance, heart rate, and muscle action potential, correlate with the MAS questionnaire. Most correlations are small or nonsignificant, but larger ones (.60) have occasionally been found.

Discriminant validity. Byrne (1966, pp. 365-367) describes an equally ambiguous situation for correlations of MAS and intelligence (discriminant validity). Many studies have been done, and most—but not all—find no significant correlation.

The more serious discriminant validity problem involves social desirability. Edwards (1957) selected 39 items that judges could agree had a socially desirable and undesirable way of answering. These questions were intended to have nothing else in common, so that a high score would reflect a consistent tendency to pick the socially desirable alternative. This scale correlated −.84 with the MAS! Note that this is as high as the test/retest reliability and much higher than any convergent validity correlation. This high correlation is somewhat misleading, however, because both Taylor and Edwards selected their items from the MMPI, and some items are in fact identical. When this overlap is eliminated, the correlation is still −.55 (Edwards, 1957, p. 88), which is about the same size as the convergent validity correlations. There seems no question that people who get low scores on the MAS obtain high scores on social desirability as measured by Edwards. This could be because they do not wish to agree with such MAS items as "I have diarrhea once a month or more," or "I cry easily" (Taylor, 1953, p. 286). That is, the MAS may only be measuring those anxiety symptoms that people wish to report, or it may not be measuring anxiety at all.

A social-desirability scale that does not ask about symptoms of psychopathology (Crowne & Marlowe, 1960) does not correlate significantly with the MAS. Therefore, the MAS cannot be measuring a broad trait of generalized social desirability; rather, it seems to be contaminated by the specific tendency to acknowledge or deny behaviors that are considered symptomatic of psychopathology.

There has been a considerable controversy as to whether social desirability is a real or a false problem (see Anastasi, 1976, pp. 515-521, for a brief discussion and the major references). My own view is that the defenders of the MAS (and MMPI) have to demonstrate convincingly that social desirability is *not* a factor. The reason for putting the burden of proof on the defendants, so to speak, is to prevent the use of measures that may later be shown to be invalid. The TAT scored for achievement motivation, for example, was used for 20 years before serious validity questions were raised. One way to prevent this is to shift the burden of proof for validity to the proponent of the measure. Remember, these assessments are often used clinically to make decisions profoundly affecting the lives of individuals.

There is a second, related reason that is especially important when discriminant validity is the issue. We have seen (pages 111-113) that undiscovered discriminant-validity problems can lead to misleading positive results, in which the measure appears to have an interesting relationship in a general hypothesis-testing study. For example, suppose the MAS correlates with another questionnaire measuring the degree of psychopathology by the number of symptoms reported. How do we know whether anxiety is really related to the degree of psychopathology *or* whether both tests are reflecting social desirability? In short, both practical and theoretical uses of a test are impaired by the suspected presence of an unwanted variable.

LOCUS OF CONTROL

A recently very popular personality dimension is *locus of control*, proposed by Rotter (1954, 1966). Rotter proposes that individuals vary in where they believe the control over important events in their lives lies. Some attribute the outcome of events to factors within their own, personal control (*internal* locus of control). Such people would believe, for example, that good outcomes are due to their own actions, rather than to luck. At the other end of the continuum are those people who attribute the control of events to outside influences, or factors that they personally do not control (*external* locus of control). Such individuals would believe more in fortune, fate, luck, or the actions of inaccessible others ("they") than in their own efforts. Rotter's *I-E* (for internal/external) *Scale* was devised to measure this trait as a general disposition. This or other measures of locus of control have been correlated with so many other personality characteristics that extensive bibliographies have been required just to keep track of such research (see, for example, MacDonald, 1972; Throop & MacDonald, 1971).

Rotter's I-E scale (Rotter, 1966) is a questionnaire that aims to measure the internal/external locus-of-control dimension. An example of external locus of control, leading to a high I-E score, would be agreement with this item:

> This world is run by the few people in power, and there is not much the little guy can do about it [Rotter, 1966, p. 11].

Empirical Status

Reliability.   Interjudge reliability is not needed. Rotter (1966) reports the internal consistency to be .69 to .73; his test/retest reliability was .55 to .78 over a one-month interval. Hersch and Scheibe (1967) have found reliability to be .43 and .84 over two months and .72 for one year.

Convergent validity.   For convergent validity, Rotter (1966) cites two studies that showed correlations of .56 and .58 between the I-E scale and other questionnaires. More recently, Powell and Centa (1972) have found a similar result: $r = .51$ with another questionnaire. Rotter (1966) also describes two studies using nonquestionnaire methods for measuring locus of control (an interview and story completions resembling the TAT procedure). But both studies aimed only to separate individuals into high and low categories on the locus-of-control dimension (that is, internal versus external). Thus, although statistically significant separation was achieved, it is not possible to know the size of the relationship across the entire dimension.

Discriminant validity.   Rotter (1966, p. 14) intended that the I-E scale should be discriminantly valid for both intelligence and social desirability. He obtained satisfactorily small correlations ($-.01$ to $-.11$) with measures of intelligence, but subsequent studies have had mixed results. Hersch and Scheibe (1967) also found no significant relationship between the I-E scale and measures of intelligence. Gold (1968) found a small but significant correlation of $-.17$ with an academic aptitude test. Brecher and Denmark (1969) as well as Powell and Centa (1972) found somewhat larger and significant correlations ($-.28$ and $-.34$). Finally, Powell and Vega (1972) found that an alternative questionnaire, the Adult Locus of Control scale, correlated as highly as .51[1] with intellectual ability.

Rotter's (1966) initial correlations between I-E and social desirability were inconsistent (r's $= -.12$ to $-.41$), and subsequent studies have not clarified the picture. Altrocchi, Palmer, Hellmann, and Davis (1968) found no relationship for females but significant correlations for males ($-.29$ and $-.34$). To confuse things further, Gold (1968) had the opposite results: the correlation was significant for females ($-.27$) but not for males. Using the Adult Locus of Control scale

[1]This scale is scored in the opposite direction to the I-E scale, with *internal* scores high. The change of sign in this correlation thus means that the nature of the relationship is the same, namely, "external" people tend to have lower intelligence scores than do "internal" ones.

and an all-female sample, Powell and Vega (1972) found a highly significant correlation (.47) for one measure of social desirability, but no relationship with an alternative measure.

Rotter's measure of locus of control, then, has only moderate reliability (a minimum of 27% error due to content plus 16% due to time). Convergent validity is only fair with other questionnaires and virtually unknown with other kinds of measures. Similarly, discriminant validity for social desirability and intelligence is not yet clearly established. Clearly, some large-scale and comprehensive studies are needed.

SUMMARY

Looking over these results as a whole, it is clear that each measure has its strengths and weaknesses. Some general problems typical of the field also emerge. Internal consistency and test/retest reliability are usually good for questionnaires, but these two reliabilities are very poor for the projective measure of achievement motivation.

Convergent validity for all five traits was restricted mostly to questionnaires. While questionnaires are convenient and efficient for assessment, their utility depends on whether or not they can be shown to correlate with a much broader spectrum of behavior. Frankly, any trait that only emerges on a questionnaire is of little interest. Thus, the convergent validity of most personality traits needs substantial broadening.

Finally, each measure had moderate to severe discriminant validity problems. None has achieved straightforward measurement of a single trait without contamination. Such potential contamination makes exactly what is being measured ambiguous. More important, these discriminant validity problems render premature and suspect the copious work in general hypothesis testing that has been done for each of these traits. Any of these findings may be vulnerable to an alternative explanation invoking the discriminant validity variable.

The reader may be beginning to wonder if any personality measure has ever passed Campbell and Fiske's tests. The answer is—maybe. The picture of failure presented so far is typical and not exaggerated, but more recent research may be showing better results.

For example, Mosher (1966, 1968) has achieved relative validity for his measures of guilt. However, his convergent validity correlations were based only on different questionnaires—a severe limitation of methods. Also, Mosher's success seems ironically to demonstrate the specificity of the trait. He had to define three specific areas of guilt (guilt about sex, about hostility, or about morality) that were empirically unrelated. Thus, the validity refers to a considerably redefined concept of guilt.

D. N. Jackson (1967, 1968, 1969) claims to have shown multitrait/multimethod validity for his Personality Research Form (PRF). However, he evaluates the matrix in an unconventional way, using factor analysis. Others (see Edwards & Abbot, 1973, pp. 257-258) have suggested that this method unintentionally stacks the data in favor of the PRF. That is, the results will be more likely to show relative validity than they would if evaluated in the more usual way. So the PRF remains up in the air.

Perhaps our progress should be measured in another way. We have discovered fairly recently, as the history of psychology goes, some tough standards for our personality measures. One result has been that persons proposing such measures have begun to pay serious attention to whether these standards have been met. Some (such as Rotter, 1966) explicitly aspire to the criteria of convergent and discriminant validity in devising their measures. It would be nice if I could offer one outstanding example of success. Personally, though, I am satisfied to know that psychologists are becoming aware of the problem and are trying to solve it. If you are ready to give up on trait assessment at this point, at least wait until you have read the arguments against packing it in (at the end of Chapter 14 and all of Chapter 15).

In the meantime, perhaps a far-fetched analogy will convey the reasons for my lack of pessimism. If you follow athletic events, especially the Olympics, you know that records are broken almost as often as these events are held. We recognize this as progress, brought about by advances in technique and training. Looked at another way, one could say that the earlier athletes were really very poor: their record-breaking performances would not now even qualify them to enter a final event, much less to win it. But of course it would be silly to call these earlier performances "poor," just because we now know how to do better. The same may be true for personality assessment. Technical improvements make it easier for us to locate problems; they may also make it possible for us to improve our methods. The single-trait measures we have looked at were good enough in their time. They are not good enough now, but that is because our standards—and therefore our possibilities—have gotten better.

Thus, the work that lies ahead for personality trait measurement is clear-cut: (1) Identify validity problems by multitrait/multimethod evaluation studies. (2) Use these results to correct failures of reliability and validity. (3) Where correction is not possible, reexamine the basic assumptions being tested. The rest of this book will, in effect, consider alternative assumptions and approaches.

14

Current Criticism of the Individual Paradigm

If we take the beginning of Freud's work to be around 1900, then the material we have covered so far spans the 20th century until about the early sixties. The last individual "name" theory to enter the field was Kelly's in 1955. Several specific studies on single-trait measures were dated even more recently, but the reader may have noticed a distinct lack of recent theoretical work. The purpose of this chapter is to give an account of developments in the past ten years. The following chapter will attempt to foretell the future of individual personality theory, by examining some of the directions it might take. These are, in one sense, the most important chapters of this Part for the introductory student: they describe the field as you will inherit it.

The past decade has been an exciting time for the field of personality. In retrospect, the work of previous years seems to have been almost glacial—somber, weighty, and slow. Suddenly, the glacier seems to have broken loose, changed forms, or to have been left behind altogether. We are all on toboggan rides in different directions. I believe that the directions that will prove to be worthwhile will be those that are guided in part by a knowledge of where we came from and where we are now.

Four trends can be seen in this recent period. First, the age of major individual personality theories has ended, almost without comment. For over 20 years now, no new theory in the mold of the seven we have examined has been proposed. To a certain extent, the "name" theories seem to have been crowded out by single-trait theories during this period. However, there may even be a slight but perceptible slowing in the proliferation of the single-trait theories quite recently. It is difficult to say much about something that has simply stopped happening after 50 years of regular occurrence. Only a future historian of science will have the perspective necessary to venture an explanation. Perhaps the widespread lack of empirical support for each of these major theories became tacitly clear; certainly no explicit criticism of any of the theories was loudly voiced. Perhaps these theories simply fell out of fashion or were pushed out by the brash new social-learning theories (see Part 2); certainly the social theories have been their successors. It is tempting to say that awareness and criticism of the individual paradigm, as opposed to any particular theory, was responsible. However, as will be seen below, the dates of explicit awareness and criticism do not support this. Rather, they support the reverse: that the hiatus in individual theories came first. Perhaps this was a period in which the general pattern of these theories as a group became clear, as the events of our past often do with the passage of time.

Thus, the second major development during the past ten years has been a rapidly growing and increasingly articulate awareness of the individual paradigm. The emphasis has shifted from distinctions among the various theories to similarities among them. By 1965, J. McV. Hunt, for example, could refer unambiguously to "traditional personality theory," meaning the individual theories as a group. The individual paradigm had become clearly visible. As we shall see, the most visible part of the individual paradigm was the emphasis on individual differences, especially traits. The "trait approach" has become a working synonym for the individual paradigm.

The third development has occurred simultaneously with the second: criticism of the individual paradigm. Psychologists have become aware of the individual paradigm as they have become aware of its empirical failures, of the cumulative weight of evidence against it. The rest of this chapter will be devoted to this critical awareness. The next chapter will explore the fourth and perhaps more hopeful development: the search for new alternatives within the individual paradigm.

MISCHEL (1968)

In 1968, under the innocent title *Personality and Assessment*, Walter Mischel presented a critical review of the evidence bearing on traditional personality measurement. As Bem and Allen (1974, pp. 506-507) pointed out later, similar criticisms had been made as early as 1928. Somehow, though, the timing and the wide-ranging detail of Mischel's book made it a singular event in the recent history of personality. Most readers were convinced by his thesis, and those who were not felt required to attack this particular book. Virtually all discussions of the current state of the field of personality implicitly or explicitly divide its recent history into two parts: before and after Mischel (1968). We should look, therefore, at what this influential book had to say. Much of it will already be familiar, as this text is avowedly "post-Mischel (1968)."

Mischel's guiding premise (pp. 1-2) was that assessment practice had been cut off from developments in theory and research, so that the practical activity of assessment seemed independent both of theoretical models and of research results. While theory and research should respond to practical needs, the reverse should also be true.

The Issues and Evidence

Mischel aimed to evaluate typical assessment practices in the light of theoretical and empirical advances in the field of personality. One way to look at his book as a whole is to consider it as answering, in sequence, a related set of five major questions:

Q: What do most of our personality theories and assessment procedures have in common?
A: The assumptions that behavior is both stable and cross-situationally consistent (Chapter 1).

Q: What is the evidence for these assumptions?
A: Mostly negative (Chapter 2).

Q: Why, then, do personality tests seem to work?
A: Artifacts and contaminants (Chapters 3 and 4).

Q: Even if they aren't reliable and valid, might not these tests still be useful?
A: The evidence says no (Chapter 5).

Q: What is the alternative?
A: Social-learning theory (Chapters 6-9).

These questions and answers will be described further here, but the full impact of the argument can only be conveyed by reading the original. Perhaps, even then, the student who has read this far in the present text will not now be as shocked as were those already in the field who saw the evidence gathered together, for the first time, in all its merciless bulk.

First of all, Mischel makes common cause between individual personality theories and traditional personality assessments of all kinds:

> Statements that deal with personality describe the inferred, hypothesized, mediating internal states, structure, and organization of individuals. Traditionally, personality psychology has dealt with these inferences about the individual's personality, focusing on behavioral observations as signs of underlying attributes or processes within the person that serves as clues to his personality. This strategy has been the most dominant one in the field [p. 4; italics omitted].

Individual personality theories have proposed these internal attributes, and traditional assessment procedures have simply acted on these proposals and set out to measure them. Personality assessment as described in Chapters 11-13 of this text is both an extension and a test of individual personality theory. Both theory and assessment assume that people have significant stable and general characteristics—that is, individual differences. Although trait theories (such as Allport's, Cattell's, or the single-trait theories) are more straightforward and less complex than what Mischel calls "state theories" (Freud, Murray, and other psychoanalytic approaches), they both assume individual differences.

Stability and consistency of traits. It all comes down to *stability* over time and generality across situations; Mischel called the latter *cross-situational consistency*. If individual differences have these two characteristics, then they are well worth measuring and would tend to confirm the individual paradigm. If on the other hand, individual differences do not show these two characteristics, then it is useless to assess them, and the individual paradigm can be seriously questioned.

Since these two vital characteristics correspond to empirical tests of test/retest reliability and convergent validity, a great deal of important evidence is already available. In the second major step of his book, Mischel surveys a wide range of available evidence under these two topics. For virtually all personality variables, cross-situational consistency is seldom above an r of .30, a value that Mischel wickedly calls the "personality coefficient." Frequently, the correlation is nonsignificant. The traits examined include cognitive styles, attitudes toward authority, moral behavior, dependency, aggression, rigidity, cognitive avoidance, and conditionability. Based on evidence from Chapters 5, 12, and 13, we can now add Allport and Vernon's expressive movements, authoritarianism, need for achievement, introversion/extraversion, anxiety, and locus of control—all of which show poor convergent validity.

The evidence for temporal stability is more variable, but not encouraging. Most traits, such as need for achievement, show little test/retest reliability. To Mischel's list of temporally unstable traits, we can add expressive movements (Chapter 5) and traits measured by Kelly's Repertory Grid (Chapters 10 and 12). Recall from Chapter 13 that authoritarianism has not been evaluated, but introversion/extraversion, anxiety, and locus of control are fairly stable. Mischel's review has produced a similarly mixed picture, with different traits.

If we look over both Mischel's and my reviews of the evidence, one possible explanation for whatever temporal stability can be found is the testing format: all the traits with any stability were measured by questionnaires, not by interviews, projective tests, or other methods. This means that the measurement situation was identical on both occasions, and the questions and answers were easy to remember. Assuming that people want to be consistent, it would be easier for them to do so on a questionnaire than on any other method. So it may be that some traits are stable and some are not. *Or* it may be that the stability found is simply an artifact of memory.

A parallel-form questionnaire would not be vulnerable to this artifact. A parallel form is an equivalent test with entirely different items; it is the best way to measure content reliability. The two forms can also be used as "test" and "retest," in order to eliminate memory effects. However, there are virtually no parallel forms for personality measures. This may be because these traits lack generality even across items. Until parallel forms are devised, we cannot tell whether the traits measured by questionnaires are really stable or not. Another interesting experiment would be to deliberately vary the amount of similarity between the two assessment situations, to find out whether the correlation increases as a function of similarity or of ease-of-remembering.

To return to Mischel's second main point, it is clear that stability and cross-situational consistency are not in fact properties of most personality measures.

Artifacts and contaminants.   Turning to the next point, Mischel suggests that the reason personality trait measures appear to be valid by other criteria may be simply a matter of artifacts. He discusses the problem of stereotypes in raters which, for example, produced misleading results with Cattell's measures (see Chapter 6). Another major artifact is the lack of discriminant validity. We have seen that personality traits may correlate with each other in ways which are "interesting" until one sees that an unintended variable or methods effect is responsible.

Practical and clinical utility.   Fourth, Mischel responds to a position that might not appear often in the technical literature but is frequently encountered in less formal discussions. This is the proposal that measures lacking in reliability and validity might still be useful for practical decisions, especially clinical work. Mischel therefore examines the evidence for the *utility* of traditional personality measures of various forms, particularly as compared to simpler and cheaper sources of information. Again, the evidence is against such measurement. Even the two old standbys of assessment, the test battery (combining many trait measures) and clinical judgment (by a trained individual), are not as accurate as, for example, nonprofessional judges or simple biographical information.

Alternatives.   Having concluded that the above evidence is against the trait approach, Mischel considers which way we should turn. He interprets the evidence as suggesting that behavior is situationally specific and turns to social-learning theory as an alternative. Social theories of personality will dominate Part 2 of this text. It is important to mention here a point that will be discussed in greater detail in Part 3 (pages 241-242): even if we accept entirely the evidence that Mischel presents against the trait approach, we are not logically required to turn to a social approach, much less to a social-learning approach. The evidence against the cross-situational consistency of traits as currently measured might come from many causes, only one of which is the hypothesis that behavior is principally determined by the situation in which it is measured.

An interesting complement to Mischel's book *Personality and Assessment* is that of Peterson (1968). This book conveys the same sense of malaise but emphasizes clinical psychology—that is, treatment more than assessment. Peterson's book is almost autobiographical, conveying the personal dilemma that befalls the practitioner when basic assumptions begin to be questioned. Again, there is a consideration of the evidence that the individual approach is not working and, finally, an exploration of a more social approach.

The strongest response that was made to Mischel's (1968) book was that of Alker (1972), who attacked Mischel's data on cross-situational consistency and also drew attention to an alternative approach. This approach, which combines individual and social variables, is the subject of Chapter 24. Most of Alker's criticisms of Mischel's evidence were rebutted by Bem (1972), who also suggested alternate strategies in the search for consistency in behavior. Finally, Bem offered a calmer perspective on the key issue of whether cross-situational consistencies exist:

> There was nothing silly about the initial assumption of personologists that everything was glued together until proved otherwise. But since it has now proved otherwise, it seems only fair to give a sporting chance to the counter-assumption that nothing is glued together until proved otherwise. Instead of assuming cross-situation correlations to be +1.00, let us begin by supposing them to be 0.00 until we can explicitly construct them to be otherwise. The heuristic value of this assumption and the strategy here outlined is not guaranteed of course. But the real world will bite back soon enough [p. 25].

OTHER CRITICISMS OF THE INDIVIDUAL APPROACH

Although the issue of cross-situational consistency has dominated criticism of the trait approach, there have been other important discussions of the broader status of individual personality theory and its manifestations.

Gullibility

Some observers of the current scene have been dismayed, discouraged, or even outraged by the resistance of the field to empirical evidence, even as it affects practical work. O. K. Buros, who has for 40 years edited the *Mental Measurements Yearbook,* an excellent source of information about and reviews of personality and ability measures, finally concluded:

> Test publishers continue to market tests which do not begin to meet the standards of the rank and file of . . .reviewers. At least half of the tests currently on the market should never have been published. Exaggerated, false, or unsubstantiated claims are the rule rather than the exception. Test users are becoming more discriminating, but not nearly fast enough. It is still true, as I said over ten years ago in *Tests in Print,* that "At present, no matter how poor a test may be, if it is nicely packaged and if it promises to do all sorts of things which no test can do, the test will find many gullible buyers." [Buros, 1972, pp. xxvii-xxviii.]

We might easily generalize Buros's statement beyond testing: for "test," read "personality theory and research."

Ignoring Evidence

Heine (1971) has a similar opinion about the state of theory and practice:

> A very large number of trained psychologists are completely unimpressed by the demonstrated difficulty of confirming propositions advanced by personality theorists. . . .

Training in the methods of science is supposed to discipline the student to accept the outcome of properly conducted research whether the results please him or not. Moreover, the well-disciplined scientist does not permit himself the luxury of rationalizing away results which are contrary to his theoretical projections. This seems not to have occurred among many of those applied psychologists in whose work the concept of personality is important.

Perhaps many psychologists and laymen alike believe observations on personality functioning are too close to everyone's heart—and therefore too important—to be constrained by scientific protocol. Other psychologists sincerely believe that research methods must be far more sophisticated than they now are to capture the complexity they perceive in clients who consult them. Consequently these psychologists are well pleased with their elaborate speculations about personality functioning as working tools—even though it is more intuitive "feel" than confirmed fact on which they rest. Since social and behavioral scientists who attempt to apply their knowledge to the solution of practical problems must fly most of the time by the seat of their pants, freehand theorizing is not to be condemned. At the same time, *if unconfirmed theory is confidently presented as fact, such misrepresentation can be highly detrimental to scientific progress* [pp. v-vi; italics added].[1]

As we shall see, this lack of discriminating standards for evidence of a theory or assessment technique is not confined to individual personality theory; it afflicts work in the social paradigm as well.

Loose Concepts

In a thoughtful article, Fiske (1974) discusses the possibility that we have nearly reached "the limits for the conventional science of personality." He emphasizes three major, if not fatal, flaws in present approaches. First, they rely almost completely on words, but without any guarantee that these words mean the same thing to everyone. For example, a review of seven different studies of several of Murray's needs (achievement, affiliation, aggression, and so on) suggested that these terms had entirely different empirical meanings to the different investigators. They were certainly not functionally, and probably not conceptually, equivalent. Similarly, we often use words loosely when gathering data from our subjects: how frequently is "often"; and how fervent is "strongly disagree"?

Second, we rely almost entirely on data based on observers' judgments. These may be trained observers, ratings by peers, or self-descriptions as on most personality questionnaires. The result is, in one sense, always the same: our data consist of what someone *says* about behavior, not of the behavior itself. A careless reliance on words is a particular handicap for this kind of data.

[1]From the Foreword to *Measuring the Concepts of Personality*, by Donald W. Fiske. (Chicago, Illinois: Aldine Publishing Company.) Copyright © 1971 by Donald W. Fiske. Reprinted by permission.

A final and related problem is the offhand but often breathtaking leap from data to concept:

> We have been misled by the apparent objectivity of our data protocols. There is perfect consensus on the location of marks on a rating scale or a questionnaire. . . . Unfortunately, investigators are not interested in studying checkmarks . . .per se. Making large, inductive leaps, they ascribe broad meaning to such objective data: the average response to a set of items is taken to [indicate the trait of] dominance [Fiske, 1974, p. 2].

As emphasized in Chapter 1 of this text, the vital connection between a conceptual and research hypothesis cannot be made either by leaping or by what Fiske earlier described as

> the path of least resistance, the easy tactical decision to accept some term current in conceptual thinking as if it were an adequate scientific construct and to employ accessible measuring procedures simply because others have used them and they seem rather applicable to the investigation being planned [1971, p. 274].

Faddish Topics, Poor Research, and Weak Theory

Another source of evaluation of the present status of individual personality theory and research is the *Annual Review of Psychology* series. Yearly reviews of the field of personality in the past decade have been disappointingly restrained. Most have echoed Sanford's observation that "the trend of the discipline, as of the city, is toward a disconcerting sprawl" (1968, p. 602). There has been occasional uneasiness about empirical problems and the lack of theoretical guidance (nostalgia for the grand old "name" theories?). But, on the whole, these reviews have been all-embracing rather than critical; they have ignored or even dismissed major criticisms. The Emperor's latest clothes might be subject to some minor and vague criticism, but he seemed, if anything, overdressed.

In 1976, the review by Sechrest took a different approach. Instead of just an annual review, he looked back a decade and came to some stronger conclusions than had previous reviewers. As if making up for years of neglect, his criticisms are numerous:

Research has not been useful. Over the period covered, the popular topics have changed from hypnosis, conformity, and needs, to obesity, sexroles, and aggression. The change, however, does not seem to reflect progress so much as fickleness. That is, the earlier topics were not resolved and finally understood but simply abandoned because the investigators ran out of steam or interest. Sechrest asks where the current "hot" topics will be five years from now. I would add that the cumulative list of such disposable or repeatedly recycled topics in personality is very long, from anxiety to XYY syndrome (see Chapter 26).

It may be that Sechrest's other criticisms of personality research follow directly from this short-sighted, faddish following of popular topics. He criticizes the methods being used as poor and not improving, producing results that are not cumulative or even replicated. Also, "most research—the *vast* proportion of research—in personality is inconsequential, trivial, and pointless even if it is well done" (p. 2). One effect is to obscure by sheer volume the good and important work that is done. One of the definitions of "personology" is that it encompasses most human activities and processes; this definition risks making the field the wastebasket of general psychology.

Finally, before listing some "nagging and persistent" methodological problems, Sechrest calls for a Law of Symmetry in Data Interpretation. That is, whatever faults you can find in your opponent's research have to be accepted as flaws if they occur in your own. The spirit behind this appeal seems to be a commendable emphasis on what's right, rather than who's right.

Sechrest's view of the state of theory is no less scathing:

> When new textbooks come out, whether in personality or introductory psychology, the discussion of theory is almost invariably organized around presentations of Freud, Jung, Adler, the neoFreudians, etc., with a usual bow toward the end in the direction of "social learning theory." In no other field purporting to be scientific are the current heroes of theory nearly all dead. And in every other field of science the current basic research is directed toward the testing of the theories being taught to students. Even in other areas of psychology things are nowhere near so bad as in personality. The theories of Pavlov, Watson, Tolman, and Hull are not taught because they are assumed to be correct, but rather for the historical perspective they afford in relation to current work. Why for so many psychologists in personality is the major theory one which was formulated more than a half century ago? [p. 3.][2]

(The reader must notice that, being only human, I am much impressed with someone who agrees with me on a point I feel strongly about.)

If the theories being taught to students are not current, what is current theory like? Sechrest describes it as modest, lacking in scope, integration, and rigor. Most of the faddish topics have this quality. Sechrest also makes an insightful criticism of the theoretical insufficiency of what he calls "surrogate variables." An example is sexual gender. This easily identified variable in fact includes and obscures other variables such as sampling, child-rearing, hered-ity, and experience. It is easy to look for and to find male/female differences in a study. The question that should be answered before the study begins is: what would this mean? Then more precise variables might be chosen. In general, Sechrest openly prefers that theories attend to basic processes, to human nature, rather than to particular topics. He even suggests that personality as a field has an "identity crisis," being something of social and clinical psychology and little of itself.

Sechrest concludes his review on this note:

> The field of personality, at least the experimental study of personality, needs a tonic—several of them, in fact. It needs better methodology, more truly experimental work, and better and more integrating theory. It needs to divest itself of 50-year-old theories and 25-year-old measures and methods. . . . Most [recent studies] are likely, however dazzling they may be, to have little longer life and impact than the rockets of the Fourth of July [p. 22].

THEN WHY BOTHER?

Some serious and distressing questions must have entered the reader's mind by now, if not much earlier. Why are we bothering with this field? Isn't it hopeless, useless, and going nowhere? At the very least, why bother even to review the older work in the individual paradigm?

The answer lies in Santayana's words (see page v): "Those who cannot remember the past are condemned to repeat it." But merely studying history is not sufficient, or else all historians would be paragons. The problem is how to learn from history in order to produce a better present and future. To accomplish this, at least in the field of personality, I think we must adopt two assumptions: First, the directions our predecessors have taken were reasonable ones at the time, worth trying. They are ones we might be taking now ourselves, had they not gone before. Second, we must learn to benefit from their failures as well as from their successes. I firmly believe that the other side of a criticism is a constructive solution. They are two sides of the same tool, although one is often more used than the other.

Throughout Part 1, I have tried to emphasize these two points. Each of the individual personality theories, and the whole idea of individual differences, has an intuitive and theoretical appeal that made it well worth trying. We are therefore the beneficiaries of years of experience that we might otherwise have endured ourselves. A scientific field is like a miniature civilization. The legacy to its heirs includes both progress and defeats. The wise inheritor learns from both, by humbly assuming that the errors were there waiting for anyone, but confidently knowing not to repeat them. Someone had to try these ways, even if only to show their folly. It is always clear after the fact what was wrong. It is precisely this clarity and hindsight that is our legacy.

The job that falls to us, then, is to do something with this accumulated knowledge—much of it knowledge of dead ends and wrong leads. What is the secret, the alchemy, of turning criticism into positive knowledge? In brief, learn to criticize well. Be precise and fair; don't accept blanket criticism any more than blanket praise. The *Shorter Oxford English Dictionary* gives two relevant definitions of the adjective *critical*:

1. Given to judging; *esp.* fault-finding, censorious.
2. Involving or exercising careful judgment or observation.

The first is cheap and easy; it is the second kind of criticism that is required for our work. So be critical in the sense of carefully assessing the merits and faults of a particular piece of work—be it measurement, research, theory, or paradigm. It is on the foundation of this careful critical work that alternatives will be based. In short, when you see something wrong, don't turn off, start thinking.

A careful observation or judgment of a particular piece of work will usually take the form: the author did this, and that's wrong for this reason. The next step is to complete that train of thought by adding: *this* should have been done instead. This addition is the key. By saying what should have been done, we not only make our criticism more precise but, at the same time, we open the door to a constructive alternative. This is not to say that anyone who criticizes must then devote personal attention to correcting all the flaws identified. We do, after all, have some choice about how we choose to spend our time in psychology, and we may not be that interested. But we must make it clear that the door is open, if it is. For example, some time was spent (pages 37-38) suggesting improvements on Hall and Van de Castle's dream study. I do not have enough interest in Freudian theory to do the necessary study, but that does not entitle me to close the door on anyone who might, by omitting these suggestions and simply concluding that it was an inadequate study. The latter conclusion would be incomplete, misleading, and irresponsible.

The question is not, why bother, but *how* to bother. If one of the individual personality theories, or some variation on it, appeals to you, work with it. Take the criticisms made of it and all the other criticisms made of other theories and the paradigm as a whole, and use them as a navigational aid, as a chart of rocks and currents to be avoided. You can avoid going aground because someone before you already did: now you know there is a danger there. You may even learn the signs of yet-uncharted shoals.

Suppose you have no interest in any of the individual personality theories, nor even in the paradigm itself. Perhaps you agree with many contemporary psychologists that the social paradigm is the way of the future. Even so, as we will see in Part 2, there are lessons to be learned. Over and over, we have seen theories that, on close examination, were not logically clear or coherent; theories whose basic premises had not been identified, much less tested; theories whose data were insufficient to the job at hand. All of these, and most of Buros's, Heine's, Fiske's, and Sechrest's criticisms of work in the individual paradigm, are lying in wait for social theories as well: we will see these same errors repeated. We have learned some of the general problems of theory construction and testing, but we need not accept them as inevitable. Having seen these problems, we can strive to avoid them. Even—or perhaps especially—if you choose neither the individual nor the social paradigm but prefer to find an entirely new way, you will need to know these general guidelines. They are the enduring tools of our trade.

15

Current Alternatives within the Individual Paradigm

In the first Part of the book, we have evaluated, both logically and empirically, seven of the major and typical individual personality theories, as well as five examples of single-trait theories. As the paradigm itself became clear, it was possible to propose a general method for validating its assumption of measurable individual differences. Finally, some contemporary criticisms of the state of individual personality theory were reviewed, followed by a promise that none of these constituted an obituary for individual personality theory, or for personality as a viable field of endeavor. The present chapter is in large part aimed at making good on that promise—that is, to propose some prospects for future work within the paradigm. These will be suggestive, not exhaustive. I hope that the reader will have thought of some others already, and perhaps this chapter will stimulate still more ideas that none of us has yet considered.

In choosing potential paths to take, one faces probabilities, not certainties. The only two alternatives I would eliminate altogether would be either to continue working in the field as if nothing had been happening in recent years, or to abandon the field as hopeless. Neither is justified, logically or empirically. Between these two extremes, there is a variety of alternatives, none guaranteed to be successful, but all interesting, promising, and worthwhile. Where to begin is ultimately a matter of personal taste.

The most popular current alternative is to leave the individual paradigm altogether. The reason Part 2 is devoted to detailed consideration of social theories is that they represent a robust and reasonable response to discouragement with the basic tenets of the individual paradigm. In Part 3, the possibility of combining the two paradigms will be discussed. So, in one sense, most of the rest of this book is devoted to possible alternatives.

As has already been emphasized, however, it is not necessary to give individual personality theory up for lost. Three broad classes of alternatives will be proposed here: to revise and build on one of the already existing major theories; to address oneself to essentially technical but vital improvements in the present methods of individual personality theory and assessment; or to explore a different model of individual differences, namely, the idiographic approach.

REVISING THE MAJOR THEORIES

It is important to recall that the final verdict on most of the individual "name" theories was that the jury is still out. For the most part, they were inadequately tested rather than disconfirmed. In each chapter, criticisms that suggested alternative approaches were made. These will be briefly summarized here.

Freudian theory would probably have to be broken into manageable parts, liberated of tautologies, and subjected to rigorous empirical tests—tests that put something at risk (see pages 34-35).

Allport (1966) suggested possible hopes for his trait theory (see page 43), despite the current evidence against it. One important revision would be to set empirical standards for positive evidence, rather than treating research as illustrative but not conclusive (page 45).

A similar standard must be established for the replication of Cattell's factors (pages 49-50). Additionally, this approach must divest itself of the possible artifact of stereotypes and, in general, broaden its behavioral base (pages 50-53).

The necessary next steps for Sheldon's theory seem quite clear: establish a truly genetic somatotype measure that is independent of environmental influences and pay more attention to the validity of the temperament measures (pages 58-59).

Murray's theory is open to almost any kind of revision, having remained aloof from objective testing other than the projective measurement of needs, which has been uniformly unsuccessful. Fiske (1971, p. 181) asserts that needs are one of the "highly stable and persistent" characteristics of human beings; perhaps his realistic but hopeful handbook on assessment could be applied to measurement of Murray's needs.

Rogers's theory in its present form has serious ambiguities or inconsistencies, as described earlier on pages 69-71. The basic concepts of phenomenology, self, and motives are unclear. These must be clarified before adequate testing can be done.

Kelly's theory at present depends intimately on the Rep Test. Some problems for its idiographic uses were described on pages 85-87; Bavelas, Chan, and Guthrie (1976, pp. 35-36) suggested possible revisions for nomothetic trait measurement.

In addition to the above, there are other personality theories not described in this relatively brief review. These include the post-Freudians, such as Jung, Adler, Rank, Horney, Fromm, Sullivan, and Erikson. There are also existential theorists such as Maslow, Frankl, and May. (The text by Hall and Lindzey, 1970, is a good source of starting references for all of these.) Note, however, that these are not included here principally because they have not even approximated adequate theory construction or empirical research. Anyone who wants to explore these theories should be constantly aware of the need for clear, logical, and testable theoretical statements plus the urgency of obtaining empirical evidence. One lesson from the past: don't spend years on a theory before testing its major premises. Elaboration can come later; reasonable hope must be established first.

There is no rule that says we must stay within the bounds of some established theory. Psychological theories are public property, open to radical revision as long as credit is given where credit is due. Some combination, variation, or total break from the above theories is equally possible. But a new theory alone is not the answer to the present problems with the individual personality paradigm. As emphasized above, the broad failures of past work must be overcome as well. The burden of evidence has shifted to those who propose such a theory to show that it can work better than its predecessors.

INDIVIDUAL DIFFERENCES: TECHNICAL IMPROVEMENTS

Most challenges to the individual paradigm have been aimed at the measurement of individual differences. This is an appropriate focus for our efforts, as the demonstrable existence of such differences is vital to the individual paradigm. The individual's behavior is seen as generated from within, and variations in behavior are attributed to the inherent characteristics of different individuals. For such a model to be supportable or even useful, these characteristics must be shown to be stable and general. Otherwise, apparent individual characteristics may just as well be situational or even random. As noted in the previous chapter, the evidence is running against the stability and generality of personality traits *as currently measured*.

If revised measures could reverse this trend, then we might have new faith in the paradigm itself. Both this and the next section of this chapter accept the present evidence against individual differences. It may be that this evidence shows that individual differences as we have conceived them do not exist. But equally logical is the possibility that the evidence reflects empirical rather than theoretical inadequacies. It is possible that individual differences do exist, but we have not yet been able to measure them adequately—that is, to translate our conceptual hypotheses into suitable empirical form. Several improvements along this line will be suggested.

The Diagnostic Approach

The first improvement would be diagnostic. We won't know whether a measure is adequate until appropriate validation has been attempted. Despite Campbell and Fiske's clear warning (see page 113) that crucial assumptions should be tested first, that is not general practice. For example, articles involving a locus-of-control measure constitute a large proportion of recent articles in personality journals. None of these measures has passed the multitrait/

multimethod validation procedure. So the first suggestion—no, I should say, plea—is that any measure be immediately subjected to validation. This would serve to diagnose particular problems that could be corrected. For example, contamination by a discriminant validity variable such as intelligence or social desirability might well be overcome by rewriting items.

Statistical Approaches

Several methodological suggestions have been made by other writers. Block (1963) emphasizes that poor reliability leads inevitably to poor agreement among measures. The reason is a statistical phenomenon called *attenuation* (in the sense of weakening or diluting). If a measure is itself unreliable, then any correlation obtained between it and any other measure will be less than the true possible correlation, had a reliable measure been used. Intuitively, it is obvious that a poor instrument will not reveal the true state of affairs. For a statistical proof and discussion, see, for example, McNemar (1969, pp. 171-172).

I cannot agree, however, with Block's suggestion that we should therefore apply a statistical correction for attenuation to all convergent validity correlations. There are two reasons for my reluctance. First, as revealed by a careful examination of the statistical derivation of the formulas regarding attenuation, there are numerous uncheckable assumptions behind the so-called correction. It is, in fact, an estimate of what the true cross-situational correlation would be *if* certain conditions held, and we cannot be sure that they do hold. Some evidence that they frequently do not is the fact that some of these "corrected" correlations reach impossible values over 1.00!

My second objection to a statistical solution is that it bypasses an important theoretical issue: the lack of reliability. As noted in Chapter 12, reliability coefficients reveal the degree to which certain assumptions about the measure have been met. Poor reliability is not merely a technical inconvenience to be overcome by statistical devices. In short, my recommendation based on Block's initial thesis is that the reasons for the lack of reliability should be identified and corrected. For example, good interjudge reliability is mostly a matter of hard work. The concept being measured must be specified, defined, and illustrated until two observers can agree. If they cannot, then it is unlikely that the investigator knows exactly what the trait means, conceptually and empirically. Internal consistency and test/retest reliability depend in part on the nature of the people being studied and are therefore not totally within the investigator's control. Still, it might well be possible to establish a known range of content and a known range of time over which the measure is reliable.

Alker (1972, p. 5) points out another statistical artifact in present data. If the individuals being studied are pretty much alike, then the correlation will be lower than it would be if individuals were more heterogeneous (see Nunnally, 1970, pp. 95-96; or McNemar, 1969, pp. 162, 170). This particular lowering of the correlation affects the reliability coefficient as well as any other correlations involving a measure for which the range of scores is limited. This kind of limitation is especially likely to occur when investigators rely on the people most conveniently available—namely, undergraduate psychology students. Compared to the full range of people in North America, university students are likely to be at one end of distributions of intelligence, achievement motivation, adjustment, and other measures. The solution is to sample more broadly, to seek out and measure the full range of people for whom the measure is intended.

Reliable measures based on the maximum obtainable range of scores are more likely to lead to higher correlations, including those correlations needed as evidence for cross-situational consistency. A note of caution: increased reliability and range may, for the same statistical reasons, also increase *discriminant* validity correlations. This would be an unwanted effect to which one must remain alert. Although it is true that poor reliability and restricted range will lower correlations artifactually, they are not the only possible cause. Some correlations may be low because there really is no relationship between the variables. One can only proceed in the hope that the convergent correlations were artifactually low but the discriminant correlations were truly low—and await the results.

The Naturalistic Approach

Fiske (1974) has suggested another methodological alternative, particularly as a remedy for the global, judgmental observations that he has criticized (see page 132). He recommends the study of "naturalistic molecular acts" (pp. 7-9). Two changes are involved. First, he suggests that we study small and specific behaviors that require little inference as to their occurrence—for example, nonverbal gestures. There would be no doubt that the behavior did occur, as observers could readily agree. Consider, for example, the difference between asking observers to count the number of smiles and asking them to judge the amount of friendliness.

Second, Fiske suggests, in effect, that we abandon our a priori, verbally based preconceptions about what behaviors go with what other behaviors. We usually assume, for example, that aggression consists of such behaviors as hitting, sarcasm, and reluctance to cooperate. Instead, we could proceed from the specific behaviors to empirically justified groupings. He suggests that naturalistic observation can be "construct-seeking":

> Starting with observed behavior, they [naturalistic studies] can avoid the difficulty faced by conventional concept-testing studies, namely the gap between the a priori concept and the particular operations believed to elicit behaviors relevant to it. They can start with low-order concepts which simply label a class of acts that are defined ostensively [i.e., by direct demonstration, by pointing at]. More abstract constructs can be built explicitly on these [p. 8].

The object would be to secure a more reliable and straightforward data base on which to build up to new concepts. To paraphrase Fiske's suggestions more loosely, we have been assuming that we know what our trait labels mean because we all "know" what the words involved mean. We have assumed that we can agree on observations simply by using verbal directions on what to observe. We have, finally, assumed that we know which behaviors go together because these behaviors all seem to be in the same verbal class. Perhaps the results have been so dismal because these assumptions are wrong. The great, global leaps have not worked; why not try smaller steps?

Alker (1972), Block (1968), and Carlson (1971) have also made some suggestions regarding alternative research strategies for the study of individual personality characteristics. These, however, are much vaguer than those described above and would require considerable elaboration to become actual research projects. Note also that Bem (1972) suggests that some, but not all, of Alker's suggestions have already been tried, to no avail. Two possibilities that recur in these and other articles resemble the idiographic approach, which will be discussed next, and the trait-plus-situation approach, which will be described in Chapters 24 and 25.

INDIVIDUAL DIFFERENCES: IDIOGRAPHIC MEASUREMENT

Allport (see pages 41-42) proposed that a trait could be conceived as common to all individuals and measured in the same way for everyone. He called this nomothetic measurement. Alternatively, a trait could be seen as unique to one individual, to be assessed differently for each individual. Allport called this idiographic measurement. Virtually all personality measurement has been nomothetic. If, however, people do not have nomothetic traits, then this strategy will have failed—not because traits do not exist, but because common traits as currently measured do not exist. This possibility has been raised by a number of writers. The best recent development of the idea is by Bem and Allen (1974), whose approach will be described here first.

Nomothetic Fallacies

Bem and Allen point out that most individual difference measurements (that is, traditional personality measures) are constructed in such a way that they can only be valid if nomothetic measurement is valid. If traits are idiographic, then nomothetic measurement will necessarily fail, but idiographic measurement would not. They accept the lack of reliability and cross-situational consistency that has been typical of personality measures. But they go on to attribute this failure to the use of nomothetic measures. In short, they suggest that we have been using the wrong methods to answer an important question.

In order to uncover alternative methods, Bem and Allen first pinpoint some of the characteristics of nomothetic measurement. They discuss three insufficiently acknowledged assumptions underlying nomothetic measurement, assumptions that must be true for such measurement to be valid. They call these assumptions "nomothetic fallacies" because they seriously doubt whether these particular assumptions are true.

The equivalence class.   First, there is the assumption of a known and shared *equivalence class.* An equivalence class is, for example, all the items on a personality questionnaire measuring a single trait. By putting all these different questions into the pot, the assessor is assuming that these items are equivalent in the sense of measuring the same thing. They are a class of items reflecting the same trait equivalently.

Let me give some examples. A standardized, Rogerian measure of adjustment (Dymond, 1954, p. 79) assumes that describing oneself as "worthless" or "really disturbed" indicates maladjustment. Two other items on the same test are describing oneself as "shy" or "disorganized." Thus, it is implicitly assumed that there is a class of self-descriptions that are equivalent, in the sense of measuring adjustment/maladjustment, and that class includes items as different from one another as "worthless" and "really disturbed" are from "shy" and "disorganized." Intuitively, the latter seem much less indicative of maladjustment than do the former.

Another example is the Manifest Anxiety Scale (Taylor, 1953, p. 286). The items

It makes me nervous to have to wait.

and

I worry over money and business.

are treated as equivalent to the item

I feel anxiety about something or someone almost all the time.

All three of these items are assumed to be in the same equivalence class for all individuals—namely, that of manifest anxiety. It seems equally plausible that the first item may reflect impulsiveness, and the second either responsibility or greed. Only the third seems unequivocally indicative of anxiety. More important, each item may reflect a different trait to a different person. Indirect evidence of this is the fact that individual items on any personality measure typically do not correlate highly with one another. Across all possible pairs of items, "mean correlations of .04 to .08 are typical; means above .20 are rare" (Fiske, 1971, p. 228).

The first potential nomothetic fallacy is, therefore, the assumption that a set of items or behaviors that in the mind of the person who constructed the measure all reflect the same trait also reflect the same trait to the individuals being measured. If this is indeed a fallacy, then behavior will be inconsistent in the eyes of the investigator, to whom the items are equivalent, but not in the eyes of the subject, to whom they are not:

> The research will yield the conclusion that a sample of individuals is inconsistent to the degree that their behaviors do not sort into the equivalence class which the investigator imposes by his choice of behaviors and situations to sample [Bem & Allen, 1974, p. 509].

Bem and Allen echo Allport's critique of a classic study of honesty

(Hartshorne & May, 1928, 1929). In this study, cheating, stealing, lying, and other behaviors were virtually uncorrelated; even cheating was inconsistent across situations. It is possible that to the children involved, these were not all manifestations of the trait honesty/dishonesty. Cheating in some exams may be principally achievement-oriented. Stealing (such as shoplifting), particularly with young adolescents, may be conformity or fear of peer disapproval. The behaviors studied were seen by the investigators as evidence of moral character, and this is one possible interpretation. The question is: was it the subjects' interpretation?

Scaling the items.   The second nomothetic fallacy is related to the first. Having assumed or defined a group of behaviors into an equivalence class, the investigator then makes additional assumptions about their *scaling*. Scaling refers to the methods by which the items are counted or scored. The most common method is the simplest: add everything in equally. For example, in the adjustment measure cited above, "shy" and "disorganized" count exactly as much as "worthless" and "really disturbed." In the Manifest Anxiety Scale, the two items about waiting and money worries count twice as much, together, as the third item about pervasive anxiety. Even if one could accept that all these items had something to do with adjustment or anxiety, it is unlikely that they are all equally strong or important as indicators. There are more elaborate forms of scaling, but these still impose the investigator's view of how the items should be scaled.

The first two nomothetic fallacies are, therefore, that (1) all items or behaviors assessed are interpreted by the subjects in the same way as the psychologist interprets them, and (2) all items or behaviors are scaled (added up or otherwise weighted) in the same way for all subjects—namely, the way the assessor scales them. The reader will notice a strong phenomenological "bias" behind these two points. That is, Bem and Allen would obviously prefer that assessment be done "in terms of the individual's own phenomenology, not the investigator's" (p. 518).

To the extent that assessment has reflected the investigator's rather than the subject's view of the world, the implication for traditional measurement is clear:

> the traditional trait-based research study will yield evidence of cross-situational consistency only if the individuals in the research sample agree with the investigator's a priori claim that the sampled behaviors and situations belong in a common equivalence class *and* only if the individuals agree among themselves on how to scale those behaviors and situations [Bem & Allen, 1974, p. 510].

The answer is to develop measures for which this is true. Here, however, we come to an apparent dead end. Bem and Allen point out that none of the interest in turning from nomothetic to idiographic measurement has ever been translated into a research program capable of studying more than one individual at a time. Therefore, they propose to push on to uncover a third fallacy, for which they do have a solution. So let's put aside for a moment the unsolved problems of the first two nomothetic assumptions; we will return to a possible solution to them at the end of this chapter.

Universal consistency. The third nomothetic fallacy is one that Bem and Allen first identify and then set out to remedy. This is the assumption of *consistency* itself—namely, that everyone is equally consistent across situations on a given trait. Maybe, they suggest, some people are and some are not. For example, perhaps some people do define honesty in the same way the investigator does (that is, they use the same equivalence class and scaling), and they are also quite consistent in how honest or dishonest they are. In that case, the investigator should study those who can be studied:

> Our advice to such an investigator, then, follows directly: Find those people. Separate those individuals who are cross-situationally consistent on the trait dimension and throw the others out, for by definition, only the behavior of consistent individuals can be meaningfully characterized by the investigator's construct; only their behaviors can be partitioned into the equivalence class under investigation [p. 512].

If you can't study all of the people all of the time (nomothetically), it is better to study some of the people some of the time (idiographically) than none at all.

Studying consistency as a trait. Bem and Allen are suggesting that even our present nomothetic measures can be used if we accept their limitations. They describe a study in which they tried to do this. The new variable was an a priori assessment of cross-situational consistency. That is, they wanted to separate individuals into those who would be consistent on a given trait and those who would not. They decided to rely on the subject's own judgment of how consistent he or she was.

Two traits were studied: friendliness and conscientiousness. Subjects were asked to rate themselves on a scale from "not at all" to "extremely" on both the trait value and trait variability. For example, each was asked:

In general, how friendly and outgoing are you?

and

How much do you vary from one situation to another
in how friendly and outgoing you are?

Similar questions were asked for several other traits. Thus a person could be extremely friendly, but not consistently so; extremely friendly and consistently so; moderately friendly, but not consistently so; and so forth in all possible combinations.

Then several convergent measures were obtained: the score on a questionnaire measure; mother's, father's, and a peer's reports; and two or three more direct measures. For example, friendliness was also rated in a group discussion, and conscientiousness was also measured by rating the neatness of the person and his or her living quarters. This choice of measures provides a good example of the variety of methods that should be used for evaluations of convergent validity.

The hypothesis was that those subjects who rated themselves as consistent on a trait would, as a group, show good correlations across situations. Those who rated themselves as not being consistent—that is, highly variable—would, as a group, show lower correlations. This was confirmed for the trait of friendliness. When subjects were divided into low- and high-variability groups by their self-ratings, the two groups differed significantly in the variability actually shown across the convergent measures. For the persons who identified themselves in advance as highly variable, the correlations ranged from −.20 to .59, with a mean of .27. For the low-variability group (self-rated as very consistent), the convergent validity correlations ranged from .34 to .75, with a mean of .57. Referring to Mischel's definition of the "personality coefficient," Bem and Allen point out that "the magic +.30 barrier appears to have been penetrated" (p. 514). In summary, it was possible to sort people out so that those for whom the measure was appropriate could be identified. Some of the people could be studied some of the time.

Two clouds on this bright horizon must be acknowledged. First, the correlations for the low-variability group are still not large by absolute standards. They are better than most convergent validity correlations, but they only account for an average of $.57^2$ or 32% of the variance. Perhaps the use of nomothetic scales is still exacting its price in terms of variance unaccounted for.

The second problem for this method is that it did not work for their second trait, conscientiousness. A post hoc, statistical (rather than the self-rated) definition of consistency had to be used to pull the two sets of correlations apart. All this means is that Bem and Allen have not found the end of the rainbow for us. But they have pointed out several paths well worth following. The reader who is interested should examine their article carefully for what they were trying to accomplish, the procedures they tried, their results, and their discussion of these results.

Two other sources might be useful as well: Fiske (1961) and Campus (1974) have discussed variability as a personality trait. Note that in all of these proposals, including Bem and Allen's, consistency (low/high variability) has become a personality trait in itself. It is what is sometimes called a *moderator variable* (Kogan & Wallach, 1964). That is, it is a trait that moderates or affects the relationship between two other variables—in this case, two convergent validity variables. Two cautions are in order: First, with a fairly large number of ways of identifying or defining any such moderator variable, there is the risk that the investigator will find such a variable, purely by chance, through post hoc analysis. Replication is mandatory. Second, a moderator variable, such as consistency, is itself being treated as a personality trait; therefore, it, too, requires appropriate validation.

Finding Shared Equivalence Classes

Barriers to idiographic measurement. The identification of consistent individuals is admittedly a compromise of necessity. Bem and Allen acknowledge (p. 511) that they have left the first two nomothetic fallacies intact.

The only purely idiographic alternatives they can suggest are limited to the study of one individual at a time. This apparent necessity to create a new, individually tailored assessment procedure for each person has been the major objection to idiographic assessment. One critic points out why this option has not often been exercised:

> The idiographists may be entirely correct, but if they are, it is a sad day for psychology. Idiography is an antiscience point of view: it discourages the search for general laws and instead encourages the description of particular phenomena (people). The idiographist is like the astronomer who despairs of finding any general laws relating to heavenly bodies and instead devotes the rest of his life to describing the particular features of the planet Neptune [Nunnally, 1970, p.356].

Bem and Allen are not as pessimistic as Nunnally. But they do, in effect, accept the nomothetic measures available and explore only the possibility of finding out for whom these measures are appropriate. Is this compromise necessary?

Equating idiographic measurement with the study of one individual at a time assumes that no two individuals are in significant respects alike. Specifically, it assumes that every individual has a different equivalence class and scaling for every trait. But this seems to overstate the case. Surely we would be virtually unable to communicate, or to describe ourselves and other people, if this were true. We must have some common phenomenological experiences.

Let us try another assumption. There may be some constructs for which *some* people share the same equivalence class. If so, a measure of such a construct could be developed and applied to these people, and it would be idiographically appropriate for all of them. In other words, rather than accept the nomothetic/idiographic dichotomy, we might imagine something in between. To paraphrase Kluckhohn and Murray (1961, p. 53):

> Every person is in certain respects
> a. like all other people.
> b. like some other people.
> c. like no other person.

The nomothetic position corresponds to *a* and the idiographic to *c*. Position *b* might be more realistic: every person is in certain respects like some other people, like some significant subpopulation.

If so, then we need to specify these subpopulations. And we also need a method for identifying such groups' equivalence classes and, if possible, their scaling of items within these classes.

A possible method. Such a method was proposed (although for other purposes) by Alex Bavelas (1942), working in the context of Lewin's theory of personality (see Chapter 17). Lewin's is a social but also a phenomenological theory, and we might consider whether this phenomenological technique could be borrowed for use in the individual paradigm.

Over several years, Bavelas developed this method for the phenomenological assessment of values—which Lewin called valences (see page 162), and which most social-learning theorists would probably call instrumental behaviors and reinforcers. First the procedure will be described in its present form; then the possibility of modification for the measurement of individual differences will be discussed.

At the outset, a specific population is identified. This might be young women in a southern California college; elementary school teachers in Victoria, British Columbia; Mennonite children of school age; nurses in training at a particular hospital; Cuban emigrants; or people in a small Midwestern town. Such populations are highly specific yet contain significant numbers of individuals who are assumed to share some common outlook. That is, their views are somewhere between those of all the people in the world and those of a single individual. Because most people belong to several such groups (some "nurses in training," for example, might also be "parents of young children"), it is important to make their membership in the population of interest quite salient to them. In addition to pointing it out to them, one might also conduct the research in the relevant location (school, home, work site).

A sample of the particular population is asked, individually, the following questions:

> What could a person like you [for example, a boy of your age at school] do that would be a good thing to do , so that someone would praise him? Who would praise him?

> What could a person like you do that would be a bad thing to do, so that someone would criticize [or, for a child, scold] him? Who would criticize him?

Note that the wording asks about the behaviors and values of people like himself, in the context being studied. The subject is thus further reminded of the relevant population, and he is also free to answer what he feels others like himself would think, whether or not he agrees with them. Each is a representative of the identified group, answering in its language, as he perceives their shared ideas.

The "praise" questions (what and who) are asked nine times, for a different answer each time. The approved behavior is written on one side of a card, and the source of approval is written on the other side of the same card. The same procedure is then followed for the "criticize" questions. There is nothing magical about the nine repetitions, but it does seem to get people past the first cliche answers into a greater variety, without requiring more than they can legitimately think of.

The procedure so far results in 18 cards for each subject in the sample— that is, N times 18 cards in all—with each card containing a behavior and a source. These are the items that presumably belong in four broad equivalence classes: approved behaviors, disapproved behaviors, sources of approval, and sources of disapproval. For children in school, for example, approved behaviors might include:

Not talking back to the teacher.
Having your hands clean.
If someone needs a handkerchief, lending them yours.

Especially after the first, usually general, responses are given, the others typically appear unique, diverse, unexpected, and often bemusing to the outsider. For example,

> If a girl had to go up to the bathroom and her house was locked, let her go up to your house [A. Bavelas, 1942, p. 377].

Let that be; they're idiographic.

For purposes of illustration, let us focus only on the set of approved behaviors; the same procedure is followed for disapproved behaviors and for the sources. These N times 9 cards can be numbered to identify both the subject and the order (1-9) in which each was given, should this information be desired later. In any case, they are all shuffled together in preparation for the second stage, in order to produce a large group of cards generated by the first sample as a whole.

Then a second sample of individuals is drawn from the same population. These people will meet as a group to sort the cards (items) into more refined equivalence classes. Each person is given a random subset of the cards, until all are distributed. Their first job is quite simple: put together all those cards that mean exactly the same thing, creating as many piles of cards as there are different categories of items on those cards. For example, "not talking back to the teacher" would probably be seen as identical to "not talking back to teachers." More abstract grouping (for example, including "not sassing teachers") is not encouraged at this point.

When everyone has done this for his or her own set of cards, the investigator begins to act, as a helper only. The subjects are the experts. The largest stack of cards—that is, the largest pile of items deemed identical by someone in the group—is taken first. The investigator begins to read items from this stack, asking others who have identical items to contribute them to this stack. (Remember that each sorter had a different set of cards.) In the process of merging stacks, the categories become refined and verbally labeled by the participants. Some stacks are broken up and recombined, always by consensus.

Because the sorters have to talk about how each was doing the original sorting, and why they are combining items, the names of categories occur naturally. Abstract and logical category schemes are not required; the natural perception of identical items is encouraged. A startling and (to me) rather sad example is, for a group of college women, a category they agreed to call "affection." It included behaviors toward pets and animals only—no humans. Examples were "taking care of my horse," and "be good to your pets." Dates and other interpersonal relations were seen as social (another category), not affectionate.

When the group agrees that the entire set is in homogeneous groupings, they stop. There are typically a few very large stacks, followed by rapidly decreasing sized stacks, and many single cards alone. Five or six stacks will probably contain 80% of the cards. The large, shared groups are the ones of interest. They contain the following information: descriptions of approved behavior, written in the language of the people in whom one is interested (the cards themselves); various equivalence classes of different kinds of approved behaviors, as constructed by these people (the stacks); the names of these classes, as given by these people (during the sorting); and a frequency distribution enabling one to see how salient each class is for the population of interest (the number of cards in each stack).

Applying the method in research.   This procedure was originally developed by A. Bavelas to enable Kalhorn (1941) to study rural children in Iowa. It has subsequently been used to study the Hopi (Thompson & Joseph, 1947); the Papago (Joseph, Spicer, & Chesky, 1949); a small Midwestern town (Warner et al., 1949); children in New Zealand (Havighurst et al., 1954); a comparison of Indian and White children (Havighurst & Neugarten, 1955); nurses in a California hospital (Rice, 1965); women clerks in a large insurance company (Barthol & Bridge, 1968); and various other groups in many unpublished or unlocated studies. The sorting by the second sample rather than the investigators is a fairly recent and significant addition, as it permits the people to make their own equivalence classes.

The method has been used to obtain a description of an unknown culture. It can also be used to identify those who are "marginal" within their group—that is, those who do not share the common outlook and might therefore be expected to drop out. Developmental changes are interesting, as they show changes in what a child feels expected to do over the years. Who approves and disapproves of what is also significant. Messages written merely by randomly sampling items from stacks, in frequencies proportional to the size of the stacks, are judged by a new sample of the population to be more credible, sensible, and persuasive than any other messages written by experts or outsiders. For this reason, the method was later dubbed the "Echo" technique (A. Bavelas, 1967): it repeats back what the people themselves have said.

Constructing new measures.   How might this method be used to measure individual differences idiographically? Begin by defining the population for which an idiographic measure is desired—for example, middle-class university students or an outpatient group in a mental-health clinic. Each is considered to be a subculture, as different in some respects from other groups as are the cultures that anthropologists contrast. The resulting items and equivalence classes for the usual question (approval/disapproval) could then be used, for example, to generate a questionnaire assessing individual differences in self-perceived worth. That is, those who say they are doing most of the important "good" behaviors would presumably have higher opinions of themselves than those who are not. The items would be scaled (weighted) by the frequency of items in the category.

The question does not have to be good versus bad. It could, for example, be "What could a person like you do that would be a *friendly* thing to do, so that others would think it was a friendly act?" The trait of interest is defined by the form of this basic question. The essential procedures that must be retained are to clearly identify the group, including its salience to the subject; to elicit items from the group itself; and to let them sort and label them in their own way. These items can then be used to construct an idiographic measure for this group.

This last step has not been done formally yet, but remember that this is a chapter for the future, to suggest possible lines that might be followed. There are many interesting options available, of which this particular method is only one.

In this Part, we have covered the central tradition of the field of personality, the individual paradigm. Seven of the most important individual theories have been presented and examined, both logically and empirically. Five single-trait theories typical of the individual paradigm have been evaluated according to the standards appropriate to their assumptions. The major bridge between this past and the future is a critical awareness of the common paradigm behind them all. Serious questions have been raised by the available empirical evidence, especially the evidence regarding individual differences as presently defined and measured. This final chapter has explored, however speculatively, revisions or improvements that promise new possibilities. There is plenty of life in the old paradigm yet.

Part 2
Social Personality Theories

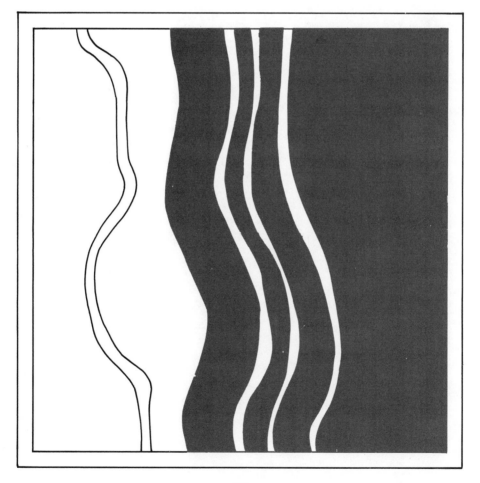

16

Introduction
to the Social Theories

Although the tradition in the field of personality has been to emphasize the individual, there have always been a few theories that did not fit this paradigm. The number, variety, and prominence of such theories has been increasing since about 1960, and the line is now clearly drawn between the traditional, individual focus and a newer interest in social factors.

These social theories of personality differ as much among themselves as do the individual personality theories, but they, too, share a common paradigm in the form of a set of assumptions about human nature. Social personality theories assume (1) that the major influences on human behavior come from the environment and, therefore, (2) that situational rather than individual differences should be the primary focus of attention.

The social personality theories consider the individual to be continually open to his or her environment and greatly influenced by it. This is the first major assumption; the various theories focus on precisely how this influence occurs. Therefore, most of the major terms in a social theory—terms such as goal, stimulus, reinforcement, imitation—refer to the environment or to relations between the individual and the environment. Most social theories also include some terms describing the individual—terms such as drive, cognition, response—but these, too, are used primarily to explain how the environment is able to influence an individual and how the individual reacts to it.

These are called social, rather than environmental, theories of personality because they specify that the most important aspect of the environment for any individual is social—that is, other people and everything they do to and for us. While all admit that the physical environment has an influence, they argue that personality is primarily affected by the social environment.

Thus, social personality theories focus either "outside" the individual or on the individual-in-relation-to-the-social-environment, and only rarely on properties exclusively "inside" an individual. Inasmuch as the characteristics of individuals are not very important in social theories, it follows that in-

155

dividual differences would not be important either. One cannot propose intra-psychic variations in individuals when the theory has no terms for the individual in isolation from the environment. Still, the variations observed in human behavior must be accounted for, and social personality theories propose that this variation arises in the social environment. This is the second major assumption. Systematic differences in situations, in stimuli, or in social settings are the major interest of social theorists—not differences in traits, needs, constructs, or other properties of individuals. Rather than classifying individuals, the social theories will classify situations.

It might seem, with all this emphasis on the environment and situational differences instead of the individual and individual differences, that these are not in fact personality theories. Surely personality, however defined, is a property of a person and not of the environment. Therefore, some have asked, where is the person in social personality theories? The answer is that the person is still there, but rather than operating in isolation, the individual is interacting with an environment. According to social theories, *personality is a set of principles by which an individual interacts with an environment.*

The environment can influence people only if, and to the extent that, people have certain characteristics. The characteristics that determine how and why a person will respond to and act upon an environment are the central part of any social personality theory. The tendency to respond to reinforcement (Dollard and Miller, Skinner), or to learn by observing others (Bandura), or to structure the environment into a patterned whole (Lewin) is an essential principle in each of these theories. These tendencies are characteristics of the human personality, attributed to people in general. Variations in individual behavior will occur because individuals experience different situations. Thus, the input may differ, while the principles for handling this input remain the same. These principles are the essence of personality for a social theorist.

Finally, it is worth noting that, while the social personality theories are "deviant" in the context of individual personality theories, they are much more like theories in general experimental psychology. Whereas individual personality theorists are interested in how people in particular behave, regardless of situation, most other psychologists—including social personality theorists—are interested in how people in general behave, depending on the situation. Most social theories have in fact borrowed a great deal from the fields of learning and perception and have sometimes even made the principles of such fields the basis of their theories of personality.

Part 2 will present four theories almost as heterogeneous as those in Part 1. What they have in common—the social paradigm of personality—is their emphasis on events occurring outside the individual, particularly in the social environment, and on transactions between individual and environment. As in Part 1, this paradigm will be applied specifically to each theory after the basics of the theory have been explained.

A special introductory comment should be made about the three theories of Dollard and Miller, Skinner, and Bandura. These are usually called *social-learning theories,* social-behavior theories, or sometimes (less accurately) stimulus-response theories. All build on the fundamentals of learning:

stimulus, response, and reinforcement. They extend these ideas, derived from the study of animal behavior, to humans, focusing particularly on stimuli and reinforcers that are social in nature. That is, they are more interested in how a child learns to respond to its mother because of the affection and attention she offers than in how a rat learns to press a bar for a food pellet. Although they disagree mightily on what the exact principles of learning are, all agree that these principles are the basis of human personality. In contrast, the first theory to be considered, Lewin's field theory, gives much more detailed attention to the nature of the stimulus or social situation and to the intricacies of transactions with the social environment that extend beyond its stimulus and reinforcement functions.

Each theory will be presented and examined as a theory, and then its empirical status will be considered—just as in Part 1. Social-learning theories, and to a lesser extent Lewin's theory, are "in favor" at present. Particularly because of the criticisms of the individual personality theories discussed in Chapter 14, many psychologists interested in personality have shifted (or even converted) to a social theory. While this is a reasonable choice, it is important to be just as critical of the new theories as of the old. We must not ignore logical or empirical problems with these theories, especially while emphasizing such problems when they occur in the individual personality theories. Recall Sechrest's "Law of Symmetry in Data Interpretation" (1976,p.7). If it is not applied, these theories will be the fads and "sky rockets" of our time. Our hope lies in open-minded evaluation and criticism, in the constructive sense, and not in blind conversion to a new theory.

17

Lewin

THE THEORY

Kurt Lewin's is the earliest social personality theory, dating at least from the publication of *A Dynamic Theory of Personality* in 1935. It has remained a respected but somewhat peripheral personality theory, partly because it was a social theory in the era of the individual paradigm and partly because Lewin and his students became much better known in the field of social psychology than the psychology of personality. As the social paradigm has emerged more clearly, however, Lewin has been recently rediscovered (for example, Bem & Allen, 1974; Ekehammar, 1974; see also Chapter 25).

Perhaps the most important contemporary role this theory can play is to offer an alternative to the social-learning theories. For those who are convinced that the available evidence requires a social rather than an individual view of personality, yet who are not attracted to or satisfied with any of the social-learning approaches, Lewin offers a considerably different social theory. As Hall and Lindzey point out:

> Perhaps the most important critical objection to S-R [social-learning] approaches is the assertion that they do not provide adequate prior specification of stimulus and response. Traditionally, learning theorists have been concerned almost exclusively with the *process* of learning and have not attempted to identify the stimuli occurring in the natural environment of the organisms they study or to develop a suitable taxonomy for these stimulus events. Further, these learning processes have been investigated in restricted, controlled settings in which it is relatively simple to specify the stimuli eliciting observable behavior. The challenge to the personality theorist is to understand the human organism operating in his real-world environment and it can be cogently argued that if the psychologist cannot fully define the stimulus for behavior his task has barely begun [1970, p. 469].

Lewin's theory concentrates precisely on the complexity of the stimuli that influence human behavior.

Lewin's conception of the human organism operating in the real-world environment is called the *life space*. This is the "totality of facts which determine the behavior . . . of an individual at a certain moment" (Lewin, 1936, p. 216). The life space consists of the person in his or her environment, as the environment exists for that person at that moment. The life space includes the self and also objects, people, or even intangibles to which the self has some relationship.

This central concept will be clearer if we identify the assumptions that Lewin wanted to build into his theory through his definition of the life space. There were three lines of thought that determined Lewin's theory: phenomenology, Gestalt psychology, and the dynamics of motivation. Fortunately, each of these ideas is easier to understand intuitively than its intimidating formal name suggests. Each will be explained and applied to the concept of life space.

The Life Space as Phenomenological

Two phenomenological theories in the individual paradigm have already been introduced, those of Rogers and Kelly (Chapters 9 and 10). In Lewin's theory it becomes obvious that the phenomenological approach can fit a social theory as well. His, too, is a "first-person" theory. Recall that the phenomenological approach in psychology emphasizes my view of the world from my own perspective, rather than from that of an outside or objective observer. Thus Lewin would describe me in my environment *as this environment exists for me.* The life space does not, therefore, correspond strictly to the physical environment or to the individual's actual relation to the physical environment. For example, I can be in a particular room but mentally miles away. I may be "close to" someone who is not physically near and not at all "close" to the person next door. A friend may become "distant" or "more open" phenomenologically but not physically. Someone may be "unapproachable" although there are no visible barriers. A deeply held belief may become "part of me" psychologically but of course not literally. "Insiders" and "outsiders" are seldom determined by real fences. All these examples suggest that we use physical analogies quite easily for psychological events. Thus, Lewin chose the term life *space,* which expresses phenomenological reality by an extended analogy to physical space.[1]

This phenomenological life space is, for Lewin, what affects behavior. Only that which is part of the life space is important. If you do not know someone is standing behind you, then she is not in your life space. As soon as you become aware of her, she enters into your life space. If you mistakenly think she is still there after she has left, she is still in your life space and affecting your behavior. Thus Lewin suggests a difference between the life space and "a

---

[1]Readers who are familiar with topology will soon recognize that Lewin used the mathematics of spatial relations, specifically hodology, for the formal relationships in his theory.

multitude of processes in the physical or social world, which do not affect the life space of the individual at that time" (1943, p. 306).

There is also a most important *boundary zone,* through which things in the physical or social world can enter the life space. Perception is the translation of physical stimuli into events in the life space—for example, recognizing something. Going in the other direction, one's own actions affect the physical or social environment as well. If a person is aware of hurting another's feelings, this is part of the life space. If not, it is outside and cannot affect behavior. The fact that physical and social events can be introduced into the life space via the boundary zone is, among other things, what makes psychological experiments possible. Rather than always being inferred from behavior, particular life spaces (such as a choice between two alternatives) can be arranged for the purpose of testing the theory.

As is obvious from these examples, many parts of the life space are transient and changeable. It is not a permanent, static view of the world, nor is it one's personality. The life space changes with changes in perception and action. Parts that were formerly seen as separate may become the same thing, phenomenologically—for example, a fear of dogs in general. Or one thing may become finely differentiated—for example, learning to distinguish sailing boats as sloop, ketch, yawl, schooner, cutter, marconi- or gaff-rigged, and so forth. Lewin also proposed a principle of *contemporaneity*: in representing the life space, only what is contemporary, or in the immediate present, is included. Therefore, past events can influence behavior only if they are currently represented in the life space. Future events can be included as goals, expectations, or intentions, presently held.

The Life Space as a Gestalt

Besides being composed of phenomenological events, the life space is a *Gestalt*—that is, a patterned whole. It is not a random collection of thoughts or a haphazard stream of consciousness. It is what the psychology of perception means by a Gestalt: the whole is not the sum of its parts but the relations among them. Lewin was a student of Max Wertheimer, the founder of Gestalt psychology,[2] and it was his explicit intention to extend these principles into a theory of personality. The essence of the Gestalt point of view is to pay attention to the relation between events rather than to the events in isolation. Just as the perceived darkness of a color depends on what surrounds it, other psychological events depend on each other as their context. A sandwich may look like a feast or a wretched necessity, depending on the context in which it is available. The old joke, "How do you like your wife?" "Compared to what?" makes the same point.

Events in the life space are called *regions*, in keeping with the analogy to physical space. The regions are all the possible events at that time. The person is also a region in his or her own life space; that is, I see all these events in relation to myself as well as to each other. The Gestalt of a life space is the connection among regions, which makes up the whole.

---

[2]No relation to the more recent "gestalt therapies."

Regions are closer if they are more similar. For example, reading books on different topics in psychology probably involves a greater degree of similarity than does reading a psychology book and a book on fishing. All the ''reading regions'' are probably more similar to one another than they are to, say, painting. To the degree that two adjacent regions are similar, their common boundary is called permeable—that is, they are close to being one region.

The arrangement of regions represents their psychological distances and relations as well. If I think of two events as necessarily occurring in a given order, then these regions lie nearer and farther from me in my life space, like two towns along a single road. One must be entered before the other. If I feel I must be dressed in a certain way for a particular occasion, then all the activities of preparing myself comprise a region or regions that must be passed through before the second activity-region can be entered.

Notice that the notion of moving around the life space has been suggested. Such movement from one region to another is called (psychological) *locomotion*. The relations among regions can be thought of as potential paths, as ways from one region to the next. I am a region in my own life space; this region changes its relation to other regions when such locomotion occurs. This is one of the ways the life space changes. Having done something (entered that region), the other regions may change—that is, look different now that I have acted in a particular way. I may be closer to some regions and further from others. Some regions may no longer be available, while new ones may appear, or the relation between previous regions may change. Just as the life space is phenomenological rather than physical, so is locomotion. The firm decision to take a certain course of action, even before embarking on overt behavior, constitutes psychological movement. Having "made up my mind," I now see things differently.

Psychological locomotion is not bound by the barriers of physical space: we can imagine ourselves anywhere, albeit on the level of unreality, even into regions which cannot be physically reached. But paths may also be phenomenologically absent or closed. People are often incapable of certain actions that they are physically, but not psychologically, able to do. For example, in stage fright the individual may be unable to move from the wings on to center stage. Even when such intense emotion is not involved, psychological paths may not be present. There may be, for the moment, no conceivable route between the heap of 5000 tiny, unassembled pieces and the picture on the cover of the jigsaw-puzzle box. Many of life's larger puzzles are similar. We cannot see a way from where we are to where we know we want to be. Only if we can restructure the life space to make a route—perhaps by discovering new, connecting regions—can locomotion begin.

The Life Space as Dynamic

The life space is an attempt to picture the person's world at a given time. It is phenomenological—that is, a picture seen from the person's own eyes. And it is a Gestalt: it includes the connections and relations among parts of the picture. How and why locomotion, or psychological action, occurs depends partly on the structure of the life space. But it also depends on what the person wants—that is, on motivation. If the person is equally near to two regions, and paths to both exist for him, then no prediction is possible without adding what each region means to him. Lewin's entire theory of motivation is complicated, but it can be accurately presented in somewhat simplified terms.

Lewin suggested that a region may have a positive or negative *valence*— that is, it attracts or repels me. Complex regions or systems of regions (such as other people) may have both positive and negative aspects. *Conflict* is induced by valences that pull or push in opposite directions.

Whether positive or negative, conflictual or straightforward, the valence creates tension in the person which creates a force towards action. This adds a dynamic aspect to the otherwise static structure of the life space. There is a force for action as long as the tension created by the valence exists. The tension will be reduced only when the valence is reduced or eliminated. This can be accomplished by entering, attaining, or enjoying a positive region. If the region is negative, its tension can be reduced by escaping or avoiding the region or, alternatively, by entering the region and "getting it over with." Once the inner tension aroused by the valence is reduced, that particular impetus to locomotion is removed.

Thus, Lewin's is in some ways a dynamic theory like Freud's. Drives or needs give rise to action, and their satisfaction leads to an equilibrium. There are, however, important differences. Freud and most other need theorists (such as Dollard and Miller, see Chapter 18) emphasize the biology of needs, assuming that all needs ultimately derive from primary or innate needs essential to survival. Lewin, on the other hand, is much more interested in the psychology of needs, in two senses.

First, without denying the existence of biological needs, he implies that they are relatively unimportant in ordinary life. Rather, he speaks of *quasi-needs*, which arise, for example, because the individual has formed an intention to do something—mail a letter, finish a task, or make a decision. These quasi-needs are psychological rather than biological, and they are the needs that pervade Lewin's writings.

The second sense in which Lewin's theory of needs is predominantly psychological is that, again, the phenomenology of the situation is uppermost. The belief that I have finished a task, rather than the objective completion, satisfies the need. For example, after working a long time on a puzzling assignment and finally seeing the solution, it is sometimes difficult to go ahead and write the necessary final report or paper. The work is psychologically finished when the solution is found, and the formal write-up for others to read may have little positive valence. Thus, in the end, we return to the individual's phenomenological situation. The life space is what is perceived, how the perceptions are seen to be related, and how they are valued by the individual. This Gestalt of person and environment is what determines behavior.

Lewin's Theory as a Social Personality Theory

One of the best-known aphorisms of Lewinian theory is that *behavior is a function of the person and his environment*. Clearly, then, Lewin's is a social personality theory. Rather than emphasizing exclusively individual or environmental terms, Lewin has tried to blend the two together as if the distinction were artificial in the first place. The life space is not a property of the individual, because it incorporates a highly articulated and structured environment. The social-learning theorists will suggest that the environment should be seen as consisting of stimuli and reinforcers. Lewin does not tell us what the environment is, in any such fixed terms, but rather how to examine it and how to talk about it. Nor is the life space purely environmental, because it is always filtered through the individual's perceptions. This is a social theory that emphasizes the relationship of the person to the environment. Separately, neither has any meaning.

Besides this emphasis on the individual in relation to the environment, Lewin leans more toward situational than individual differences (the second characteristic of a social theory). Certainly, he proposes no fixed traits except mental ability (Lewin, 1935, Chapter 7). If the situation is always understood to be phenomenological (the life space), then variations in behavior are due to situational differences. Note, however, that the situation does not have a unilateral influence on the individual. I often construct my own situation by my perceptions, my intentions, and my actions.

EMPIRICAL STATUS

There are at least two obstacles to empirical testing of Lewin's theory. First, the theory is not critically centered on any single issue or set of issues. This has been noted for most of the personality theories already presented. Only the exceptional theory can be reduced to a crucial question—such as whether trait factors replicate, or (as we will see) whether response and reinforcement are necessary for learning. Lewin's theory, like most, is an umbrella for many possible experiments, none of which is more central than any other. The second problem is one common to phenomenologists. It is vital but difficult to construct a known phenomenological situation in the individual for the purpose of one's study. Inferring the life space from the behavior would be circular.

In the face of the second problem, it is surprising that Lewin's has been one of the most empirically productive of all personality theories. Cartwright (1959) and Deutsch (1968) have reviewed many of these studies. Phenomenological experiments can be done. For the student who wants to sample the particular blend of rigorous logic and acute sensitivity to the subject's experience that is perhaps the best legacy of the Gestalt school, including especially Lewin, a study by Henle and Aull (1953) is recommended.

The best-known line of research on Lewin's personality theory is the work on tension systems using the technique of interrupted tasks. A task that the individual intended to complete is experimentally interrupted, creating, according to the theory, an unsatisfied quasi-need. Such tasks are more likely to be remembered than are comparable completed tasks. This is known as the Zeigarnik effect, after the woman who first demonstrated it (Zeigarnik, 1927/ 1938). They are also more likely to be resumed than are tasks begun by someone else (see a description of Ovsiankina's work in Lewin, 1935). The effect can also be used to study the characteristics that make tasks (regions) similar, by predicting which task will act as substitute for another in discharging the residual tension (for example, Henle, 1942). This area of research is very large and heterogeneous, with so many twists and turns that it is beyond the scope of the present book to review all this work in the necessary detail. Therefore, another area of research will be discussed here.

The Study of Conflict

A relatively simple issue that still includes the basic concepts of Lewin's theory is the study of conflict. What happens when there are two regions of equal valence, one and only one of which can and must be entered? For example, there may be two equally attractive alternatives or a choice between "the frying pan and the fire." Conflicts such as these can be described in Lewinian terms, with testable consequences.

Following Lewin (1938), Barker (1942) made the following initial assumptions: (1) Positively valenced regions attract the person, while negatively valenced regions repel the person. (2) These valences are at least slightly variable, so that the relative strengths of valences in the life space continually change by small amounts. (3) The force of any valence is stronger if closer. That is, a positive valence becomes more attractive as one approaches it, and a negative valence becomes more repellent as one approaches it. This is sometimes called the goal gradient. (4) As time passes, there is increasing pressure to make a decision; that is, the predecision region itself becomes negative.

When these assumptions are applied to a conflict situation, some interesting conceptual hypotheses result. In a conflict situation, the individual must choose between two essentially equal valences. The person must be unable *not* to choose—for example, by leaving the field. When both choices (regions) are positive, this is called an *approach/approach* conflict. When both are negative, this is called an *avoidance/avoidance* conflict. This distinction follows from the first assumption above.

Rather than being caught perpetually between the two choices, which would be the case if the valences were fixed and unvarying, the individual oscillates, by the second assumption. Each valence, whether positive or negative, changes slightly in relation to the other, so the individual will begin to move toward one and away from the other. This slight change in valence may occur for any number of reasons, or it may be random. In any case, it serves to get the person off of dead center and into locomotion.

What happens then is determined by the third assumption, the goal gradient. As the individual moves closer to one region, the valence of that region acts more strongly, while the valence of the other region recedes in distance and in force. If the two valences are positive (approach/approach conflict), then the region toward which the person is moving will become more attractive, and the alternative less attractive, simply as a result of having moved slightly in one direction. The person should therefore continue to go in that direction.

But if the two valences are negative (avoidance/avoidance conflict), then the region toward which the person begins to move will become more negative. It will repel the person, while the other alternative, which is now more distant, will not appear as bad as before. Therefore, the individual will reverse course, avoiding the region toward which he or she was moving. Now that the person is closer to the other alternative, however, it becomes worse and causes another reversal—and so on.

The fourth assumption, an increasing pressure to make a decision, is necessary to get the person out of this vicious cycle. The individual will eventually make a decision, but compared to the approach/approach decision, it will involve more ambivalence—more psychological movement back and forth between the two alternatives. This should be felt subjectively as more uncertainty and should also be reflected empirically in longer decision times.

To test this deduction (and several others), Barker (1942) asked each of 19 boys, 9 to 11 years old, first to drink a small amount of each of seven liquids: orange juice, pineapple juice, tomato juice, water, unsweetened lemon juice, vinegar, and salt water. Then the subject sat in front of a display that presented him with two cards at a time, each bearing the name of one of the liquids (for example, "tomato juice" and "orange juice"). Directly in front of the child was a lever that could be tilted toward one card or the other, by degrees, until at its farthest reach, a buzzer sounded. The child was to choose which of the two liquids he would like to drink by moving the lever all the way over in one direction and sounding the buzzer. He could, however, move the lever back and forth as much as he wanted up until the time he indicated his final choice. Barker measured both the amount of such wavering before the choice (weighted according to how far the lever was displaced each time) and also the total time between the presentation of a pair of cards and the final choice of one card.

Although all possible pairs of the seven choices were presented (in random order), the ones most relevant to the conceptual hypothesis here were those between highly preferred (approach/approach) alternatives and between less preferred (avoidance/avoidance) alternatives. The rank-order of preference was inferred for each child separately by adding up the number of times a drink was chosen over another in a pair. The drink consistently chosen over each of the others would have the highest possible score and would be ranked first, and so on. Exactly how Barker arrived at his independent- and dependent-variable scores is illustrated in Figure 17-1.

The choice that involved the bottom two, least preferred choices (usually salt water and vinegar) should be preceded by more wavering and a longer decision time than a choice between the top two (usually pineapple and orange juice). Both measures did differ in the predicted direction, but only the time scores were significantly different for the approach/approach and avoidance/ avoidance situations.

This experiment is a good translation not only of the conceptual hypothesis but of the phenomenology of conflict into the life space of the subject. The child faced clearly defined regions (the two cards) and a means of locomotion towards those regions (the lever). His personal valences were used, not a group average. The situation was made engaging and real by having the child actually taste the liquids at the outset. Barker (1942, pp. 26-29) even describes

INDEPENDENT VARIABLE: AMOUNT OF PREFERENCE FOR EACH DRINK

for orange juice		for pineapple juice	
left card vs.	right card	left card vs.	right card
orange juice	pineapple juice	pineapple juice	orange juice
orange juice	tomato juice	pineapple juice	tomato juice
orange juice	water	pineapple juice	water
orange juice	unsweetened lemon juice	pineapple juice	unsweetened lemon juice
orange juice	vinegar	pineapple juice	vinegar
orange juice	salt water	pineapple juice	salt water
pineapple juice	orange juice	orange juice	pineapple juice
tomato juice	orange juice	tomato juice	pineapple juice
water	orange juice	water	pineapple juice
unsweetened lemon	orange juice	unsweetened lemon	pineapple juice
vinegar	orange juice	vinegar	pineapple juice
salt water	orange juice	salt water	pineapple juice

The preference rating for orange juice, for example, was established by the total number of times it was chosen over the other drinks in the twelve paired comparisons shown in the first two columns. Similarly for pineapple juice, using the third and fourth columns. Note that the two pairs in dotted lines are identical to pairs already given: Orange vs. pineapple was presented only once to a subject, as was pineapple vs. orange. Each of these pairs was, however, counted twice—in the preference rating for orange juice and also for pineapple juice—since they are relevant to both.

DEPENDENT VARIABLES: PRECHOICE BEHAVIORS (WAVERING, TOTAL TIME)

The solid boxes above indicate the pairs on which prechoice data were based. For example, the total amount of lever movement before a choice between

orange juice vs. pineapple juice

was added to the similar amount for the choice between

pineapple juice vs. orange juice.

This sum was the prechoice wavering for this particular approach/approach conflict.

Figure 17-1.   Example of the research definitions of the concepts in Barker's study

the entire life space of the experiment in which the conflict situation was created—including the initial conversation with the experimenter and the final goal of being paid 15¢ for having participated.

Methodological Problems

There might, however, be flaws in the experiment as conducted. The valences of the drinks were inferred from the final choice itself, so that the independent and dependent variables are confounded. *What* choice was made each time ultimately determined the valence assigned to each drink. This valence was then used to predict *how* a particular choice was made (wavering, total time). In effect, Barker was predicting backwards, from the choice to how it had been made. If the wavering and time that preceded the choice affected the final decision, then these two variables were not distinct from each other.

However, this overlapping of the variables is not important if it cannot plausibly have affected the outcome. (In this case, the criticism becomes aesthetic rather than substantive.) So let us look more closely at the situation. Suppose the actual choice between alternatives had not even been recorded, only the wavering and time. Instead of inferring the valences in order to identify the two kinds of conflict, Barker could simply have assumed that a choice between two sweet juices (orange and pineapple) would be an approach/approach conflict and a choice between salt water and vinegar would be an avoidance/avoidance conflict. Few would dispute this assumption. So, in effect, Barker did not need the complex system of ranking to convince us that he had established the two different kinds of conflict. His tailoring of the conflict to the individual subject, in this case, made little difference, especially at the extreme positive and negative ends. If so, then the procedures by which he derived the valences are unlikely to have influenced these valences, because they are so obvious and generally shared, particularly when the subjects had previously tasted all the drinks and nothing was left to their imaginations.

Barker's method of calculating the valences also helped to avoid any artifactual influence of the prechoice behaviors (wavering, time) on the valences of the drinks. Let's look even more closely at how the independent and dependent variables were arrived at, using Figure 17-1 as an aid. All possible pairings of the 7 drink cards were presented twice, so that the position of the card (left or right) could be eliminated as a factor. The predecision score for any particular choice was the average of the 2 presentations of that pair of cards (the 2 solid boxes in Figure 17-1). But the valence of each drink was summed over the total of 12 presentations in which that drink appeared (twice with each of the 6 others). Of these 12 pairings, only 2 overlapped with another set of 12 pairings that determined the valences of any other particular drink—namely, the 2 pairings in which they were pitted against each other.

Specifically, then, the 2 valences that determined what was an approach/approach (or avoidance/avoidance) conflict were based on a total of 22 independent choices: 12 involving one drink, plus 12 involving the other drink, minus the 2 duplicates (in dotted lines in Figure 17-1). Furthermore, the measured prechoice behaviors overlapped with the final choice that determined the valences in only 2 of these 22 cases (the 2 in solid boxes in Figure 17-1). Therefore, the valences were determined by a much larger sample of behaviors than were the prechoice measures in each particular conflict situation. It is not plausible to argue that the 2 valences were greatly affected by the behavior preceding the choice between them, because in 20 out of 22 pairings these particular prechoice behaviors were not involved at all.

This detailed analysis of the experiment raises an interesting methodological point. In general, it is wise to avoid confounding the independent and dependent variables. But the fact that they are not entirely separate does not automatically invalidate the result. Only a careful look at the experiment can tell you that.

Recall that the independent and dependent variables were confounded in the studies by Hall and Van de Castle (page 37), Sheldon (page 58), and Chodorkoff (page 75). The problem was the same in all three cases: someone making a judgment about the subject's behavior had information about the subject that constituted the independent variable. For example, Sheldon could tell the body type when he judged temperament. It was altogether plausible in all three cases that the judgments could be affected by knowledge of the independent variable. This was later confirmed in the one case tested, by the lower correlations between body type and temperament when the ratings were made independently. When the independent and dependent variables meet, so to speak, inside the same person's (the judge's) head, it is difficult to argue that the two variables will not be confounded. Indeed, it is the rare case, like Barker's study, in which contamination of results can be convincingly rebutted.

There is, however, still a problem with the Barker study. The decision times differed significantly for the two types of conflict, but the wavering-behavior measure did not. Barker himself was not happy with measuring ambivalence by physical movement. He noted that some locomotion would probably be purely mental and therefore not translated into lever action, and that some lever action might be the result of accidental pushes, not true ambivalence. In any case, and possibly for these reasons, the lever measure did not show the expected result. At most, Barker had shown that avoidance/ avoidance conflicts take longer to resolve. He had not established *why* they take longer—namely, that they induce more ambivalence.

Further Research

In a subsequent study, Barker (1946) tried to study the same ambivalence with a different research hypothesis, this time including mental uncertainty that is not limited to physical movements. He gave college students questionnaires to take home and fill out at their leisure. These contained 18 kinds of personal characteristics or life situations that might be desirable or undesirable (for example, good or poor health, cheerful disposition, educational advantages, no friends). The positive alternatives were paired with each other in all possible combinations, as in the choice between 1 and 2 in the following:

1. good health (with less than average good humor)
2. cheerful disposition, good humor, gaiety (with
   less than average good health)

The subject was asked to make each choice and then to indicate whether or not that choice had been an uncertain one. A parallel questionnaire made up of choices between negative alternatives was administered to another group. Lewin's conflict theory suggested that there would be more choices marked uncertain in the negative questionnaire (avoidance/avoidance conflicts) than in the positive questionnaire (approach/approach conflicts). This was confirmed.

It is unfortunate that a classic experimental error can be found in this study. The groups to which the two different conflict situations were given were not initially comparable. The positive questionnaire was given to classes in educational and experimental psychology at two universities, and the negative questionnaire was given to an introductory psychology class at a third university. If, for any reason, students in introductory psychology at the third university were generally more uncertain (or more inclined to say they were) than the other students, this would be an alternative explanation of the results. It is desirable to have a diversity of subjects in an experiment, but the independent variable must be randomly assigned. Pure chance rather than who a subject was should have determined which questionnaire he or she got. A proper replication is needed.

In any case, the result depends on whether the indicated uncertainty reflected psychological ambivalence in the sense intended by the conflict theory. The pertinent instructions were as follows:

> Assume that you could choose *one* of each of these pairs of alternatives. Place an x before the alternative you would choose. In some cases your choice will be obvious and clear to you. In other cases your choice will be very uncertain, and you will have to force yourself to indicate a choice; in these cases draw a circle around the x. . . . [Barker, 1946, pp. 42-43; italics original].

Barker has assumed that an "obvious and clear" choice is equivalent to going directly to one alternative, and that a "very uncertain" choice is equivalent to vascillation toward and away from each alternative. Perhaps it is. It "feels" like that, and no incompatible interpretations offer themselves readily. This point is only mentioned to illustrate the difficulty in experimentally showing psychological locomotion. The phenomenologist takes on a much harder methodological task than does the nonphenomenological researcher.

With some qualifications, Barker has established a difference in choice time as predicted. His data also suggest a difference in what goes on during that time, but this would require at least an improved replication of the second study. Guthrie (1976) has successfully confirmed some of Lewin's conflict theory, with still a different research procedure.

What bearing does all this have on Lewin's theory as a whole? Certainly it does not corroborate the entire theory. Such research is too simple, too limited to a few issues. But, just as certainly, negative results would have been damaging to the theory. That is, at least part of the theory was put at risk in these experiments, and so something can be claimed for their partial success. For further evaluation of the theory as a whole, two things are needed: the same kind of careful statement and analysis of each area of research; and a knitting together of these areas into a more coherent statement of the entire theory. Enough research on very different topics has been begun to show that experimental work follows easily from Lewin's theory. The next step should be to bring all this together to assess the total picture.

18

Dollard and Miller

THE THEORY

John Dollard and Neal Miller (1950) proposed to organize a theory of personality out of three different lines of thought: Freudian personality theory; learning theory as developed by Clark Hull in general experimental psychology; and the perspective of modern social science. In essence, they translated parts of Freud's theory into learning-theory terminology and added the social conditions of learning and personality development.

Principles of Learning

The learning principles upon which Dollard and Miller depend are a highly abbreviated form of Hull's elaborate learning theory. Learning, for Dollard and Miller as for Hull, includes both trial-and-error (instrumental) learning and Pavlovian classical conditioning. They propose that four elements are necessary and sufficient to produce learning: *drive, cue, response,* and *reinforcement,* in that order.

Because drive and reinforcement are two sides of the same concept, they are best defined together. Drive, or motivation, is any stimulation strong enough to cause action (for example, intense hunger, pain, or longing for someone). Reinforcement, or reward, is the reduction or removal of these drive stimuli—eating, escape or relief from pain, or reunion with the loved one. The drive stimuli can be internal (hunger, a toothache) or external (ear-splitting noise or a fearsome threat).

Early in life, all drives are primary or innate, satisfying biological requirements. Later, learned or secondary drives are aquired through association with primary drives and reinforcement. For example, mother is associated with eating and therefore takes on reinforcing properties; that is, this particular person becomes a positive reinforcer herself. A dentist associated with pain comes to evoke the acquired drive of fear; avoiding this particular person is drive- (fear-) reducing and therefore reinforcing.

The relation of drive and reinforcement to learning in Dollard and Miller's theory is that both are necessary, in either primary or secondary form, for learning to occur: what is learned is whatever achieves reinforcement and thereby reduces an aroused drive.

Cue and response correspond to *when* to do *what* for reinforcement. To Dollard and Miller, learning consists of pairing a cue (now more commonly called a stimulus) with a response. What is being learned is a stimulus-response connection—for example,

stimulus	→	*response*
Hear "thank you."	→	Say "you're welcome."
Feel leg going to sleep.	→	Shift position.
Phone rings.	→	Answer it.
See face of clock.	→	Think "It's almost 3 o'clock."
Hear silence.	→	Go check on what the children are up to.
See leader's behavior.	→	Follow the leader.

Even in these simple examples, note the variety of cues and responses. Cues can be anything we perceive from outside or even within our bodies. They may be discrete events (the phone bell), a pattern (such as the clock face), or even no stimulus (silence when noise is usual). Responses may be simple or complex acts, either words or deeds, or even thinking.

The last, "follow the leader" example is one in which Dollard and Miller were particularly interested (Miller & Dollard, 1941). They called this *imitation* or, more specifically, *matched-dependent behavior*. The imitator matches his or her behavior to that of the leader; the imitator's response is in that sense dependent on the leader's as a cue. Imitation of adults and older siblings is very likely to be rewarded in young children and—quite apart from games such as "follow the leader"—is a fundamental part of the socialization process. The imitation sequence, once learned, could account for the rapid acquisition of many other stimulus-response sequences. According to Dollard and Miller, an S-R sequence must occur before it can be rewarded and thereby learned. A previously learned tendency to imitate one's elders increases the likelihood that grown-up responses will be made and rewarded.

The fundamental unit that is learned is a stimulus plus a response. However, most human acts are made up of more complex sequences in which many cues and responses follow one another in rapid succession. Many links in this chain may be unobservable thoughts connecting the initial cue to the final response. The stimulus "How many days in June?" might be followed by the quick flow of responses "Thirty-days-have-September-April-June-JUNE-30," of which only the last part, the number, may be spoken aloud. Each of the earlier thoughts is a *cue-producing response*, by which we prompt ourselves by one thought to arrive at another. Thus, a cue-producing response serves both as a response and as a cue for the next response. ("April," in the above example, is cued by "September" and in turn cues "June.") The important point is that Dollard and Miller, especially through the cue-producing function of language, have deliberately allowed a wide range of higher mental processes into their theory. It is not a theory that reduces all behavior to simple physical reflexes such as knee jerks or salivation.

According to Dollard and Miller, drive, cue, response, and reinforcement must all occur, in that order, for learning to take place. In more familiar words, the learner must want something, notice something, do something, and receive something. If drive reduction follows fairly quickly after a particular stimulus-response combination, then that combination will tend to be repeated—that is, that cue will tend to evoke that particular response rather than any other.

In addition to the four basic elements of learning, Dollard and Miller adopt many auxiliary concepts from general learning theory, including the following: Most learning appears to be *gradual*, requiring several repetitions of the basic sequences before it is firmly established. If reinforcement ceases, the response gradually ceases, a situation called *extinction* (of the S-R connection). Under ordinary reinforcement, the learner will initially *generalize*—that is, respond in the same way to cues similar to those originally experienced. (For example, a child applies its new, highly praised word "Daddy" to every male it sees.) Conversely, with differential reinforcement, the learner will *discriminate* among stimuli, learning which cues do and which do not lead to reinforcement of a particular response.

Personality, then, to Dollard and Miller, is the combination of a very large number of individual learning units (called *habits*, following Hull) acquired and modified by reinforcement. Friendliness would be a complex of behaviors generalized over a wide range of social situations (cues) because of consistent reinforcement for such behaviors. Persons who are unfriendly would never or only rarely have been reinforced for friendly behaviors and, therefore, would not have learned to make such responses; they may even have learned to avoid such behaviors because of previous rebuffs. Thus, personality is as much a process (of constant learning and relearning) as it is a product (what has been learned at any given time).

Freudian Concepts

It is this emphasis on the process of personality development that is one of the reasons Dollard and Miller find Freud's theory (see Chapter 3) so compatible with their learning theory. In this developmental process, Dollard and Miller's reinforcement principle and Freud's pleasure principle have the same central function. The child is born with certain primary drives, or instincts. It is driven by these instincts to make responses, both real and fantasied, to objects (cues) in its world. Those responses that are gratified (reinforced) are continued and become part of the personality. In both theories, the individual's actions are ultimately compelled by and for the satisfaction of drives. Because direct satisfaction of sexual or aggressive drives is seldom reinforced in children and is in fact usually punished, less direct responses (such as sublimation) that still reduce the drive must be found.

One of these indirect responses, the defense mechanism of repression, is crucial to translating Freud's concept of the unconscious into learning theory. Recall that aversive stimuli (such as pain) are reduced by escape. One way to escape such stimuli, mentally at least, is *not to think* about them. To the extent that the response of not-thinking permits one to escape the painful drive stimulus, that response will be rewarding and therefore learned and repeated. Repression is the learned response of not-thinking about something because the thought either is painful in itself or has been associated with pain.

For example, if sexual thoughts and actions have been punished, these thoughts come to arouse the acquired drive of fear, which Freud called anxiety. Repressing these thoughts is a way of escaping the painful anxiety. Because it reduces a drive, repression is reinforced and becomes the usual response to any stimuli that arouse sexual interest. Thus do the forbidden instincts become unconscious—actively kept unconscious, just as Freud proposed.

Note that a sexual stimulus has two roles in this sequence of events. It arouses the sexual drive, which must be satisfied; and as a cue that has been associated with punishment, it also evokes the acquired drive of fear. Both Freud's and Dollard and Miller's theories recognize this situation as one of conflict.[1] What is desired is also forbidden. Thus, the desire and even conscious awareness of the primary drive are repressed, but an indirect response that is satisfying to the libido will be found.

Such indirect responses are, of course, defense mechanisms and the many adult manifestations of various psychosexual stages. Loving a girl "just like the girl that married dear old Dad" is presumably close enough to the Oedipal fantasy to be satisfying but disguised enough to avoid castration anxiety. Thus, the sequence

$$\text{impulse} \longrightarrow \text{conflict} \longrightarrow \text{anxiety} \longrightarrow \text{defense}$$

has been translated into a learned pattern of behavior. Although conflict, neurosis, and psychotherapy are included in great detail in this theory, it is intended to be a description of normal as well as abnormal personality, just as Freud's theory was.

So far we have seen how Dollard and Miller began by describing personality in terms of Hull's learning theory; then proposed that this approach ran parallel to Freud's theory of personality; and so proceeded to follow the track of the two theories. Most Freudian concepts are adopted and given a learning as well as psychoanalytic definition. For example, the ego is associated with acquired drives; with learned skills for coping with both drives and reinforcement conditions; and with higher mental processes.

This renaming of concepts would be superficial if the theories did not share their most basic assumptions. Both begin with the premise that human behavior is essentially motivated by primary drives (or needs) and their reduction. Freud called the reduction of drives gratification or satisfaction, whereas

---

[1]This conception of conflict is different from Lewin's.

Hull called it reinforcement. The effect of drive reduction is the same in either case: to perpetuate any behavior that gives pleasure or avoids pain.[2] Historians of science would point out that this obvious similarity between Freud and Hull (and other theories as well) is probably not a coincidence, but rather that the theories are two independent manifestations of the intellectual climate of the late 19th and early 20th centuries. Hedonism, biological adaptation à la Darwin, and even the concept of energy from physics can be seen as influences on both theories.

Social Conditions

By the time Dollard and Miller formulated their theory, there was, in addition, a new and different idea in the air: the realization that humans are social as well as biological. Therefore, the social environment must be included in any complete description of human nature. This is the third line of thought mentioned at the beginning of this chapter—the social setting into which Dollard and Miller placed their psychoanalytic learning theory. The social context seemed to them to be essential to both other theories. Learning theory requires knowledge of the stimulus conditions in which learning occurs: what are the cues, what responses are reinforced? Similarly, Freudian theory emphasizes the reality principle by which the ego must cope: what is this reality? The answer to these questions must be sought

> in terms of the physical and social conditions of learning, especially the conditions provided by the social structure of a society. In order to predict behavior we must know these conditions as well as the psychological principles involved. Psychology supplies the principles while sociology and social anthropology supply the systematic treatment of the crucial social conditions [1950, p. 10].[3]

For example, the case of Mrs. A. (1950, pp. 16-21) included a harsh foster mother, repressive sexual training, and a disparity between the patient's social class and her husband's, all as causal factors in the development of a severe phobia.

In both normal and abnormal development, the social conditions of learning would include language, imitation, and acquired drives. Dollard and Miller get even more specific about the social conditions of the early developmental sequence. They emphasize four sets of "social conditions for the learning of unconscious conflicts": the feeding situation (including weaning); cleanliness (or toilet) training; early sex training, including taboos on masturbation and on homosexual and heterosexual responses; and "anger-anxiety conflicts," the result of parental punishment of anger and aggression (1950, pp. 132-156). These seem to correspond to the Freudian oral, anal, and phallic

---

[2]A good general discussion of the many similarities between learning and Freudian theories can be found in Kimble (1961, Chapter 14).

[3]From *Personality and Psychotherapy*, by J. Dollard and N.E. Miller. Copyright 1950 by McGraw-Hill, Inc. This and all other quotations from this source are used with permission of McGraw-Hill Book Company.

stages, with the last including both phallic sexuality and aggression toward the parent.

Dollard and Miller wanted to demonstrate that these stages involve not only erogenous zones and experiences but a set of social conditions laid down by the culture through the parents. The confrontation between these can be dramatic:

> If the child has come safely and trustfully through the early feeding and weaning experience it may learn for the first time in its cleanliness training that the culture patterns lying in wait for it have an ugly, compulsive aspect. No child may avoid this training. The demands of the training system are absolute and do not take account of individual differences in learning ability. The child must master cleanliness training or forfeit its place in the ranks of socially acceptable persons. . . . On pain of losing the parents' love and so exposing itself to the high drives and tensions which occur when they do not support it, and on further pain of immediate punishment, the child must learn to attach anxiety to all the cues produced by excretory materials—to their sight, smell, and touch. It must learn to deposit the feces and urine only in a prescribed and secret place and to clean its body. It must later learn to suppress unnecessary verbal reference to these matters, so that, except for joking references this subject matter is closed out and excluded from social reference for life [1950, pp. 136-137].

While the customs and taboos enforced on the child may vary from culture to culture, and even among families, the customs of the particular culture and family are crucial to the development of personality.

Thus Dollard and Miller have extended Freudian theory to include not only psychological and biological processes occurring within the individual, but also conditions external to the individual (stimulus, punishment, social class, culture) and transactions between the individual and the environment (reinforcement, which consists of getting something that is wanted—both the wanting and the getting must be present for reinforcement to occur). The importance of these factors makes theirs one of the early social theories of personality.

The second characteristic of a social theory is emphasis on situational rather than individual differences. Although they are not elaborated in detail in Dollard and Miller's theory, situational differences are considered important—for example, social-class differences in sexual attitudes and cross-cultural differences in child-rearing patterns. They seem particularly aware of the need for understanding the social circumstances that lead to normal or neurotic personalities:

> We must admit that we do not know the exact conditions under which the common conflict-producing circumstances of life generate severe conflicts in some and not-so-severe conflicts in others. We know that the conditions and factors described here *do* occur in those who later turn out to show neurotic behavior. It may be that the circumstances of life are not really "the same for normals and neurotics," that this sameness is an illusion based on

[the observer's] poor discrimination of the actual circumstances [1950, p. 155].

And, later, they suggest

therapists will have to acquire more specialized knowledge of social conditions. . . . Behind the notion of "reality" is hidden the great variability incident to social and cultural conditions . . . . The psychologist . . . may err by putting too much emphasis on constitution and habit, thus underestimating the variability that may be produced by specific social conditions. As far as psychotherapists are concerned, we feel that a knowledge of social conditions is underdone rather than overdone [1950, pp. 419-421].

By emphasizing major influences on behavior from outside the individual, and by at least aspiring to describe situational as well as individual differences, Dollard and Miller fit the paradigm of social personality theories.

EMPIRICAL STATUS

The empirical-status sections of the three social-learning theories will differ somewhat from similar sections in the book so far. Rather than being completely independent of data regarding other theories, these sections will be interwoven and cumulative. As these three theories overlap substantially in their approach and issues, it is natural that research on one theory would also be relevant to one or both of the others. Therefore, this research will be distributed among the three sections according to where it fits best without anticipating material not yet covered. For example, research on the nature of reinforcement is equally pertinent to Dollard and Miller's and to Skinner's theory. However, since the particular research to be discussed derives directly out of Skinner's theory, it will be presented there rather than here. Similarly, Bandura disputes a fundamental assumption both of Dollard and Miller and of Skinner—namely, the necessity for response and reinforcement to occur before instrumental learning can take place. Experiments on this issue will be described in the chapter on Bandura.

In the present section, then, we will cover issues limited to Dollard and Miller's theory alone. When all three theories have been described and all the pertinent studies finally covered, that will be a good time to summarize the empirical status of the social-learning approach to personality. Meanwhile, what can be said about Dollard and Miller's theory in particular?

Dollard and Miller saw their theory as a synthesis and application of three already established approaches: general learning theory, Freudian clinical psychology, and sociology. They were cautious, however, about its empirical status or even its readiness for rigorous empirical testing. In the preface to their major work, they emphasized:

Most of the ideas in this book are hypotheses, the basis for research, not proven principles. Furthermore, it has not been possible to formulate these hypotheses in as rigorous, systematic, and quantitative a form as will eventually be desirable [1950, p. ix].

Unfortunately, little subsequent theoretical or empirical work has been done on their personality theory. Probably because of its close historical links to the experimental lab, their theory is often credited with more precision, completion, and empirical support than the authors would have claimed or, indeed, than the facts justify.

Their work draws evidence principally from clinical or social examples and from studies of animal learning. The deficiencies of clinical case histories as objective evidence have already been described (pages 32-34). Sociological and anthropological examples are subject to the same criticism: they illustrate but do not offer objective, repeatable evidence.

Evidence from Animal Studies

Animal studies, no matter how objectively and carefully conducted, cannot confirm a theory of *human* personality. To explain this bald assertion, consider an example of such "borrowed" evidence. A study shows that rats shocked in a white box begin to act as though they fear the white box itself. Assume that this study, or several such studies, show that rats can acquire secondary drives by learning experience. It was just such evidence that led Dollard and Miller to suspect a similar mechanism for learned fear in humans. That is, the animal studies were an inspiration for a new idea about human personality. But they do not confirm that new idea as well as inspire it, for two reasons.

First, what is true of rats in certain conditions may or may not be true of humans (or any other species) in other conditions. It is a basic principle of comparative psychology that both similarities and differences among species must be demonstrated and not assumed.

Second, the reasoning that connects the two phenomena is faulty on another ground. In the animal study, the experience of shock in the white box was shown to be the antecedent to the consequent fear of the box. If shock (punishment) in the box is known to precede fear of the box, and if other antecedents (such as an innate fear-of-white-boxes in rats) have been ruled out by good experimental design, then it is reasonable to conclude that the shock caused the fear. But in the human case to which this experiment is being extended by analogy, only the *effect* is known. The cause (prior punishment) is inferred from the effect; it has not been directly observed. The reasoning goes something like this: if punishment has been shown in one case to cause fear, then whenever fear exists, punishment must have preceded and caused it. An absurd example of exactly the same reasoning would be the claim that since shaving can be shown to cause hairlessness, all cases of hairlessness anywhere on any person, animal, or inanimate object must have been caused by (unseen) shaving.

This is not to demean the animal studies as valid studies of acquired drives in rats, nor to minimize Dollard and Miller's creativity in suggesting that these findings resemble human neurosis. But that is enough mileage for these studies. They cannot in addition carry the human case. In general, good research may serve several roles, in different settings, and we must be alert to the differences among inspiration, illustration, and evidence. It is unlikely that the same results can play all three roles for any theory.

The main reason that experiments similar to the animal studies have not been done with humans was well put, if understated, by Dollard and Miller in another context:

> It is difficult to secure opportunities for subjecting young infants with malice aforethought to those drastic conditions of controlled primary drive and reward which are essential to a successful experiment [Miller & Dollard, 1941, p. 98].

The necessary conditions for testing certain hypotheses can be created for animal but not for human subjects. Even so, this does not make animal research suffice for knowledge of human personality. To accept this substitution is to act like the fool who, in the old story, is looking for his keys under a street light. A helpful bystander asks him exactly where he lost the keys. "Back there," says the fool, gesturing down the block where there is no street light, "but the light's much better here." Researching only other species, even under the best conditions, will not uncover laws of human behavior.

Reinforcement in Classical Conditioning: Empirical Tests

It might seem, then, that for ethical and practical reasons Dollard and Miller's personality theory cannot be subjected to empirical tests. Certainly most of the extreme and complicated elaborations of their theory are out of our experimental reach. But what about their most basic premise? The assertion that drive, cue, response, and reinforcement are necessary and sufficient for learning to occur can be and has been tested in quite innocuous experiments.

This conceptual hypothesis is relatively easy to test, for logical reasons. If Dollard and Miller claim that four elements are necessary for learning to occur, then we need only show that learning can occur without one or more of these elements, and we make their hypothesis untenable. It is desirable for a theory to be so apparently vulnerable because the relevance of data to theory becomes quite clear. Recall that because of the logical looseness of Freud's theory, for example, there was no important assumption that could be readily confirmed or disconfirmed—thus leaving the theory in limbo. Popper's *Logic of Scientific Discovery* (1959) suggests that we should proceed ruthlessly and efficiently by trying to *disconfirm* theories, and thus find out which survive. The result would be a quicker arrival at a theory that will fit the available data. This is more valuable than the mere survival by default of even a favorite theory.

The test of what is necessary for learning to occur may depend on which kind of learning is being examined. Dollard and Miller have the only major social-learning theory that relies heavily on classical as well as instrumental conditioning, and that in fact treats them as the same kind of learning. Inasmuch as the others do not emphasize classical conditioning, and in any case treat it as a different kind of learning, only classical conditioning will be considered here. The role of the four basic elements (particularly response and reinforcement) in instrumental learning will be taken up when Bandura's theory has been presented.

Classical conditioning is the kind of learning that Pavlov discovered when his dogs began to salivate at the sight or sound of a once-neutral stimulus (such as a bell) that had been associated for some time with food. Classical conditioning is based on an innate reflex, such as the dog's tendency to salivate when food is placed in its mouth. It is often called stimulus substitution because, after learning, a new stimulus (the bell) can act as a substitute for the original stimulus (the food) in the sense that the new stimulus can now evoke the reflexive response.

Instead of food, a noxious or unpleasant stimulus can be the basis for *aversive* classical conditioning. Individuals who have been severely nauseated on a car or boat ride may find later that the very sight or smell of the car or boat is enough to bring on the nausea. Dollard and Miller use this kind of learning to explain acquired drives, especially the acquired fear or anxiety that plays such an important role in the psychoanalytic aspects of their theory. A neutral or even positive stimulus, such as a sexual cue, is paired with a painful experience, such as severe punishment, that evokes reflexive withdrawal and fear. After training (repeated experience), the sexual cue now evokes fear and avoidance itself. This learned response will eventually cause conflict that must be handled by repression and other defense mechanisms. According to Dollard and Miller, classical conditioning is the mechanism by which society not only represses forbidden drives directly, but also teaches the individual a more indirect response—to fear these drives.

(*Instrumental* or trial-and-error learning is not based on a reflexive response. Any response that is instrumental in achieving reinforcement is repeated. It is seldom or never a reflex response. Examples of instrumental learning in Dollard and Miller's theory are the learning of imitation or of repression when these responses achieve reward or avoid pain.)

Whether or not classical conditioning has the role in personality development that Dollard and Miller propose, the question here is how it works. Specifically, is reinforcement involved? Dollard and Miller insist that all four elements, including reinforcement, are necessary for any kind of learning to occur. To test their conceptual hypothesis, we'll have to be quite specific about what reinforcement is, how it operates, and how these principles apply to aversive classical conditioning.

The basic research procedure is as follows: The unconditioned stimulus is an electrical shock. Even shock mild enough to be given to human subjects causes reflexive increases in responses presumed to indicate fear or arousal, such as heart rate and the galvanic skin response (GSR). After the shock has been repeatedly paired with a neutral stimulus such as a light or tone, this stimulus itself begins to lead to increased heart rate or GSR. Now the light or tone alone, without any shock, leads to the physiological fear response. Learning, in the form of aversive classical conditioning, has occurred.

For Dollard and Miller, the reinforcement in the above situation must be the shock, specifically the termination of the shock. Recall that they define drive as strong stimulation—the pain of the shock going on. Reinforcement is drive-reduction—here, the shock going off. If, as seems highly plausible, the end of the shock is reinforcing *and* if reinforcement is necessary for classical conditioning, then better or poorer reinforcement should result in better or poorer conditioning. It is generally accepted that immediate reinforcement is more effective than delayed reinforcement. Keeping the shock on longer delays its termination, thereby delaying any reinforcement. Thus, a short shock would deliver quick reinforcement (in effect, getting the pain over with quickly), while a prolonged shock would delay the reinforcement (the pain lasts longer). As Miller proposed, generally:

> Other things being equal, a signal followed by a brief noxious stimulus should acquire the capacity to elicit stronger fear than one followed by a prolonged noxious stimulus [1951, p. 375].

However, the data contradict this prediction. Bitterman, Reed, and Krauskopf (1952) used the same intensity of shock but with either .5 or 3 seconds duration. Conditioning did occur within the 16 experimental trials in which a light was paired with the shock, but the duration of the shock did not make any difference to this conditioning. Similarly, Wegner and Zeaman (1958) used shock durations of .1, 2, 6, and 15 seconds and found no difference in conditioned cardiac responses (heart rate in response to a tone paired with the shock). The termination of the shock is undoubtedly a reinforcer in Dollard and Miller's terms, but it is apparently irrelevant to the establishment of aversive classical conditioning.

It might have occurred to you that Miller derived the wrong prediction. A longer shock is (cumulatively) a stronger shock and therefore much more reinforcing when it stops. By this reasoning, longer shocks should produce stronger conditioning. But even if we accept this opposite derivation, the above results showed *no* difference, not even one in the other direction. In a more direct experiment, Runquist, Spence, and Stubbs (1958) varied only the intensity, not the duration, of a noxious stimulus (a puff of air to the eyelid), and they, too, found no significant difference between conditioning at the two intensities.

In sum, these studies (and others, with both humans and animals) have shown that it does not matter when the shock or other aversive stimulus stops (Kimble, 1961, pp. 273-274). *Aversive classical conditioning depends only on the onset of the unpleasant, drive-inducing stimulus and not at all on its termination.* Therefore, no drive-reduction is required. Classical conditioning—particularly the aversive kind so important to Dollard and Miller's theory—seems to depend solely on the contiguous pairing of the neutral and reflex-provoking stimuli, and not at all on drive reduction or reinforcement. Thus, we have the first important exception to Dollard and Miller's most basic principle—that all learning depends on drive-reducing reinforcement.

19

Skinner

Some authors of personality theories are well known outside personality textbooks. B. F. Skinner is, like Freud, known to all who study psychology and to many laypersons as well. There are similarities between the two that may account for their widespread recognition. Both are excellent writers who have used this gift to explain and advocate their theories with great skill. Each has extended a theory of personality into a full-fledged examination of human nature and society (Freud, 1930/1961; Skinner, 1971). Skinner's position on free will and behaviorism has probably incited as much controversy as did Freud's theory of sexuality a generation earlier. All these reasons may explain why there are many pro-Skinnerians and many anti-Skinnerians, but few neutrals. However, the controversy usually does not center on Skinner's relatively simple personality theory. Rather, partisans argue either about philosophical issues (human nature) or about essentially political issues (the nature of an ideal society). Somewhere in between, the theory of personality gets lost. We will try to look solely at Skinner's personality theory, which is quite straightforward. The crucial psychological issues for Skinner's theory, as for Freud's or anyone else's, will be whether it is logically coherent and whether it is empirically supported.

THE THEORY

Just as Dollard and Miller's personality theory is based in large part on Hull's learning theory, Skinner's personality theory is virtually equivalent to his own learning theory. Theories of learning are often general theories of behavior; that is, they aim to account for the acquisition and change of behavior in the broadest possible sense. Thus, the affinity of learning theories and personality theories is quite natural, being based on a common ambition to encompass human behavior. When learning theories become personality theories, however, they must concentrate on human rather than animal subjects and on general learning principles rather than rules covering only specific phenomena (such as verbal learning). Typically, as we saw with Dollard and Miller, they choose to focus on social and abnormal behavior as well.

Skinner's Principles of Learning

Skinner makes little distinction between his learning and personality theories: personality is, like anything else, acquired by reinforcement. It can be shaped, modified, and selectively extinguished by the same process. *Operant conditioning* is the main learning principle that Skinner uses to explain personality. (He does include some role for respondent, or classical, conditioning.) Operant conditioning resembles what other learning theories call trial-and-error or instrumental learning. In the presence of a stimulus, the organism (animal or human) happens to emit a particular response. If reinforcement follows quickly—that is, if it is contingent on that response—then a similar response is likely to be repeated, especially in the presence of that stimulus.

The class of behaviors to which the reinforced behavior belongs is called the operant: "the behavior *operates* upon the environment to generate consequences. The consequences define the properties with respect to which responses are called similar" (1953, p. 65). Thus, a pigeon comes to peck at a target when such pecking is reinforced. A child speaks until it hears "That's right" for the appropriate word, which now becomes more probable than the previous baby-talk. Another child misbehaves, gets its parents' attention, and subsequently misbehaves when it has been deprived of their attention.

Reinforcement that works by presenting a stimulus (such as food or approval) is called a *positive* reinforcer. A stimulus whose removal acts as a reinforcer (such as shock or scolding) is a *negative* reinforcer. Reversing the reward conditions—that is, removing a positive reinforcer or presenting a negative reinforcer—is *punishment*. (The usage of negative reinforcer and punishment is a bit slippery and often inconsistent. Anyone who wants to be precise would be well advised to look at the discussion by Michael, 1975.) In general, terminating a reinforcement contingency leads to *extinction*—and eventual decline of the learned behavior—after some initial display of emotion (such as kicking the broken vending machine or pestering the unyielding parent).

The operant may become more closely controlled by a particular stimulus following training in *stimulus discrimination,* in which operant responses are reinforced only after a certain stimulus and not after others. Similarly, the response may be differentiated from other responses that do not produce reinforcement. For example, there is usually *response differentiation* of the force used to shake someone's hand: too little is "limp," too much is painful. If narrowly contingent consequences such as these do not occur, then *stimulus* and *response generalization* are likely. That is, barring any specific experience to the contrary, similar stimuli will be treated as if they are the same as the original stimulus, and similar responses will often be made in place of the original, reinforced response. For example, despite wide differences in design, we treat all brake lights on the car ahead as the same signal or stimulus. On the response side of the same situation, the physical movements by which we step on the brake probably vary according to car, footwear, posture, and so on, but we do not notice these variations. They all comprise the operant "braking," because they all achieve the same desirable result. Thus, both the stimulus and response are defined either broadly or narrowly depending on the reinforcement contingencies.

Reinforcement

A great deal of Skinner's work has been devoted to the intricacies of reinforcement, his central principle. He defines reinforcement in practical terms: whatever works, in the sense of increasing the frequency of the operant response. "The only defining characteristic of a reinforcing stimulus is that it reinforces" (1953, p. 72). We can make a guess about what will reinforce a particular organism under given conditions only to the extent that we resemble that organism and can guess what would reinforce us (1953, p. 73). Notice that Skinner does not claim that primary drives and their reduction are the basis of reinforcement. He substitutes a purely empirical identification of reinforcers, aided by a little introspection at the outset.

Skinner did accept the notion of *conditioned* (what Dollard and Miller would call secondary) reinforcers, which, although initially neutral, have acquired the capacity to reinforce by their association with a reinforcer. A light that goes on whenever food is presented to a pigeon will eventually reinforce on its own. For example, the pigeon will peck a target more frequently if that makes the light come on—the empirical test of a reinforcer. (However, the evidence suggests that these secondary reinforcers lose their power very quickly if the primary reinforcer is not paired with them occasionally.)

There is a special class of conditioned reinforcers that is important to the development of personality and social relations. *Generalized* reinforcers are those that have been paired with several primary reinforcers, and thus do not depend on a particular state of deprivation or satiation. (The light would only act as a conditioned reinforcer when the pigeon is hungry.) Skinner proposes that through early association with many primary reinforcers, such events as attention, affection, control (of the environment or of other people), and tokens such as money become generalized conditioned reinforcers for most people.

Skinner has introduced at least two new aspects of reinforcement both to learning and to personality-as-learning. Both are especially useful for going beyond simple responses to the complex and lasting behaviors we associate with personality.

Shaping or, more formally, the "method of successive approximations," is a process whereby current, simple behaviors can be shaped into a new, complex behavior by carefully managed reinforcement. The organism is successively reinforced for closer and closer approximations of the desired behavior. For example, according to Skinner, parents initially reward any sound the baby makes. Over time, they stop rewarding nonspecific babbling and shift the contingency to closer approximations of real words. Then, even the right words do not elicit reinforcement unless they are grammatically arranged as well. Shaping, then, is done as follows: A response that does occur is rewarded, making similar behaviors more likely by response generalization. Then one of the similar behaviors that is closer to the ultimate goal becomes the new operant and is rewarded, while the initial behavior is no longer rewarded and therefore extinguishes. The process is repeated, with each step leading to a closer approximation of the final response.

The other major contribution is the study of various *schedules of reinforcement*. Skinner discovered (almost accidentally, he claims; Skinner, 1959, p. 368) that reinforcement need not be delivered every time the operant is made. Such *partial* (as opposed to *continuous*) reinforcement results in slower but satisfactory learning. It also produces more resistance to extinction; that is, the organism continues to respond long after all reinforcement has stopped. This effect appears to be one answer to the problem of explaining why early training should last so long without reinforcement and without extinction. Skinner would argue that we continue to do things for which we were reinforced in childhood, but not subsequently, because the original training was likely to have involved partial reinforcement. Parents cannot be present or attentive to every correct response and, therefore, would be naturally likely to produce a partial-reinforcement schedule. Precisely this kind of schedule, it turns out, will result in more stable and long-lasting performance, even when reinforcement is so infrequent as to resemble extinction conditions. Ferster and Skinner (1957) went on to examine many, many different kinds of reinforcement schedules and showed that, for pigeons at least, each schedule produces typical response patterns and extinction curves. To my knowledge, there is no comparable body of data for humans.

It is obvious that much of the above is quite similar to terms and concepts already described for Dollard and Miller's theory. In fact, most of the basic phenomena of learning (reinforcement, extinction, generalization, discrimination, secondary reinforcement, and so on) are universally accepted as the basis of any learning theory. The difference is not about what the facts are, but about how and why they occur.

Skinner's Behaviorism

The major theoretical difference between Dollard and Miller and Skinner is the degree to which they are willing to infer unobserved, hypothetical states to account for behavior. Note, for example, that Dollard and Miller list drive, stimulus, response, and reinforcement as the essential elements of learning. Skinner refers only to stimulus, response, and reinforcement—no mention of drive. His objection to the concept of drive is that it is an inferred state of the organism, whereas stimulus, response, and reinforcer can all be observed directly. He prefers to describe conditions of deprivation and satiation (for example, 48 hours without food versus all-you-can-eat) that can be observed and even controlled. These conditions, he argues, predict very accurately whether or not food will be reinforcing, and they do not require any inferences about internal, unmeasurable psychological or physiological states.

Skinner's preference for avoiding what he calls "conceptual inner causes" (1953, p. 31) and building a theory based instead only on behavioral descriptions makes him a *behaviorist*. This term has two possible meanings.

Most psychologists today are *methodological behaviorists*, in that they believe that the only objective knowledge we can have of others comes from their behavior. For example, a teacher cannot assess how well a student is able to do in a subject except by arranging to observe some behavior that will reveal that ability: test responses, an interview or discussion, or solving a problem that requires mastery of the subject matter. In fact, most of us are methodological behaviorists in our everyday lives. We judge, for example, how another person feels about us by what this person says, does, or looks like (including subtle nonverbal behaviors). Another person's private experiences are not available to us in any other way. We might be surprised to find out later that he acted aloof because he felt uncomfortable, or was preoccupied, or whatever. Indeed, we only know this later because he tells us—behavior again. Methodological behaviorists find behavior a necessary route to any psychological phenomenon, but they do not equate behavior with the phenomenon itself. Drives, motives, needs, cognitions, feelings, perceptions, and other psychological phenomena may best be studied via their behavioral manifestations. Although the method is behavioral, the terms in the theory are not.

What is usually meant by the term *behaviorist*, however, is not the ordinary methodological behaviorist but a *substantive behaviorist* (sometimes also called a conceptual, theoretical, or radical behaviorist). The substantive behaviorist, such as Skinner, goes a step further and makes observed behavior the sum and substance of the theory. That is, the substantive behaviorist prefers not to go beyond the observed and measured behavior to infer psychological processes, but rather to build a theory on behavior alone.

The reasons for wanting to do it this way are understandable. First, if it is not necessary to propose any concepts or processes other than the stimuli and responses, then the theory will be simpler than one that requires extra concepts to explain the same data. Furthermore, inferred and unobserved concepts have often (but by no means always) been misleading and unproductive in psychology. For example, circularity may result. When an observed behavior is "explained" by an unobserved, inferred drive, this is really no explanation at all: Eating occurred because of a hunger drive. How do you know there is a hunger drive? Because eating occurred! A single observation is used to demonstrate the concept that explains the observation. At best, we are no further ahead than if we had simply observed the behavior. At worst, we may be deceived into thinking that the behavior has been explained, when it has only been relabeled.

This is the problem Skinner and other substantive behaviorists would like to avoid. If description of the observed relations between behaviors and external events (a certain response always follows a certain stimulus) will suffice, then no nonbehavioral inference (such as learning) is necessary. But if such description will *not* suffice, and a logically satisfactory inferential theory will fit the data better, then the latter must be accepted. In the end, the choice between substantive behaviorists and other psychologists will be dictated, not by whim or preference, but by which kind of theory works better.

For our purposes, the major difference between Dollard and Miller's and Skinner's social-learning theories is Skinner's substantive behaviorism. Indeed, Skinner differs from virtually every other personality theorist in this regard. Dollard and Miller freely use inferred concepts to explain behavior. Many were adopted from Hull's theory, with which Skinner clearly disagrees on this issue (Skinner, 1959). Recall also that one of Dollard and Miller's major aims was to add behavioral definitions to Freudian concepts such as instinct, gratification, conflict, anxiety, and repression.

Given, for example, that a child is openly aggressive toward other children of the same age, the two theories would explain the behavior quite differently. Dollard and Miller would propose that any child has strong, instinctual, aggressive drives that are initially directed at the parents. Such aggression is severely punished by the parents, however, and is therefore not expressed directly. This causes conflict and anxiety, which result in the displacement of the aggression (by defense mechanism) to safe but satisfactory objects—namely, the peers. Skinner would describe this aggression as the result of simple discrimination learning. The parents punish or at least do not reward the child for aggression toward them, but they typically reward aggressiveness in interaction with peers, especially by male children. The operant, aggression, comes to be attached to certain stimuli rather than others by differential reinforcement.

Skinner's Theory as a Social Personality Theory

Skinner is more exclusively a social personality theorist than any other social-learning theorist. He rejects the inferred, internal characteristics of individuals that all individual personality theories emphasize, and that most social theories include as well. Instead of merely adding external factors, he builds his entire theory on them. The only terminology that refers to the individual is the response and its characteristics (differentiation, generalization, frequency). All other terms are interpreted as situational. Reinforcement is a special kind of stimulus—one that increases the frequency of the preceding response. It does not depend on any drive state in the individual, only on environmental conditions of deprivation or satiation.

Similarly, variations in behavior are attributed exclusively to situational differences, past or present. The main determinant of behavior is *prior reinforcement history*. Any behavior is as it is, not because of any lasting characteristic of the individual, but because of a particular kind of reinforcement experience: continuous or partial schedule, training in discrimination, in differentiation, or in generalization, and so on. Even the operant itself is determined entirely by exactly how and when reinforcement is presented. One implication of this emphasis on situational differences is even stronger here than it is for Dollard and Miller's theory: if situations cause individuals to behave as they do, then an individual will change whenever the situation changes. Thus, Skinner expects change rather than stability, and specificity rather than generality in behavior. This is exactly the opposite of individual personality theories, which expect behavior to be stable over time as well as general—that is, cross-situationally consistent.

EMPIRICAL STATUS

In his own writing on personality, Skinner relies almost exclusively on examples, anecdotes, and animal studies. The reasons for rejecting these as hard evidence of a personality theory have been discussed earlier. The example of the aggressive child, described above, illustrates the problem with speculative evidence for Skinner's theory. Skinner's explanation of the aggression is simpler and less inferential than Dollard and Miller's. But it does infer a prior reinforcement history (the discrimination learning) that has not been directly observed. To the extent that this is typical of Skinner's evidence-by-example, he is subject to the same logical criticism as Dollard and Miller were (page 178). Antecedents cannot be rigorously inferred from consequences. There is a tendency for Skinner and his followers to explain current behavior by past reinforcement. That is, a prior reinforcement history that would explain the present behavior according to the theory is, therefore, assumed to have occurred. But if this reinforcement history has not been documented, then such an explanation is just as circular (and just as inferential) as explaining the behavior by drives or traits.

However, many other researchers who follow Skinner's personality theory have been actively engaged in empirical work with humans. For example, there are two psychological journals (the *Journal of Experimental Analysis of Behavior* and the *Journal of Applied Behavior Analysis*) devoted exclusively to operant conditioning, including human studies. This work includes both operant conditioning of social behaviors and psychotherapy by operant conditioning (usually called behavior modification; see Bandura, 1969; Krasner & Ullmann, 1965; Ullmann & Krasner, 1965). Two major issues emerging from such studies will be discussed here: (1) evidence for the operant origin of most behavior and (2) evidence on the nature of reinforcement. A third issue, whether response and reinforcement are necessary to produce learning, is common to all three social-learning theories and is therefore being deferred until Bandura has been heard from.

Questioning the Operant Etiology of Behavior

Skinner holds that a major goal of psychological science is to understand the causes of behavior. This is certainly one of the goals of personality theory. Skinner believes that the major cause of most behavior is operant conditioning. We behave as we do because we have been operantly conditioned to do so. Our personality is a composite of operant responses. Skinner further proposes that this can be demonstrated by what he calls the *functional analysis* of behavior:

understanding cause and effect relations by controlling the external causes of behavior—specifically, the reinforcement contingencies.

Literally hundreds of studies have been conducted to show that many and diverse behaviors can be operantly conditioned. For example, Azrin and Lindsley (1956) reinforced cooperative behavior in a game played by children and demonstrated that the frequency of cooperation increased. Operant conditioning, then, is an antecedent of cooperation. It may even be said to be a cause of cooperation. But it would be very wrong to leap to the conclusion that operant conditioning is *the* cause or antecedent of cooperation—that is, the usual or only reason children cooperate. Azrin and Lindsley did not conclude this, but many do.

The widespread use and effectiveness of behavior modification using operant conditioning has fostered this belief. For example, Etzel and Gewirtz (1967), using operant techniques, were fairly effective in decreasing the amount of crying by two institutionalized infants. However, their description of the original behavior as "caretaker-maintained high-rate operant crying" and of the therapeutic procedure as "extinction" (p. 303) makes unwarranted assumptions about the origin of the crying in the first place. That is, they are assuming, with only anecdotal evidence, that the babies had been crying because they were being reinforced for it, probably with attention. Crying is described as an operant maintained by the well-meaning caretakers. Only if it were such an operant would extinction, by removing attention, be an appropriate description of how the therapy worked. Extinction refers to the termination of an operant by removing precisely the reinforcer previously maintaining it. This means there must be evidence that the behavior was in fact being maintained by the reinforcer. Etzel and Gewirtz do not offer such evidence.

An alternative explanation of this study would be that the infants were crying for some unknown reason, perhaps physical discomfort. Removing attention whenever they cried (but not at other times) acted as punishment and, therefore, decreased the frequency of the behavior. This would be not extinction (of crying) but acquisition (of not-crying). The latter interpretation does not require the assumption that the crying had previously been operantly conditioned.

The main point is that it is wrong for any theory to conclude that whatever changes a behavior also illuminates the original cause of the behavior. For example, this author's vision is improved by wearing glasses. Does this mean that poor vision is caused by being born without eyeglasses? (In that case, everyone with good vision would have come forth into the world wearing glasses.)

Surmising the cause of a behavior from factors that later change or eliminate it is seductive but unsound reasoning. Behavior may arise for reasons other than those that later change it. In fact, it may arise and be modified by several different causes. Therefore, evidence that demonstrates that operant conditioning is *sufficient* to cause changes in behavior does not in addition demonstrate that operant conditioning is *necessary* to cause the behavior. To demonstrate that operant conditioning is the only antecedent of a behavior, it would be necessary to observe real-life child-rearing and to show that the behavior emerged only when operant conditioning of it had been previously observed. For any Skinnerian who wishes to make strong causal statements, this kind of research should have a high priority. Functional analysis of current behavior has more to do with the control than with the etiology of the behavior. It only shows that it can be done.

If a behavior can be operantly conditioned, then it is possible that the behavior may have originated in this way—possible, though not inevitable. However, there are some cases for which operant conditioning is not even a likely possibility. Consider some examples.

First, Breland and Breland (1961) and Bolles (1972) have shown that there is a wide range of behaviors in many different animal species that simply cannot be operantly conditioned, even by long training or under intense motivation. The authors' conclusions range from calling these "some failures of reinforcement to control behavior" (Bolles, 1972, p. 394) to "a clear and utter failure of conditioning theory" (Breland & Breland, 1961, p. 683).

Before accepting the latter conclusion, however, recall that all the examples are of animal experiments. The diversity of species used, from rat and pigeon to racoon and pig, certainly suggests that the phenomenon might be general. But we necessarily lack similar studies with humans because of the less severe training and motivation typically used. If a human does not respond to operant conditioning, it is always possible to assert that the training was too gentle—an explanation that is, fortunately, not challenged by further and harsher experiments. Thus, humans and animals have not been subjected to the same conditions of learning. Furthermore, the principal explanation for these failures of conditioning seems to be that inborn behaviors interfere with the operant. For example, pigs that were being trained to carry large wooden coins to a "piggy bank" for deposit inevitably gave up this operant to persistently drop and root at the coins instead. Rats innately react to shock by freezing or running; operants that are not compatible with one of these behaviors are difficult or impossible to train. Only if there are equally strong inborn tendencies in humans would the same interference with the operant be expected. If not, we might even expect humans to be *more* conditionable than animals. Thus, this first example has less relevance to the operant origin of human behavior than it seemed at first.

The next example raises the question whether what appears to be simple operant conditioning with humans is indeed purely behavioral, as Skinner maintains. An often-cited study involved reinforcing individuals with "mmm-hmm" for uttering predetermined classes of words (such as plurals) in conversation (Greenspoon, 1955, 1966). However, DeNike (1964; see also Spielberger & DeNike, 1966) showed that this procedure was effective only for subjects who became aware of the contingency. Those who did not figure out what was going on performed as poorly as the unreinforced control group. A nonbehavioral variable, awareness, must be invoked to explain why operant conditioning worked for some but not for others. This does not mean that awareness is necessary for all learning—an issue that is still in dispute. But

Skinner holds that it is *never* necessary for learning. The above evidence contradicts him.

The general relevance of operant conditioning to that most important behavior, language, has been seriously attacked by Chomsky (1959). Skinner's book *Verbal Behavior* (1957) proposed that language is acquired and used just as any other operant—by reinforcement, stimulus generalization, and so on. The book is "the most extensive attempt to accommodate human behavior involving higher mental faculties within a strict behaviorist schema" (Chomsky, 1959, p. 28). The particular criticism that is relevant here is the implausibility of the thesis that language is acquired by no more and no less than reinforcement:

> It is simply not true that children can learn language only through "meticulous care" on the part of adults who shape their verbal repertoire through careful differential reinforcement.... It is a common observation that a young child of immigrant parents may learn a second language in the streets, from other children, with amazing rapidity, and that his speech may be completely fluent and correct [Chomsky, 1959, p. 42].

Chomsky goes on to point out that children begin very early to use phrases they were never explicitly taught. Indeed, the great usefulness of the tool of language is that we constantly see or hear entirely new stimuli—that is, new arrangements of words—and yet understand their meaning the first time. It is not plausible to propose that each component of adult language was shaped and reinforced separately: it would take too long. Explaining this vast capacity by stimulus generalization will only work if the characteristics that make the stimuli similar are known. Chomsky believes that humans are born with a special capacity to perceive and learn language and that explanations, such as Skinner's, that are limited to external influences simply do not fit the rapidity and flexibility with which most children learn to speak.

The psycholinguist Roger Brown agrees that reinforcement is not important in shaping children's language. Brown and his colleagues have studied the development of language in the kind of naturalistic observation of parent/child interaction most suited to exploring Skinner's causal hypotheses. They have found "[not] a shred of evidence that approval and disapproval are contingent on syntactic correctness" (Brown & Hanlon, 1970, p. 47). Instead, parents seem to reinforce the accuracy of the child's speech—that is, whether it is true, not whether it is grammatical. Brown and Hanlon conclude:

> Explicit approval or disapproval of either syntax or morphology is extremely rare in our records and so seems not to be the force propelling the child from immature to mature forms [of speech] [1970, p. 48].

Thus, there is no evidence for parental shaping of grammatical speech by reinforcement of successive approximations.

To summarize all of the above, the first empirical issue is: what does the existing research tell us about the proposition that most human behaviors originate by operant conditioning? The answer is, very little. Functional analysis can demonstrate that a particular behavior can be produced operantly, but not that it necessarily or even usually has been produced that way. In addition, there is some evidence, particularly in the area of language, that operant conditioning alone cannot account for the acquisition of the behavior. Variables *inside* the organism—from awareness of the contingency to a genetic program for learning language—seem to be necessary.

Defining Reinforcement

The second major empirical issue for Skinner is: what is reinforcement? As a substantive behaviorist, Skinner rejected any definition based on the state of the organism (hunger, thirst, pain, need, or want). Instead, he defined reinforcement empirically, by its capacity to increase the frequency of an operant—that is, to produce operant conditioning. If food, water, escape from shock, a toy, a puzzle, or a smile is effective for operant conditioning, then each is a reinforcer.

The problem with this definition arises when the corresponding definition of operant conditioning is examined. Operant conditioning is the increase in the frequency of a response following reinforcement. Reinforcement is defined in terms of operant conditioning, and operant conditioning is defined in terms of reinforcement. Conditioning is what happens because of reinforcement, and reinforcement is what causes conditioning. As Meehl (1950) and others have pointed out, this is a circular pair of definitions. A reinforcer is a stimulus that reinforces, and it reinforces because it is a reinforcer. As with most circular propositions, it is both logically and empirically unsatisfactory. It is not possible to predict in advance what will be a reinforcer. It is necessary to cast about for stimuli that will increase the rate of operants and to be satisfied with knowing, after the fact, that a stimulus that did so is a reinforcer for that organism in that situation.

Meehl (1950) has proposed a way in which an empirical definition of reinforcement could be made more general and predictive. He suggests that once something has been shown to reinforce in one situation, a second empirical test should be made. Something that has reinforced in one situation can then be, so to speak, nominated as a potential reinforcer in a more general sense. The empirical test of whether it is indeed a *transsituational reinforcer* is to predict that it will reinforce another operant in another situation. Thus, if candy increases the frequency of putting toys away, it should also increase saying "please." The second operant is a test of whether candy has general, transsituational reinforcing properties. This definition is not circular because it makes predictions about the reinforcer in a situation other than the one by which the reinforcer was originally identified.

Many reinforcers can be shown to be transsituational, and Meehl's solution was held to be satisfactory for many years. Eventually, however, Premack (1959, 1965) pointed out that the definition was still empirically unsatisfactory. The transsituational-reinforcement theory, like virtually all theories of reinforcement including Skinner's, assumes that the capacity to reinforce is a property of the reinforcer. That is, some things are inherently desirable and others are not; the problem is simply to sort out which are which. Behind this, Premack pointed out, is hidden an assumption: once a reinforcer, always a reinforcer. Whether they are supposed to reinforce in one situation (according to Skinner) or in many (according to Meehl), those stimuli that are labeled reinforcers are implicitly endowed with a special, permanent property—the capacity to reinforce.

But there are many cases where this seems not to be true. A child may be polite as an operant for food. Later, however, the same child may eat a particular food in order to be polite. Food has now become part of an operant, and an operant has become a reinforcer. And again, many people will solve puzzles in order to get a prize of money. But the same people might, on another occasion, pay for a puzzle to solve (that is, buy one).

In these examples, operants and reinforcers are changing roles in a very confusing way. But the confusion arises only because reinforcers, once identified as such, are implicitly supposed to hold still and reinforce. They should never become part of an operant, and an operant should never include a reinforcing activity. The error, Premack pointed out, lies in assuming that reinforcement is the *property* of a stimulus (such as food) or of an activity involving that stimulus (such as eating). Premack proposed an alternative definition of reinforcement that would still be empirical and behavioral, but neither circular nor so rigid as to exclude examples of reversability, such as those suggested above.

To present Premack's theory, it is convenient first to change the standard definition of reinforcement slightly and call it a response (eating) that includes a stimulus (food). In fact, this usage has been around for some time (see Kimble, 1961, Chapter 9). Consuming the reinforcer is what is reinforcing. Food is not reinforcing if you don't get to eat it, nor is a compliment if you don't hear it. So Premack describes reinforcement as a response—namely, consuming the reinforcer. This change of terminology is unimportant empirically as long as the consumption is observable because the probability that food will be eaten by a hungry organism is very high. So presenting food and having it eaten are virtually the same thing empirically. But the change is useful theoretically because both operants and reinforcers are now responses—responses that under earlier theories belonged to two separate classes, reinforcers and nonreinforcers, the latter being potential operants.

Premack suggests that the notion of reinforcement as a class of behaviors distinguished by some permanent property is wrong. His alternative is quite simple: given several possible responses, the reinforcer is the preferred one; the others are operants that it can reinforce. That is, reinforcement is a *relation between responses* and not a property of the response itself. If an individual prefers eating to being polite, eating will reinforce being polite. If being polite is preferred, then it will reinforce eating. Relativity is the rule.

In general, reinforcers are identified in the context of other available responses. For any organism at any time, there is an identifiable ranking of preference for the responses available. A behavioral way of identifying this ranking is to give the organism free (noncontingent) access to all the responses and to rank the frequency with which the organism engages in each. The more frequent is assumed to be the more preferred, and it should then reinforce anything less frequent. If it does, then this theory of how to identify reinforcers is both correct and noncircular.

In an experiment with animals, Premack (1962) first deprived rats of water for some time, although they had all the food and activity they wanted. Under this deprivation, the free-access frequencies of drinking and running (in an activity wheel) were definitely different, with drinking exceeding running. Then, after the same deprivation, the animals were placed in an operant conditioning situation where drinking was contingent on running in an activity wheel. The frequency of running increased, confirming that the relative ranking of responses could accurately predict that drinking would reinforce running. But any primary-drive theorist, or even a Skinnerian who had previously observed that water acted as a reinforcer, would have predicted the same thing. The more interesting part of the experiment involved a second group of rats who were given all the food and water they wanted but no activity. This deprivation rearranged the ranking so that running was more frequent than drinking in free access. When the comparable test by conditioning was made, running was shown to reinforce drinking. So the first group ran to drink while the second drank to run. This reversal can only be accounted for or predicted by Premack's theory of the relative ranking of responses. All other theories would have to say that one and only one of the responses can have the properties of a reinforcer. In this experiment, the hierarchy was experimentally arranged by deprivation, a procedure that Premack points out has been usual even if not intentional in most conditioning studies.

But the hierarchy can be merely discovered as well as manipulated. Premack (1959) gave children free access to both candy and a pinball machine and observed which one each child spent the most time on, eating or playing pinball. These frequencies were used to infer a ranking for each child, and then the appropriate tests were begun. Those who preferred candy were required to play one ball before getting each candy. The operant (playing pinball) increased. The other children had to eat one piece of candy before they could play a ball, their highest frequency response. Again, the less preferred operant response increased.

Ayllon and Azrin (1965) used this theory and procedure to discover reinforcers for behavior modification of psychotic patients. The most frequent behaviors in free access, such as privacy or commissary items, were effectively used to reinforce nonpsychotic behaviors, which were previously infrequent. Thus, the theory works for humans as well as for animals.

Premack's theory has, by substantial revision (and only with these revisions) saved Skinner's empirical and behavioral approach to reinforcement. There are some other implications as well. This theory defines reinforcement not only as relational rather than absolute, but also as idiographic and situational. Each individual's ranking depends on what is available. It can vary from time to time and situation to situation, and it can differ from the rankings of others, because no ranking is assumed to be permanent. Premack noted, for example, that with sufficient food deprivation, the pinball players would have come to prefer candy, which would then be the reinforcer. Similarly, the candy-eaters would presumably have been satiated eventually, so that candy would no longer be a reinforcer for them.

There are two other, broader implications. First, it is foolish to try to list basic needs or primary drives (as Murray and Dollard and Miller have done), or to add psychological drives such as curiosity and competence (for example, Maslow, 1967; R. W. White, 1959) to such a list. A fixed list of drives for all people ignores the relational definition of reinforcement and assumes that reinforcement is a property of each item on the list. The need-list approach cannot predict or explain items on the list that act as operants rather than reinforcers under certain conditions. Nor can it account for the easy reversability of items on the list—for example, exploring in order to eat (finding a restaurant) and eating in order to explore (trying out a new restaurant).

The second, broader implication is that, using Premack's theory, we can know what will reinforce when but not *why*. To say that running or drinking or eating candy or playing pinball are reinforcing because they top the ranking says nothing. The ranking method of identifying is purely descriptive and empirical, consistent with Skinner's behaviorist approach. A nonbehaviorist might ask subjects which they preferred and then predict that their subjective preference determined what would be a reinforcer. But the behavioral approach permits no inference beyond the relative frequency of behaviors in a free-access situation.

This behaviorist orientation may be the reason why Premack, as he points out (1965, pp. 176-177), cannot account for the efficacy of such reinforcers as "yes" or "that's right." It is unlikely that anyone would, given free access, spend much time listening to someone else say "yes." Yet this is a powerful reinforcer in many situations. Obviously its power resides in what the "yes" means in a particular situation. There is a methodological, but not substantive, behaviorist alternative dating back to Tolman (1932) that proposes that reinforcement has informative as well as motivational effects. That is, reinforcement not only gives the organism something preferred, but it indicates what response is correct. This is probably the function of "mmm-hmm" in verbal conditioning experiments mentioned earlier (Spielberger & DeNike, 1966).

According to this view, an operant followed by reinforcement is not simply a barter for something preferred but an inquiry into the contingency currently operating. This may then also explain such reinforcers as "yes." But an informative role for reinforcement is only compatible with a cognitive theory that is not tied to substantive behaviorism. One such theory will be discussed in the next chapter, and some of these issues will be reexamined in Chapter 21.

Where does all of this leave the empirical status of Skinner's theory? As we have seen, the original theory is for the most part so encumbered with logical problems as to preclude meaningful empirical testing. As we will see in greater detail in the next chapter, there is also some empirical evidence that Skinner's theory of learning is wrong and must be replaced by a more cognitive approach. Before you suggest that Skinner merely tolerate some cognitive concepts, consider the following.

One of the most important qualities of Skinner's theory, its behaviorist simplicity, can be viewed either positively or critically. In a constructive view, the major strength of the theory is its parsimony and closeness to observables. To violate this principle casually is to do a serious disservice to the theory. Put more negatively, substantive behaviorists cannot have it both ways—claiming the ascetic virtues of their plain, unadorned theory, yet slipping in to non-behavioral concepts when necessary. Having strayed into cognitive territory, they must then compete with theories (both social and individual) that use these concepts openly and with some precision.

20

Bandura

THE THEORY

Albert Bandura and Richard Walters introduced a new approach to personality in their earliest book, *Social Learning and Personality Development* (1963), and then continued to work separately along similar lines until Walters's death in 1968. Bandura particularly has developed the social-learning basis of the theory (1971, 1977).

This social-learning theory is the only one to begin as a personality theory rather than as a general learning theory. From the beginning, it focused on human rather than animal learning and almost exclusively on the development of personality, both normal and abnormal. Instead of emphasizing the similarity of human learning to the simplest classical and instrumental or operant learning in animals, Bandura and Walters have stressed the complex learning of which humans are perhaps uniquely capable. The major theme of Bandura's most concise, recent statement of theory is the human's "superior cognitive capacity," including "higher mental processes [that] permit both insightful and foresightful behavior" (1971, pp. 2-3). In keeping with this theme, he emphasizes (1) learning from models, as opposed to learning from direct experience; (2) the symbolic and cognitive aspects of learning, as opposed to stimulus-response behaviorism; and (3) self-regulation, in addition to external regulation of behavior by reinforcement.

Learning from Models

The first of these three emphases is the best-known aspect of Bandura and Walters's original theory. Learning through *modeling*, also called *observational learning* or vicarious learning, is still the most prominent part of Bandura's current theory. The individual learns observationally—not by being in a learning situation, making responses, and directly experiencing reinforcement, but rather by observing someone else do so. Someone else, the model, makes the response and experiences the consequences. Anyone whose behavior is witnessed by the learner is called a model, regardless of whether the model intends to be copied or is even aware of the learner's observation.

Bandura argues, on practical grounds, that none of us has the time, even in a lifetime but much less in the developmental years, to make and directly experience the consequences of all possible responses. Nor does a family or society have the time or the heart to rigorously impose these time-consuming and even dangerous contingencies directly (such as learning how to cross a busy street). So a child can watch a parent or other adult, a sibling or peer, or even a fictitious character on television, and still learn both how to make the same response and what consequences follow from it. Bandura is proposing, in brief, both that learning without response and reinforcement does occur and that it is usually more efficient than learning by direct experience.

Early experiments (for example, Bandura, 1965) showed that mere exposure to a model was not sufficient to guarantee much learning. Therefore, the theory has been elaborated to include the following necessary subprocesses: *attention, retention, motoric* (behavioral) *reproduction,* and *motivation.*

The learner must attend to the model. This might be, for example, because of the model's attractiveness or because the medium itself is intrinsically attention-getting, as television seems to be for children.

After sufficient attention to ensure accurate selection of the important features of the model's behavior, the learner must be able to retain the information thus acquired in order to make these responses later, even when the model is no longer available. In some way, what the model did must be converted into a symbolic representation—usually in images or words—that can effectively store the behavior. Mental rehearsal can often aid this storage.

Motoric reproduction is the stage in which the learner puts the symbols into action. That is, recalling what the model did, the learner must put together a pattern of responses that resembles the model's. In some cases, the component responses will be readily available, such as simple words and unskilled movements. But if the modeled behavior was a skilled performance, such as learning a precise pronunciation or the movements of an experienced athlete, then the learner will not be able to perform them even after attention and retention. A certain amount of practice, guided and greatly assisted by the modeling observed, will be necessary.

Finally, even if all of the above conditions are met, and learning has occurred, the learner will never perform the modeled behavior unless he or she anticipates some kind of reinforcement for it. That is, the individual must be motivated to perform.

One way in which the learner might be influenced to perform or not would be by the motivation provided by *vicarious reinforcement.* These are observed rewards and punishments given to other people as a consequence of particular actions. Typically, the learner witnesses not only the modeled behavior but the reinforcement received by the model for the behavior. If the model has been rewarded, the behavior is likely to be performed spontaneously when the occasion arises. If the model was punished, the behavior will be inhibited unless another contingency replaces the observed one. A child may see a friend punished for interrupting its (the friend's) parents. This will tend to teach but also to inhibit interrupting, unless or until the observing child expects that the consequences to it will be different—for example, by seeing different consequences in the child's own home, or by being told that similar behavior will not be punished.

Recall that Miller and Dollard (1941) described imitative behavior, which may sound quite similar to observational learning. There are important differences, however, between Bandura's learning by observation and Miller and Dollard's matched-dependent behavior (see page 172). Observational learning is a process encompassing many stages and subprocesses, as well as the stimuli, responses, and reinforcement involved. In Miller and Dollard's theory, and in subsequent Skinnerian and other behaviorist versions, imitation is only a response that is learned like any other response, by reinforcement. The stimulus is the model, whose behavior provides a cue to which the learner responds with imitation. If this response is rewarded, then it is likely to increase in frequency, and it may also generalize to other models and other behaviors.

This drive-stimulus-response-reinforcement interpretation (without the drive, for Skinnerians) fits such social-learning theories very well. Bandura finds it restrictive, though, and incapable of encompassing several important circumstances. Although the young child tends to imitate immediately, in the presence of the model, older children and adults often do not. For example, an adolescent may carefully observe the behavior of a popular figure but is unlikely to repeat it on the spot. More probably, the admired behavior will be performed first in privacy, in front of a mirror. Also, new parents often find themselves acting like their own parents, many years later. Thus, the response does not necessarily or even usually occur in the presence of the stimulus (the model) and may in fact be delayed for some time. In that case, any reinforcement for making the response must also occur long after the original stimulus. The behavior may be learned even though both response and reinforcement are missing in the learning period, when the behavior is being observed but not imitated. On the other hand, when imitation finally does occur, the original stimulus (the model) is usually absent. Imitation, or matched-dependent behavior, cannot be dependent on matching another's response if the other is no longer present.

It may seem a simple matter to resolve these problems by proposing that the learner stores the information and puts it together later, rather than having to experience all of it literally and directly at the same time. But information storage and processing are cognitive operations that cannot be accommodated by Dollard and Miller's or Skinner's theories. Imitation, in such theories, describes only the immediate, overt reproduction of a response just made by another. It cannot include the passive acquisition of information about what the other did, information that may or may not lead to behavior later. Imitation, Bandura argues, is a special and limited kind of learning, much less important than the process of observational learning.

Parenthetically, this position necessarily relinquishes reinforcement as an explanation of why observational learning occurs in the first place. That is, why do people tend to notice and remember what other people do? It cannot be for reinforcement because, as has already been pointed out, both response and reinforcement occur too late to produce the strong learning of a general habit of "learning by modeling." Thus, Bandura and Walters did not treat this as a learned tendency. It is simply assumed to occur universally in humans.

Cognitive and Symbolic Processes

The essential difference between Bandura's theory of modeling and the earlier theories of imitation leads naturally to the second theme of the theory as a whole: the importance of *cognitive* and *symbolic* processes. Although these processes are not developed in detail, they pervade the theory and are explicitly held to be necessary for understanding human behavior. One example is the set of mechanisms for observational learning already described. Selective attention, symbolic representation and storage of information, and the translation of this information back into behavior are all cognitive operations. They require, in plain words, someone who thinks. This is in strong contrast to the automatic stimulus-response learning proposed by the first two social-learning theories.

Bandura's treatment of the concept of reinforcement also reveals his cognitive approach. He proposes that reinforcement seldom operates merely as the automatic fixative of behavior. More often, it serves two other functions—as *information* and as *incentive*. Reinforcement following a given response indicates, or at least permits the individual to form hypotheses about, what the correct response is. This informative function (mentioned in the discussion of Premack's theory on page 195 can operate whether the reinforcement is experienced directly or vicariously. Thus, seeing someone else punished for a certain behavior is as informative as being punished oneself.

In addition, reinforcement teaches what to expect as a result of the correct or incorrect response. This special kind of information is usually called incentive—that is, an expectation of future outcomes. Again, incentive can be acquired by either direct or observational experience. Indeed, Bandura's explanation for the effectiveness of vicarious reinforcement is solely that such observed reinforcement provides information and incentive. It cannot act to increase the frequency of the previous response, because there has been no response by the observer yet. Direct, as opposed to vicarious, reinforcement is likely to be a powerful regulator of already learned behavior (via incentive) but an inefficient teacher by trial and error, because it yields information so slowly and haphazardly: "Under most circumstances, a good example is . . . a much better teacher than the consequences of unguided actions" (Bandura, 1971, p. 5).

Even in accepting most of the other basic phenomena of learning, such as classical conditioning, discrimination learning, and learning by direct, reinforced experience, Bandura emphasizes that these processes are regulated cognitively. Experience does not control behavior. The awareness and expectations one has as a result of experience determine behavior. A person in

Bandura's theory is one who is constantly observing, thinking, forming hypotheses and expectations, and finally deciding what to do—based on what this person wants and on what he or she judges the situation to be.

Self-Regulation

At the outset, three distinguishing characteristics of Bandura's theory were mentioned. Observational learning and the cognitive approach have been introduced. The last, briefly, is *self-regulation* of behavior by self-reinforcement. This is in some senses a reaction to the exclusive control by external reinforcement that other social-learning theories imply. From the earliest version of the theory (Bandura & Walters, 1963), it was emphasized that not all consequences are externally imposed, especially for adults. An important part of child-rearing is to replace the carrot and stick of parental or societal reinforcements with self-set standards, enforced by self-administered rewards and punishments. Each of us is often his or her own harshest critic as well as most appreciative fan. We can decide to give ourselves a work break, a banana split, or a compliment. Although overt, physical self-punishment is considered deviant, it is normal to criticize one's own performance and to withhold rewards because they are not yet deserved. Bandura redefines self-concept and self-esteem, as used by Rogers and others, in terms of the standards set for oneself, the degree to which one approaches those standards, and the consequences in terms of self-reinforcement.

Bandura's as a Social Personality Theory

Looking back over the whole of the theory, the social paradigm becomes apparent. Learning by modeling requires the presence of another person, making the learning at least a minimally social phenomenon. To the extent that the environment provides information and often controls reinforcement or incentive as well, another external factor has been added. The cognitive emphasis of Bandura's theory may appear to be nonsocial—that is, referring to processes inside the individual. But these cognitive and symbolic operations are for the most part representations of external events. They are the vital intermediaries between situation and response; they constitute transactions between the individual and the environment rather than closed, purely internal events.

Furthermore, no individual differences as such are suggested. All differences, however enduring, are presumed to be the result of experience. Insofar as the essence of any learning theory is to show how experience can change the individual, these differences are essentially situational. The only exception is Bandura's notion of self-standards, which implies a certain imperviousness to experience:

> If actions were determined solely by external rewards and punishments, people would behave like weathervanes, constantly shifting in radically different directions to conform to the whims of others. . . . Close scrutiny of

social interactions would most likely reveal, barring powerful coercive pressures, steadfast adherence to ideological positions rather than compliant behavior reversals [Bandura, 1971, p. 27].[1]

Bandura and Walters were quite aware of the "inner" and "outer" models of personality. Their book is often cited as one of the first explicit expressions of an alternative to the individual paradigm. Much as he rejects the individual view, however, Bandura has not found the behaviorist label congenial, insofar as "it unfortunately implied a one-way influence process that reduced man to a helpless reactor" (1971, p. 2). He rejects any one-way influence, either of internal factors or of external ones, and aspires to a theory that would ultimately encompass interaction between the individual and the environment. "Behavior partly creates the environment and the resultant environment, in turn, influences the behavior. In this two-way causal process the environment is just as influenceable as the behavior it controls" (1971, p. 40).

There is an unfortunately common but inaccurate tendency to polarize the individual and social positions, with all individual theories seen as nomothetic trait theories and all social theories as S-R behaviorism. Bandura has been helpful in questioning these stereotypes. Here is a modern social-learning theory, clearly within the social paradigm, but based on cognitions and even hinting at some individual differences. This is a good antidote to simpleminded caricatures of either paradigm; it may also, as will be suggested in Chapter 25, be capable of moving us into a new paradigm altogether. Because it promises to accommodate both paradigms, Bandura's theory has been given by many the burden of being *the* answer to problems in modern personality theory. Whether it is yet ready to carry this heavy burden is the question to be examined next.

EMPIRICAL STATUS

Tests of Observational Learning

There is one empirical issue on which Bandura and Walters flatly disagree with the other two social-learning theories. This is the issue of whether reinforcement or even a response is necessary for learning to occur. For Dollard and Miller the fundamental necessary and sufficient conditions of learning are drive, cue, response, and reinforcement, in that order. For Skinner, stimulus, response, and reinforcement are the essence of learning. There is no question, and Bandura and Walters do not dispute, that these are sufficient to produce learning in many cases. But are they necessary?

The question is whether learning can occur *only* when this sequence is directly experienced by the learner; or whether learning can also occur merely

[1]From *Social Learning Theory*, by Albert Bandura. © 1971 General Learning Corporation (General Learning Press). This and all other quotations from this source are reprinted by permission of Silver Burdett Company.

by watching a model (the stimulus), although the observer makes no imitative response and therefore cannot be and is not reinforced for such a response. A direct test of this conceptual hypothesis is Bandura's 1965 study of children's learning from televised film. In addition to investigating whether children would imitate a filmed model, the study also examined the effects of vicarious reinforcement on learning and on spontaneous performance.

Nursery school boys and girls (3½ to 6 years old) were seated, alone in a darkened room, in front of a television set on which the same 5-minute film was played for each child. The film featured a man and an adult-size "Bobo doll" (an inflated plastic figure painted like a clown and weighted at the bottom so as to be self-righting). The model proceeded to act "aggressively" toward the doll. He ordered it to clear out of the way, and then attacked it in four different ways—for example, by kicking it around the room while saying "Fly away!" After the sequence of four attacks had been repeated twice, a closing scene showed what happened to the model after such behavior. There were three different endings, each seen by one-third of the children. Each child saw only one ending. One experimental group saw a second man enter the room and reward and praise the model for his behavior. The second group saw the same man enter, scold, and spank the model. The third group saw no consequences at all; the film simply ended after the sequence of attacks had been repeated twice. Then each child was taken to a room containing a Bobo doll and many other toys. The child was left alone for 10 minutes, after being told it was all right to play with anything in the room. Observers recorded how many responses matching the model's each child made. Finally, the experimenter entered with juice and sticker-pictures, which the child was offered for each response like the model's that it could reproduce. Matching responses were recorded in the same way, by observers.

Thus, there were four stages to the experiment: the opportunity to learn without responding or being reinforced (watching the first part of the film); observation of vicarious reinforcement (what happened to the model at the end of the film); the opportunity to perform the observed responses spontaneously (being alone in the room); and then the request to perform them with a positive incentive.

According to modeling theory, the child should be learning while passively watching the film. Moreover, it should learn both what the model did and what happened as a consequence. In the first opportunity to perform spontaneously, both these aspects would operate. That is, the child would expect the same consequences for itself as the model received and would act accordingly. Therefore, the first research hypothesis was that children who saw the model rewarded would imitate his behavior, and those who saw him punished would not. But this would not mean that the latter group had not learned anything from the film, only that they chose not to make the responses because they had also learned the expected consequences. The second opportunity to perform, when the expected consequences were explicitly changed and every child knew it would be rewarded for imitating, is the crucial test of observational learning. The research hypothesis is that now all children should perform the model's actions, regardless of the film ending they had seen.

The results seem to support these hypotheses. There was an effect of the three different film endings on spontaneous performance. The group who saw the model punished performed significantly fewer of the model's responses when left alone in the room than did children who saw the model rewarded or saw no consequences to the model. When positive incentives were offered, these differences due to vicarious reinforcement disappeared. All groups made matching responses. This was not imitation or matched-dependent behavior because the model was obviously not present. Observational learning had occurred.

But there are some difficulties with this experiment. The first result— lower spontaneous performance across all children when the model had been punished—was due entirely to the girl subjects' behavior. The boys' spontaneous performance was unaffected by the model's punishment, even though the model was male, like them. If anything, a same-sexed model should have increased observational learning.

The second effect, showing modeling under positive incentive, was actually quite small. The average number of different matching responses was between 3 and 4 per child for all groups. The article does not report the maximum possible number of different matching responses. Because the model made four distinct attacks, each including both verbal and physical components, which were counted separately, there must have been a minimum of eight possible responses. Furthermore, the responses seem to have been counted even when repeated, so the number possible in 10 minutes is probably much higher.

Thus, although the children did show that they had learned something observationally, they did not learn very much of what they had observed. In fact, without a control group who had not seen the film, it is not possible to know exactly how much was learned from the film itself. The responses were chosen for their novelty, and a previous study had shown that children were unlikely to think of these exact responses on their own. Still, the amount of observational learning would best be evaluated by the *difference* between children who saw the film and those who did not. It is not good research design to "borrow" a control group from an earlier, different experiment.

Bandura was himself dissatisfied with the total amount of performance in the last phase of the experiment:

> It is evident from the findings...that mere exposure to modeling stimuli does not provide the sufficient conditions for imitative or observational learning. The fact that most of the children in the experiment failed to reproduce the entire repertoire of behavior exhibited by the model, even under positive-incentive conditions designed to disinhibit and to elicit matching responses, indicates that factors other than mere contiguity of sensory stimulation undoubtedly influence imitative response acquisition [1965, p. 593].

The factors he went on to suggest correspond very closely to what he later called the subprocesses of attention, retention, and motoric reproduction. (As indicated in the quotation, the fourth subprocess, incentive motivation, was present in the experiment and had a demonstrable effect.)

It is widely believed that modeling—that is, unreinforced learning by observation—has been clearly demonstrated. A closer look at the available evidence reveals a picture as confusing as the study just described. Some learning by modeling does occur, but it also does *not* occur. Most important, the factors that count are not yet understood, leaving an almost whimsical pattern of results that defies prediction. Several prominent examples will illustrate.

Bandura and MacDonald (1963) divided children into two groups according to whether, in judging others' behavior, they typically responded to the subjective intention or to the objective effect. An example of objective effect would be when wrong was done but not intentionally. For each group, the subjectively and the objectively oriented, the experiment included exposing the children to modeling and vicarious reinforcement of the opposite orientation. It was predicted that this would be more effective than operant conditioning of the opposite orientation. It was—for the subjectively oriented children only. Besides this inexplicable failure to obtain a significant effect for the other half of the children, the absolute size of the effect was not impressive. The proportion of objective judgments made by originally subjective children, after modeling, was slightly over 50%.

Bandura and Mischel (1965) also divided children into two groups, this time according to whether they typically preferred small immediate rewards or larger but delayed rewards—for example, 25¢ today or 35¢ next week. Each child watched a model consistently demonstrate the opposite preference and both explain and praise himself for his choice. As in the Bandura and Mac-Donald study, the child's preference was assessed before the modeling, and the child made no responses in the presence of the model. Children who had previously preferred delayed rewards shifted to choosing immediate rewards 60% of the time, which was significantly more than children of the same original preference who had not seen the opposite behavior modeled. But, again, the other half of the children did not show a significant effect of modeling over the control group who saw no model. That is, the "low-delay" children were not affected by the modeling experience.

Bandura and Harris (1966) tried to influence language development by modeling and found no effect of modeling alone, either on a frequent language behavior (use of prepositional phrases) or on an infrequent behavior (use of the passive construction). There have been no explanations of why some behaviors can be changed with modeling while other, apparently similar, behaviors cannot. After-the-fact explanations abound, but these are an insubstantial base for a theory.

In a naturalistic study of parents' modeling of language for their own children, Brown (1973, pp. 356-368) found indirect but compelling evidence that such modeling is unlikely to be important. He and his colleagues studied the degree to which an individual child's language development followed the idiosyncratic frequencies with which its parents typically spoke in certain forms. The reasoning was that, if modeling or imitation were important, then children should adopt their parents' distinctive speaking patterns, so that forms used more frequently by their parents should develop earlier. There was no such correlation, and Brown concluded:

> In sum, there is no clear evidence at all that parental frequencies influence the order of development of the forms I have studied. I am prepared to conclude that frequency is not a significant variable [1973, p. 368].

Recall that Brown also found no evidence for operant conditioning of language. Language acquisition will apparently be as difficult for Bandura to handle as it is for Skinner.

Where does this leave the issue that divides the social-learning theories? Because Dollard and Miller as well as Skinner assert strongly that response and reinforcement are always necessary for learning, their position is undermined even by this weak evidence, because some observational learning has been shown. One counter-example is enough to dispute their generalization: it is not the case that all learning requires response and reinforcement. But that is all that this evidence shows. Some learning may require response and reinforcement; some learning may be more effective with modeling; and there may be yet other ways of learning as well. We have been forced from simple principles to unknown complexities. But these complexities cannot be ignored. If nothing else, social-learning theories must specify the antecedents of learning and show that they hold true.

Theoretical Problems

Leaving this issue, which spans the three social-learning theories, there are some aspects of Bandura's particular social-learning theory that require closer scrutiny. Other than demonstrating that strict stimulus-response-reinforcement theories are not general, how does the theory stand? Although it has developed substantially since the early days when observational learning was all that distinguished it from the other social-learning theories, this theory is only beginning to take a coherent, systematic shape. The three major themes that Bandura currently stresses—observational learning, cognitive and symbolic functions, and self-regulation—all suffer to some degree from a sprawling, superficial treatment. These inadequacies are barriers to more precise empirical development of the theory, just as theoretical problems have held back research on Freud's and Rogers's theories (recall pages 34-35 and 69-71).

Having made this broad criticism, it is only fair to add that this theory is the youngest we have considered so far. Most of the much older theories, both social and individual, have shown the same diffuseness, without the plausible excuse that they are still developing.

There are two major flaws in the observational-learning part of the theory. First, the subprocesses of observational learning have not yet been explored or defined in sufficient detail to make predictions as easily as post hoc explanations. Since Bandura acknowledged in 1965 that mere exposure was not sufficient to produce observational learning, it falls on this theory to identify the necessary additional factors. Bandura and Jeffery (1973) have explored some of the subprocesses that might determine observational learning of a complex and arbitrary motor sequence. They found that coding and symbolic or motor rehearsal in various combinations and conditions sometimes facilitated observational learning, but sometimes did not.

It is not yet possible to say, for any given situation, whether the necessary factors are present and, therefore, whether observational learning will occur:

> If . . .one wishes to explain why modeling does or does not occur, a variety of determinants must be considered. In any given instance lack of matching behavior following exposure to modeling influences may result from either failure to observe the relevant activities, inadequate coding of modeled events for memory representation, retention decrements, motoric deficiencies, or inadequate conditions of reinforcement [Bandura, 1971, p. 8].

At present, none of these subprocesses is so clearly defined that one can tell, other than by knowing whether learning does occur, when they are present or absent in sufficient degree to expect learning or not. Without a definition both independent of and prior to any consequent learning, these subprocesses remain principally after-the-fact rationalizations for failures to obtain observational learning from modeling.

The second problem with the present conception of observational learning is the inclusion of verbal instructions (also called induced awareness) as a kind of modeling. Bandura points out that verbal instructions, either in person or in print, play a major role in transmitting information to the learner. Two examples are instruction manuals on a wide variety of topics and instructions telling the person that painful consequences will follow the signal in classical-conditioning experiments. Bandura calls instructions "verbal modeling" (1971, p. 10), apparently in order to subsume them under a single general learning process. The first example seems to be treated as analogous to vicarious learning, whereas the second would have to involve both vicarious learning and vicarious reinforcement. But if learning by modeling involves watching another person perform the behavior to be learned, then clearly these are not instances of modeling. The verbal model is often a book or written note, with no other person present.

It is curiously difficult to find a rigorous definition of what a model is, in order to settle this issue. Throughout his work, Bandura refers to the model as an example, or as another person experiencing direct learning. In contrast, verbal instructions are already-symbolized pieces of information that the learner can use to guide behavior. In other words, instructions entirely omit the first subprocess—attention to a performing model. Being already in symbolic (verbal) form, they also eliminate the symbolizing stage of the retention process. Still, Bandura implies that the two are essentially interchangeable:

> Much social learning is fostered through exposure to behavioral modeling cues in actual or pictorial forms. However, after adequate language development is achieved, people rely extensively upon verbal modeling cues for guiding their behavior [1969, p. 145; italics omitted].

Unfortunately, all of this implies that anything that produces the same result as an observed model, as long as it is not direct, reinforced experience, is also a model. The test of whether such stimuli act as models seems to be whether learning occurs—as it certainly does in the case of verbal instructions. But if the concept of model is defined by learning, and learning is explained by modeling, then Bandura's theory is in the same logical fix as Skinner's circular use of reinforcement and learning (page 192). It would be far better to propose a more general category of "learning without direct experience," of which observing a model is only one instance. Learning by instruction, without a performing model, would then be a different case.

Besides getting the theory out of a logical difficulty, this approach would force closer attention to exactly how and when instructions work. For example, in a study that seems almost a satire on operant-conditioning procedures, Ayllon and Azrin (1964) found that establishing a reinforcement schedule with psychiatric patients was almost totally ineffective until someone told the patients about it! Given the present state of the field, an informative and important research design in social learning would be one that compares learning under experimental conditions of modeling, operant conditioning, and verbal instruction, plus the necessary control group or groups.

Moving on to Bandura's conception of self-regulation and self-reinforcement, we find that this does not include any specification of when these will override external reinforcement. Granted that we feel that we are able to reinforce ourselves, what happens when society does not agree? Bandura points out that conflict between external and self-produced reinforcement may arise, but he does not say how it will be resolved. Which will dominate must be inferred from behavior in a circular manner.

This problem points up a larger issue: the lack of a reinforcement theory. Bandura does not say what makes anything a reinforcer (or an incentive) but, rather, relies on intuition and effect, just as Skinner does. The only difference is that Bandura's intuitions about reinforcement are different from Skinner's. The entire discussion of circularity of a definition of reinforcement, the trans-situational solution, and Premack's critique (pages 192-193) could be repeated here just as pertinently.

The third major emphasis that distinguishes Bandura's social-learning theory from the others is the theme of cognitive and symbolic processes. As already discussed, these assumptions are often used throughout the theory to explain, for example, incentive as opposed to reinforcement; modeling as opposed to imitation; and awareness as opposed to automatic learning. Similarly, the process of translating experience into symbols, either as images or words, is essential to the theory of observational learning. Yet the precise way in which cognition and symbolization operate is not elaborated. These concepts are used as explanations without being adequately explained themselves.

As readers, we are all so immediately aware of our own thinking, remembering, planning, and verbal coding (such as thinking in words) that we do not question the validity of these processes. But exactly how do such processes occur? Are they the same for all people? These are complex, fascinating questions. They have occupied psycholinguists as well as researchers on attention, memory, and recall, and have led to a whole new experimental area called cognitive psychology (for example, Neisser, 1967). Yet Bandura does not draw on this information at all, relying instead on examples and intuitive notions to illustrate what ought to be technical terms—information, incentive, symbolic coding, and so on. Often, too, the cognitive explanation is after-the-fact, and therefore circular.

If the problem of circularity seems to have been overemphasized throughout this book, from Freud to Skinner and now Bandura, I offer two justifications: in defense of these authors, circularity is rarely immediately apparent, as it seems to hide in plausible and useful, if vague, aspects of the theory, especially in the early stages. These appear to be plausible and useful precisely because they are circular and, until the circularity is recognized, irrefutable. Second, in defense of my own dogged pursuit of circularities, I would point out that they are a serious handicap to the theory itself. A theory is not logically coherent or empirically testable to the extent that it contains circular definitions of major concepts. Indeed, the student who wishes to make the most effective and direct analysis of any theory will be well prepared if he or she has mastered three basic logical concepts: circularity; tautology; and necessity and sufficiency.

21

Summing Up: Social Learning and Social Theories

In this chapter, we will take a broader look at the recurring issues raised in Part 2. First, all three social-learning theories will be compared in a summary of social-learning issues. This overview is particularly important because of the dominance of social-learning theories in contemporary personality theory and research. Then, the social paradigm as a whole will be summarized, as it applies to the four theories covered and to others as well.

SOCIAL-LEARNING ISSUES

It is curious that, as a cognitive-learning theorist, Bandura has omitted any mention of earlier cognitive work in general learning theory, which dates back to E. C. Tolman's *Purposive Behavior in Animals and Men* (1932). It is not that work such as Tolman's constitutes anything resembling a personality theory. But a debate between the cognitive and behavioral positions was conducted over a period of 20 years by some of the best minds in psychology. The result was a distillation of issues that is still useful to any cognitive-learning position. Today, the three major issues can be applied directly to the social-learning theories, which are in some senses reliving the past. These issues, which will be used as a convenient summary of the three social-learning theories, are (1) learning versus performance; (2) *how* learning occurs (the role of reinforcement); and (3) *what* is learned (S-R versus S-S connections).

Learning versus Performance

Cognitive-learning theory is responsible for the distinction between learning, or acquisition, and performance. In stimulus-response-reinforcement learning (learning by direct experience), these two processes are not easily separable and are often treated as identical. When does a response cease to be part of the learning sequence and become instead the outcome or performance of that learning? When learning occurs other than by direct experience, the distinction becomes clearer. For example, observational learning is behaviorally passive. The learner does not make the response during acquisition. Later, when the new response is made for the first time, and correctly, this is clearly not learning or practice but performance of what has already been learned.

Performance always requires a response, in order that we can be assured that the behavior has indeed been learned. This corresponds to methodological behaviorism. But learning does not necessarily require a response, as we have already seen. The individual may learn by observing or by being instructed, and perhaps by other indirect means such as reasoning. Learning refers to changes in the organism—changes that may not be visible to someone else. Performance has to do with evoking and controlling the behavior; it reveals the learning but is not conceptually identical to it. The distinction between learning and performance will emerge again below.

Parenthetically, Bandura (1971, p. 9) suggests that the necessity to infer learning from performance is irrelevant for humans because one can simply ask them what they learned, bypassing performance altogether. However, verbal behavior is still behavior, and if the learning is complex it will be commensurately difficult to judge whether or to what degree the verbal statement accurately reflects learning (see Wilson, 1973). Furthermore, knowing how to do something and knowing how to say how to do it are two different things. Try—without any practice—to say *exactly* how to tie your shoes.

How Learning Occurs

The dominant behavioral theories have also been reinforcement theories. Thus, the second question—how does learning occur?—is answered simply: reinforced practice. Cognitive theorists propose and offer evidence that reinforcement is unnecessary for learning. Responses made without reinforcement can be learned. Responses not even made, and thus not reinforced, may be learned (for example, by observation). It is sometimes held that reinforcement is still necessary for performance. Even this is not correct if reinforcement is interpreted in the usual way, as reward *after* the response. What is needed for performance is incentive—that is, a reason to perform what has been learned. Incentive can be introduced by instruction, vicarious reinforcement, or any other procedure that leads to the expectation that the behavior *will be* reinforced. Of course, one way to induce this expectation is to make the organism go through the stimulus-response-reinforcement sequence at least once. This experimental procedure has tended to confound the distinction between the reinforcing and incentive functions of the reward.

What Is Learned

Finally, cognitive and behavioral theories usually disagree about what is learned. All three social-learning theories have followed Dollard and Miller's assertion that stimulus-response (S-R) connections are learned. That is, the individual learns to make certain responses on certain occasions. Earlier cognitive theories, however, suggested that learning often consists of stimulus-stimulus (S-S) connections, sometimes called a cognitive map. For example, "that door leads to food" represents the stimulus *door* as connected to the stimulus *food* in a specific way. Naturally, if the individual wants food, he or she is very likely to go through the door. But that is mere performance, according to the cognitive theorist. The person may go through the door frontwards, sideways, or backwards; he or she may push open the door with hand, arm, foot, or hip. These responses are irrelevant alternative ways of implementing the knowledge. The cognitive map need not be geographic or spatial. "Talking back leads to scolding" is an S-S connection that is psychological but not spatial.

Bandura speaks mostly of response learning—that is, of learning to make "new behavioral configurations" (1971, p. 8). However, he implies an S-S position as well. For example, vicarious reinforcement, the informative and incentive functions of reinforcement, and awareness of a contingency all involve using expected consequences to guide behavior. This implies that the consequences must have been learned as stimuli in an S-S connection. ("Kicking the Bobo doll leads to punishment.")

Similarly, symbolic representations of behavior are stimuli, not responses. Consider the following statement:

> By observing a model of the desired behavior, an individual *forms an idea* of how response components must be combined and temporally sequenced to produce new behavioral configurations. The *representation* serves as a guide for behavioral reproduction [Bandura, 1971, pp. 8-9; italics added].

This sounds very much like stimulus learning. Thus, it would be more consistent for Bandura to move further over to the cognitive position and include S-S learning explicitly in his theory. It is ironic that, according to Tolman, rats learn cognitive maps; but, according to the social-learning theorists, humans learn simple S-R connections!

Current Empirical Status: A Summary

The empirical status of the three social-learning theories is no better than that of the individual personality theories included in Part 1. Too little research has been directed at issues that lie at the heart of any of these theories. Dollard and Miller are shaky on three grounds. Their theory of aversive classical conditioning as reinforced learning is wrong; there is at least some evidence that behaviors that they assumed to be acquired only by instrumental learning do not require response and reinforcement; and, finally, their theory of reinforcement based on drive reduction is invalidated by Premack's data. Skinner's theory also suffers on the last two points. Even a Skinnerian who incorporated Premack's revised reinforcement theory (and most seem not to) would be left with the problem of the informative function of reinforcement—for example, the powerful "mmm-hmm" and "yes." Bandura's evidence may be sufficient to raise questions about S-R-reinforcement theories, but it is not yet adequate for building a satisfactory and convincing alternative. Surely, social-learning theories must face these central issues: what is learning, and how does it occur?

Rotter's Social Learning Theory

One social-learning theory that has not yet been mentioned is that of Julian B. Rotter (1954, 1955, 1967; Rotter, Chance, & Phares, 1972). Rotter in fact named his theory "social learning theory," or SLT. It is a highly eclectic theory, acknowledging the major influences of Lewin, Tolman, Skinner, and Hull. This tolerance is its greatest weakness. As has been shown in recent chapters, these theories are not at all compatible with one another in their fundamental premises. Even the most similar of the four, Tolman and Lewin, who were both cognitive theorists, sometimes disagreed, especially about learning. In accepting all these theories, Rotter creates a theory that is logically inconsistent. For example, he propounds Skinner's empirical definition of reinforcement, yet also emphasizes its cognitive opposites, goals and needs. He accepts Tolman's principles of expectation and hypothesis-formation in cognitive learning, yet equates experience with reinforcement. One is unable to find a clear statement of the necessary and sufficient conditions for learning to occur—a minimum criterion for a social-learning theory.

Rotter is explicit about belonging in the social paradigm:

> The unit of investigation for the study of personality is the interaction of the individual and his meaningful environment [1954, p. 85; italics original].

It is ironic, therefore, that his major impact has been through his locus-of-control trait measure (1966; see Chapter 13, above). Recall that locus of control is, according to Rotter, a learned expectancy about one's ability to control outcomes (such as reinforcements). This expectancy results from early interaction with the environment. But according to Rotter it becomes generalized and largely independent of the present environment—in short, a trait. Whatever Rotter's intentions, locus of control has become a single-trait theory with little connection to its original context. One almost suspects that, because it employs the language (but not the premises) of the social paradigm, locus of control has become a popular topic for "closet trait theorists," who feel they must hide their real orientation because of the present climate of criticism of the individual paradigm.

THE SOCIAL PARADIGM

Social-learning theories are the salient but not the only instances of the social paradigm. Lewin's theory is also social, and there are other, less well-known social theories of personality (including those of Andras Angyal, Kurt Goldstein, and Gardner Murphy; see Chapter 25). Just as with the individual personality theories, behind their differences these social theories share a common paradigm. All, as we have seen, emphasize external more than internal causes of behavior. All explain behavior by situational more than individual differences.

Just as with the individual theories, there are occasional deviations from the paradigm: Murray includes press; and Bandura includes self-standards. But these are minor, relatively undeveloped aspects of each theory. The reader should try the same exercise as was proposed in Chapter 11: look back over all the major terms of each social theory. The vocabulary of the social theories—life space, stimulus, reinforcement, model—is a vocabulary describing events to a substantial degree outside the individual. The focus is on the individual in an environment, not the individual in isolation. The implications of this difference in focus will be the sole topic of Chapter 23, in which the two paradigms will be compared in detail, revealing both real and pseudo-differences between them.

22

Validation
of Social-Behavior Measures

As noted at the beginning of Chapter 12, personality theory and measurement are inseparable. Clearly, measurement is necessary in order to bring any theory to an empirical test. In a more subtle but equally important way, personality theories influence personality assessment as a practical activity. It may seem that the assessment of personality characteristics in an applied setting and for purely practical purposes would owe little to the sometimes remote and abstract theories of personality. Indeed, such assessment is usually taught in separate courses on psychometrics or psychological measurement (rather than in courses on personality theory). The former courses, furthermore, typically include only trait measurement. However, as was shown in Chapters 12 and 13, personality trait measures follow directly from the individual paradigm, and this relation between paradigm and procedure in fact tells us how to validate such measures.

The same reasoning will be extended here to assessment in the social paradigm. This paradigm dictates distinct and different assessment procedures from those in the individual paradigm. This is true whether or not the assessment procedure derives directly from a major theory. Most assessments of social behavior are analogous to single-trait theories, in that they follow the general paradigm, not any particular theory of personality. Because of their recent origin, these procedures are not nearly so highly developed as the trait measures are, but they are probably just as widely used at present. An example of such a procedure will be given to make clear what is meant by social-behavior measurement; then the validation issues can be discussed.

THE CASE OF ANN

One of the early classics of the social-learning literature is the behavior modification of social isolation in a little girl (Allen, Hart, Buell, Harris, & Wolf,

1964). We will focus on the method by which her behavior was assessed, not on the treatment itself.

The Method of Assessment

Ann was about 4 ½ years old, enrolled in a university preschool. For 5 days, two observers each spent half of the morning recording Ann's social behavior. Specifically, her proximity to and interaction with adults and other children were recorded every 10 seconds. For each 10-second interval, it was noted whether Ann was near or interacting with an adult, a child, or both. On two of the mornings during the study, both observers recorded all morning, and these records agreed 81% to 91%.

The data for each of the 5 days were converted to percentages of time spent in social interaction with adults and with children. When Ann was interacting with both an adult and a child, this was counted in both categories—except for the daily 15-minute scheduled group activity, which was not scored at all. A graph showed that during the first 5 days of observation, Ann spent about 50%, 50%, 40%, 30%, and 40% of the morning sessions interacting with adults and about 10%, 20%, 10%, 10%, and 10% of the same sessions interacting with children. The rest of the time she was alone.

According to the authors, "Analysis of the data indicated that her isolate behavior was being maintained and probably strengthened inadvertently by adult social reinforcement" (p. 516). Although general, anecdotal examples of this pattern of reinforcement are given, no data are presented, and no procedures for systematically recording the teachers' behavior are described. The rest of the report describes the teachers' subsequent, planned use of smiles, approval, and so on, to reinforce Ann's interaction with other children. The same recording procedures were used throughout so that the effect of changes in reinforcement contingencies could be compared. (She did increase her interactions with children.)

Comparison with Trait Assessment

Several differences from (and some similarities to) traditional trait measurement are evident. The procedure was designed for and applied to a single subject, Ann. There is no explicit intention that this particular system of recording would be useful or relevant for other individuals. In other words, it is an idiographic procedure. The assessment was also oriented exclusively toward the subsequent treatment conditions. That is, it was conducted partly to verify the solitary nature of Ann's behavior, but mostly to provide a baseline against which to compare increases in peer interaction after reinforcement.

An important difference from trait assessment is the emphasis on overt behavior, using observers rather than questionnaires, interviews, projective tests, or other more indirect techniques. The aim is clearly that the behavior should "speak for itself," without the need for any inference about why it occurred, the feelings that accompanied it, or any trait that caused it.

The purpose is also to observe the behavior continuously, rather than to summarize it as one might do by questionnaire or peer judgments. Note, however, that although the assessment is based on much more data than is the usual trait measure, it is still based on a sample rather than the whole. The pattern of interaction observed for the 5-day period was considered to be typical of Ann's interactions with adults and children. Her behavior was described in the article as having developed within a few days of beginning nursery school and as being well established after 6 weeks of school, when the formal 5-day observation was done. The rationale for the behavior modification is obviously that the behavior would have continued if not modified. Thus, the 5 mornings of observation are treated as a sample of all the other days.

Another major difference from trait measurement is the attention paid to the stimuli preceding or accompanying the responses. Ann was not described simply as alone or interacting but as interacting with one class of persons or another (adults or children). It is implicit that these classes of people are discriminative stimuli for different responses, and indeed Ann was described as "isolating herself from children and [seeking] the attention of adults" (p. 512). The precise goal was not to describe how isolated or outgoing Ann was, but rather *with whom she did or did not interact*. In addition to recording various stimulus conditions, there was some attempt to differentiate among responses—for example, proximity versus interaction. Finally, there were at least anecdotal descriptions of the reinforcement consequences of various stimulus-response combinations:

> The teachers responded warmly to Ann whenever she contacted them and remained in conversation with her for as long as she desired. When she stood about alone, they usually went to her and tried to get her into play with children. If they succeeded, they left shortly, to allow Ann to play freely with other children. All too frequently, Ann was "out" again as soon as the teacher left, standing on the periphery, soliciting teacher attention, or playing alone [p. 516].

In short, the method of assessment is perfectly consistent with the social paradigm—in this case, particularly with Skinner's social-learning theory. It focuses on environmental influences and identifies situational rather than individual differences. There is no inference about traits and very little about any internal processes (the latter, for example, does occur when it is strongly implied that Ann wanted attention from adults). Because these methods differ from trait assessment in the individual paradigm, the validation procedure will differ. How to validate social-behavior measures will be the main topic of this chapter. First, however, it might be a good idea to point out some defects in the procedure while the case is still fresh in our minds.

Problems with the Observation of Ann

Although some stimulus differences were noted, others were ignored. Only behavior in the morning at the nursery school was observed. Ann was not observed at home. We do not know if she had siblings or neighborhood friends, or how she interacted with children and adults in other settings. Thus, when Ann is described as exhibiting "a low rate of social interaction with her peers" (p. 511), this should have been qualified by adding "in the nursery school setting." In general, we do not know how good this sample of Ann's behavior is, or how well it represents her typical behavior, in school or out.

There is also a practical question of how continuous such observation is, or should even try to be. Even assuming that a determined observer can watch *constantly* for up to 2 hours, the behaviors within any observation interval were not fully differentiated. Behaviors were broken into 10-second units, during which time Ann could be described as near both an adult and a child, but not both near someone and alone. The latter would occur, for example, whenever Ann was joined by someone during the 10-second interval. There is no description of how such transition periods were counted (whether as alone or as interacting); yet how this problem was resolved by the observers clearly influenced the final percentages.

Further, although the behavior was classified into three categories (proximity, interacting, alone), only interacting and alone are reported on the summary graph. We do not know whether proximity was subsequently counted as interaction or simply left out.

There is another area in which specificity was intended but not actually obtained. Recall that the reinforcement consequences of Ann's behaviors were assumed but not assessed formally. The conclusion that she did increase interactions with her peers in the experimental part of the study is not convincing evidence of the unobserved previous reinforcement contingencies. Even the new reinforcement pattern was not systematically observed, so we have no strict evidence that it was implemented as described. An important situational variable was left to informal impression.

Finally, the reliability of the observations is open to some question. Because they are reported in percentages, rather than correlation coefficients, it is difficult to know what the figures represent. Only interjudge reliability was reported, not internal consistency—for example, the consistency of Ann's behavior over the 5 days before treatment began. For the interjudge reliability, the two judges matched their observations under conditions different from their usual procedure. That is, they usually observed only half the morning, but on the days when reliability was checked, they observed for the full 4 hours. We do not know when during the course of the study the reliability was checked between judges. It appears to have been before treatment only; yet Ann's behavior became more variable after treatment, and observation may have become more difficult. Since the observers undoubtedly knew when treatment began, the potential for observer bias also exists. Finally, we do not know if the two observers randomly varied the half of the morning each observed, or whether one observer always did the first half and the other the second half. In summary, there are many questions about the assessment procedure unanswered in the published report. None of us could repeat this procedure with only the article in hand.

There is a great variety in social-behavior measures. The kind of direct observation illustrated above is probably the most common and the most attractive to social-learning theorists. But the practice of such assessment is far from standardized (for example, Kanfer, 1972), and one may also encounter structured interviews or experiments, diaries kept by the individuals recording their own daily or weekly activities, checklists of typical behaviors, and even automatic recording by cameras or other mechanical devices. The whole field is in urgent need of a thorough organizing and categorizing review, which is beyond the scope of this book. Meanwhile, Mischel (1968, Chapters 7 and 8) and Wiggins (1973, also Chapters 7 and 8) are good introductory sources of information. H. F. Wright (1960) and Weick (1968) are detailed sources on observation as a particular technique. It is interesting but not coincidental that virtually the earliest observational studies were conducted by Lewin and his students (for example, Lewin, Lippitt, & White, 1939; Barker, Dembo, & Lewin, 1941; Barker & Wright, 1949, 1951, 1955). The social paradigm leads inevitably to the assessment of behavior in situations.

SIGN VERSUS SAMPLE

The essential difference between assessment in the individual and in the social paradigm is the inference made from the assessment. In trait assessment, any response is treated as a *sign* of the hypothetical trait; that is, it serves to indicate the degree to which the person "has" a certain amount of the trait being measured. For example, the amount of agreement with items on the F scale is meant to be interpreted as a sign of the amount of the construct, authoritarianism. The behavior, marking "yes" or "agree" on the paper, is only of interest to the extent that is does indeed reflect this trait.

In contrast, the social theorist makes a different inference from behavior—namely, that it is a *sample* of the person's responses to various situations. Ideally, the social-behavior assessor would like a complete census of all behaviors by the individual in all situations, plus the responses of others to these behaviors. Since this is seldom practical, a sample of behaviors in a sample of situations is used.

The distinction between treating behavior as a sign and treating it as a sample goes back to Goodenough (1949). Loevinger (1957) explains it as follows:

> In referring to some test responses as signs, Goodenough meant that they represented and indicated the presence of traits and of other behavior which they did not resemble. In referring to test responses as samples, Goodenough was describing tests in which the items are essentially similar to the behavior which it is desired to predict [p. 644].

As the social model has emerged, the distinction has become more important and more explicit:

> In one sense, all psychological approaches are based on behavioral observation: check marks on MMPI answer sheets and stories in response to inkblots obviously are behaviors just as much as crying or running or fighting. . . . The difference between approaches depends on how these

behaviors are used. [In the individual paradigm] the observed behaviors serve as highly indirect *signs* (symptoms) of the dispositions and motives that might underlie them. In contrast, in [social] behavior assessments the observed behavior is treated as a *sample,* and interest is focused on how the specific sampled behavior is affected by alterations in conditions. Behavioral approaches thus seek to directly assess stimulus-response covariations [Mischel, 1976, pp. 199-200].

Both kinds of assessment involve inference: the behavior is used as a means to an end. The ends are quite different, however, because the basic conception of human nature differs for individual and social theorists. The former hold that inherent individual differences determine behavior; therefore, they seek to infer these characteristics from a person's behavior. The latter hold that external, situational differences cause behavior; therefore, they seek to make inferences about situation-behavior relations in the life of the person being assessed. In this case, the inference is from the observed sample of behaviors and situations to a conclusion about typical behaviors in all such situations.

Recall that validation was described (page 93) as any objective way to answer the question: does the procedure measure what it says it measures? We cannot legitimately ask whether a social-behavior measure validly measures a personality trait (construct validity, as in Chapter 12), because such measures do not claim to measure traits or any other constructs. They claim to measure "stimulus-response covariations." With two such different kinds of measures in mind, a broader conception of validation seems appropriate. The purpose of personality measurement is to make inferences from behavior. Different kinds of measurement make different inferences and are used for different purposes. Therefore, the more precise questions underlying validation become: Can the assessment procedure be used for this particular purpose? Is the inference made from the measure justified? It follows that different kinds of validation will be required for measures that have different purposes—that is, from which different inferences will be made (see also pages 270-271).

An assessment such as the observation of Ann aims to measure behaviors that are a sample of the total behaviors of interest. This total set of behaviors is sometimes called the *population,* the *universe,* or the *domain* of behavior. The behaviors actually observed, as well as the assessment procedure itself, are called a *sample* of the domain of behaviors. This means that they have the relation of a part to the whole. The term *universe* is a bit misleading: the whole does not have to be *all* behaviors. The total set of interest may be, as in the case of Ann, only behaviors having to do with social interaction, only in the nursery school setting, and further differentiated by the stimuli that precede or accompany them (the presence of children or adults, and their responses). Thus the 5 mornings of observation of Ann's proximity to and interaction with adults and children were intended to sample Ann's typical interactions with adults and children in that setting. The inference made was clearly that Ann usually interacted more with adults than with other children. That is, an inference was made from the sample to the whole.

The assessment procedure is valid if that inference is justified. This kind of validity is called *content validity*, because it focuses on the actual content of the test—that is, on the behaviors themselves, rather than on any construct to be inferred from them:

> Evidence of content validity is required when the test user wishes to estimate how an individual performs in a universe of situations the test is intended to represent [*Standards for Educational and Psychological Tests*, 1974, p. 28].

The earliest kinds of assessment procedures for which content validity was required were achievement tests—spelling, reading, math, or any school test. The universe of situations might be, for example, all the problems in a fourth-grade arithmetic book. Some of these are randomly sampled for the test, and the student's total performance in arithmetic is inferred from performance on that sample. What this test has in common with behavioral assessments of personality is that observation of a sample of responses to a certain situation is used to infer what all responses would have been, had all of them been observed. No trait or construct (such as ability) is inferred. The universe of situations might be divided into distinctly different sets of situations, especially if we expect that responses will vary according to situation. One situation, or kind of stimulus, might be simple addition, another, long division, and so forth. Then there will not be one single "score" for the person being assessed but potentially different assessments for each of the situations observed.

In other words, a content-valid measure asks simply: what does the individual usually do? Thus, this kind of validity suits behavioral assessment, in which the same question is being asked, but about social behavior rather than school performance.

An example may make clear the difference between content and construct validity in personality assessment. Suppose we observe an individual in a group discussion, sampling the amount of time this particular person talks. If this number is interpreted as a measure of the individual's social dominance, then a personality trait is being inferred from the behavior. This construct would have to be validated by procedures such as those outlined in Chapter 12. On the other hand, the sample of talking time might be used to infer how talkative the individual is in group discussions. This use infers a universe of behavior from a sample of behavior; therefore, it requires content validity. The validation process would emphasize the adequacy of sampling of group discussion situations, as well as how the talking responses were sampled within the particular discussion observed.

Assessment within the social paradigm virtually always implies content validity. The assessment procedure represents a sample of the behavior of interest. Indeed, the only difference between the measured behavior and the inferred behavior is that one is the observed part, or sample, and the other is the unobserved whole, or universe.

What about reliability? As will be seen shortly, certain kinds of reliability apply to all measurements. And, as was obvious in Chapter 12, reliability blends naturally into validity, since it too depends on the assumptions behind the assessment procedure—that is, on the conceptual paradigm within which the measure exists.

STANDARDS FOR RELIABILITY

Objectivity is necessary for any measurement. Therefore, interjudge reliability must be demonstrated for social-behavior measures. This is particularly important when observers are watching, categorizing, and recording classes of behavior as the behavior occurs. We require evidence that the observer saw the behavior of interest, categorized it correctly, and recorded this accurately. In short, we need to know how the scores came to be and that they can be independently verified. Wiggins (1973, p. 376) points out that it is surprising how often the advocates of functional analysis and of radical behaviorism rely on subjective impressions of behavior, rather than on controlled and demonstrably objective observation. Recall that a key variable in the case of Ann, the teachers' reinforcing behavior, was based only on impressions, not on systematic observation.

In order to demonstrate interjudge reliability, the researcher must specify a set of rules for observation in such a way that independent observers can use them. Two or more observers must then apply the assessment procedure to the same ongoing behavior without consulting one another. Their agreement is a measure of how explicit, public, and objective the observation is. A loss of accuracy (reliability) here is a severe handicap. If two trained observers do not agree, then the procedures are not replicable, and they are probably also unclear, contradictory, or otherwise inadequate. Each judge is not trying to guess what the other one is writing down; each is trying to apply the same assessment procedure to the case at hand.

Many of the problems of obtaining satisfactory reliability are too particular to a given assessment procedure to be discussed here. Some general problems can be described, however. The situation in which reliability is checked should be typical of the situations in which observations are made without checking reliability. That is, unless two or more observers are used all the time, care must be taken that the reliability check is made on typical behavior. An example would be dual observation only at the beginning of the assessment, when it is unfamiliar to everyone, including the subject. Many people might restrict their behavior until they got used to being observed, after which they might behave more variably. Early reliability checks would be unrealistically high because of the limited range of behaviors emitted.

Obviously, one observer should not be able to see what the other is doing. When the recording consists of marking or not marking a category of behavior, as is frequently the case, then the observers should not be able to take clues from each other's actions that a recordable event has occurred. Other demonstrable artifacts affecting reliability are described by Reid (1970) and Taplin and Reid (1973).

Finally, the method of evaluating reliability is often problematic. If the data consist of a range of numbers—for example, the degree of attentiveness or the intensity of reinforcement—then the correlation coefficient can be used, and inferences about the amount of error can be made as described in Chapter 12. However, many or even most behavioral observations are dichotomous or qualitative. For example, the behavior occurred or it did not, or one of several possible behaviors occurred. Such data are not readily amenable to correlational statistics and are usually reported in percentages, as in the case of Ann. Percentages do not tell us the proportion of error in the measurement, as correlations do (see page 96). They are merely descriptive statistics, with no general properties or interpretations.

As Bijou, Peterson, Harris, Allen, and Johnson (1969, pp. 194-199) point out, even how to calculate these percentages is not clear. We can guess that the reliability percentages reported by Allen et al. (1964) for the observation of Ann represented the number of 10-second intervals for which the observers made the same mark (for example, Ann was in proximity to a child) divided by the total number of 10-second intervals of observation that day. This method may result in highly inflated percentages, however, because many intervals are easy to agree upon—for example, when Ann plays alone for a half-hour. The observers' ability to judge is not being taxed as much during such periods as when Ann is near others or approaching and leaving them quickly.

Another method that Bijou and colleagues describe in their article—and one that is in common use—is to have observers record over a longer period, without subdivision into intervals, and compare the total number of incidents recorded. For example, one observer might record 10 disruptive acts and the other observer, 8. By this method, one can only put the smaller over the larger number and report 80% agreement. First, this figure is quite arbitrary; it merely avoids the embarrassment of 10/8 = 125% agreement. Using the higher figure as the base of the percentage must assume that the observer who recorded more incidents was more correct; the other observer recorded only 80% of them. Second, and more fundamentally, the figure does not tell us whether or not the observers are reporting the same incidents. They might easily have recorded different behaviors but ended up with similar numbers.

Bijou et al. (1969) discuss but do not resolve this problem, and there are clearly deficiencies in present procedures. For example, in a study taken at random from a recent journal, Zlutnick, Mayville, and Moffat (1975), in assessing epilepticlike seizures prior to and after behavior modification, report at least 90% agreement on five subjects. The procedure for obtaining this reliability was as follows: two observers watched for one hour or more, until six seizures (which might be only "vacant staring") had been recorded, and then computed the smaller-over-larger percentage described above. With such infrequent behavior, it is highly likely that the observers could observe each other recording. Since sometimes one was a trained observer and the other a parent, it is plausible that the parent followed the lead of the trained observer in recording. Furthermore, the rest of the assessment was done by one observer, up to 6 consecutive hours a day! The authors imply that the subject could get out of sight of the observer during the main assessment periods, when reliability was not being checked. The subjects had good reason to do so: they were being punished for the seizures. The point is that, even with a relatively simple and dramatic behavior such as a seizure, the interjudge reliability as reported is inadequate.

A further problem is the random probability of agreement. Suppose that two observers are to say only whether a behavior occurred or not. Suppose, for the purpose of illustration, that neither observer even watches the subject but merely flips a coin at the end of every recording interval to decide whether the behavior occurred or not. If heads, the behavior occurred; if tails, the behavior did not occur. Then the two observers might, for any particular recording interval, have the following results:

Observer #1	Observer #2
heads	heads
tails	tails
heads	tails
tails	heads

In short, they will agree 50% of the time. If we have no other way of knowing whether the behavior occurred or not, we must focus on their agreement, not their accuracy. To give a more extreme but more plausible example, suppose that both observers know that the behavior occurs frequently—say, 90% of the time. The best strategy for agreement would be to record that the behavior occurred *all the time*. The interjudge agreement would be 100%; each observer would be right 90% of the time; and the observers would both agree and both be right .9 times .9, or 81% of the time. That's not bad for pure guesswork. (Such issues are discussed in the field called signal detection; see, for example, Galanter, 1962, especially pp. 94-114.)

CONTENT VALIDATION

Once objectively reliable measures have been demonstrated, we must start to ask whether they have content validity. A behavioral assessment will have content validity to the extent that it is an *adequate* sample of a *specified* domain. That is, the assessor must tell us what was the intended domain of behaviors and/or situations and how the sampling was conducted in order to justify a generalization to that domain. It is generally agreed that content validation is at present more a logical than an empirical procedure. It depends primarily on the assessor's being explicit, clear, and sensible about the procedure—and on our judgment of how well this has been done. There is, however, some role for empirical testing of content validity of behavioral assessments.

Defining the Domain of Behaviors

Let's hypothetically redo the observation method for the case of Ann so as to establish content validity. The domain should be specified as the social-interactive behaviors of the child in the nursery school during free-play periods (to exclude the structured activities, home activities, and other categories of behavior, such as aggression, dependency, and so on). The categories of interacting and alone could be the target behaviors, but made into a continuum (to facilitate reliability calculations as well as to provide more precise information), as follows:

1. Alone—actively excluding others: withdrawing or turning away from, keeping her back to an adult or child or both; for example, when Ann was described as having "retired to a make-believe bed in a packing box in the play yard to 'sleep' for several minutes" (Allen et al., 1964, p. 512).
2. Alone—passively excluding others: remaining at some distance from others, while engaged in a solitary activity at which she could be joined if someone else initiated it; for example, gathering pebbles (p. 513).
3. Proximity: physical closeness not required by the size of the area; for example, hanging around someone without interacting.
4. Interaction—acceptance: responding to an interaction initiated by someone else (where refusal would be actively excluding others, as above).
5. Interaction—continuing: after the interaction begins, count this category as long as it continues.
6. Interaction—initiation: actively seeking an interaction with another.

The major stimuli of interest are (1) adult and child as discriminative stimuli and (2) adult attention as a presumed reinforcer. Thus, when Ann is interacting, we would note whether this interaction includes an adult, a child, or both. Judgment would be required when, for example, Ann is talking to an adult with a child standing nearby, listening. This might be counted as interaction with an adult, as the other child is merely a bystander. The converse would be true when an adult is watching Ann play with a child. Only when both adult and child are participants in the interaction would both be judged to be the discriminative stimuli. Obviously some training would be required to enable judges to make this subtle distinction. Note that Ann could be initiating interaction with an adult while actively excluding a child.

The adult reinforcement also requires definition and judgment. The class of adult behaviors defined as reinforcing might include anything from attention to praise. It might include withdrawal of reinforcement, such as leaving Ann's presence either physically or socially (for example, starting to talk to someone else), and of course, not being there at all. Perhaps reinforcement could be put on a continuum from negative through neutral to intensely positive. A Premack-type hierarchy (see pages 193-194) would be the best procedure.

All of the above is an effort to define the domain of behaviors and stimuli to be assessed. I cannot emphasize strongly enough that it is only an armchair effort to revise the original observation system for Ann. Actual use would undoubtedly dictate many additions, decisions, and changes until a final workable version was ready for use. The principal goals of the revision are to put the behaviors on a meaningful continuum, to continue to specify stimuli, and to add explicit observation of adult reinforcement. Interjudge reliability could be measured by correlation, except for the adult/child/both distinction. The latter could be treated conservatively by assessing the percentage of agreements when a stimulus is relevant—that is, not counting those cases when the child is passively excluding others (when no social stimulus is recorded).

Having defined the domain of behaviors and situations, a time period for which the assessment is intended to be valid must also be stated. The choice between, say, 1 day and 6 weeks has implications for how stable the behavior is assumed to be. Since the original study had assumed that Ann's behavior was stable, several weeks would be an appropriate period. Several years would be inappropriate, as most social theorists would assume that change would be very likely over such a long period. In summary, the assessment would aim to describe Ann's behaviors of a specified kind, in specified situations, with specified consequences, over a specified time period.

Sampling Behavior

Next, the behavior must be sampled. Continuous observation might be possible with "relays" of observers, but it would be an unwieldy operation. Note that continuous means literally all the time, without the convenience of 10-second intervals. A "real-time" recording system, such as holding down the appropriate lever to record marks on a continuous moving tape, would be required. If, however, we assume some short-term stability and consistency in Ann's behavior, then sampling becomes possible. That is, we can assume that an appropriate part will be like the whole. It is not necessary to assume that Ann's behavior is unvarying—indeed, the inclusion of stimuli and reinforcers implies the opposite. But it is necessary to specify in advance which stimuli will cause behavioral variations, so that these can be recorded. It is impossible to record everything, and some hypothesis about the major situational variables must guide the observation. This might come from a theory, or from previous, informal observation, but it must finally be examined formally. This is, after all, a main purpose of assessment in the social paradigm: to examine situational influences on behavioral variation.

The usual method of sampling in behavioral assessment is time sampling—that is, observing some period of time less than the whole. This was implicit in the case of Ann, where 5 mornings stood for an unspecified longer period. It is also possible to sample events (for example, H. F. Wright, 1960, pp. 104-108)—that is, to observe continuously but to record only predetermined events such as quarrels, games, laughing, crying, or playing with other children.

Assuming that we decide to sample times from the entire period of interest, the question is how to sample adequately—that is, in such a way as to obtain a good representation of the whole. A sampling procedure that to some degree spans the entire period of interest is preferable to the concentrated sampling of 5 days used in the case of Ann. A *random* sample of appropriate time units across the entire period of interest is the ideal. A nonrandom concentration of units within the period, such as the 5-day series for Ann, has obvious bias and cannot claim to represent the entire period. Other systematic, nonrandom time-sampling methods, in which the subject is observed every X minutes, have been shown to be discrepant from continuous observation of the same period (Thomson, Holmberg, & Baer, 1974).

The number of time units to be sampled depends principally on the variability of the behavior or situations being sampled. If there is little variability, then a small sample will do. If variability is greater, then more samples must be taken to obtain a true picture. For example, if Ann were totally withdrawn, never interacting with anyone, then a single sample would be a true picture of the entire period. If, on the other hand, Ann's behavior were totally unpredictable, changing minute by minute from isolated to intensely social, then continuous observation would be required. Most behavior is somewhere between these two extremes, and the sampling frequency must be chosen accordingly.

There is also a second, more microscopic level of sampling to be considered. What size should the sampled time intervals themselves be? If, for example, the observer takes a "snapshot" approach and records the behavior occurring at a particular instant, then the sampled time interval is very small. As a result, some behaviors cannot occur within it; for example, it is difficult to judge whether or not "helpfulness" occurred within a fraction of a particular second. If, on the other hand, the sampled interval is too large, too many behaviors will occur within it and information will be lost. The size of the sampled interval must be suited to the behavioral unit of interest. Again, hypothesis and experience will help the decision.

As noted at the beginning of this section, content validation is more a logical than an empirical procedure. It is built into the assessment procedure, rather than evaluated afterwards. The construction of a content-valid assessment procedure can only be achieved by constantly asking oneself: what is it that I want to measure, and why? The solution to any particular problem will be dictated by the best answer to that question. It is vital that these decisions and their rationale be a part of the published report, so that others can judge whether the procedure is valid for their purposes as well.

There are, however, some empirical aids. Obviously, interjudge reliability can be measured empirically. The homogeneity and stability of behaviors within the period of interest can also be measured by other reliability procedures. For example, if the behavior is assumed to be homogeneous, as was clearly implied for Ann's preference for adult over child interaction, then the internal consistency of such behaviors should be high. This would mean that, at any particular time, the responses should be similar. Alternatively, the same amount of consistency might be expected across time. That is, the proportion of adult to child interactions would be expected to be stable across the period of interest. Thus, while perfect homogeneity and unlimited stability are not expected by social theorists, some specified degree of each can be expected and empirically assessed.

THE STATUS OF SOCIAL-BEHAVIOR ASSESSMENT

No final statement can be made about the current, overall reliability and validity of social-behavior assessments. Two tentative conclusions, however, can be drawn.

First, although the general paradigm behind such assessments is now clear, the actual techniques used have little uniformity. Each investigator seems to use a new procedure designed for a new subject. It is not possible even to survey all the techniques available, much less to begin to make summary statements about particular techniques as was done for the single-trait theories (Chapter 13). In other words, our knowledge is not accumulating.

A fortunate exception to this lack of uniformity is the Behavioral Coding System, reviewed by Jones, Reid, and Patterson (1975). This observational system is aimed particularly at the measurement of aggressive behaviors in family interaction. The authors review the development, rationale, and problems of their procedure. They present some evidence on its reliability, emphasizing the problems in obtaining and maintaining interjudge reliability (pp. 73-80). Unfortunately, these authors seem to argue for content, construct, and other validities all at once (pp. 82-88), so that it is not clear exactly which kind they mean to establish. It is, however, a large step forward in terms of standardization and detailed consideration of practical problems to be solved.

Second, the standards for evaluating such assessment procedures are clear, but their implementation is not. Nothing comparable to Campbell and Fiske's explicit and orderly standards exists for these techniques. We do know that a different kind of validity is required, but the application of this validity standard is not well developed. Furthermore, most of those who practice behavior-modification techniques based on the social paradigm seem unaware of the appropriate validity standards and have even exempted themselves from validity issues. Yet a measurement procedure of unknown or doubtful reliability and validity cannot have any clinical utility.

The field, in short, requires not only a systematic review but a conceptual breakthrough that will facilitate the validation of its assessment procedures. Behavioral assessment may or may not be the bright new answer to problems in personality assessment, as many have claimed (for example, Bersoff, 1973; Goldfried & Kent, 1972; Mischel, 1968). Criticism within the field can also be found (see, for example, Goldfried & Pomeranz, 1968; Parton & Ross, 1965; and other references in this chapter). We will not know if their promise is well founded until these procedures have shown themselves to be reliable and valid.

The current state of the field is well summarized by Johnson and Bolstad:

> If a behaviorist wants to convince someone of the correctness of his approach . . .it is most likely that he will show his behavioral data with the intimation that this data speaks eloquently for itself. Because he is aware of the research on the low level of generalizability of behavior across settings (e.g., see Mischel, 1968), he is likely to be more confident of this data as it becomes more naturalistic in character, i.e., as it reflects naturally occurring

behavior in the subject's usual habitat. As a perusal of the behavior modification literature will indicate, these data are often extremely persuasive. Yet, the apparent success of behavior modification and the enthusiasm that this success breeds may cause all of us to take an uncritical approach in evaluating the *quality* of that data on which the claims of success are based. A critical review of the naturalistic data in behavior modification research will reveal that most of it is gathered under circumstances in which a host of confounding influences can operate to yield invalid results. The observers employed are usually aware of the nature, purpose, and expected results of the observation. The observed are also usually aware of being watched, and often they also know the purpose and expected outcome of the observation. The procedures for gathering and computing data on observer agreement or accuracy are inappropriate or irrelevant to the purposes of the investigation. There is almost never an indication of the reliability of the dependent variable under study. . . . Thus, by the standards employed in some other areas of psychological research, it can be charged that much behavior modification research data is subject to observer bias, observee reactivity, fakability, demand characteristics, response sets, and decay in instrumentation.[1] In addition, the accuracy, reliability, and validity of the data used [are] often unknown or inadequately established [1973, pp. 7-8].[2]

No one can escape certain minimum standards for research evidence; these are the ground rules of psychology. Johnson and Bolstad go on to examine in detail the problems they have named and to suggest solutions. It is a prescription for work yet to be completed.

[1]"Instrument decay" is a rather vivid way of describing changes in recording standards or precision over time. For example, observers have been shown to become less accurate when they believe that their reliability is not being checked (Reid, 1970). In this sense, the instrument of measurement (observation) decays, especially if the reliability is checked only at the beginning of the study, as is usual.

[2]From "Methodological Issues in Naturalistic Observation: Some Problems and Solutions for Field Research," by S.M. Johnson and O.D. Bolstad. In L.A. Hamerlynck, L.C. Handy, and E.J. Mash (Eds.), *Behavior Change: Methodology, Concepts and Practice.* Copyright 1973 by Research Press. Reprinted by permission.

Part 3

Current Issues
and Prospects

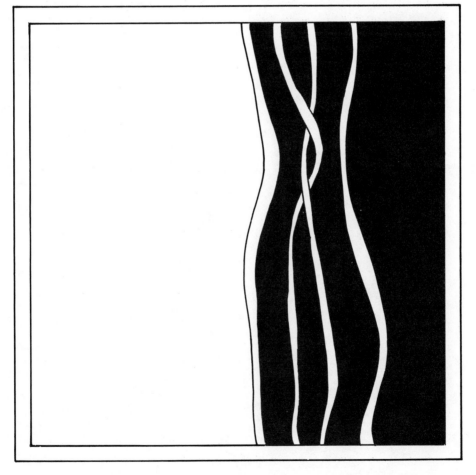

23

Individual versus
Social Theories

The most important recent development in personality theory has been the clear awareness of two different families of theories—the individual and the social. To the extent that these rival paradigms encompass all the important personality theories, they simplify the field in two significant ways. First, once we have identified a theory as individual or social, we can quickly and easily go beyond its particulars to its more basic and general assumptions about personality. These characteristic differences between the two paradigms will be reviewed and contrasted in this chapter. Second, an appreciation of the essential differences between the two paradigms enables us to design studies that test the two head-on against each other, at least on some issues. The next chapter will introduce such designs, and the chapter after that will consider the possibility of an empirical and theoretical compromise between the two positions.

FIVE MAJOR DIFFERENCES

Two of the contrasting assumptions of individual and social personality theories have been stressed throughout this book. Three others follow as consequences of the second assumption.

Internal versus External Factors

The first premise has to do with where the personality is located. Individual theories hold that personality is *inside* the individual. That is, all individuals have certain intrapsychic characteristics that determine their behavior: an unconscious, traits, needs, self-concept, personal constructs, and so on. In contrast, social theories describe important determining events *outside* the individual as well: stimulus, reinforcer, model, events that become regions in the life space, and the like.

233

Most individual theories have no formal terms for environmental phenomena. All personality theories acknowledge, informally, that the environment makes a difference. But with most individual theories, this observation remains casual and anecdotal. Precisely how the environment influences personality is not spelled out by these theories. This emphasis on formal terminology may seem pedantic, but it is necessary. The main advantage of any theory is that it goes beyond informal, common-sense description to make definite statements. Vague notions should become precise definitions and principles. Formal terminology both facilitates the accurate communication of the theory to others and enables the theory to be empirically tested. We must hold, therefore, that individual theories do not include the effects of the environment. This is not necessarily a defect, only a difference from the social theories. This difference will ultimately be resolved by the evidence—that is, by what concepts are necessary to account for human behavior.

Of all the major social theories, only Skinner's, being substantively behaviorist, has no formal terms for intrapsychic phenomena. The other theories add the environment to the individual, rather than replacing one with the other. Concepts such as drive, self-reinforcement, and quasi-need are inside the individual, just as with individual theories.

In addition, social theories have terms for phenomena that are neither completely individual nor completely environmental but incorporate both: Reinforcement and incentive refer both to the individual's desires and to an environmental event. The life space is a representation of the individual in the environment. Observational learning requires both an observer and a model. Finally, as noted at the outset, social theories have some terms that refer exclusively to the environment. By scanning the basic terminology of any personality theory, one should be able to identify it as individual or social, depending on whether only individual or individual-plus-social factors are included.

Individual versus Situational Differences

The second major assumption that divides individual and social theories is the emphasis on individual versus situational differences. Any theory of personality must explain why people act differently from one another—why there is not one standard personality for all human beings. The individual theories propose that, by adulthood, individuals are inherently different from one another. People behave differently because there are different kinds of people. Usually, though not necessarily, these differences are cast as nomothetic traits. This means that all individuals can be placed somewhere on a common dimension that identifies their behavior with regard to this trait. Social theories of personality propose that variations in behavior arise because of current variations in situations—reinforcement contingency, learning experience, life space, and so on.

Strictly speaking, individual and situational differences fall on a continuum rather than being dichotomous. The rare theory that emphasizes hereditary differences is implicitly proposing differences that are totally inside the individual, unaffected by the environment. But most individual theories, such as Rogers's and Freud's, suggest that individual differences arise out of early childhood experiences. Frustration, satiation, or conditions of worth leave their permanent mark. The question therefore becomes not whether the environment has any influence, but *when* that influence operates.

Individual theories explicitly or implicitly propose an early period of massive environmental influence, while the personality is developing. Thereafter, and especially in adults, the effects of this early developmental influence are considered virtually permanent. (The only change-producing event in adult life that these theories systematically propose is psychotherapy.) Thus, environmental differences in childhood become individual differences in adults. Social theories simply extend this early period of influence from childhood throughout life. They assume that environmental forces continue to act on individuals, so that individuals continue to change and differ from one another according to situational differences. At no point are these differences considered permanent. If the environment remains the same, the individual may appear to "be" a certain way. But according to a social theory, this appearance should not obscure the constant possibility of change introduced by a changing environment.

Stability versus Change

These contrasting views on individual versus situational differences lead to a third point that divides individual and social theories. After the personality has developed, an individual theory emphasizes and predicts stability, whereas a social theory emphasizes and predicts change.

Recall that individual differences are only meaningful if they persist over some period of time; otherwise, they might as well be chance or situational fluctuations in behavior. Thus, for example, individual theories expect substantial test/retest reliability, which is a measure of temporal stability, in any assessments of individual differences. Social theories and assessments, on the other hand, expect changes in behavior on the assumption that, as time passes, the situation will probably change. For example, psychotherapy by behavior modification is not assumed to have a permanent effect unless the conditions that maintain the new behavior can be made permanent. Traditional psychotherapy, on the other hand, is assumed to change the personality and, therefore, to be permanent in its effect.

Cross-situational Consistency versus Situational Specificity

The importance or unimportance of the situation in maintaining behavior over time is closely related to the fourth major difference between the two paradigms. Individual theories assume that behavior is fairly general across situations, whereas social theories assume that behavior is quite specific to the situation.

Individual differences are not only stable but general—that is, manifest in any relevant situation. People should be cross-situationally consistent. This is why, for example, convergent validity must be demonstrated. An oral character type, low self-esteem, or cerebrotonic temperament is each supposed to pervade the individual's behavior. One particular method, such as a standardized personality measure, may be a convenient way to assess the personality, but it is not supposed to be the only way. The trait should reveal itself in a wide variety of behaviors in different situations. This is precisely why the trait is worth measuring, because of its presumably broad predictive power.

In contrast, social theories do not expect so much generalization. They focus on the changes in the situation that can evoke wholly different behaviors—for example, how discrimination learning takes place; which behavior is modeled; or how the regions of the life space are related. Behavior should be situationally specific. As we have seen, social-behavior measures include the situation as an important factor. This is why social theories emphasize change rather than stability: with the passage of time, an individual's situation often changes; if it does, then the behavior is likely to change as well.

Just as the individual theorist is obliged to expect stability and generality of individual differences, it falls to the social theorist to predict when and how specificity and concomitant change will occur. These two kinds of prediction, which follow from the emphasis on individual versus situational differences in the two paradigms, lead to the fifth major difference, which is methodological.

Correlational versus Experimental Methods of Research

In order to ask the kinds of questions that their theories require them to ask, individual and social theorists usually must use different research methods—namely, correlational versus experimental methods. These refer to the general research procedures, not necessarily to the specific statistical analysis afterwards. An *experimental* design is one in which the independent variable is deliberately produced and randomly applied to subjects. In *correlational* design, the major variable is found as it exists—in the case of personality traits, as a characteristic of the subjects themselves.

To understand why the individual theorist uses correlational methods and the social theorist uses experimental methods, consider the nature of the essential proposition each is testing. The individual theorist assumes that individual differences are stable and general. To test this assumption, we cannot simply observe one response and declare that to be the individual's typical response. The same response must be shown to occur in a different situation or at a different time. Thus, the various first responses made by a group of individuals should be the same, for each individual, the second time they are measured. For example, highly anxious persons, as identified by their responses when first measured, should be highly anxious according to their responses on any subsequent measurement. Moderately anxious and nonanxious individuals should show the same consistency of responses. They should not suddenly make responses typical of highly anxious individuals, nor vice versa. The essential design amounts to observing whether responses agree for two different times or situations. This is often called response/response or R-R research because the two sets of responses are being compared (and usually correlated statistically). The situation, whether held constant, varied, or ignored, is not supposed to matter and is not, therefore, an essential element of the design.

The social theorist, on the other hand, proposes that the situation very much matters and aims to demonstrate changes in response attributable to the situation. Typically, then, some people are treated to one situation and some to another. Which individuals experience which situations must be determined randomly, so that any differences in response between groups of people can be attributed to the difference in situations. For example, some children might be reinforced for agreeing with an adult, and others for disagreeing. If the two groups then show different amounts of agreement, according to their reinforcement contingency, then a situational difference has been shown. This kind of research design emphasizes the correlation of a situation (or stimulus) to the response and is sometimes called S-R research, in contrast to R-R research. S-R research can be done with individuals as well as with groups. One individual may experience both situations, in which case the response at any particular time should correspond to the situation just experienced (for example, learning versus extinction trials). Experimental research requires the investigator to arrange different situations. Correlational research requires the investigator to assess already existing differences in responses.

Although each paradigm tends to use its own method, the choice is dictated solely by the nature of the problem at hand. Individual personality theorists may have occasion to do experimental research. For example, if psychoanalytic theory assumes that everyone learns to repress sexual material, then groups of individuals might be exposed to sexual versus nonsexual stimuli and then tested for recognition or recall (for example, Kline, 1972, Chapter 8; MacKinnon & Dukes, 1962). This is an experimental design, focusing on variations in stimuli, not in individuals. Or a social theory might combine a correlational variable (individual differences) with an experimental variable (situational differences). For example, individual differences among subjects may be assessed before beginning (as in Bandura's modeling studies, page 205); then a situation is introduced to alter or even reverse the original individual differences. But when the main aim is to establish individual differences, correlational design is necessary; when it is to establish situational differences, then an experimental design is preferable.

PSEUDO-DIFFERENCES

A great deal has been written about other supposed differences between the two kinds of designs, and indeed between the two major theoretical paradigms. Cronbach (1957), for example, suggested that historically the two methods, especially as they correspond to two different theoretical paradigms, constitute two different disciplines of scientific psychology. It is therefore worthwhile to consider briefly some ways in which the two major paradigms do *not* differ.

Methodological Rigor

First, there is no virtue in any research method beyond using it appropriately. It is true that random assignment and the creation of known experimental conditions have advantages when causal inferences are important (see Blalock, 1961). But when correlation rather than causation is of interest, and especially when the necessary conditions (such as different personality types) cannot be created experimentally, this difference is irrelevant. A correlational design must and should be used.

The individual theorist using correlational methods is not thereby less rigorous, more humanistic, more intuitive, or a more fuzzy or free-ranging thinker. Nor is the experimental psychologist (in this case the social personality theorist) automatically more precise, surer of cause-effect relations, less interested in individual human beings, or inclined to mistake rats and statistics for people. All these errors and virtues must be earned; they are not bestowed by the choice of a particular method. Many psychologists, including this author, use both methods at different times, and no Jekyll and Hyde changes have been observed!

The Importance of the Individual

Another difference commonly attributed to the two personality paradigms is what might be called the "empty organism" debate. Recall (page 43) that Allport rejected the situationist or social approach because he felt such theories proposed an empty organism pushed and pulled solely by environmental forces, rather than an individual human being with his or her own capacities, thoughts, needs, desires, and self.

This debate between the so-called humanistic and behavioristic approaches has been perpetuated by Rogers and Skinner (1956). In fact, however, the only social personality theory to ignore intrapsychic factors entirely is Skinner's. And to the extent that he cannot account for such phenomena as language or observational learning without invoking cognitions, his theory is inadequate. Each of the other major social theories—Dollard and Miller, Bandura, Lewin—includes purely individual concepts. Dollard and Miller include many of Freud's traditional concepts. Bandura emphasizes the need for "inner" as well as "outer" concepts. Lewin combines social influence with a truly phenomenological approach. Virtually all modern approaches to personality (see Bowers, 1973; Mischel, 1973) include at least cognitive factors. None proposes an empty organism.

This debate seems to arise out of a confusion between (1) the assumption of internal versus external factors and (2) the assumption of individual versus situational differences. Social theories virtually never propose individual differences. If it were true that the only possible intrapsychic qualities were individual differences, then the social theories would be implying an empty organism. But both individual and social theories (except Skinner's) propose internal characteristics that are *universal* rather than varying among individuals (the unconscious, responsiveness to reinforcement, a self, phenomenological experience). They differ only in whether these universal characteristics are exclusively internal and in whether, in some of their essential psychological qualities, individuals differ from one another in ways that are both permanent and pervasive.

A related argument is that individual personality theories respect human individuality and uniqueness, through individual differences, whereas social theories favor an anonymous, deterministic version of human nature. But both kinds of theories assume individual variability in behavior. Neither an individual nor a social theorist would be surprised to see a wide variety of individuality and uniqueness among human beings. The two differ only in how they account for this variation, and in whether they consider it stable and general. They do not differ in whether it occurs. Mischel (1968, pp. 188-190) has described how idiographic behavior can arise from nomothetic social-learning principles. On the other side, Bem and Allen (1974) have pointed out that most traditional assessments of individual differences are not at all idiographic but rather may contain "nomothetic fallacies." All this is not to suggest that the social theorists are really the good guys and the individual theorists the villains. Given the wide variety within each paradigm, the individual and social approaches simply cannot be polarized on the issue of human individuality.

Intuitiveness

Finally, individual personality theories are often described, even by their critics, as more congruent with our intuitions than social personality theories (for example, Bem & Allen, 1974; Mischel, 1968, Chapter 3). It is commonly assumed that we intuitively perceive people as consistent in their behavior across situations and as self-determined rather than situationally determined. Is that your intuition about yourself, your friends, or people in general? There is no evidence that we all have the same intuitions or, even if we do, that these intuitions correspond to the individual paradigm.

The role of intuition in psychology is subtle but important (see Polyani, 1958). Perhaps the issue of what everyone's common intuition might be is irrelevant. But one's own personal intuition is relevant. We are inclined to choose or create theories that develop out of our own intuitions and observations. This is a rich and valuable source of ideas, certainly more interesting and congenial than forcing oneself to adopt an intuitively unappealing though fashionable and authoritative position. Intuition should help to shape and decide how to test a theory, but its truth or falsity must be tested by the appropriate objective evidence. Again, this is a false dichotomy between individual and social theories. Either may be intuitive or not, to different people. But either will be proven or not by proper research.

A Note on Psychology and Human Nature

Before closing, I would like to interject a personal view on two of these pseudo-issues—the empty organism and individuality—which deserve some special comment. These effective, if emotional, arguments are frequent themes of individual personality theories, which are often cast as the last bastions of "individualism." But it is an illusory argument. For one thing, this ignores social theories, notably Lewin's, that fully integrate social influence with the phenomenological individual consciousness. More to the point, an equally frightening caricature could be drawn of the person described by the trait theories: a mindlessly consistent, blind automaton unresponsive to the immediate, surrounding world and incapable of novel action. This "person" cannot tell one situation from another nor one response from another, being programmed (possibly by neuropsychic structures) to behave with unvaried consistency from childhood to death. Obviously, this is no more an accurate representation of individual theories than the "empty organism" is the ideal of most social theories. The latter is no more valid when Skinner defends it than when Allport or Rogers attacks it.

The error that leads to such propaganda on both sides is in believing that one's theoretical position is a complete and final statement on human nature. None of the theories we have encountered encompasses all of human nature; all are tentative bets on where the major causal factors of some behaviors lie. Jumping several vital steps to controversies outside the domain of science is a common fault among psychologists and other scientists, many of whom seem to be incipient philosophers or poets. Viewed as psychology, these are all inaccurate generalizations from the issues and evidence at hand and, as such, produce only endless, sterile arguments full of opinion, not facts or proper theories. A more plodding approach through real issues answerable by specifiable evidence is more likely to yield the kind of progress that psychology can offer in the understanding of human nature.

The rest, as suggested in Chapter 1, is best left to other disciplines or modes of thought, including simple personal belief. I do not mean, however, to portray scientists, including psychologists, as objective, value-free machines for knowledge. As just noted, our intuitions and beliefs should influence our work at certain stages. Moreover, we are entitled to all manner of untested personal opinions—so long as they are not labeled scientific psychology. Indeed, the point is that scientists have a special duty to make the general public understand when they, the scientists, speak as individuals and when they speak in the role of scientist. There is a further duty to make clear which issues science can settle, and which ones it cannot.

24

Person and Situation: Statistical Interaction

Until recently, the study of personality has been virtually dichotomized by the individual/social difference. Empirical studies were either in the individual or in the social format, usually focused on individual or situational differences. This is appropriate when the aim is to examine a particular theory, and the success or failure of a particular theory does contribute some information about the standing of the paradigm to which that theory belongs.

For example, the repeated failure of personality measures to show satisfactory reliability and convergent validity suggests that temporal stability and generality are not easily demonstrated. Mischel's review (1968, Chapter 2) summarizes abundant evidence that these assumptions may not be viable. This has led many psychologists to abandon the individual paradigm for a social approach—for example, to give up personality testing for behavior modification or situational assessment (see Bersoff, 1973). But the logic behind this shift is weak.

First, the failure of some or even a great number of individual differences to show stability and generality does not prove that valid individual differences do not exist. It is logically possible that some individual differences may yet be established. Perhaps, as suggested in Chapter 15, we have only been clearing the ground, eliminating simplistic and relatively easy measurement procedures and will now be forced into better conceptions of assessment. In short, it is hasty and premature to abandon the idea of individual differences *if* one is prepared to look hard at where the old measures may have gone wrong.

There is another reason why it is not logical to embrace situational differences automatically because of the failure of trait measures. *Evidence against the one paradigm is not necessarily evidence for the other.* The low correlations showing poor reliability and convergent validity have often been interpreted as evidence for situational specificity of behavior. But they can just as well be interpreted as evidence of randomness or errors of measurement, or of more complex causes of behavior. If the individuals' scores at one time do not correlate well with their scores at another time, the social theorist may infer that the situation must have changed. But there is no evidence beyond the low correlation: the inference of situational change in this case is circular.

When there is a low convergent validity correlation, the situation has been explicitly changed and can more reasonably be invoked as the cause of the change in scores. But this inference is valid only if everyone's score has changed in the same way—that is, if everyone's score is determined by the situation. There should be a significant difference between group scores in the two situations. Actual evidence of a difference between situations, rather than indirect inference from a low correlation, is needed to justify the situational hypothesis. Yet this evidence is seldom mentioned, much less examined, when the social theorist reinterprets low correlations but does not check differences between means. In any case, unless everyone behaves like everyone else within each situation, these variations among individuals may still be attributed to true individual differences, randomness, errors of measurement, or more complex causes.

This problem illustrates the methodological issue: what is failure (or error variance) in correlational design includes exactly what the social theorist wants to study. Similarly, what is failure (or error variance) in experimental design is not separated from what the individual theorist is interested in. Neither design can deliver good evidence for the other side. In correlational studies, one either finds a sufficient correlation or one does not. Failure is uninformative, as it may be due to situational effects *or* to randomness, errors of measurement, or more complex causes. Similarly, in experimental studies, one either obtains a significant difference between groups or one does not. Failure may be due to (unmeasured) individual differences or to the same alternatives that plague correlational studies: randomness, errors of measurement, or more complex causes. The more complex causes of behavior are precisely the subject of this chapter and the next.

A RESEARCH DESIGN

If the purpose of a particular study is to decide between individual and situational differences, then obviously neither of the usual designs will do. What is needed is all the information missing in either of the usual designs used alone. Both experimental and correlational designs must be combined in the same study, so that the situation is experimentally changed and individual differences are measured as well. This has been done in several studies (see Bowers, 1973, for a summary).

A schematic version of such a design is shown in Figure 24-1a. Each individual is identified as a "1" or a "2" on the trait being studied (for example, extraverted or introverted, or high or low in friendliness). Two situations relevant to the trait are created experimentally (for example, being in a group of strangers or in a group of friends). Each individual participates in each situation. Reading across the figure, all the 1's are put in situation 1 and also in situation 2; so are the 2's. (For example, both the introverts and the extraverts

Situation

	1	2
1	(individuals who are "1" on the trait, responding in situation 1)	(individuals who are "1" on the trait, responding in situation 2)
2	(individuals who are "2" on the trait, responding in situation 1)	(individuals who are "2" on the trait, responding in situation 2)

Trait (label on left side between rows)

a.   General Design

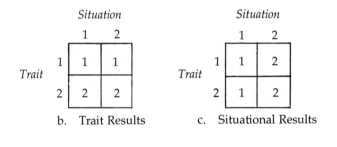

b.   Trait Results   c.   Situational Results

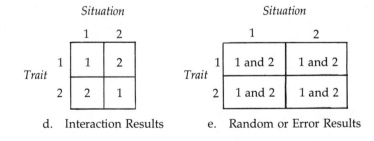

d.   Interaction Results   e.   Random or Error Results

Figure 24-1. Trait versus situation design

are with friends at one point in the experiment and with strangers at another point.)

In each situation, some aspect of the individual's behavior is measured—say, how much conversation he or she initiates. The pattern of responses, according to trait and situation, can be entered in the four cells.

There are several possible patterns of results, each of which should tell us something about the role of trait and situation in this study. Figure 24-1b shows the results that a strict trait or individual-differences theory would predict. Responses correspond completely to the person's trait, so that the 1's make the same response, regardless of situation; so do the 2's.

Figure 24-1c shows the results that would support a purely social or situational-differences theory. Responses correspond to the situation, changing when the situation changes, regardless of trait.

But these two obviously do not exhaust the possibilities, once such a design is executed. There may be mixed and more complex results, not corresponding strictly to either trait or situation. One example is given in Figure 24-1d. In this example, what happens depends on both trait and situation. For example, introverts do not initiate conversation with strangers but do so with friends, while extraverts do the opposite. This kind of result is called an *interaction* of trait and situation. This does not mean interaction in the sense of interpersonal relations. Rather, it is a statistical concept meaning that two factors—namely, trait and situation—act together to determine an individual's behavior. This result is more subtle than either the strictly individual or strictly social approach. It suggests that behavior may depend on who the person is *and* on what the situation is. Certain people act one way in one situation but differently in another, but this pattern is systematic and predictable.

All of the above results assume systematic behavior: everyone in a particular cell acted the same way as everyone else in that cell. Figure 24-1e suggests a fourth possibility: that people will not act systematically at all. Some of the 1's in situation 1 make one response, some another, and so forth for all combinations of traits and situations. This result would mean either that behavior in the study is random (truly unpredictable) or that we do not know yet how to measure the behavior accurately.

In Figure 24-1, only two kinds of people, two situations, and two responses were used purely for convenience. People can be assessed (and usually are) on a much more discriminating dimension, with many different levels of the trait. The situations can also be more varied, as can the responses being measured. The essence of the design, in any of these variations, is that it combines experimental and correlational design: it includes both trait and situation.

Because the question of individual versus situational differences is a major issue between individual and social theories, such designs are potentially very important empirically. They might tell us which paradigm's interpretation of the cause of variability (individual or situational differences) is better able to predict behavior. Conceptually, such designs are interesting because they include a possible compromise between individual and social influences—namely, the possibility of trait/situation interaction. Ekehammar

(1974), for example, proposes that the interactionist alternative could not flower conceptually until this method had emerged. The previous dichotomy between experimental and correlational research tended to emphasize the schism between the two paradigms and to make intermediate positions awkward and untestable.

PROBLEMS AND PROSPECTS

Research designs should be thought of as tools to be used for certain problems. If one wants to ask a question involving both trait and situation, then this kind of design is the suitable too!. Unfortunately, it has not yet been perfected, and there is a danger of misreading the early results. There has been a recent upsurge of interest in such designs (for example, Argyle & Little, 1972; Bowers, 1973; Endler, 1973, 1975; Goldberg, 1972; Golding, 1975; Mischel, 1973), and it is likely that the problems will be attacked vigorously in the near future. The known deficiencies of trait-versus-situation designs are both statistical and theoretical. The first will be discussed as nontechnically as possible. The second is just as important and is not at all technical.

Statistical Issues

The student with intermediate statistics will have recognized this kind of design as amenable to two-way analysis of variance (see, for example, R. L. D. Wright, 1976, Chapter 14, for a painless introduction). In fact, the main purpose of the earliest explicit work in this format (Endler, Hunt, & Rosenstein, 1962) was to assess the respective contributions of trait and situation to response variance in the case of anxiety. The statistical interaction term corresponds to trait/situation interaction. Each of the main effects (trait and situation) and their interaction can be tested for significance—that is, whether each is substantially larger than the variance within each cell.

Furthermore, this design has been used to assess the *relative* importance—in terms of variance accounted for—of trait, situation, and their interaction. This is an appealing model because it avoids the simplistic, all-or-none tendency of the two major paradigms. The results might show that a certain percentage of the response variance is due to the trait (individual differences), another percentage can be attributed to the situation (situational differences), still another percentage can be traced to the interaction of the two, and the rest is due to error.

Bowers (1973) surveyed 11 articles reporting results using this method (and the statistic called eta- or omega-squared). His conclusion was that

> neither trait nor the situationist predictions are borne out. Far too little of the total variance ($\overline{X}$ = 12.71%) is due to the person to justify a thoroughgoing trait position. On the other hand, the percentage of variance due to situations is also meager ($\overline{X}$ = 10.17%). In fact, in 11 out of 19 comparisons, the percentage of variance due to situations is *less* than the variance attributable

to persons. Furthermore, the interaction of persons and settings accounts for a higher percentage of variance than either main effect in 14 of 18 possible comparisons, and in 8 out of 18 comparisons the interaction term accounts for more variance than the sum of the main effects. The mean percentage of variance attributable to the Person X Situation interaction is 20.77% [p. 321].

Thus, Bowers and many others began to accept the greater importance of the interaction between trait (which Bowers calls "person") and situation. It began to look as though a compromise between the two major paradigms was empirically justified.

Then Golding (1975) pointed out some defects in the statistical basis of this conclusion. First, the percentage-of-variance statistic (eta- or omega-squared) used to draw these conclusions is inappropriate for the issue at hand. It does not indicate how generalizable behavior is over situations or how generally situations affect persons.

Second, this statistic is, in any case, quite vulnerable to variations in the sample of people or situations. Different values can easily be obtained by using individuals who vary more or less from one another on the trait being studied (or by choosing traits on which little or great variation is expected). Similarly, the sample of situations used—how similar or dissimilar they are—affects the variance estimate.

Third, the interaction term, which has assumed primary importance in this research, is especially vulnerable to sampling, measurement, or other sources of error. In some cases, for example, this term has been statistically inseparable from error or residual variance. In all cases, the interaction term must be replicated in another sample before being relied upon.

Finally, the data on which Bowers's summary is based is "too fragmentary and fallible" (Golding, 1975, p. 286) to support a major theoretical position. Most of the studies have some troublesome aspect, such as asking about hypothetical situations rather than creating different situations experimentally; observing trivial behaviors; or using different observers at different times in such a way that the effects of observer and time could not be separated. Golding concludes that the present data and statistical technique used do not justify *any* conclusions about the relative importance of trait, situation, and their interaction. He does, however, suggest procedures that could answer these questions in future studies.

Theoretical Issues

The other, nonstatistical defect of this line of research, as carried out to date, has been acknowledged in one way or another by most writers on the topic (for example, Endler, 1975). This problem is the lack of any theoretical formulation of the trait/situation interaction. The term *interaction* has a statistical but not necessarily a psychological or theoretical meaning. There has been a tendency to pick traits and situations for the sake of obtaining data. When the question being asked is formulated almost entirely in statistical terms, it often (but not necessarily) loses any other meaning along the way.

For example, it would be psychologically and theoretically meaningless to ask whether authoritarianism interacts with different athletic situations (water polo compared to soccer) to determine smiling responses. The data could be obtained so as to permit a statistical answer, but it could hardly be of any general (or even particular) interest. None of the trait/situation interaction studies has been so patently arbitrary and devoid of conceptual hypothesis in their choice of trait, situation, and response as this example; but neither have they had a clear and compelling theoretical reason for expecting a particular combination of trait and situation to be important. Endler (1974) has begun to propose such a theory for trait and situational anxiety, and Ekehammar (1974) has given an overview of the general problem: the latter will be discussed in the next chapter.

It may have appeared to the student at some point in this text that the differences between individual and social approaches have been overdrawn. It seems dogmatic to insist on either individual or situational differences, with no position in between. Thus, the suggestion that they might be combined in some way appeals to our common sense. *But common sense is not sufficient.* The choice of trait and response, the choice of particular situations, and especially the combination of this trait with these situations and this response in a particular study, must follow some conceptual hypothesis. If this line of research is to continue, as seems desirable, then a theory combining individual and situational differences in a new terminology will be necessary.

This is a subtle and interesting challenge. For instance, once the possibility of situational influence has been accepted, even in interaction with traits, then the first assumption of the individual paradigm has been exchanged for that of the social paradigm. But some form of individual differences must be retained; therefore, the new approach is not identical with the social paradigm.

Recall that the difference between the two paradigms on the issue of individual versus situational differences is often a matter of degree. No social theorist proposes that every situation and every moment produces a different response. That is, individual differences are simply more stable and more general than situational effects. Where do they meet? When (say, in childhood) do specific and changeable situational influences become both general and lasting? A new paradigm incorporating both positions must address the question: what are the limits of generality and change in human behavior?

25

Person and Situation: Theoretical Interaction

Perhaps it is a stroke of good luck, historically, that the statistical design described in the last chapter was shown to be deficient at just this time—no earlier and no later. Earlier criticism would have precluded the many studies that have been done. Although their results cannot be relied upon, these studies do serve to draw attention to the empirical possibility of person/situation interaction. They may have led us away from a prolonged and sterile war between the individual and social positions into a more fruitful reconciliation.

Had the criticism come later, however, the unchecked repetition of a solely statistical design would probably have been equally prolonged and sterile. As Kaplan (1964) has pointed out, scientists tend to follow the "law of the instrument"—to wit, "Give a small boy a hammer, and he will find that everything he encounters needs pounding" (p. 28). Every trait and situation does not need pounding into an analysis-of-variance design right now. The field may need instead to catch its breath from the empirical exertions of recent years and to begin a more thoughtful consideration of alternative paradigms.

In his historical review, Ekehammar concludes, "if interactionism is not the Zeitgeist[1] of today's personality psychology, it will probably be that of tomorrow's" (1974, p. 1045). Interactionism now has a name and many advocates, but there is as yet more enthusiasm than substance. We need ways to think about what person/situation interaction means—how to encompass and express it conceptually, in order that we may subsequently find useful empirical translations of this new approach. This chapter will describe some of the options available.

There are three potential sources of interactionist theory: Situational elements can be added to existing individual theories. Individual differences can be added to existing social theories. Or we might turn to less well-known,

[1]"spirit of the times"

preexisting interactionist theories that, until recently, have been out of the mainstream of personality theory.

MODIFICATION OF INDIVIDUAL OR SOCIAL THEORIES

It is hard to judge whether the first two options, remodeling individual or social theories, are prudent or overly conservative. About the first, little can be said because there is so much to be done. Recall that there were suggestions of social phenomena in some of the individual theories covered: Cattell's specification equation; Murray's press; Rogers's self-in-the-world or self-and-experience; Kelly's experience corollary. There is not much to work with in any of them, but the social aspects might be developed.

The second alternative is to add more about individuals to present social theories. There seems to be some confusion about what changes are required to make a social theory into an interactionist one. It depends on what is being called a social theory in the first place. Some psychologists have called "social" only those theories that have *no* reference to characteristics of individuals in any form—in short, only Skinner's substantive behaviorism, or variations on it. In that case, the addition of any variables referring to unobservable psychological processes of individuals would produce an interactionist theory. By this definition, all other social-learning theories are already interactionist: Dollard and Miller, as well as Bandura, already include such variables as drive, habit, retention, and motivation.

This definition seems too narrow to me, and it has not been used in this book. A social theory here is one that (1) puts major, but not necessarily exclusive, emphasis on environmental factors, and (2) identifies only situational and not individual differences. These theories often include mediating processes located within individuals rather than in the environment. None, however, develops any individual differences. The addition of individual differences would make such a theory interactionist, in the sense of possessing all significant aspects of both paradigms.

The social-learning theories as a group seem to have one major possibility: to make explicit an individual difference often found implicitly in these theories—namely, prior reinforcement history. A favorite post hoc explanation of social-learning theories is that the behavior exhibited is the result of unobserved previous learning. Used this way, it is of course circular, but this concept could be rehabilitated. It is perfectly consistent with the basic theory that an individual, in effect, carries within a constantly updated reinforcement history, which reflects itself in current behavior. The inferred but unobserved prior reinforcement history might be deemphasized and the current state of the individual accepted for what it is: short-term, mutable individual differences.

It follows that one would then pay more serious attention to assessing the state of the individual prior to experimental reinforcement. For example, the Skinnerian preoperant or base-rate behavior would become an explicit statement of how the person *is* at that point, rather than merely a point of departure for inferring what the situational contingencies are or were. Improvements in the procedures for behavioral assessment are essential to establishing the validity of such descriptions.

As we saw, Bandura seems further along than most social theorists in accepting and defining characteristics of persons—for example, self-reinforcement. Mischel (1973) has also proposed the addition of "cognitive social learning person variables" as individual differences. Certainly, cognitive theories will be more comfortable adding such variables than will the more extremely behavioral positions. They have already defined the situation at least partly according to how the person sees it, rather than as a totally external variable. For example, a fuller treatment of individual differences in the life space would make Lewin's an interactionist theory. However, there may be a more imaginative use of Lewin's theory, to be discussed shortly.

INTERACTIONIST THEORIES

The third approach is more subtle and far-reaching. Rather than "cut and paste" parts of two paradigms to produce a patchwork, the relation of person and situation might be entirely reconsidered. That is, rather than simply adding on the missing parts to one paradigm or the other, one might invent an entirely new paradigm—a truly interactional paradigm. Obviously, it is impossible to describe any such paradigms that are yet to be invented. There are, however, some possibilities that already exist, at least in outline.

The past is often rediscovered, sometimes having lain neglected in corners while more fashionable notions flourished. So it seems for several interactionist theories of personality. Ekehammar (1974) found at least seven such theories already waiting to suggest how to conceptualize person and situation together. Most will be only mentioned here. We have been on a long journey, through 11 major theories and many other issues. Detailed consideration of all these new alternatives is beyond the scope of this book. Like the alternatives in Chapter 15, these are suggestions for the future, aimed to whet your appetite rather than to satisfy it. The interested reader who wants to go further might begin with Ekehammar's article and the references given both there and here.

Ekehammar finds the first modern interactionist position to be that of J. R. Kantor, who as early as 1924 suggested that psychology should study "the individual as he interacts with all of the various types of situations which constitute his behavior circumstances" (1924, p. 92). It is interesting that Kantor was apparently also a substantive behaviorist, emphasizing the physical rather than the psychological environment.

Next, and by far the most influential of all, was Lewin's theory (Chapter 17). Lewin's short-hand expression $B = f(P, E)$—meaning behavior is a function of the person and the environment—has appeared in almost every recent article advocating the interactionist alternative. It is the bumper-sticker of the new movement. It is partly for this reason that Lewin has already been included as a major theory. Lewin (see 1936, Chapter 1) felt that his approach was fundamentally different from most other personality theories, individual or social.

Lewin's overall approach is often called *field theory*, and it is this more general perspective that has clear implications for interactionist alternatives. The field concept is borrowed from modern physics and refers to a shift from emphasis on objects (such as particles or planets) to a focus on the relations between them (for example, electromagnetic or gravitational fields). An analogous conceptual shift from the properties of people or of situations to relations between them has been proposed in psychology as well:

> The field concept in physics has served as a stimulating analogy for scientific workers in other areas. Essentially, "field theorists" in the non-physical sciences have attempted to consider the phenomena they investigate as occurring in a *field;* that is, as part of a totality of coexisting facts which are conceived as mutually interdependent. In other words, "field theory" as it is employed in the social and biological sciences does not refer to theories about physical phenomena, for example, gravitational or electromagnetic phenomena; rather it refers to a "method of analyzing causal relations and of building scientific constructs" (Lewin, 1943, 1951). This method, in a manner analogous to that of field theory in physics, assumes that the properties of any event are determined by its relations to the system of events of which it is a component and that "changes here and now depend on changes in the immediate neighborhood at a time just past."
>
> The term "field theory" in psychology has been applied primarily to the work of the Gestalt psychologists [e.g., Koffka, 1935], and it has been employed to characterize particularly the work of Kurt Lewin and his students. However, in view of our previous discussion of the meaning of "field theory," it should be evident that there are many possible approaches to theorizing in the social sciences which could be "field-theoretical" in spirit [Deutsch, 1968, p. 412].[2]

If you reread Lewin's theory (Chapter 17), it becomes obvious that the life space is a field containing both person and situation. Kurt Goldstein (1940) formulated a similar theory, applied to clinical psychology.

There are two other psychological field theories, in the general mold of Lewin's. Andras Angyal (1941) proposed his concept of "biosphere" as the basic unit of personality, suggesting that the original separation of person and situation had been a conceptual error:

> The biosphere includes both the individual and the environment, not as interacting parts, not as constituents which have independent existence, but as aspects of a single reality which can be separated only by abstraction [p. 100].

---

[2]From "Field Theory in Social Psychology," by M. Deutsch. In G. Lindzey and E. Aronson (Eds.), *The Handbook of Social Psychology* (2nd ed.) (Vol. 1), 1968, Addison-Wesley, Reading, Mass. Reprinted by permission.

The book, *Foundations for a Science of Personality*, develops his theme at length. It does not contain any empirical research, however.

Gardner Murphy (1947) called his a "biosocial" approach to personality. He later explained this approach colloquially as follows:

> I have believed for a long time that human nature is a reciprocity of what is inside the skin and what is outside; that it is definitely not "rolled up inside us" but our way of being one with our fellows and our world [1958, p. viii].

More formally, Murphy postulated that:

> A personality is a structured organism-environment field, each aspect of which stands in dynamic relation to each other aspect. There is organization within the organism and organization within the environment, but it is the cross organization of the two that is investigated in personality research [1947, p. 8].

Murphy's major theoretical statement is *Personality: A Biosocial Approach to Origins and Structure* (1947).

Two more recent but much less systematic possibilities are Rotter's social-learning theory (1954), which the reader may recall has both social and individual differences as well as a strong Lewinian influence, and Jessor's (1956, 1958) emphasis on the psychological environment. The essence of all the above interactionist theories, as I understand them, is their suggestion that we stretch our minds to begin with, to include *both* person and situation as the proper unit of study.

INTERPERSONAL INTERACTION

There is one other approach that will be given more detailed coverage here, for two reasons. First, because it comes from outside psychology (from psychiatry), it is easily overlooked by psychologists: Ekehammar mentions it only tangentially. Second, it is the approach that I personally have found most interesting over the past several years and one on which I continue to work, principally because it seems to me both unique and promising. This is not simply a personal indulgence, however. Carson (1969) found enough of importance to devote an entire text to this interpersonal theory of personality.

The basic idea is as follows: Let us assume the importance of external influences on the individual—that is, the significance of the environment. Most social theories equate the environment with the social environment and emphasize situations involving other persons. Let us then go one step further. For those situations in which the environment is another person, is not *each* person the social environment of the other? For example, when the parent rewards the child, is not the child's behavior also rewarding to the parent? (We all know the old joke about the rat who claims to have its experimenter well trained. . . .)

Looked at this way, there is no one "individual" and another "environment": each individual is the social environment of the other. The unit of study becomes their behaviors toward each other—in short, their interaction. Now we have to stop and point out that we have three distinct uses of this ubiquitous term. There is *statistical interaction*, as described in Chapter 24. There is *conceptual interaction* of person and situation—that is, theories that include both concepts as indistinguishable, as described in the previous section of the present chapter. Now there is *interpersonal interaction*—that is, the actual behaviors occurring between two or more individuals as they interact socially. Although it is by no means an organized and tested theory, this approach does offer a new concept of personality that is neither individual nor social.

Historical Background

Many personality theories have come from clinical psychology and psychiatry. Freud, Murray, Rogers, Kelly, and Dollard and Miller all began by observing and treating disturbed individuals. Each assumed that there is a continuum rather than a dichotomy between normal and abnormal personalities. Each proposed that the principles of human behavior are universal; only the details of individual lives differ to produce pathology or health. This same process of evolution from a special to a general theory seems to be producing a theory of personality based on communication and interaction between individuals.

There is no single name associated with the interpersonal approach to personality. If a beginning can be found, it is probably the publication of Bateson, Jackson, Haley, and Weakland's "double bind" theory of schizophrenia (1956). About the same time, Laing (1960, 1961) and others began to take a similar approach to mental illness, calling attention to the importance of other people and to the often bizarre and difficult interpersonal environment of the patient. For more recent theoretical summaries, see Watzlawick, Beavin, and Jackson (1967), Laing (1969), and Sluzki and Ransom (1976). For clinical examples that are both engrossing and useful for understanding this approach, see Laing and Esterson (1964) and Watzlawick (1964).

The common point shared by the half dozen or more authors who take this approach is the assumption that the principal influence on people is other people. Recall that Sullivan defined personality as "the relatively enduring pattern of interpersonal situations which characterize a human life" (1953, pp. 110-111). For Sullivan, personality was "an illusion" that cannot be separated from interpersonal situations (Hall & Lindzey, 1970, p. 140). The ultimate aim of an interpersonal theory is to identify these interpersonal situations and to understand how they influence the individual.

The family context of schizophrenia was the first, dramatic focus of all these theories. Schizophrenia, a severe mental illness often characterized by thought disorder, had previously been treated as a condition or "trait" of the patient, and causes were therefore sought in the patient's personality. In the mid-1950s, however, several groups of investigators began to look at the kinds of families schizophrenic patients had, in order to find out what kind of interpersonal situation schizophrenia thrived in. Bateson, Jackson, Haley, and Weakland (1956) proposed that the families of schizophrenics communicated in an unusual manner. They proposed the term *double bind* for a communication that contains two incompatible messages—for example, "I love you" in a cold tone of voice; or "Don't obey me." A person constantly subjected to such impossible communications might begin to appear, or actually to be, thought-disordered. The patient might then begin to "double bind" the family.

Interaction as Communication

The important point here is not a particular theory of the etiology of schizophrenia, but the broader implication that an individual's behavior might be shaped by how others interact with him or her, particularly by how they communicate with each other. Communication and interaction become the social environment that determines the behavior of the persons involved. Behavior is understood in its interpersonal context. Most versions of this loosely knit theory assume that *communication*

> is synonymous with what is observable in [human] interaction. That is, communication is seen not as just the vehicle, not as just the manifestation, but as a better conception of what is often loosely gathered under the rubric "interaction" [Watzlawick & Beavin, 1967, p. 4].

This implies that individuals treat all behavior of others, verbal or non-verbal, as communication—whether it is intentional or not. Thus, if someone's facial expression seems sour to you, then that expression, along with the words, posture, and so on, is part of the total communication you receive and react to. According to the communication approach, the individual lives in a world of messages, with acute sensitivity to the behavior of others as it bears on the self. Intuitively, this is plausible, if we find that our greatest joys, sorrows, angers, pleasures, and other concerns involve our relationships to and inter-actions with other people.

Communication thus becomes all of behavior and the inferences that can be drawn from behavior. Both verbal and nonverbal communication are in-cluded: the exact words, tone of voice, pauses, intonations, emphasis, facial expression, eye contact, posture, gesture, and the context or setting in which the communication occurs (such as mother and child versus a pair of strangers in a queue). What counts is what is said *and* how it is said.

Two logically equivalent statements such as "that's good" and "that's not bad" may each have a different impact as a compliment. The use of first names may convey informality, friendliness, intimacy, superior/inferior status, or even disrespect, depending on the context and tone of voice. Note that com-munication conveys not only factual information about the world but also important information about the relationship between the communicants. If a student addresses a professor as "Pat," the student not only indicates which person (out of all the people present) is being addressed, but also a certain level of informality in the relationship between the two of them.

Each individual not only receives communication but originates it as well. If all behavior is communication, then the behavior of each person is communication to the other person. Therefore, one cannot focus on what A does to B without also looking at what B does to A. The individual is, in any particular interaction, necessarily part of a reciprocal interpersonal system, which he or she both influences and is influenced by.

We must therefore study *"the reactions of individuals to the reactions of other individuals"* (Bateson, 1958, p. 175; italics original). This describes an ongoing process in which everyone is both communicator and receiver. The minimum unit of study is two people—the dyad rather than the monad (Sears, 1951). One must observe the context of their interaction and at least one exchange of messages in order to understand what is going on. The concept of individual personality is replaced by that of interpersonal system. Not only does the theory focus on the relation of the individual to the social environment, it makes the individual *part* of this social environment. It denies the validity of viewing a person either solely as an individual or as a pawn of the environment.

In this approach, many differences in behavior are ascribed to situational differences—that is, to communication or interpersonal context. Laing and Esterson (1964), Jackson and Weakland (1959), and others have proposed that schizophrenia is a reasonable reaction given the family environment in which the schizophrenic lives. Fry (1962) proposes that neurotic anxiety often reflects an unfortunate pattern of marital interaction. In these cases, the symptom (schizophrenia or anxiety) is treated simply as behavior that is part of the total communication between individuals. For example, withdrawal or "talking nonsense" clearly conveys the message "I am not communicating with you" (Haley, 1959). This suggests that there is method in all madness. The patient may be disguising important messages in carefully phrased nonsense, just as Hamlet did. Recall that Hamlet's family situation was a difficult one, and direct communication would have been dangerous. It is important to add the view from the other side as well: it is difficult to respond to someone who speaks bizarrely. Sluzki, Beavin, Tarnopolsky, and Verón (1967) have described such confused communication and its effect on the recipients. In such cases, the reciprocity of communication takes on a tragic character.

Once one begins to pay careful attention to the communication of others (and oneself), a new world of previously unnoticed behavior may emerge. One can easily observe double-binding communications in everyday life; for example, "You *should* be spontaneous," or "I'm only kidding, but...." The emotional impact of a single word or gesture can be understood once its context is elucidated.

The Task for the Future

However intuitively fascinating this approach may be, what happens if the same standards of logic and evidence used throughout this book are applied? The result is that this approach does not even approximate a proper theory. Critics have pointed out that the double bind is not adequately defined

(Schuham, 1967); that research on the familial etiology of mental illness is logically flawed (Fontana, 1966); that defining all behavior as communication, without any reference to intention, is questionable (Wiener, Devoe, Rubinow, & Geller, 1972).

Just as important is the lack of objective, empirical evidence for any of the assertions made by advocates of the theory. The communication approach has not yet replaced clinical observation with objective evaluation of evidence.

But we can hope that these steps in the evolution of a theory still lie ahead. For example, Laing, Phillipson, and Lee (1966) have developed both a terminology and a way of measuring subtle interpersonal expectations and perceptions. Wiener et al. (1972) have proposed a method for establishing what is a communication and what is not. J. Bavelas (1975, 1976) has demonstrated an experimental method for studying at least simple interpersonal systems.

If you find this (or any other) approach appealing, you should steep yourself in the folklore that has been developed so far, learn from the critics, and then strike out on your own. Formulate an interesting and testable idea, and then take a chance: find out if it is true.

26

Problems in Personality
Theory and Research

It is clear that the field of personality is currently too broad and incomplete, too much in flux and controversy, to permit any facile summary statements. Furthermore, this book has aimed to give the student the information and skills necessary to form his or her own ideas and conclusions. This chapter is, therefore, personal and speculative. To the extent that the book has been successful, what I have to say will be in some ways the same and in some ways different from the conclusions each reader has reached. Still, it would be cowardly not to answer here the question my students always ask: what do *you* think?

My first and dominant impression is that there is an abundance of personality theories and data, but that we are starving in the midst of plenty. Both the sheer bulk of published work and the respect it commands give the appearance of a continuously active field of endeavor. Yet the activity has been remarkably slow in producing the progress that could be reasonably expected.

The formulation of personality theories has been almost casual with respect to ordinary standards for scientific theories. Definitions, premises, logical coherence, and the overall organization of the theory have been to some degree inadequate in all of the theories described. Awareness of metatheoretical assumptions, particularly of two distinct paradigms within the field, has been slow to develop. Debate over the two paradigms, once they emerged, has often been relatively superficial, focused heatedly on pseudo-issues.

There has been virtually no emphasis on the gathering of objective evidence that would make a difference to the theories. Theories have been illustrated or used as a general framework or approach, but they have seldom been put to a crucial test. The work that has been done has seldom been replicated, even when marred by serious deficiencies. Negative, disconfirming results have usually been ignored. This is in stark contrast to some other areas of psychology (such as perception and general learning theory) and to other sciences, where criticism and replication are the heart of empirical work.

Finally, there has been little change in each of the theories. New theories have been added through the years, but the old ones remain sacrosanct, as if it would be irreverent to modify or amend them. Eventually, they seem to fade imperceptibly into the history of psychology. They may be periodically revived and enjoy a brief new popularity, only to decline again for no clear theoretical or empirical reason. There is no reason to expect that their successors will fare any differently. The cause or causes of all these failings must be sought, at both the theoretical and empirical levels, if future work is going to be any better.

One possible cause, which must at least be considered, is that the work in this particular field is simply not good enough—not that it has not been perfect, but that it has not been as good as even our present knowledge of theory and method permits. This suggestion is not arrogant or insulting. Excellent work in any field is rare. Of all the artists taught the same basic skills, only a few produce great works. A handful of physicists win Nobel prizes. In psychology, too, there is a wide variation in that combination of talent, persistence, and flair that really good work requires. But this answer alone is not satisfactory. Obvious as the errors we have seen may seem in retrospect, few of us would have easily seen them in advance, *given the state of the field at the time.* That is, the errors arose from the historical nature of personality theory and research.

Thus, the blame cannot be laid entirely on the persons working in the field. I suggest that the problem is the field itself, as defined by those working in it. The people working in a field define the field, its goals, and its methods. Nature does not tell us how best to approach it in order to solve its puzzles. It will answer honestly when questions are put, but it does not tell us which questions to ask. People decide that a certain approach is desirable and, having done so, they have constructed the problem whose solution they seek. Some ways of constructing the problem are better than others. I believe that, inadvertently and often with the best of intentions, we have defined the field of personality in such a way as to actually impede our own efforts.

There have been two ways of defining the field. First, and most common, is defining it in terms of the major "name" theories. That is, personality as a field is this collection of larger-than-life theories. Second, and more recent, is defining the field as a collection of popular topics—dependency, aggression, obesity, achievement motivation, and so on. I propose that both approaches are too extreme, either too general or too specific, to lead to fruitful work.

THEORETICAL SPRAWL

The fundamental goal of all global personality theories (individual or social) has been to develop a general theory of behavior—a theory of nothing less than human nature itself. Such a sweeping goal is quite appealing. It corresponds to our intuitive notion of psychology as knowledge of people in general, rather than bits and pieces of conditioning, perception, motivation, and the like. Furthermore, such a theory would serve a unifying function, bringing together the odds and ends of psychology into a coherent whole, from which interrelated special cases could be derived.

Finally, the strong tradition of applied psychology within personality (especially assessment and psychotherapy) has exerted pressure towards this holistic goal. Although personality theory, assessment, abnormal personality, and psychotherapy are usually divided up academically into different courses, each of the theories we have covered has clearly influenced and been influenced by the practical, clinical aspects of personality. One of these influences has been the desire for an all-embracing theory. We recoil from assessing or treating less than the whole person and, similarly, from personality theories that aim for less than a theory of the person as a whole.

I would like to argue that this goal has been a poor way to set the problem—that it has inevitably if subtly led to the very difficulties that now make the goal itself so unattainable. Despite its appeal, the goal of an encompassing personality theory may be the major barrier to significant advances in the field. The two major lines of my argument are that attempts at general theories of behavior have resulted in (1) poorly constructed theories and (2) a fatal dichotomy between theory and research.

Any effort at a comprehensive theory of human behavior will have little probability of success if one accepts, first, that humans are wondrously complex and, second, that precise theory-building on any topic is demanding and painstaking. It is an awesome task to attempt a complete theory of human nature in all its aspects. Such a theory must somehow find some order, some simplification of human complexity, yet without specializing and leaving out any significant aspect. Ironically, as noted in Chapter 1, one of the first traps is usually that of oversimplification: personality is proposed to be based entirely on traits, learning, the unconscious, or some other single, unifying concept.

Another result has been to create theories with a broad brush, impressive in their scope but often flawed on closer inspection. These theories are usually vague and disjointed, sacrificing precision for comprehensiveness, and clarity for speculation. Crucial terms (self, experience, reinforcement) are often inadequately defined. The causal connections among important concepts are not spelled out, and the necessary conditions for the development of, say, fixation, self-esteem, or observational learning are not carefully dealt with. A theory that relies on vague or intuitive definitions, and that avoids the commitment of firm prediction by using anecdotal evidence interpreted after the fact, is seriously deficient as a theory. It is also virtually untestable.

Being merely mortal, our personality theorists have not completed the task they set for themselves of an adequate comprehensive theory. Yet none would forsake the criterion of comprehensiveness for a more modest, but more clearly and carefully formulated, "middle-range" theory (Merton, 1957).

My second observation on the fate of personality theories, as presently conceived, is that for the most part they have favored broad speculation. This is compatible with the goal of a general theory. But historically, the result has been to remove these theories from the empirical fray. Speculation itself becomes almost a virtue, as if these theories were broader than any mere experiment, tossing only an occasional bone of evidence to those who insist. A choice among theories becomes, of necessity, a matter of eloquence, fashion, and personal preference. Even when this aloofness from the "manual labor" of empirical work is not prized, it has been difficult to test such broad theories. Few have defined their terms and principles carefully enough for empirical translation, much less made the priority of their assertions clear enough to know where to begin.

The result has been to cast empirical work adrift—to the detriment of both theory and research. Neither alone is fertile. Personality theories have truly suffered from their isolation from research. Such testing as has been done often comes too late. Questions about the heritability of the somatotype measure, about the necessary and sufficient conditions of learning, about the adequacy of factor analysis, could have been asked much earlier in the development of the theories that relied heavily on the answers to those questions.

Ideally, theory and research should weave back and forth, so that an important assumption is tested as soon as possible. The theory can then proceed on a firmer basis, confirming its assumptions as often as feasible, rather than building a house of cards that can be blown over by a single study. Research should have the healthy role of changing opinions; it is perfectly appropriate to build a theory as one proceeds, being guided by the data. But a theory should always dictate which data are important, and when.

EMPIRICAL TOPIC-HOPPING

Similarly, the aloofness of personality theories from research has had the effect of casting empirical work adrift. Probably as a direct result, there is a trend toward studying particular phenomena as topics in their own right, without any guiding theoretical context.

Pure empiricism, like pure speculation, is usually sterile and is perhaps even less appealing. In the individual paradigm, it sometimes seems that every existing personality measure has been correlated with every other personality measure, for no apparent reason. Within the social paradigm, it seems that children have been reinforced into every conceivable behavior, again without any apparent theoretical point. The dogged accumulation of data does not demonstrably lead to a basis from which a theory can be constructed.

A look at the table of contents of any personality journal, or the subjects of any *Annual Review* of personality, will reveal an endless list of such topical work: anxiety, aggression, cognitive style, altruism, self-concept, sex roles, birth order, alcohol and drug use, and so on and on. Typically, each topic is an initially interesting, real-life problem. It is then intensively dissected with whatever procedures are conveniently at hand—for example, sex differences in I-E Scale scores, or the operant conditioning of aggressive responses. There is virtually no conceptual hypothesis. Finally, the topic simply drops out of sight. I have yet to see a review that after, say, ten years of such research can offer a coherent and informative statement of cumulative results on such a topic. More often, reviewers simply list all the studies done, mention conflicting results, make up a post hoc theory, or perhaps simply conclude that the problem is more complicated than was originally thought. Meanwhile, the doers of research have gone on to another, different topic, leaving only the poor students to memorize the accumulated droppings.

Experience alone should tell us that such atheoretical gathering of data does not, by alchemy, create theory, nor even any simplification or refinement of the problem. Even a claim of relevance is misleading—relevance to what or to whom? The study of altruism in experiments does not help anyone out there in the world who needs helping; it does not lead to a basic theory of helping behavior; it does not lead to a set of coherent rules by which we might induce more altruism in our fellow human beings. It may make the experimenter feel as if he or she is doing something worthwhile, but this seems to be the only benefit.

Even more misleading than purely descriptive work is research that, while on a fashionable topic, is sophisticated enough to don a theoretical disguise. The actual study is the usual combination of convenient procedures with popular topics, but a theoretical "word from our sponsor" is added by reference to several articles or even books. One or several theories are cryptically cited to account for the results. The uneasy reader cannot quite see the connection. The skeptical reader sees that the same global theories could have accounted for any set of results. At best, such research nibbles around the edges of a theory. At worst, it represents one or several theories as confirmed or disconfirmed that, in fact, remain untouched. One method of testing for the presence of such research is to ask the simple question: did the investigator *risk* anything in this study? A study that is certain to be right about something is not likely to be informative.

THE ALTERNATIVE

My conclusion is that the two dominant strategies in the field lie at two extremes, both too exaggerated to be of use. Theory without data is opinion. Data without theory are trivia. Both pure speculation and pedantic empiricism are antiscientific; neither tests an idea.

We must go beyond the mere description of data; the issue is how far beyond. I believe the appropriate principle is to go as far as you can while remaining meaningfully connected to data. It doesn't matter so much whether one starts with a broad theory or with a narrow, empirical topic. What does matter is that one should reach as far as possible in the other direction—toward data or toward theory—without losing a firm grip. The result will be an empirically examined theory. The theory will undoubtedly not be so grand as those we have seen, but it will not be so trivial as purely topical research.

In other words, it would be better to build from theories of moderate scope. These may eventually unite to form a general theory of behavior. They might even be guided from the outset by some looser, general framework. But the specific parts that are asserted as facts should be modest enough to permit tight formulation and relevant empirical examination. Conant (1951) points out that modern science is a blending of speculation and empiricism, which were previously conducted as separate activities. Neither should dominate.

The problems of a proper balance between theory and research and, ultimately, of how to set problems we can solve, are not unique to the field of personality. My favorite words on the topic are attributed to Pavlov (in Morison, 1960, pp. 187-188). As it turns out, this is such a free translation from the Russian that the unknown translator, not Pavlov, should be given credit. But who cares, it's still good advice:

> Firstly, gradualness. About this most important condition of fruitful scientific work I never can speak without emotion. Gradualness, gradualness, and gradualness. From the very beginning of your work, school yourselves to severe gradualness in the accumulation of knowledge.
>
> Learn the ABC of science before you try to ascend to its summit. Never begin the subsequent without mastering the preceding. Never attempt to screen an insufficiency of knowledge even by the most audacious surmise and hypothesis. Howsoever this soap-bubble will rejoice your eyes by its play, it inevitably will burst and you will have nothing except shame.
>
> School yourselves to demureness and patience. Learn to inure yourselves to drudgery in science. Learn, compare, collect the facts!
>
> *But learning, experimenting, observing, try not to stay on the surface of the facts. Do not become the archivists of facts. Try to penetrate to the secret of their occurrence, persistently search for the laws which govern them.*

27

Implications for Practice

To those of you who plan to practice psychology outside of the university, it may have seemed at times that this book was written with someone else in mind. The dominant themes have been theory and research, which are the stuff of academic psychology and not of practical or applied psychology. Certainly, at many points, I have been explicitly hopeful that some of you would become research psychologists and do the necessary theoretical and empirical work that lies ahead. Many of you, however, may have interests or opportunities more in the direction of application, such as clinical or counseling psychology, psychological assessment, personnel work, child care, or education. This chapter will consider some of the many direct implications of the rest of the book for applied psychology.

Far from being an afterthought, practical psychology has in fact been the source of most personality theories. Virtually all of the "name" theories grew out of clinical practice. Almost all of their authors were practicing psychotherapists who developed their theories out of human nature as they saw it in the counseling room. Most have theories of abnormal psychology and psychotherapy as well, although these were not included in this text. The assessment procedures have a similar leaning towards application. Both paper-and-pencil and behavioral assessments have been used—and often invented—in practical settings, for practical purposes. Since applied psychology has led to most of the theories and research covered in this book, it should not be surprising to find many parallels between "basic" and "applied" issues. Whether theory grew out of practice or the reverse, it is a good idea for the two branches to keep in touch.

THE ADEQUACY OF THEORY AND RESEARCH

I would like to propose that applied psychology will prosper or suffer in direct proportion to the adequacy of relevant theory and research. In other words, if our theories or the empirical basis for these theories are poor, then

263

many applications of psychology will be poor practice. The basis for this proposal is the above-mentioned parallelism. Most applied psychology is, implicitly or explicitly, closely related to theory and research. Practitioners usually assume that certain theories hold, that certain facts have been established, and in this sense they are dependent on these theories or data. Several illustrations will help make the point.

Anyone who applies behavior modification by operant conditioning is assuming that a certain theory of human behavior has been empirically verified. Specifically, this person assumes that human learning proceeds in a certain way—or, at the very least, that human performance can be controlled in a certain way. In either case, the necessary and sufficient conditions for changing behavior are implicit: they are the procedures used. In short, anyone who uses operant conditioning assumes that the principles behind operant conditioning—Skinner's personality theory—are valid. It matters how people typically, probably, or necessarily learn, if their behavior is to be changed by a learning procedure. Similarly, it matters what reinforcement is, if the identification and use of reinforcers is an important part of practice. A circular theory of reinforcement is not merely logically untidy, it is useless for guiding the selection of a reinforcer in an applied setting. An empirically demonstrated theory of reinforcement, such as Premack's (with the reservations noted), is much more likely to be useful and practicable.

Another example: Many forms of psychotherapy and evaluation are based on essentially Freudian assumptions about the unconscious mind. Anyone who assumes that an individual is disinclined to, or even incapable of, true self-knowledge, that instead there is a natural tendency toward self-deception, is building on psychodynamic theory. This is often reflected in practice by relying more on the interpretation of experts than on the individual's own report, or by seeking to convince the patient or client of his or her own "true" mental state. If there is no credible evidence for this assumption, then there is no justification for the practice.

And another: Many contemporary educational practices seek to prevent the student from experiencing failure of any kind. Such experiences are assumed to lower the student's self-esteem in a devastating and general way. This assumption can be traced directly to Rogers's theory about the global nature of self-concept or -regard (see page 67). Rogers assumes that the child cannot distinguish between "Your understanding is wrong or incomplete" and "I don't like you," with the result that any criticism is crippling to self-regard. This assumption is not supported by any research, but it is the basis for certain teaching practices, such as emphasizing the affective (emotional) aspect of teacher/student interaction, rather than the informative aspect.

As a final example, psychological assessment is based on assumptions about its validity for particular purposes. Anyone who gives a "personality test" before hiring an individual assumes that this measure is capable of giving reliable and valid information of some kind. Anyone who conducts a behavioral assessment before or after treatment is assuming that this procedure is objective, reliable, and valid for the purpose at hand. Otherwise, there would be no point, in either case, to making the assessment.

In all these examples, decisions are being made that influence the lives of individuals, and these decisions rest implicitly on the adequacy of their theoretical and empirical basis. This suggests, first, that practitioners should learn to recognize the implicit assumptions in their procedures and, second, that they should be able to find out whether these assumptions hold. That is, practitioners should be good *consumers* of theory and research information, even if they do not do the original work themselves. They should not have to rely on authorities.

THE INDIVIDUAL/SOCIAL CONTROVERSY

As we have seen, the two paradigms that have dominated the field of personality represent two substantially different scientific views of human nature. The issues currently being debated have implications (1) for the assessment of individual differences; (2) for concepts of psychopathology; and (3) for the choice and evaluation of psychotherapy.

Individual Differences

The acceptance or rejection of the existence of individual differences has widespread consequences for any application of psychology. As Vernon said succinctly, "We could go a long way towards predicting behavior if we could assess these stable features in which people differ from one another" (1964, p. 181). If individual differences exist, and if we can measure them adequately, surely we would be foolish not to. On the other hand, if they do not exist, or if our measures are incapable of assessing them, then we would be equally foolish or even irresponsible to act as if we can make such measurements. All traditional personality measures make some assumptions and, therefore, some claims about individual differences. Children are selected or rejected for special educational opportunities on the basis of measures of their achievement motivation (Entwisle, 1972). Adults are hired or not on the basis of personality inventories. Treatment programs are designed for patients on the basis of psychological assessments. All of these practices assume that significant, stable, and general individual differences exist and can be measured.

Indeed, the assumption of individual differences is found far beyond professional psychology. For an extreme but thought-provoking example, consider the recent interest in the possibility of genetic engineering—for example, by eugenic selection, genetic counseling, or even cloning. Advocates of genetic intervention propose that we are capable of producing individuals with desirable personal characteristics by these means. Besides physical and intellectual characteristics, aspects of personality are also mentioned. Depending on what is valued, these characteristics might include leadership, mental stability, aggressiveness or passivity, cooperativeness or competitiveness, honesty, and so on.

Let us put aside for the moment issues of morality, ethics, and social policy (which are not the property of psychology but of all of us) and look at a purely technical issue that is in the domain of the psychology of personality. Such proposals assume that personal characteristics are genetically based and, therefore, certainly assume that trait-based individual differences exist. They assume further that we are capable of identifying who has how much of these characteristics, so that certain genes might be perpetuated or not. If there is substantial doubt about any of these assumptions, as there is in the field of personality today, then such proposals are meaningless in any practical sense and doomed to failure—a costly failure by any method of calculating human costs.

Another way of looking at the issue is to suggest that psychology as a field has spent over 50 years convincing both public and practitioner that individual differences in personality exist and can be measured. Now it is necessary to reevaluate practices based on these assumptions—practices that now seem quite remote from particular theories and measures.

Psychopathology

A second manifestation of the individual/social distinction is our concept of mental illness, or psychopathology. Given the close relationship between personality and abnormal psychology, it should not be surprising to find the same two paradigms in the latter field. What is surprising is the almost perfect concordance between current issues in psychopathology and those we have been studying in personality.

Let us take the debate as initiated by the psychiatrist Thomas Szasz (1961). Szasz argues that the usual medical concepts of mental illness are based on an inappropriate metaphor to physical illness and should be replaced by a situational approach. I would like to argue that this concept is as much the product of individual personality theory as it is of the much-maligned "medical model." Szasz assumes that because psychiatrists, being physicians, think in terms of medical diseases and symptoms, they continue to use a medical model for mental as well as physical diseases. Whether or not that is true, it is obvious on examination that the mental-disease model is also analogous to the individual personality paradigm and is therefore possibly derived from, or at least reinforced by, the long unquestioned dominance of this paradigm in psychology.

The term *mental illness* implies a condition in the mind of the patient—that is, something is wrong *with the patient*. For example, behaviors such as extreme suspiciousness, acting as if one is being persecuted, and perhaps delusions of grandeur or exaggerated self-importance, are traditionally taken to indicate the mental condition called paranoia. This mental condition is essentially a trait, of which the symptoms are behavioral signs. Just as many normal behaviors are used, in the individual paradigm, to infer the presence of a certain degree of a trait, so the abnormal behaviors we call symptoms are used to infer the presence of a special kind of trait, a certain mental illness.

With personality traits, the behavior is used to infer the trait; with mental illnesses, the symptoms are used to infer the illness. There are many other parallels. Personality traits are assumed to be both stable and general—that is, cross-situationally consistent. Similarly, mental illness is assumed to be both stable (unless treated) and highly general; it is presumed to pervade most of the patient's behavior. From the observed behaviors, inferences are made about other kinds of behavior in other situations. I recall the first time I met a patient labeled schizophrenic. Given my traditional (and purely textbook) knowledge of this condition, I could not have been more startled by his first words to me: "Do you have any matches?" No thought disorder, no withdrawal, no wild flights of fantasy, simply an ordinary human interaction. I had naively assumed, according to the individual paradigm underlying classical psychopathology, that his mental condition would produce behaviors that were consistently pathological—that is, that such a patient was incapable of normal behavior.

Another parallel between the mental-illness and trait models is that the mental condition is a psychological fiction: it is not supposed to have a tangible existence. Just as a trait is a convenient summary label for certain behaviors, the mental illness is a summary explanation of certain behaviors called symptoms. People who use the term do not ordinarily expect to find physical evidence of a neurosis, nor even of the presumed psychological cause (repression, conflict, impulses, or whatever).

Whereas the distinction between literal and metaphorical traits is relatively unimportant in personality theory, it is quite important in the study of abnormal personality. Here it is necessary to distinguish between mental illness (a metaphor) and organic brain disease (a literal reality). There do exist physical diseases that produce psychological and behavioral disturbance. For example, general paresis is a psychosis produced by syphilis of the nervous system. Porphyria is a metabolic disorder that is accompanied by psychological disturbance. Brain damage from a stroke or accident often produces personality changes as well as intellectual or physical incapacities. There are many psychiatrists and psychologists who believe that most mental disorders will eventually be shown to have a physical basis. Therefore, it is important to distinguish whether the usage is literal or metaphorical. That is, does the person using the term *mental illness* mean to imply the presence of a potentially identifiable physical condition, or simply a hypothetical state of mind?

Both these positions contrast with that of Szasz and many contemporary clinicians, especially the social-learning theorists. Having adopted the social paradigm, they propose that the deviant behaviors are primarily situational in origin. They look for situational differences rather than individual differences. They do not infer any intrapsychic, mental entity behind the behavior. The behavior is not a symptom of an internal mental process or trait; it is the result of an external situation. It is a response to social stimuli, reinforcement, or the like. Psychopathology also has its substantive behaviorists, who refuse to make any inferences about mental states of the patient. For them, behavior is not a symptom of anything at all; it is a functional consequence of observable environmental events. Even the more moderate social theorists are cautious about psychological inferences, preferring to emphasize the ultimately external causes while admitting some cognitive mediating process (see, for example, Bandura, 1969, especially Chapters 3 and 9).

In summary, theories about abnormal personality are divided along exactly the same lines as are the general theories described in this book. Some cite principally internal, mental causes and study individual differences. Others cite external, social causes and study situational differences. The implications for what to do about the patient's problem are similarly divergent.

Psychotherapy

If the patient's condition is situational, then it would be meaningless to try to assess the patient in isolation from the social environment or to try to treat a psychological aberration that, in this view, does not exist. In clinical terms, these two schools of thought not only differ on etiology; they also, as a direct consequence, differ about diagnosis and therapy. The traditional psychopathologist working in the individual paradigm would logically attempt to diagnose the patient's precise condition, because the identification of individual differences is essential. The social theorist would make a situational and behavioral assessment instead, looking for covariations between stimuli and responses. Evidence about the reliability and validity of either kind of assessment bears on the probable strength of its guiding theory. A concern with lack of reliability and consistency of traditional methods of diagnosis (for example, Zubin, 1967) has led many to question the existence of the traits ostensibly being diagnosed. There have been multitrait/multimethod studies of psychopathological traits (for example, Goldberg & Werts, 1966; Lorr & Hamlin, 1971; Zuckerman, Persky, Eckman, & Hopkins, 1967).

In deciding how to treat a problem, it matters what you think the problem is. If the problem is seen as essentially mental, then these mental processes must be changed. Thus, insight therapy, emphasizing the patient's understanding of his or her mental condition, is typical of the individual approach, be it Freudian psychoanalysis or Rogerian client-centered therapy. If mental illness is causing the symptoms, then the illness—not the symptoms—should be attacked directly. If only the symptoms are removed, then others will replace them, as the essential cause has not been removed. If, on the other hand, the behavior is situationally controlled, then the situation should be changed and the behavior will change. There is no need for insight and no fear of symptom substitution.

A great deal of heated misunderstanding has resulted from debates about psychotherapy derived from the two different paradigms. Each side is logical, responsible, and even necessary *given its assumptions about human nature*. The failure to realize that each side is working out of an entirely different paradigm focuses the argument on false issues.

For example, the effectiveness of the two schools of psychotherapy is often compared. However, it is questionable whether the outcomes can be directly compared, as each has quite different goals from the other. A behavior modifier attempts to change behavior because of a sincere belief that this is all that is wrong. The insight-oriented therapist attempts to change mental attitudes, processes, and understanding because of an equally sincere belief that these are the essential problem. To ask whether each has been successful, one must use different criteria of success. The behavior modifier has not attempted to change the way the patient thinks or feels and should not be faulted for not doing so. The insight therapist does not attempt to remove symptomatic behavior, even feels it would be irresponsible to do so, and should not be evaluated by purely behavioral criteria.

This is not to suggest that the evaluation of psychotherapeutic outcomes is unimportant. Quite the contrary, it is a subject about which I frequently become righteously aggressive. It is to suggest that evaluation is so vital that it should be done with precision and not with arbitrary or merely convenient criteria. The standard or standards by which the effectiveness of therapy is judged should be suited to the goals and basic assumptions of the particular therapy. (The goals and basic assumptions of the patient might also be considered: does he or she want insight, behavior change, both, or neither?)

I have tried not to take a position on any side of the debate about the nature of psychopathology and its consequences for assessment and treatment. The current evidence suggests plenty of room for debate rather than certainty. The purpose of this section has been to demonstrate how the paradigms that have been emphasized and examined in this book are directly related to how we think about, assess, treat, and evaluate psychopathology. The relevance of evidence for or against either paradigm is implicit. Should an interactionist theory be preferred, remember that it, too, requires evidence.

THE VALIDITY OF ASSESSMENT PROCEDURES

One of the most common activities for applied psychologists is assessment. Psychological testing is common in schools, clinics, business, government, and other institutions. The behaviors or traits being assessed tend to fall into two broad categories: ability and personality, or to paraphrase Cronbach (1970), what we can do and what we usually do. Ability tests include measures of intelligence, academic achievement, and special skills such as music or sports. They also include assessment of disabilities, such as mental retardation or specific neuropsychological deficits. Personality assessment includes almost all the rest: measures of motivation, character, preferences, interests, social behavior, and so forth. It also includes personality disturbance and psychopathology.

Although this book has not dealt with ability measures except as discriminant validity variables, these measures will be included here. Like personality measures, ability measures can be treated as trait constructs, as behavioral samples, or in a third way, as we shall see. Again, we will focus on the information of interest to practitioners who will be principally consumers rather than researchers. How can one judge whether an assessment procedure is appropriate to use?

The way *not* to make this judgment is by relying on someone else's opinion. The rules that place logic and evidence over any kind of authority are as true for the users of psychological procedures as they are for those who do research. Practical psychologists are not second-class citizens who must rely on the authority of their "betters," the research psychologists (see pages 7-8). If psychological assessment is to be objective and scientific, as it claims to be, then any informed individual can ask questions about its validity and evaluate the answers received according to known standards. The questions to ask, and the standards to apply to the answers, are the keys to being able to judge for yourself.

Matching Ends and Means

The essential job of psychological assessment is to match the means and the ends—that is, the method and the information desired. Sometimes only the goal is known, and one must then select among available measures for the one(s) best suited to that goal. Sometimes the job is to ask whether the assessments currently being used are serving the ends for which they are intended. Finally, in some institutions, the job seems to be to discover anew the goal for which the measures are being given, have always been given, and apparently always will be given.

As emphasized in Chapters 12 and 22, the validity of a measure is directly connected to the purpose for which the measure is intended. If the means and ends match, the measure is valid. I will try to suggest a series of questions that can be asked about any psychological measure in order to establish its validity. There are three classes of validity for psychological assessment procedures, corresponding to three broad purposes for which tests are given. We have already encountered two of them: inferences about a trait construct (Chapter 12) and inferences about behavioral content (Chapter 22). Here we will add a third, to complete the picture.

In many practical settings, an assessment is made in order to make an inference about an entirely different but important behavior, called the *criterion*. For example, an assessment is made in order to predict whether the person will be a good employee, succeed in graduate school, profit from psychotherapy, or be a good astronaut. The criterion might be, for example, whether the supervisor's rating at the end of 6 weeks on the job is "satisfactory" or "unsatisfactory." A test given before hiring would be valid if it correlated well with this criterion. In other words:

> *Criterion-related validities apply when one wishes to infer from a test score an individual's most probable standing on some other variable called a criterion.* Statements of predictive validity indicate the extent to which an individual's future level on the criterion can be predicted from a knowledge of prior test performance; statements of concurrent validity indicate the extent to which the test may be used to estimate an individual's present standing on the criterion [*Standards for Educational and Psychological Tests*, 1974, p. 26; italics added].

Thus, *criterion validity* can be divided into two kinds, *predictive* or *concurrent*, depending on whether the criterion exists or not at the time the assessment is made. The most usual case is the predictive one, in which the assessment is made in order to predict a future state of affairs, such as performance on the job, once hired; the outcome of psychotherapy yet to be conducted; grades in courses not yet taken. The measure is valid to the extent that it gives us a peek into the future: it identifies some present behavior that tends to correlate with future performance.

An example of the concurrent kind of criterion validity is neuropsychological assessment. The assessor may wish to know whether or not an individual has suffered brain damage of a particular kind. This is the criterion, and it exists at the time of testing. Because it can only be directly observed by surgery or autopsy, however, there are excellent reasons for wanting another procedure that correlates with this criterion. If a behavioral measure has been shown to agree with the criterion during a validation period in which the brains were actually examined, then we can be reasonably sure that this measure alone will continue to agree and can be used in place of the more drastic procedures.

Note that the criterion is a specific, empirical observation, not a construct. But it is not the same as the behavior observed; that is, the criterion is not a sample of the behavior observed, as in content validity. The criterion is an observable behavior or condition that is important enough, for some practical reason, to be predicted or estimated concurrently.

In summary, validity depends on what the assessor is interested in:

> In predictive or concurrent validity, the criterion behavior is of concern to the testor, and he may have no concern whatsoever with the type of behavior exhibited in the test. (An employer does not care if a worker can manipulate blocks, but the score on the block test may predict something he cares about.) Content validity is studied when the testor *is* concerned with the type of behavior involved in the test performance. Indeed, if the test is a work sample, the behavior represented in the test may be an end in itself. Construct validity is ordinarily studied when the tester has no definite criterion measure of the quality with which he is concerned, and must use indirect measures.... Here the trait or quality underlying the test is of central importance, rather than either the test behavior or the scores on the criteria [Technical recommendations for psychological tests and diagnostic techniques, 1954, p. 14].

It follows from this definition of validity that a particular measure may be valid for more than one purpose. For example, a typing test may be a good sample of the content of interest and also a good predictor of performance on the job. These two validities would have to be demonstrated separately. A common error is to infer one validity from another. For example, an ability test is assumed to predict university performance, because we believe that intelligence plays a major role in such performance. Plausible as this hypothesis may be, it is still just an hypothesis. Even if the test were shown to be construct valid as a measure of ability, it would also have to be shown to correlate well with the criterion of interest.

The reverse error is also possible: because a measure predicts a criterion, it is assumed to be measuring a construct that we believe causes that criterion. For example, the Advanced Placement section of the Graduate Record Examination correlates fairly well with scores on comprehensive examinations in graduate school. This may be because the Advanced Placement measures general knowledge or ability in the student's field of specialization. On the other hand, the correlation may be caused by the high degree of similarity between the two measures: both are intense, timed, fact-oriented, traditional examinations. The Advanced Placement does not correlate as well with other criteria of success in graduate school—for example, faculty ratings—that do not share the same method (Willingham, 1974). The moral is to identify the kind of validity claimed or desired and then to work on that. One cannot borrow one kind of validity from another, with a plausible hypothesis as a promissory note.

Accurately identifying the kind of validity required or claimed is the first and most challenging job. It requires careful thought, the ability to look past the obvious (including, often, the test's title!), clear communication with those who want the assessment done, and, especially, an ability to avoid misleading answers. If it is not done well, it might as well not be done at all; the best one could do would be to come up with a good answer for the wrong question.

Having identified the kind of validity appropriate to the job at hand, evaluating whether the measure, or any measure, has this kind of validity (and the all-important reliabilities) is essentially a technical job, beyond the scope of this book. It is both important and interesting, if you have a taste for high-level problem solving. Some background on how to establish construct and content validity has been given in Chapters 12 and 22, respectively. For further details, the reader might begin with the thorough but concise *Standards for Educational and Psychological Tests* (1974) and then move on to a good psychometrics book such as Anastasi (1976), Cronbach (1970), Fiske (1971), Nunnally (1967 or 1970), or Wiggins (1973).

I have been assuming that the practicing psychologist will be evaluating the validity of a measure by examining the available research literature, rather than designing an original study. An example of this kind of work is the review of the existing literature on the construct validity of some common personality measures (Chapter 13). Another is the critique of the measures used in the case of Ann (Chapter 22). If the picture drawn by previous work is incomplete or ambiguous, an original study may be in order. This is particularly likely to be the case for the establishment of criterion validity, which is highly dependent on a specific population, institution, and goal. In my experience, employers of applied psychologists are much more open to innovation than the student expects. That is, most institutions may have fixed assessment procedures but welcome an evaluation of them as well as in-service research aimed at improving them.

Standardized versus Nonstandardized Assessment

There is one exception to the straightforward and optimistic description above: the use of *nonstandardized* (sometimes called clinical) assessment procedures. Examples are personal impressions, unstructured interviews, or idiosyncratic interpretations of standardized measures. By *standardized* is meant an assessment procedure that specifies (1) the stimuli to be used, (2) the responses to be recorded, and (3) the method of scoring or interpretation to be used. A standardized assessment can be used by anyone trained in its use and will have good interjudge reliability; in short, it is an objective procedure.

In practice, one often encounters assessments that do not meet these criteria, yet are firmly defended by their users. Their only validity, and it cannot really be called validity, is the personal quality or experience of the user. This firm belief in subjective impressions is often coupled with a scorn for statistics and assessment "by the numbers." This misstates the relevant issue, which is to compare a known and replicable procedure with one that depends on the personal skill and authority of an individual. Let us compare the two approaches assuming the *best* use of each; it is easy but useless to criticize one or the other for its misapplications.

First, some pseudo-differences: Although the results of nonstandardized assessments are usually qualitative, while standardized measures are usually quantitative, exceptions can be found on both sides. Thus, an aversion to or preference for numbers is irrelevant. Standardized assessment is not limited to group testing, with nonstandardized assessment the only individualized approach. Many standardized measures are individually administered—for example, the Stanford-Binet or Wechsler intelligence tests. Similarly, both can be idiographic; standardized measures are usually but not necessarily nomothetic. Standardized assessments are not automatically reliable and valid; this has to be proven. Standardized means only that interjudge reliability has been established. Conversely, nonstandardized assessments are not automatically unreliable and invalid; they have simply not yet been evaluated.

Now, some real differences: Nonstandardized assessments are usually broader and more flexible in scope than are their standardized cousins. For example, an unstructured interview can range broadly over a variety of topics, often leading to unexpected conclusions. A standardized measure will, in effect, look for one and only one thing and ignore anything else. On the other hand, it will always give the information sought. A nonstandardized assessment, by its very flexibility, may miss important information, or obtain it only on a hit-or-miss basis. A friend of mine relied on an across-the-desk interview for hiring a new employee on a loading dock. The general impression was very favorable, and the man was hired. Only when he stood up did the interviewer realize that the applicant had a prosthetic leg! The applicant had been already seated when the interviewer entered the room and had applied for work in general, assuming quite appropriately that the expert would judge whether the handicap was relevant or not. But the expert didn't think to ask. A standardized procedure would require that certain information always be obtained, thereby requiring that the necessary information be clearly specified.

The main argument for nonstandardized assessments seems to be that they "feel better" to the assessor—more intuitive, less arbitrary, somehow more satisfying. Playing the devil's advocate, I would suggest that this may be because they are more vague, less precise, and do not imply as clear a commitment as a standardized procedure. In short, there is a lot of room for waffling.

The main argument against nonstandardized assessments is, therefore, that they cannot be evaluated. We cannot know if the procedure is reliable or valid, because it cannot be specified or repeated.

Let me phrase this criticism more positively. There is undoubtedly a great deal of important information gathered in nonstandardized procedures—information that our present standardized procedures do not even aim to measure. It would be to everyone's benefit if such procedures could be made generally available and did not rest on the variable skills of individuals. A dramatic but true case in point: I knew a highly skillful clinician, apparently able to garner subtle and accurate information from a single interview. When he died young, the method—whatever it was—died with him. How much better if we could have translated the procedure into a public and enduring one.

In summary, I am suggesting that nonstandardized assessments be treated as a source of future standardized assessments. They should be seen as incomplete but promising procedures, not to be compared with standardized procedures yet. Rather, they should be converted as quickly and carefully as possible into objective procedures, which can then be used and validated. This brings us full circle, back to Chapter 1. The goals and methods of psychology include the translation of fuzzy but promising concepts into compatible objective observations. It's difficult and risky, but also exciting and creative. I enthusiastically recommend it to you.

References

Adorno, T. W., Frenkel-Brunswik, E., Levinson, D. J., & Sanford, R. N. *The authoritarian personality.* New York: Harper, 1950.

Alker, H.A. Is personality situationally specific or intrapsychically consistent? *Journal of Personality,* 1972, *40,* 1-16.

Allen, K. E., Hart, B., Buell, J. S., Harris, F. R., & Wolf, M. M. Effects of social reinforcement on isolate behavior of a nursery school child. *Child Development,* 1964, *35,* 511-518.

Allport, G. W. *Personality: A psychological interpretation.* New York: Holt, 1937.

Allport, G. W. *Patterns and growth in personality.* New York: Holt, Rinehart & Winston, 1961.

Allport, G. W. *Letters from Jenny.* New York: Harcourt, Brace & World, 1965.

Allport, G. W. Traits revisited. *American Psychologist,* 1966, *21,* 1-10.

Allport, G. W. Personality: A unique and open system. In D. L. Sills (Ed.), *International encyclopedia of the social sciences* (Vol. 12). New York: Macmillan, 1968.

Allport, G. W., & Vernon, P. E. *Studies in expressive movement.* New York: Macmillan, 1933.

Altrocchi, J., Palmer, J., Hellmann, R., & Davis, H. The Marlowe-Crowne, repressor-sensitizer, and internal-external scales and attribution of unconscious hostile intent. *Psychological Reports,* 1968, *23,* 1229-1230.

Anastasi, A. *Psychological testing* (4th ed.). New York: Macmillan, 1976.

Angyal, A. *Foundations for a science of personality.* Cambridge, Mass.: Harvard University Press, 1941.

Argyle, M., & Little, B.R. Do personality traits apply to social behavior? *Journal for the Theory of Social Behaviour,* 1972, *2,* 1-35.

Ayllon, T., & Azrin, N. H. Reinforcement and instructions with mental patients. *Journal of the Experimental Analysis of Behavior,* 1964, *7,* 327-331.

Ayllon, T., & Azrin, N.H. The measurement and reinforcement of behavior of psychotics. *Journal of the Experimental Analysis of Behavior,* 1965, *8,* 357-383.

Azrin, N. H., & Lindsley, O. R. The reinforcement of cooperation between children. *Journal of Abnormal and Social Psychology,* 1956, *52,* 100-102.

Bandura, A. Influence of models' reinforcement contingencies on the acquisition of imitative responses. *Journal of Personality and Social Psychology*, 1965, *1*, 589-595.

Bandura, A. *Principles of behavior modification*. New York: Holt, Rinehart & Winston, 1969.

Bandura, A. *Social learning theory*. Morristown, N.J.: General Learning Press, 1971.

Bandura, A. *Social learning theory*. Englewood Cliffs, N. J.: Prentice-Hall, 1977.

Bandura, A., & Harris, M. B. Modification of syntactic style. *Journal of Experimental Child Psychology*, 1966, *4*, 341-352.

Bandura, A., & Jeffery, R. Role of symbolic coding and rehearsal processes in observational learning. *Journal of Personality and Social Psychology*, 1973, *26*, 122-130.

Bandura, A., & MacDonald, F. J. Influence of social reinforcement and the behavior of models in shaping children's moral judgments. *Journal of Abnormal and Social Psychology*, 1963, *67*, 274-281.

Bandura, A., & Mischel, W. Modification of self-imposed delay of reward through exposure to live and symbolic models. *Journal of Personality and Social Psychology*, 1965, *2*, 698-705.

Bandura, A., & Walters, R. H. *Social learning and personality development*. New York: Holt, Rinehart & Winston, 1963.

Bannister, D., & Mair, J. M. M. *The evaluation of personal constructs*. London: Academic Press, 1968.

Barker, R. G. An experimental study of the resolution of conflict by children: Time elapsing and amount of vicarious trial-and-error behavior occurring. In Q. McNemar & M. A. Merrill (Eds.), *Studies in personality*. New York: McGraw-Hill, 1942.

Barker, R. G. An experimental study of the relationship between certainty of choice and the relative valence of the alternatives. *Journal of Personality*, 1946, *15*, 41-52.

Barker, R. G., Dembo, T., & Lewin, K. Frustration and regression: An experiment with young children. *University of Iowa Studies in Child Welfare*, 1941, *18*(No. 1).

Barker, R. G., & Wright, H. F. Psychological ecology and the problem of psychosocial development. *Child Development*, 1949, *20*, 131-144.

Barker, R. G., & Wright, H. F. (in collaboration with L. S. Barker and others). *One boy's day; a specimen record of behavior*. New York: Harper, 1951.

Barker, R. G., & Wright, H. F. *Midwest and its children*. New York: Harper & Row, 1955.

Barthol, R. P., & Bridge, R. G. The echo multi-response method for surveying value and influence patterns in groups. *Psychological Reports*, 1968, *22*, 1345-1354.

Bateson, G. *Naven* (2nd ed.). Stanford, Calif.: Stanford University Press, 1958.

Bateson, G., Jackson, D.D., Haley, J., & Weakland, J. Toward a theory of schizophrenia. *Behavioral Science*, 1956, *1*, 251-264.

Bavelas, A. A method for investigating individual and group ideology. *Sociometry*, 1942, *5*, 371-377.

Bavelas, A. *Echo. A method for improving understanding and communication between groups*. Unpublished report of General Research Corporation, Santa Barbara, Calif., October 1967.

Bavelas, J.B. Systems analysis of dyadic interaction: The role of interpersonal judgment. *Behavioral Science*, 1975, *20*, 213-222.

Bavelas, J. B. Systems analysis of dyadic interaction: Prediction from individual parameters. Unpublished manuscript, 1976. (Available from author, University of Victoria, Victoria, B. C.)

Bavelas, J. B., Chan, A. S., & Guthrie, J. A. Reliability and validity of traits measured by Kelly's Repertory Grid. *Canadian Journal of Behavioural Science*, 1976, *8*, 23-38.

Becker, W. C. The matching of behavior rating and questionnaire personality factors. *Psychological Bulletin*, 1960, *57*, 201-212.

Becker, W. C., Peterson, D. R., Hellmer, L. A., Shoemaker, D. J., & Quay, H. C. Factors in parental behavior and personality as related to problem behavior in children. *Journal of Consulting Psychology*, 1959, 23, 107-118.

Bem, D. J. Constructing cross-situational consistencies in behavior: Some thoughts on Alker's critique of Mischel. *Journal of Personality*, 1972, 40, 17-26.

Bem, D. J., & Allen, A. On predicting some of the people some of the time: The search for cross-situational consistencies in behavior. *Psychological Review*, 1974, 81, 506-520.

Bergin, A. E. The evaluation of therapeutic outcomes. In A. E. Bergin & S. L. Garfield (Eds.), *Handbook of psychotherapy and behavior change*. New York: Wiley, 1971.

Bersoff, D.N. Silk purses into sow's ears: The decline of psychological testing and a suggestion for its redemption. *American Psychologist*, 1973, 28, 892-899.

Bieri, J. Cognitive complexity-simplicity and predictive behavior. *Journal of Abnormal and Social Psychology*, 1955, 51, 263-268.

Bieri, J. Cognitive structure and judgment. In J. Bieri, A.L. Atkins, S. Briar, R.L. Leaman, H. Miller, & T. Tripodi (Eds.), *Clinical and social judgment: The discrimination of behavioral information*. New York: Wiley, 1966.

Bijou, S. W., Peterson, R. F., Harris, F. R., Allen, K. E., & Johnson, M. S. Methodology for experimental studies of young children in natural settings. *Psychological Record*, 1969, 19, 177-210.

Bitterman, M. E., Reed, P., & Krauskopf, J. The effect of the duration of the unconditioned stimulus upon conditioning and extinction. *American Journal of Psychology*, 1952, 65, 256-262.

Blalock, H. M., Jr. *Causal inferences in nonexperimental research*. Chapel Hill: University of North Carolina Press, 1961.

Block, J. The equivalence of measures and the correction for attenuation. *Psychological Bulletin*, 1963, 60, 152-156.

Block, J. Some reasons for the apparent inconsistency of personality. *Psychological Bulletin*, 1968, 70, 210-212.

Bolles, R. C. Reinforcement, expectancy, and learning. *Psychological Review*, 1972, 79, 394-409.

Bonarius, J. C. J. Research in the personal construct theory of George A. Kelly: Role Construct Repertory Test and basic theory. In B. A. Maher (Ed.), *Progress in experimental personality research* (Vol. 2). New York: Academic Press, 1965.

Boring, E. G. *A history of experimental psychology* (2nd ed.). New York: Appleton-Century-Crofts, 1957.

Bowers, K. S. Situationism in psychology: An analysis and a critique. *Psychological Review*, 1973, 80, 307-336.

Brecher, M., & Denmark, F. L. Internal-external locus of control and verbal fluency. *Psychological Reports*, 1969, 25, 707-710.

Breland, K., & Breland, M. The misbehavior of organisms. *American Psychologist*, 1961, 16, 681-684.

Brown, R. *A first language: The early stages*. Cambridge, Mass.: Harvard University Press, 1973.

Brown, R., & Hanlon, C. Derivational complexity and order of acquisition in child speech. In J. R. Hayes (Ed.), *Cognition and the development of language*. New York: Wiley, 1970.

Buros, O. K. (Ed.). *The seventh mental measurements yearbook*. Highland Park, N. J.: Gryphon Press, 1972.

Burwen, L. S., & Campbell, D. T. The generality of attitudes toward authority and nonauthority figures. *Journal of Abnormal and Social Psychology*, 1957, 54, 24-31.

Byrne, D. *An introduction to personality: A research approach* (1st ed.). Englewood Cliffs, N.J.: Prentice-Hall, 1966.

Byrne, D. *An introduction to personality: Research, theory, and applications* (2nd ed.). Englewood Cliffs, N.J.: Prentice-Hall, 1974.

Campbell, D. T. Recommendations for APA test standards regarding construct, trait, or discriminant validity. *American Psychologist*, 1960, *15*, 546-553.

Campbell, D. T., & Fiske, D. W. Convergent and discriminant validation by the multitrait-multimethod matrix. *Psychological Bulletin*, 1959, *56*, 81-105.

Campbell, D. T., & Stanley, J. C. *Experimental and quasi-experimental designs for research*. Chicago: Rand McNally, 1966.

Campus, N. Transituational consistency as a dimension of personality. *Journal of Personality and Social Psychology*, 1974, *29*, 593-600.

Carlson, R. Where is the person in personality research? *Psychological Bulletin*, 1971, *75*, 203-219.

Carson, R. C. *Interaction concepts of personality*. Chicago: Aldine, 1969.

Cartwright, D. Lewinian theory as a contemporary systematic framework. In S. Koch (Ed.), *Psychology: A study of a science* (Vol. 2). New York: McGraw-Hill, 1959.

Cattell, R. B. *Description and measurement of personality*. New York: World Book Co., 1946.

Cattell, R. B. *Personality: A systematic, theoretical, and factual study*. New York: McGraw-Hill, 1950.

Cattell, R. B. *Factor analysis: An introduction and manual for psychologist and social scientist*. New York: Harper, 1952.

Cattell, R. B. *Personality and motivation: Structure and measurement*. New York: World Book Co., 1957.

Child, I. The role of somatotype to self rating on Sheldon's temperamental traits. *Journal of Personality*, 1950, *18*, 440-453.

Chodorkoff, B. Self-perception, perceptual defense, and adjustment. *Journal of Abnormal and Social Psychology*, 1954, *49*, 508-512.

Chomsky, N. Review of *Verbal behavior* by B. F. Skinner. *Language*, 1959, *35*, 26-58.

Cohn, T. S. Is the F scale indirect? *Journal of Abnormal and Social Psychology*, 1952, *47*, 732.

Conant, J. B. *Science and common sense*. New Haven: Yale University Press, 1951.

Coombs, C. H., Raiffa, H., & Thrall, R. M. Some views on mathematical models and measurement theory. *Psychological Review*, 1954, *61*, 132-144.

Couch, A., & Keniston, K. Yeasayers and naysayers: Agreeing response set as a personality variable. *Journal of Abnormal and Social Psychology*, 1960, *60*, 151-174.

Cronbach, L. J. The two disciplines of scientific psychology. *American Psychologist*, 1957, *12*, 671-684.

Cronbach, L. J. *Essentials of psychological testing* (3rd ed.). New York: Harper & Row, 1970.

Cronbach, L. J., Gleser, G. C., Handa, H., & Rajaratnam, N. *The dependability of behavioral measurements: Theory of generalizability for scores and profiles*. New York: Wiley, 1972.

Cronbach, L. J., & Meehl, P. E. Construct validity in psychological tests. *Psychological Bulletin*, 1955, *52*, 281-302.

Crowne, D. P., & Marlowe, D. A new scale of social desirability independent of psychopathology. *Journal of Consulting and Clinical Psychology*, 1960, *24*, 344-354.

Davidson, M. A., McInnes, R. C., & Parnell, R. W. The distribution of personality traits in seven-year-old children: A combined psychological, psychiatric, and somatotype study. *British Journal of Educational Psychology*, 1957, *27*, 48-61.

DeNike, L. D. The temporal relationship between awareness and performance in verbal conditioning. *Journal of Experimental Psychology*, 1964, *68*, 521-529.

Deutsch, M. Field theory in social psychology. In G. Lindzey & E. Aronson (Eds.), *The handbook of social psychology* (2nd ed., Vol. 1). Reading, Mass.: Addison-Wesley, 1968.

Dollard, J., & Miller, N.E. *Personality and psychotherapy*. New York: McGraw-Hill, 1950.

Drever, J. *A dictionary of psychology* (Revised by H.Wallenstein). Baltimore: Penguin Books, 1952.

Dymond, R. F. Adjustment changes over therapy from self-sorts. In C. R. Rogers & R. F. Dymond (Eds.), *Psychotherapy and personality change*. Chicago: University of Chicago Press, 1954.

Edwards, A. L. *The social desirability variable in personality assessment and research*. New York: Holt, Rinehart & Winston, 1957.

Edwards, A. L., & Abbott, R. D. Measurement of personality traits: Theory and technique. In P. H. Mussen & M. R. Rosenzweig (Eds.), *Annual review of psychology* (Vol. 24). Palo Alto, Calif.: Annual Reviews, 1973.

Ekehammar, B. Interactionism in personality from a historical perspective. *Psychological Bulletin*, 1974, *81*, 1026-1048.

Endler, N. S. The person versus the situation—a pseudo issue? A response to Alker. *Journal of Personality*, 1973, *41*, 287-303.

Endler, N. S. A person-situation interaction model for anxiety. In C. D. Spielberger & I. G. Sarason (Eds.), *Stress and anxiety* (Vol. 1). Washington: Hemisphere Publications (Wiley), 1974.

Endler, N. S. The case for person-situation interactions. *Canadian Psychological Review*, 1975, *16*, 12-21.

Endler, N. S., Hunt, J. McV., & Rosenstein, A. J. An S-R inventory of anxiousness. *Psychological Monographs*, 1962, *76*(17, Whole No. 536), 1-33.

Entwisle, D. R. To dispel fantasies about fantasy-based measures of achievement motivation. *Psychological Bulletin*, 1972, *77*, 377-391.

Erikson, E. H. Growth and crises of the "healthy personality." In C. Kluckhohn & H. A. Murray (Eds., with the collaboration of D. M. Schneider), *Personality in nature, society, and culture* (2nd ed.). New York: Knopf, 1961.

Erikson, E. H. *Childhood and society* (2nd ed.). New York: Norton, 1963.

Erikson, E. H. *Identity, youth, and crisis*. New York: Norton, 1968.

Etzel, B. C., & Gewirtz, J. L. Experimental modification of caretaker-maintained high-rate operant crying in a 6- and a 20-week-old infant (*Infans tyrannotearus*): Extinction of crying with reinforcement of eye contact and smiling. *Journal of Experimental Child Psychology*, 1967, *5*, 303-317.

Eysenck, H. J. *Dimensions of personality*. London: Routledge & Kegan Paul, 1947.

Eysenck, H. J., & Eysenck, S. B. G. *Manual of the Eysenck Personality Inventory*. London: University of London Press, 1965.

Eysenck, H. J., & Eysenck, S. B. G. *Manual of the Eysenck Personality Questionnaire (junior & adult)*. San Diego, Calif.: Educational and Industrial Testing Service, 1975.

Farley, F. H. Social desirability, extraversion, and neuroticism: A learning analysis. *The Journal of Psychology*, 1966, *64*, 113-118.

Farley, F. H. On the independence of extraversion and neuroticism. *Journal of Clinical Psychology*, 1967, *23*, 154-156.

Farley, F. H. Moderating effects of intelligence on the independence of extraversion and neuroticism. *Journal of Consulting and Clinical Psychology*, 1968, *32*, 226-228.

Fenichel, O. *The psychoanalytic theory of neurosis*. New York: Norton, 1945.

Ferster, C. B., & Skinner, B. F. *Schedules of reinforcement*. New York: Appleton-Century-Crofts, 1957.

Fiske, D. W. The inherent variability of behavior. In D. W. Fiske & S. R. Maddi (Eds.), *Functions of varied experience*. Homewood, Ill.: Dorsey, 1961.

Fiske, D. W. *Measuring the concepts of personality.* Chicago: Aldine, 1971.

Fiske, D. W. Can a personality construct be validated empirically? *Psychological Bulletin,* 1973, *80,* 89-92.

Fiske, D. W. The limits for the conventional science of personality. *Journal of Personality,* 1974, *42,* 1-11.

Fjeld, S. P., & Landfield, A. W. Personal construct consistency. *Psychological Reports,* 1961, *8,* 127-129.

Fontana, A. F. Familial etiology of schizophrenia: Is a scientific methodology possible? *Psychological Bulletin,* 1966, *66,* 214-227.

Fowler, O. S., & Fowler, L. N. *Phrenology: A practical guide to your head.* New York: Chelsea House, 1969.

French, E. Development of a measure of complex motivation. In J. W. Atkinson (Ed.), *Motives in fantasy, action, and society.* Princeton, N. J.: Van Nostrand, 1958.

Freud, S. [The interpretation of dreams.] In J. Strachey (Ed. and trans.), *The standard edition of the complete psychological works of Sigmund Freud* (Vols. 4 & 5). London: Hogarth, 1953. (Originally published, 1900.)

Freud, S. [The psychopathology of everyday life.] In J. Strachey (Ed. and trans.), *The standard edition of the complete psychological works of Sigmund Freud* (Vol. 6). London: Hogarth, 1960. (Originally published, 1901.)

Freud, S. [Fragment of an analysis of a case of hysteria.] In J. Strachey (Ed. and trans.), *The standard edition of the complete psychological works of Sigmund Freud* (Vol. 7). London: Hogarth, 1953. (Originally published, 1905.)

Freud, S. [Analysis of a phobia in a five-year-old boy.] In J. Strachey (Ed. and trans.), *The standard edition of the complete psychological works of Sigmund Freud* (Vol. 10). London: Hogarth, 1955. (Originally published, 1909.) (a)

Freud, S. [Notes upon a case of obsessional neurosis.] In J. Strachey (Ed. and trans.), *The standard edition of the complete psychological works of Sigmund Freud* (Vol. 10). London: Hogarth, 1955. (Originally published, 1909.) (b)

Freud, S. [Leonardo da Vinci and a memory of his childhood.] In J. Strachey (Ed. and trans.), *The standard edition of the complete psychological works of Sigmund Freud* (Vol. 11). London: Hogarth, 1957. (Originally published, 1910.)

Freud, S. [Psycho-analytic notes on an autobiographical account of a case of paranoia *(dementia paranoides).*] In J. Strachey (Ed. and trans.), *The standard edition of the complete psychological works of Sigmund Freud* (Vol. 12). London: Hogarth, 1958. (Originally published, 1911.)

Freud, S. [From the history of an infantile neurosis.] In J. Strachey (Ed. and trans.), *The standard edition of the complete psychological works of Sigmund Freud* (Vol. 17). London: Hogarth, 1955. (Originally published, 1918.)

Freud, S. [Civilization and its discontents.] In J. Strachey (Ed. and trans.), *The standard edition of the complete psychological works of Sigmund Freud* (Vol. 21). London: Hogarth, 1961. (Originally published, 1930.)

Freud, S. [An outline of psycho-analysis.] In J. Strachey (Ed. and trans.), *The standard edition of the complete psychological works of Sigmund Freud* (Vol. 23). London: Hogarth, 1964. (Originally published, 1938.)

Freud, S. [*The origins of psychoanalysis: Letters, drafts and notes to Wilhelm Fliess (1887-1902)*] (M. Bonaparte, A. Freud, & E. Kris, Eds., E. Mosbacher & J. Strachey, trans.). New York: Doubleday, 1957.

Freud, S., & Jung, C. G. [The Freud/Jung letters: The correspondence between Sigmund Freud and C. G. Jung] (W. McGuire, Ed., R. Manhem & R. F. C. Hull, trans.). Princeton, N. J.: Princeton University Press, 1974.

Fromm, E. *The sane society.* Greenwich, Conn.: Fawcett, 1955.

Fry, W. F., Jr. The marital context of an anxiety syndrome. *Family Process,* 1962, *1,* 245-252.

Galanter, E. Contemporary psychophysics. In R. Brown, E. Galanter, E. H. Hess, & G. Mandler, *New Directions in Psychology* (Vol. 1). New York: Holt, Rinehart & Winston, 1962.

Gathercole, C. E., Bromley, E., & Ashcroft, J. B. The reliability of repertory grids. *Journal of Clinical Psychology,* 1970, *26,* 513-516.

Glover, E. Research methods in psychoanalysis. *International Journal of Psychoanalysis,* 1952, *33,* 403-409.

Gold, D. Some correlation coefficients: Relationships among I-E scores and other personality variables. *Psychological Reports,* 1968, *22,* 983-984.

Goldberg, L. R. Some recent trends in personality assessment. *Journal of Personality Assessment,* 1972, *36,* 547-560.

Goldberg, L. R., & Werts, C. E. The reliability of clinicians' judgments: A multitrait-multimethod approach. *Journal of Consulting Psychology,* 1966, *30,* 199-206.

Goldfried, M. R., & Kent, R. N. Traditional versus behavioral personality assessment: A comparison of methodological and theoretical assumptions. *Psychological Bulletin,* 1972, *77,* 409-420.

Goldfried, M. R., & Pomeranz, D. M. Role of assessment in behavior modification. *Psychological Reports,* 1968, *23,* 75-87.

Golding, S. L. Flies in the ointment: Methodological problems in the analysis of the percentage of variance due to persons and situations. *Psychological Bulletin,* 1975, *82,* 278-288.

Goldstein, K. *Human nature in the light of psychopathology.* Cambridge, Mass.: Harvard University Press, 1940.

Goodenough, F. L. *Mental testing: Its history, principles, and applications.* New York: Holt, Rinehart & Winston, 1949.

Greenspoon, J. The reinforcing effect of two spoken sounds on the frequency of two responses. *American Journal of Psychology,* 1955, *60,* 409-416.

Greenspoon, J. The effect of a verbal stimulus as a reinforcement. In T. Verhave (Ed.), *The experimental analysis of behavior: Selected readings.* New York: Appleton-Century-Crofts, 1966.

Groesbeck, B. L. Towards description of personality in terms of configuration of motives. In J.W. Atkinson (Ed.), *Motives in fantasy, action, and society.* Princeton, N.J.: Van Nostrand, 1958.

Guthrie, J. A. *An experimental study of information seeking in the decision process.* Unpublished master's thesis, University of Victoria, 1976.

Haley, J. An interactional description of schizophrenia. *Psychiatry,* 1959, *22,* 321-332.

Hall, C. S., & Lindzey, G. *Theories of personality* (2nd ed.). New York: Wiley, 1970.

Hall, C. S., & Van de Castle, R. L. An empirical investigation of the castration complex in dreams. *Journal of Personality,* 1965, *33,* 20-29.

Hanley, C. Physique and reputation of junior high school boys. *Child Development,* 1951, *22,* 247-260.

Hartshorne, H., & May, M. A. *Studies in the nature of character: Vol. 1. Studies in deceit.* New York: Macmillan, 1928.

Hartshorne, H., & May, M. A. *Studies in the nature of character: Vol. 2. Studies in service and self-control.* New York: Macmillan, 1929.

Havighurst, R. J., & collaborators. *Studies of children and society in New Zealand.* Christchurch, N. Z.: Canterbury University College, Department of Education, 1954.

Havighurst, R. J., & Neugarten, B. L. *American Indian and White children: A sociopsychological investigation.* Chicago: University of Chicago Press, 1955.

Hays, W. L. *Basic statistics*. Monterey, Calif.: Brooks/Cole, 1967.

Heider, F. *The psychology of interpersonal relations*. New York: Wiley, 1958.

Heine, R. W. Foreword. In D. W. Fiske, *Measuring the concepts of personality*. Chicago: Aldine, 1971.

Hempel, C. G. Fundamentals of concept formation in empirical science. In O. Neurath, R. Carnap, & C. Morris (Eds.), *International encyclopedia of unified science* (Vol.2). Chicago: University of Chicago Press, 1952.

Henle, M. An experimental investigation of dynamic and structural determinants of substitution. *Contributions to Psychological Theory*, 1942, *2*(3, Serial No. 7).

Henle, M., & Aull, G. Factors decisive for resumption of interrupted activities: The question reopened. *Psychological Review*, 1953, *60*, 81-88.

Hersch, P. D., & Scheibe, K. E. Reliability and validity of internal-external control as a personality dimension. *Journal of Consulting Psychology*, 1967, *31*, 609-613.

Hilgard, E.R., Jones, L.V., & Kaplan, S.J. Conditioned discrimination as related to anxiety. *Journal of Experimental Psychology*, 1951, *42*, 94-99.

Horney, K. *New ways in psychoanalysis*. New York: Norton, 1939.

Humphreys, L. G. Factor analysis: Psychological applications. In D. L. Sills (Ed.), *International encyclopedia of the social sciences* (Vol. 5). New York: Macmillan, 1968.

Hunt, D. E. *Studies in role concept repertory: Conceptual consistency*. Unpublished master's thesis, Ohio State University, 1951.

Hunt, J. McV. Traditional personality theory in the light of recent evidence. *American Scientist*, 1965, *53*, 80-96.

Jackson, D. D., & Weakland, J. H. Schizophrenic symptoms and family interaction. *Archives of General Psychiatry*, 1959, *1*, 618-621.

Jackson, D. N. *Manual for the Personality Research Form*. Goshen, N. Y.: Research Psychologists Press, 1967.

Jackson, D. N. Multimethod factor analysis in the evaluation of convergent and discriminant validity. *Psychological Bulletin*, 1969, *72*, 30-49.

Jackson, D. N., & Guthrie, G. M. Multitrait-multimethod evaluation of the Personality Research Form. *Proceedings of the 76th Annual Convention of the American Psychological Association*, 1968, *3*, 177-178.

Jessor, R. Phenomenological personality theories and the data language of psychology. *Psychological Review*, 1956, *63*, 173-180.

Jessor, R. The problem of reductionism in psychology. *Psychological Review*, 1958, *65*, 170-178.

Johnson, S. M., & Bolstad, O. D. Methodological issues in naturalistic observation: Some problems and solutions for field research. In L. A. Hamerlynck, L. C. Handy, & E. J. Mash (Eds.), *Behavior change: Methodology, concepts and practice*. Champaign, Ill.: Research Press, 1973.

Jones, R. R., Reid, J. B., & Patterson, G. R. Naturalistic observation in clinical assessment. In P. McReynolds (Ed.), *Advances in psychological assessment* (Vol. 3). San Francisco: Jossey-Bass, 1975.

Joseph, A., Spicer, R. B., & Chesky, J. *The desert people: A study of the Papago Indians*. Chicago: University of Chicago Press, 1949.

Jung, C. G. [Psychological types] (a revision by R. F. C. Hull of the translation by H. G. Baynes). In H. Read, M. Fordham, G. Adler, & W. McGuire (Eds.), *The collected works of C. G. Jung* (Vol. 6). Princeton, N. J.: Princeton University Press (Bollingen Series XX), 1971. (Originally published, 1921.)

Kalhorn, J. *Ideological differences among rural children*. Unpublished master's thesis, State University of Iowa, 1941.

Kanfer, F. H. Assessment for behavior modification. *Journal of Personality Assessment*, 1972, *36*, 418-423.

Kantor, J. R. *Principles of psychology* (Vol. 1). Bloomington, Ind.: Principia Press, 1924.

Kaplan, B. *The conduct of inquiry: Methodology for behavioral science*. San Francisco: Chandler, 1964.

Kelly, G. A. *The psychology of personal constructs: A theory of personality* (2 Vols.). New York: Norton, 1955.

Kerlinger, F. N. *Foundations of behavioral research*. New York: Holt, Rinehart & Winston, 1964.

Kimble, G. A. *Hilgard and Marquis' conditioning and learning* (2nd ed.). New York: Appleton-Century-Crofts, 1961.

Kline, P. *Fact and fantasy in Freudian theory*. London: Methuen, 1972.

Kluckhohn, C., & Murray, H. A. Personality formation: The determinants. In C. Kluckhohn & H. A. Murray (Eds., with the collaboration of D. M. Schneider), *Personality in nature, society, and culture* (2nd ed.). New York: Knopf, 1961.

Koffka, K. *Principles of Gestalt psychology*. New York: Harcourt, Brace & World, 1935.

Kogan, N., & Wallach, M. A. *Risk taking: A study in cognition and personality*. New York: Holt, Rinehart & Winston, 1964.

Krasner, L., & Ullmann, L. P. (Eds.). *Research in behavior modification: New developments and implications*. New York: Holt, Rinehart & Winston, 1965.

Kuhn, T.S. *The structure of scientific revolutions*. Chicago: University of Chicago Press, 1962.

Laing, R. D. *The divided self*. London: Tavistock, 1960.

Laing, R. D. *Self and others* (1st ed.). New York: Pantheon, 1961.

Laing, R. D. *Self and others* (2nd ed.). New York: Pantheon, 1969.

Laing, R. D., & Esterson, A. *Sanity, madness and the family*. London: Tavistock, 1964.

Laing, R. D., Phillipson, H., & Lee, A. R. *Interpersonal perception: A theory and a method of research*. London: Tavistock, 1966.

Lasker, G. W. The effects of partial starvation on somatotype: An analysis of material from the Minnesota Starvation Experiment. *American Journal of Physical Anthropology*, 1947, *5*, 323-342.

Lewin, K. [*A dynamic theory of personality: Selected papers*] (D. K. Adams & K. E. Zener, trans.). New York: McGraw-Hill, 1935.

Lewin, K. [*Principles of topological psychology*] (F. Heider & G. Heider, trans.). New York: McGraw-Hill, 1936.

Lewin, K. The conceptual representation and the measurement of psychological forces. *Contributions to Psychological Theory*, 1938, *1*(4, Serial No. 4).

Lewin, K. Defining the "field at a given time." *Psychological Review*, 1943, *50*, 292-310.

Lewin, K. *Field theory in social science: Selected theoretical papers*. New York: Harper, 1951.

Lewin, K., Lippitt, R., & White, R. K. Patterns of aggressive behavior in experimentally created "social climates." *Journal of Social Psychology*, 1939, *10*, 271-279.

Lindzey, G. Behavior and morphological variation. In J. N. Spuhler (Ed.), *Genetic diversity and human behavior*. New York: Wenner-Gren Foundation for Anthropological Research, 1967.

Loevinger, J. Objective tests as instruments of psychological theory. *Psychological Reports*, 1957, *3*, 635-694.

Lorr, M., & Hamlin, R. N. A multimethod factor analysis of behavioral and objective measures of psychopathology. *Journal of Consulting and Clinical Psychology*, 1971, *36*, 136-141.

MacCorquodale, K., & Meehl, P. E. On a distinction between hypothetical constructs and intervening variables. *Psychological Review*, 1948, *55*, 95-107.

MacDonald, A. P., Jr. Internal-external locus of control: A bibliography—part 2. *Catalogue of Selected Documents in Psychology*, 1972, *2*, 68-76.

MacKinnon, D. W., & Dukes, W. F. Repression. In L. Postman (Ed.), *Psychology in the making.* New York: Knopf, 1962.

Maddi, S. R. *Personality theories: A comparative analysis* (3rd ed.). Homewood, Ill.: Dorsey, 1976.

Malinowski, B. *Sex and repression in savage society.* London: Routledge & Kegan Paul, 1927.

Malinowski, B. *The sexual life of savages* (3rd ed.). London: Routledge & Kegan Paul, 1932.

Maslow, A. H. A theory of metamotivation: The biological rooting of the value life. *Journal of Humanistic Psychology,* 1967, 7, 93-127.

Matheson, D. W., Bruce, R. L., & Beauchamp, K. L. *Introduction to experimental psychology* (2nd ed.). New York: Holt, Rinehart & Winston, 1974.

McClelland, D. C., Atkinson, J. W., Clark, R. A., & Lowell, E. L. *The achievement motive.* New York: Appleton-Century-Crofts, 1953.

McClelland, D. C., Clark, R. A., Roby, T. B., & Atkinson, J. W. The effect of the need for achievement on thematic apperception. *Journal of Experimental Psychology,* 1949, 37, 242-255.

McGee, H.M. *Measurement of authoritarianism and its relation to teachers' classroom behavior.* Unpublished doctoral dissertation, University of California at Berkeley, 1954.

McNemar, Q. *Psychological statistics* (4th ed.). New York: Wiley, 1969.

Meehl, P. E. On the circularity of the law of effect. *Psychological Bulletin,* 1950, 47, 52-75.

Mehrabian, A. Male and female scales of the tendency to achieve. *Educational and Psychological Measurement,* 1968, 28, 493-502.

Merton, R. K. *Social theory and social structure.* Glencoe, Ill.: Free Press, 1957.

Michael, J. Positive and negative reinforcement, a distinction that is no longer necessary; or a better way to talk about bad things. In E. Ramp & G. Semb (Eds.), *Behavior analysis: Areas of research and application.* Englewood Cliffs, N. J.: Prentice-Hall, 1975.

Miller, N. E. Comments on multiple-process conceptions of learning. *Psychological Review,* 1951, 58, 375-381.

Miller, N. E., & Dollard, J. *Social learning and imitation.* New Haven: Yale University Press, 1941.

Mischel, W. *Personality and assessment.* New York: Wiley, 1968.

Mischel, W. Toward a cognitive social learning reconceptualization of personality. *Psychological Review,* 1973, 80, 252-283.

Mischel, W. *Introduction to personality* (2nd ed.). New York: Holt, Rinehart & Winston, 1976.

Mitsos, S. B. Representative elements in role construct technique. *Journal of Consulting Psychology,* 1958, 22, 311-313.

Morgan, H. H. Measuring achievement motivation with "Picture Interpretations." *Journal of Consulting Psychology,* 1953, 17, 289-292.

Morison, R. S. "Gradualness, gradualness, gradualness" (I. P. Pavlov). *American Psychologist,* 1960, 15, 187-197.

Mosher, D. L. The development and multitrait-multimethod matrix analysis of three measures of three aspects of guilt. *Journal of Consulting Psychology,* 1966, 30, 25-29.

Mosher, D. L. Measurement of guilt in females by self-report inventories. *Journal of Consulting and Clinical Psychology,* 1968, 32, 690-695.

Murphy, G. *Personality: A biosocial approach to origins and structure.* New York: Harper, 1947.

Murphy, G. *Human potentialities.* New York: Basic Books, 1958.

Murray, H. A. (and collaborators). *Explorations in personality: A clinical and experimental study of fifty men of college age.* New York: Oxford University Press, 1938.

Murray, H. A. What should psychologists do about psychoanalysis? *Journal of Abnormal and Social Psychology,* 1940, *35,* 150-175.

Murray, H. A., & the staff of the Harvard Psychological Clinic. *Thematic Apperception Test Manual.* Cambridge, Mass.: Harvard University Press, 1943.

Neisser, U. *Cognitive psychology.* New York: Appleton-Century-Crofts, 1967.

Newman, R. W. Age changes in body build. *American Journal of Physical Anthropology,* 1952, *10,* 75-90.

Norman, W.T. Toward an adequate taxonomy of personality attributes: Replicated factor structure in peer nomination personality ratings. *Journal of Abnormal and Social Psychology,* 1963, *66,* 574-583.

Norman, W. T., & Goldberg, L. R. Raters, ratees, and randomness in personality structure. *Journal of Personality and Social Psychology,* 1966, *4,* 681-691.

Nunnally, J. C. *Psychometric theory.* New York: McGraw-Hill, 1967.

Nunnally, J. C. *Introduction to psychological measurement.* New York: McGraw-Hill, 1970.

Parton, D. A., & Ross, A. O. Social reinforcement of children's motor behavior: A review. *Psychological Bulletin,* 1965, *64,* 65-73.

Passini, F. T., & Norman, W. T. A universal conception of personality structure? *Journal of Personality and Social Psychology,* 1966, *4,* 44-49.

Pervin, L. A. *Personality: Theory, assessment, and research.* New York: Wiley, 1970.

Peterson, D. R. Scope and generality of verbally defined personality factors. *Psychological Review,* 1965, *72,* 48-59.

Peterson, D. R. *The clinical study of social behavior.* New York: Appleton-Century-Crofts, 1968.

Polyani, M. *Personal knowledge.* Chicago: University of Chicago Press, 1958.

Popper, K. *The logic of scientific discovery.* New York: Harper & Row, 1959.

Powell, A., & Centa, D. Adult locus of control and mental ability. *Psychological Reports,* 1972, *30,* 829-830.

Powell, A., & Vega, M. Correlates of adult locus of control. *Psychological Reports,* 1972, *30,* 455-460.

Premack, D. Toward empirical behavioral laws: I. Positive reinforcement. *Psychological Review,* 1959, *66,* 219-233.

Premack, D. Reversibility of the reinforcement relation. *Science,* 1962, *136,* 255-257.

Premack, D. Reinforcement theory. In D. Levine (Ed.), *Nebraska Symposium on Motivation* (Vol. 13). Lincoln: University of Nebraska Press, 1965.

Rapaport, D. The structure of psychoanalytic theory: A systematizing attempt. In S. Koch (Ed.), *Psychology: A study of a science* (Vol. 3). New York: McGraw-Hill, 1959.

Rees, L. Constitutional factors and abnormal behavior. In H. J. Eysenck (Ed.), *Handbook of abnormal psychology: An experimental approach.* London: Pitman, 1961.

Reid, J. B. Reliability assessment of observation data: A possible methodological problem. *Child Development,* 1970, *41,* 1143-1150.

Rice, G. H. *The internalization of attitudes among nurses at the Palo Alto-Stanford Hospital.* Unpublished doctoral dissertation, Stanford University, 1965.

Richardson, J. F. Correlations between the extraversion and neuroticism scales of the E.P.I. *Australian Journal of Psychology,* 1968, *20,* 15-18.

Rogers, C. R. *Counseling and psychotherapy: Newer concepts in practice.* Boston: Houghton Mifflin, 1942.

Rogers, C. R. Some observations on the organization of personality. *American Psychologist,* 1947, *2,* 358-368.

Rogers, C. R. *Client-centered therapy: Its current practice, implications, and theory.* Boston: Houghton Mifflin, 1951.

Rogers, C. R. A theory of therapy, personality, and interpersonal relationships, as developed in the client-centered framework. In S. Koch (Ed.), *Psychology: A study of a science* (Vol. 3). New York: McGraw-Hill, 1959.

Rogers, C. R., & Skinner, B. F. Some issues concerning the control of human behavior. *Science*, 1956, *124*, 1057-1066.

Rokeach, M. *The open and closed mind*. New York: Basic Books, 1960.

Rosenzweig, S. *Freud, Jung and the kingmaker: The visit to America 1909*. St. Louis: Rana House, 1977.

Rotter, J. B. *Social learning and clinical psychology*. Englewood Cliffs, N. J.: Prentice-Hall, 1954.

Rotter, J. B. The role of the psychological situation in determining the direction of human behavior. In M. R. Jones (Ed.), *Nebraska Symposium on Motivation* (Vol. 3). Lincoln: University of Nebraska Press, 1955.

Rotter, J. B. Generalized expectancies for internal versus external control of reinforcement. *Psychological Monographs*, 1966, *80*(1, Whole No. 609).

Rotter, J. B. Personality theory. In H. Helson & W. Bevan (Eds.), *Contemporary approaches to psychology*. Princeton, N. J.: Van Nostrand, 1967.

Rotter, J. B., Chance, J. E., & Phares, E. J. *Applications of a social learning theory of personality*. New York: Holt, Rinehart & Winston, 1972.

Rudner, R. S. *Philosophy of social sciences*. Englewood Cliffs, N. J.: Prentice-Hall, 1966.

Runquist, W. N., Spence, K. W., & Stubbs, D. W. Differential conditioning and intensity of the UCS. *Journal of Experimental Psychology*, 1958, *55*, 51-55.

Sahakian, W. S. (Ed.). *Psychology of personality: Readings in theory* (2nd ed.). Chicago: Rand McNally, 1974.

Sanford, N. Personality: The field. In D. L. Sills (Ed.), *International encyclopedia of the social sciences* (Vol. 11). New York: Macmillan, 1968.

Schatzman, M. Paranoia or persecution: The case of Schreber. *Family Process*, 1971, *10*, 177-207.

Schreber, D. P. [*Memoirs of my nervous illness*] (I. Macalpine & R. A. Hunter, Eds. & trans.). London: Dawson & Son, 1955. (Originally published, 1903.)

Schuham, A. I. The double-bind hypothesis a decade later. *Psychological Bulletin*, 1967, *68*, 409-416.

Schultz, D. P. *A history of modern psychology*. New York: Academic Press, 1969.

Sears, R. R. A theoretical framework for personality and social behavior. *American Psychologist*, 1951, *6*, 476-483.

Sechrest, L. Personality. In M. R. Rosenzweig & L. W. Porter (Eds.), *Annual review of psychology* (Vol. 27). Palo Alto, Calif.: Annual Reviews, 1976.

Shakow, D. Psychoanalysis. In D. L. Krantz (Ed.), *Schools of psychology: A symposium*. New York: Appleton-Century-Crofts, 1969.

Sheldon, W. H. (in collaboration with S. S. Stevens & W. B. Tucker). *The varieties of human physique: An introduction to constitutional psychology*. New York: Harper, 1940.

Sheldon, W. H. (with the collaboration of S. S. Stevens). *The varieties of temperament: A psychology of constitutional differences*. New York: Harper, 1942.

Sheldon, W. H. (with the collaboration of C. W. Dupertuis & E. McDermott). *Atlas of men: A guide for somatotyping the adult male at all ages*. New York: Harper, 1954.

Sheldon, W. H., Lewis, N. D. C., & Tenny, A. M. Psychotic patterns and physical constitution: A third year follow-up of 3800 psychiatric patients in New York State (Psychiatric Research Foundation Lecture). In D. V. Siva Sankar (Ed.), *Schizophrenia: Current concepts and research*. New York: PJD Publications, 1969.

Shweder, R. A. How relevant is an individual difference theory of personality? *Journal of Personality*, 1975, *43*, 455-484.

Skinner, B. F. *Science and human behavior*. New York: Free Press, 1953.

Skinner, B. F. *Verbal behavior*. New York: Appleton-Century-Crofts, 1957.

Skinner, B. F. A case history in scientific method. In S. Koch (Ed.), *Psychology: A study of a science* (Vol. 2). New York: McGraw-Hill, 1959.

Skinner, B. F. *Beyond freedom and dignity*. New York: Knopf, 1971.

Skolnick, A. Stability and interrelations of thematic test imagery over twenty years. *Child Development*, 1966, *37*, 389-396.

Sluzki, C. E., Beavin, J., Tarnopolsky, A., & Verón, E. Transactional disqualification: Research on the double bind. *Archives of General Psychiatry*, 1967, *16*, 494-504.

Sluzki, C. E., & Ransom, D. C. (Eds.). *Double bind: The foundation of the communicational approach to the family*. New York: Grune & Stratton, 1976.

Smith, M. B. The phenomenological approach in personality theory: Some critical remarks. *Journal of Abnormal and Social Psychology*, 1950, *45*, 516-522.

Spielberger, C. D., & DeNike, L. D. Descriptive behaviorism versus cognitive theory in verbal operant conditioning. *Psychological Review*, 1966, *73*, 306-326.

Standards for educational and psychological tests. Washington, D.C.: American Psychological Association, 1974.

Sullivan, H. S. *The interpersonal theory of psychiatry*. New York: Norton, 1953.

Szasz, T. S. *The myth of mental illness: Foundations of a theory of personal conduct*. New York: Harper & Row, 1961.

Taplin, P. S., & Reid, J. B. Effects of instructional set and experimenter influence on observer reliability. *Child Development*, 1973, *44*, 547-554.

Taylor, J. A. A personality scale of manifest anxiety. *Journal of Abnormal and Social Psychology*, 1953, *48*, 285-290.

Technical recommendations for psychological tests and diagnostic techniques. *Psychological Bulletin Supplement*, 1954, *51*(2, Part 2), 1-38.

Thompson, L., & Joseph, A. *The Hopi way*. Chicago: University of Chicago Press, 1947.

Thompson, R. C., & Michel, J. B. Measured authoritarianism: A comparison of the F and D scales. *Journal of Personality*, 1972, *40*, 180-190.

Thomson, C., Holmberg, M., & Baer, D. M. A brief report on a comparison of time-sampling procedures. *Journal of Applied Behavior Analysis*, 1974, *7*, 623-626.

Throop, W.F., & MacDonald, A.P., Jr. Internal-external locus of control: A bibliography. *Psychological Reports*, 1971, *28*, 175-190.

Titus, H. E., & Hollander, E. P. The California F Scale in psychological research: 1950-1955. *Psychological Bulletin*, 1957, *54*, 47-64.

Tolman, E. C. *Purposive behavior in animals and men*. New York: Century, 1932.

Tyler, L. E. *The psychology of human differences* (3rd ed.). New York: Appleton-Century-Crofts, 1965.

Ullmann, L. P., & Krasner, L. (Eds.). *Case studies in behavior modification*. New York: Holt, Rinehart & Winston, 1965.

Vernon, P. E. *Personality and assessment: A critical survey*. London: Methuen, 1964.

Vingoe, F. J. Validity of the Eysenck extraversion scale: Replication and extension. *Psychological Reports*, 1968, *22*, 706-708.

Walker, R. N. Body build and behavior in young children: I. Body build and nursery school teachers' ratings. *Monographs of the Society for Research in Child Development*, 1962, *27*(3, Serial No. 84).

Warner, W.L. (and collaborators). *Democracy in Jonesville: A study of quantity and inequality*. New York: Harper & Brothers, 1949.

Watzlawick, P. *An anthology of human communication: Text and tape*. Palo Alto, Calif.: Science and Behavior Books, 1964.

Watzlawick, P., & Beavin, J. Some formal aspects of communication. *American Behavioral Scientist*, 1967, *10*(8), 4-8.

Watzlawick, P., Beavin, J. H., & Jackson, D. D. *Pragmatics of human communication: A study of interactional patterns, pathologies, and paradoxes.* New York: Norton, 1967.

Webster, H., Sanford, N., & Freedman, M. A new instrument for studying authoritarianism in personality. *Journal of Psychology,* 1955, *40,* 73-84.

Wegner, N., & Zeaman, D. Strength of cardiac conditioned responses with varying unconditioned stimulus durations. *Psychological Review,* 1958, *65,* 238-241.

Weick, K. E. Systematic observational methods. In G. Lindzey & E. Aronson (Eds.), *The handbook of social psychology* (2nd ed., Vol. 2). Reading, Mass.: Addison-Wesley, 1968.

Weinstein, M. S. Achievement motivation and risk preference. *Journal of Personality and Social Psychology,* 1969, *13,* 153-172.

White, B. L. An experimental approach to the effects of experience on early human behavior. In J. P. Hill (Ed.), *Minnesota Symposia on Child Psychology* (Vol. 1). Minneapolis: University of Minnesota Press, 1967.

White, J. H., Stephenson, G. M., Child, S. E. A., & Gibbs, J. M. Validation studies of the Eysenck Personality Inventory. *British Journal of Psychiatry,* 1968, *114,* 63-68.

White, R. W. Motivation reconsidered: The concept of competence. *Psychological Review,* 1959, *66,* 297-333.

Wiener, M., Devoe, S., Rubinow, S., & Geller, J. Nonverbal behavior and nonverbal communication. *Psychological Review,* 1972, *79,* 185-214.

Wiggins, J. S. *Personality and prediction: Principles of personality assessment.* Reading, Mass.: Addison-Wesley, 1973.

Willingham, W. W. Predicting success in graduate education. *Science,* 1974, *183,* 273-278.

Wilson, A. *The verbal report of the concept in concept-learning research.* Unpublished doctoral dissertation, University of Victoria, 1973.

Wolpe, J., & Rachman, S. Psychoanalytic "evidence": A critique based on Freud's case of Little Hans. *Journal of Nervous and Mental Disease,* 1960, *131,* 135-148.

Woodworth, R. S., & Sheehan, M. R. *Contemporary schools of psychology* (3rd ed.). New York: Ronald Press, 1964.

Wright, H. F. Observational child study. In P. Mussen (Ed.), *Handbook of research methods in child development.* New York: Wiley, 1960.

Wright, R. L. D. *Understanding statistics: An informal introduction for the behavioral sciences.* New York: Harcourt Brace Jovanovich, 1976.

Wylie, R. C. *The self concept: A critical survey of pertinent research literature.* Lincoln: University of Nebraska Press, 1961.

Wylie, R. C. The present status of self theory. In E. Borgatta and W. W. Lambert (Eds.), *Handbook of personality theory and research.* Chicago: Rand McNally, 1968.

Wylie, R. C. *The self-concept (Rev. ed.): Vol. 1. A review of methodological considerations and measuring instruments.* Lincoln: University of Nebraska Press, 1974.

Zeigarnik, B. [On finished and unfinished tasks.] In W. D. Ellis (Ed. and trans.), *A source book of Gestalt psychology.* London: Routledge & Kegan Paul, 1938. (Originally published, 1927.)

Zlutnick, S., Mayville, W. J., & Moffat, S. Modification of seizure disorders: The interruption of behavioral chains. *Journal of Applied Behavior Analysis,* 1975, *8,* 1-12.

Zubin, J. Classification of the behavior disorders. In P. R. Farnsworth, O. McNemar, & Q. McNemar (Eds.), *Annual Review of Psychology* (Vol. 18). Palo Alto, Calif.: Annual Reviews, 1967.

Zuckerman, M., Persky, H., Eckman, K. M., & Hopkins, R. R. A multitrait multimethod measurement approach to the traits (or states) of anxiety, depression and hostility. *Journal of Projective Techniques and Personality Assessment,* 1967, *31,* 39-48.

Author Index

Subject Index